Comparative Urban Research

Comparative

The Administration

Sponsored by the Committee on Urban Administration and Politics
COMPARATIVE ADMINISTRATION GROUP
OF THE AMERICAN SOCIETY FOR PUBLIC ADMINISTRATION

Urban Research

and Politics of Cities

Edited by ROBERT T. DALAND

With a Foreword by FREDERIC N. CLEAVELAND

SAGE PUBLICATIONS / BEVERLY HILLS, CALIFORNIA

For information address:

SAGE PUBLICATIONS, INC.
275 South Beverly Drive
Beverly Hills, California 90212

First Printing

Printed in the United States of America

Standard Book Number 8039-0012-0

Library of Congress Catalog Card No. 69-18751

to

FRED W. RIGGS

Scholar in his own right

Advisor and friend to other scholars

Organizer of conditions which make possible

the scholarly work of others

Contents

Foreword

THIS COLLECTION of essays brings together two themes dominant in contemporary social science: a methodological focus on comparative analysis and a substantive focus on the city. The two decades since World War II have witnessed a remarkable growth in the use of comparative analytic techniques to explore the complex problems of modern societies. The concern of researchers has been to escape the pitfalls of the conclusion drawn from a single case or the generalization bound by the experience of a single country or culture. Comparative analysis has contributed in an important way to enlarging our understanding of the dynamics of modernization at work in developing countries throughout the world. And it has also provided better clues to the student of older, industrialized societies seeking to explore changing patterns of behavior. Yet the application of comparative analysis to the study of cities has tended to lag behind its use in studying national political systems, or system components like political parties, government bureaucracies, or legislative bodies.[1]

The attraction of the city as a subject for analysis to the student of public affairs is readily understandable. Among complex institutions of twentieth-century society, none poses more severe problems for leadership groups than do cities. Increasing millions in every part of the world are dependent for the quality of their lives, indeed for their survival, on man's capacity to make the city

---

[1] See International Urban Research, Institute of International Studies, *The World's Metropolitan Areas* (Berkeley and Los Angeles: University of California Press, 1959), pp. 1–2:

> The paucity of comparative urban research is of course not due to an indifference on the part of social scientists, but to the absence of comparable, or standardized, information from one country to another, and to technical problems presented by this deficiency. The units of observation themselves—that is "cities" and "towns"—have not been standardized, nor have we information on a representative sample of those for the world as a whole. Most of our data have pertained to the "cities" of the West, although just as many "cities" are found in the rest of the world. Furthermore, the structure of urban communities has changed with increasing urbanization—a change that has gone further in some countries than in others. This dynamic element has meant that definitions of urban places adequate for one region or time have not been suitable for another region or time.

work—as a purveyor of essential services, as a source of basic amenities and of opportunities for personal development, and as an instrument for maintenance of law and order. It is imperative that we deepen our understanding about cities and their problems, about the process of urbanization and how to avoid spawning more ungovernable urban agglomerations. We have so far failed to exploit fully the contribution comparative research can make to that understanding. We can ill afford to continue tolerating that failure.

In short, the essays in this volume are concerned with a vitally important subject: the administration and politics of cities. And they seek to bring a significant perspective to bear upon this subject: comparative analysis.

This volume is a direct outgrowth of a seminar on comparative urban research sponsored by the Comparative Administration Group (CAG)[2] of the American Society for Public Administration and held at the University of North Carolina in Chapel Hill, N.C., during July and August, 1967. In contrast to most of the earlier summer research seminars conducted under the auspices of CAG, this seminar on comparative urban research was conceived and planned as a major project of a continuing CAG committee, the Committee on Comparative Urban Administration and Politics (CUAP).[3] The intellectual concerns of the Committee helped to shape the orientation of the seminar.

The Committee came into being in 1964 through the initiative of CAG chairman Fred Riggs. From its inception Committee members shared the central objective of stimulating the cross-national comparative study of urban political systems, and especially of their administrative dimensions. Yet because of the undeveloped state of comparative urban research, CUAP concluded that special

---

[2] For a brief description of the origins and purposes of the Comparative Administration Group see the foreword written by its chairman, Professor Fred W. Riggs, to a volume of papers growing out of two earlier research seminars sponsored by CAG—John D. Montgomery and William J. Siffin (eds.), *Approaches to Development: Politics, Development, and Change* (New York: McGraw-Hill, 1966) pp. ix–xii.

[3] At the time of the seminar the Committee was composed of Frederic N. Cleaveland, Robert T. Daland, William J. Gore, Daniel R. Grant, Victor Jones, Emil J. Sady, Wallace Sayre, Frank P. Sherwood, and Frank Smallwood. Following the seminar, five of its participants joined the Committee: Robert R. Alford, James F. Guyot, William J. Hanna, Francine F. Rabinovitz, and Deil S. Wright.

encouragement should also be given to two other kinds of research efforts: (1) efforts to refine the methodology of comparative analysis as applied to urban administration and politics, even when the research in question was not cross-national; and (2) efforts to carry out empirical studies of urban political systems in developing nations even when they were not comparative. These two extensions of its central purpose appeared appropriate because Committee members believed that achievement of its central goal depended upon the development of more effective analytic tools for comparing urban governments, and on the accumulation of bodies of basic data on urban administration and politics in emerging nations, so that cross-national comparative research could be rooted in empirical data.

Other problems of defining scope and determining orientation beset the Committee.[4] Was the whole field of urban studies its domain, or should its focus be confined to the study of political and administrative phenomena? Was it to be concerned alike with the scholar-researcher interested in empirical theory and with the practitioner seeking solutions to practical problems? Was its primary concern to be with urbanism as a life style, or with the process of urbanization? While these issues were discussed, sometimes at length, the Committee concluded that it might find new insights into such questions through the experience of the research seminar. Accordingly the issue of what should be the scope and orientation of the Committee on Comparative Urban Administration and Politics became an underlying question before the seminar participants throughout their time together.

Robert Daland assumed major responsibility for planning the seminar and for serving as participant-director. The CUAP chairman assisted in the planning, giving particular attention to the relation of the Committee to the seminar. During the final week

[4] Two other publications shed further light on the Committee's efforts to formulate its objectives and define its focus. These papers grew directly out of Committee discussions and were written by Committee members on request for presentation at a conference of the Comparative Administration Group held at the University of Maryland in April, 1966. See Robert T. Daland, "A Strategy for Research in Comparative Urban Administration," published as a CAG Occasional Paper (Bloomington: Comparative Administration Group, 1966 mimeographed); and Emil J. Sady, "The Need for Comparative Studies on Practical Problems of Urban Administration," published as a CAG Occasional Paper (Bloomington: Comparative Administration Group, 1966 mimeographed).

seminar members and Committee members met together to hear the final papers and discuss the implications of the seminar experience for the future of CUAP.

The primary interests of the eight seminar participants[5] reflect something of the range and diversity of scholars working in this broad field of inquiry. The group included scholars concerned with large metropolitan areas and others studying smaller cities; some were concerned with Western culture, while others worked with cultures of the developing nations of Asia, Africa or Latin America. Some were studying mass behaviors, while others concentrated their attention upon elites. Some were exploring the process of urbanization, and others were more involved with urbanism as a life style. Special effort was made to recruit for the seminar several scholars who had already completed the field work for their research and who, therefore, would come armed with data ready for analysis. For them the seminar provided opportunity to try out analytic procedures, sharpen interpretations of their data, and perhaps refine a conceptual framework devised earlier. Five of the resulting essays reflect the fruits of such efforts.

The seminar has proved difficult to assess, as it was difficult to plan. Interaction among participants was extensive; it was sharp at times, yet in every sense constructive. Despite the diversity of subjects under study, the variety of research problems, and the varied backgrounds of participants, certain common concerns emerged early, concerns which cut across all differences to provide the basis for a strong community of interest. The student of comparative urban politics in some exotic culture found new perspectives contributed by students of urban phenomena in Western societies, perspectives which added a far different dimension to his thinking from those provided by his colleagues specializing in the same cultural area.

For its part, the Comparative Urban Administration and Politics Committee found in the seminar confirmation for its central focus as tentatively formulated. The Committee thus reaffirmed

[5] The eight participants were Robert R. Alford, Robert T. Daland, Daniel R. Grant, James F. Guyot, William J. Hanna, Francine F. Rabinovitz, Frank P. Sherwood, and Deil S. Wright. Judith Lynne Hanna also participated much of the time as the research associate for her husband, and Frederic Cleaveland, CUAP chairman, attended most of the sessions.

its objective to encourage use of the comparative approach in the study of urban administration in its social and political context. Furthermore, the Committee found support for the priority emphasis it has given to the development of cross-national comparative studies and to the advancement of the theory and methodology of comparative urban research. The seminar strengthened the commitment of the Committee to the promotion, in particular, of the development of data resources for cross-national urban research. The most important activities of the Committee in this direction thus far have been in organizing discussions with the U.N. Division of Public Administration and Statistical Offices on provision of comparative international urban data.[6]

As with any complex group process, many people have contributed significantly to this enterprise. All of us associated with the Committee and the seminar acknowledge a deep sense of personal obligation to Fred W. Riggs, chairman of the Comparative Administration Group. His intellectual leadership, his organizing genius, and his untiring efforts have indeed gone far towards building a new subdiscipline of comparative public administration. In the process his work and the standards of excellence in scholarship which this work exemplifies have helped to bring new rigor and conceptual richness into the study of public administration. His initiative led to the establishment of CUAP and his wise counsel and participation in several sessions aided greatly in planning and carrying on the urban research seminar. To acknowledge formally the central contribution of Fred W. Riggs to this enterprise, we have dedicated this volume on comparative urban research to him.

Among the seminar participants, Robert Daland served not only as director but also assumed editorial responsibility for putting this volume together and, with the important help of Francine Rabinovitz, he has seen it through the production process. We thank them both for this extra effort on behalf of all of us.

Four members of CUAP—William J. Gore, Victor Jones, Emil J. Sady, and Frank Smallwood—made important contributions to the thinking and broad planning which led to the research

[6] Further light is shed on the Committee's efforts in this direction by a paper written on Committee request by Francine F. Rabinovitz on "Data Resources for Cross-National Urban Research on Administration and Politics," scheduled for discussion at the U.N. during the summer of 1969.

seminar. The latter three also helped to sharpen the seminar papers by their participation in the final week. Their valued intellectual contribution is gratefully acknowledged.

We also acknowledge our indebtedness to Robert H. Trudeau and William C. Reynolds, the two graduate student assistants to the seminar, for aid well beyond the normal call of duty. Mr. Reynolds provided specialized skills in programming and data processing which proved invaluable to some of the participants. Mr. Trudeau, in addition to serving as general administrative assistant to the seminar director, also prepared the bibliography.

Our thanks go to the University of North Carolina for providing adequate and comfortable space and general logistical support through its Department of Political Science. Mrs. Louise Richey, Mrs. Joanne Robb and Miss Mary Fletcher provided essential secretarial services to meet the immediate needs of the seminar.

Finally, the activities of CUAP and the urban research seminar were financed out of a generous grant from the Ford Foundation to the Comparative Administration Group. This support is gratefully acknowledged. It should be added that each author takes full responsibility for the statements, opinions and interpretations contained in his essay, and these do not purport to represent the position of the Ford Foundation.

FREDERIC N. CLEAVELAND, *Chairman,*
Committee on Comparative Urban
Administration and Politics, CAG

CHAPEL HILL, N.C.
January 27, 1969

1 /

Comparative Perspectives
of Urban Systems

ROBERT T. DALAND

INTRODUCTION

THE PREPARATION OF THIS volume presumes that comparative urban politics is a distinctive field of study. If this be so, one expects the accoutrements of the field to be distinctive as well, including its concepts, issues, data, methods of analysis, and findings. It is the purpose of this chapter to characterize some distinctive problems and characteristics encountered in comparative urban political studies. Our objective will be clarified by stating two things that will not be attempted. In the first place, no effort will be made to define the field by drawing an inclusive and exclusive boundary around it. This seems a sterile exercise in view of the underdeveloped status of studies in comparative urban government. Secondly, no effort will be made to explore the problems of comparative analysis in general, or of cross-national and cross-cultural analysis. Such discussions are plentiful elsewhere.[1]

A word is in order, however, concerning the values of comparative urban research as compared with the study of national and international systems. These values are both strategic and substantive.

---

[1] Of particular value is the concise statement of problems of cross-cultural study contained in William John Hanna, "The Cross-Cultural Study of Local Politics," *Civilisations*, XVI, No. 1 (1966), 81–96; see also Robert E. Ward *et al., Studying Politics Abroad: Field Research in the Developing Areas* (Boston: Little, Brown, 1964).

Insofar as the scale of the urban system is substantially smaller than that of the nation, a condition which is frequently the case, the urban unit is more researchable with any given input of finances and effort where the nature of the research involves opinion surveys, interviewing in the field, physiographic variables or anything involving numbers of people or travel time and distance. Moreover, where the urban system is the research locale there is a choice among cities, which provides a greater opportunity to select a situation where access is good, the current political climate is conducive to investigation, or support services are available locally. In a specific nation it is an all or nothing proposition. One can easily list other advantages which fall under the general rubric of flexibility.

Much more important, however, are the substantive advantages. In the case of the primate city, where it exists, the urban system is such a dominant influence in the national system that the study of one necessarily involves the study of the other. It follows that under conditions where single cities are somewhat less dominant, they are still significant in national politics, suggesting that national systems cannot really be understood until the role of urban politics is understood. This would be true even in a large, highly multinucleated country. What we are saying is that microsystems research is crucial to macroanalysis where any complete understanding of the total system is an objective. The reverse is also true, since ecological variables are recognized as significant to urban studies. It would be highly significant in understanding the national system should we find that urban communities were *not* significant political units, since we know that in so many countries urban politics is an important basis for national political behavior. It is widely presumed that the regional basis of national politics is more important in the less developed countries than in more developed ones; and it is usually presumed that urban politics is the focus of regional politics despite an occasional exception on this score. If these notions are valid, urban politics is a crucial variable in national studies.

Having said that comparative urban studies are necessary to complete the vertical dimension of political studies generally, a word may be added about the horizontal dimension. Conceivably

urban study is merely an appendage of national political research. Urban political patterns would only be used as intra system
variables in this event. This position is rejected here on the
grounds that comparative urban studies are of intrinsic interest.
It has been noted that urban politics frequently varies more within
nations than among categories of cities in different nations. One
can find more parallels between the cities of southern Brazil, northern Europe, and northeastern U.S., probably, than between northern and southern Brazil, northern and southern Europe, or perhaps northeastern and Pacific Coast U.S. The manager plan distinguishes U.S. cities from those with the mayor or commission
forms. Manager cities are found also in Canada and Europe in substantial numbers. The variable "nation" or "culture" has not been
shown to be a decisive and exclusive conditioner of urban governmental patterns. Considerable light is shed on this question by
Robert Alford's discussion in the final chapter of this book.

Of those who would reject the city as an object of intrinsic
interest in political studies it should be asked, "Would you also
reject the study of interest groups in politics?" In specific research
arenas the question of whether the political glue is economic interest or geographic propinquity is surely an empirical one. In central
Brazil is the political glue São Paulo or coffee? To explain either
by the other would be rash.

THE UNIT OF ANALYSIS:
WHAT IS URBAN?

The urban political analyst is faced with a variety of alternatives about the object of his research which the student of national
systems does not have. The analyst of nations is provided with
specifically defined geographical boundaries, data are collected
within this boundary, and international comparisons can be made.
National polities operate within a single international context. In
Eastonian terms the boundaries between the system and the external environment are rather clearly defined.

The urbanist must make a choice (or a compromise) among

both vertical and spatial units of analysis. He may choose to focus his analysis on the consequences of urbanization (or urbanism) for the national political system. He may prefer to concentrate on the urban polity itself. He may choose to study behavior of the individual in an urban setting. What does each of these approaches imply? In the first case the analyst is concerned with the political and administrative consequences for the national political system of some series of "urban" phenomena. In the present volume aggregate data on urbanization are used by Rabinovitz as the independent variable. The research question is, "What is the difference between political behavior in the less urbanized as compared with the more urbanized nation?" If the nation is approached in system terms by the urbanist, the question is, "What urban subsystem outputs constitute significant national system inputs, and with what consequences?" It is evident that there is a very great range between systems in which urban polities constitute an important input into national politics and those in which it does not. Presumably this continuum correlates highly with that which represents the range between nations with a high proportion of their citizens living in cities and those in which a high proportion do not.

   This question has received very little attention. One reason for this is that nations are not usually organized on a two-level basis consisting of the nation, and of the urban (or rural) units directly below. Rather there are varying patterns of intermediate states, provinces, and districts. Thus, when urban polity outputs are only indirectly translated into national system inputs through their impact on some intermediate polity such as the state, the independent effect of the urban polity is difficult to isolate. The dramatic case is the national capital which historically has participated in national politics, of which Paris is but one obvious example. The practice of establishing a special district controlled by the national government itself, to control the forces of urban politics on the scene, is a response to historical experiences. The role of primate cities generally has been observed unsystematically. For the most part, however, urban system inputs to the national system have not been subjected to systematic study. It even seems worthwhile to ask whether urban systems, in general, produce significant political inputs into a national system. This is an empirical question. The persistence of urban units of government suggests that they are functional from a system point of view. But are they functional to a national system of which they are a part, or to their own members who employ their influence with the national, or an intermediate, government to seek autonomy which is neither functional nor dysfunctional for the national system, and therefore tolerated? [2] The answers to this question appear to vary considerably. Some have suggested that for Brazil the municipalities may have proven politically functional to the state and national systems, but not to the local citizenry. Donald Rosenthal finds that municipal governments in India serve purposes of personal and group status for interests without access at district, state, and national levels.[3] Parenthetically, it may be noted that the existence of a very large social and physical urban community does not necessarily insure the creation of a formal local government covering the area. The state of Rajasthan in India has not provided corporate status for the city of Jaipur, with its more than 400,000 population. In fact, there were only twenty municipal corporations in India as of 1964.[4]

The second analytical perspective concentrates on the urban polity itself. It has been the habit of many analysts of U.S. city government to regard state and national contexts as relatively constant, and to treat the urban polity as though it were a more or less closed system. For some purposes this is an appropriate position. When the objective is to study community power structure, virtually by definition, it is a question of ascertaining who it is that wields the power that the urban government possesses. Implicitly, the amount of this power is roughly the same as between cities being compared, and the amount is also regarded as significant to the members of the urban system. In cross-national studies

[2] One example of direct municipal intervention in national politics is traced for São Paulo by Richard M. Morse, "The Metropolis as Polis," in *From Community to Metropolis: A Biography of São Paulo, Brazil* (Gainesville: University of Florida Press, 1958), pp. 238–56.

[3] Donald B. Rosenthal, "Problems in Comparative Analysis of Urban Political Systems" (unpublished paper based on a presentation at the University of North Carolina, January 24, 1967), p. 10.

[4] Donald B. Rosenthal, "Administrative Policies in Two Indian Cities," *Asian Survey*, VI (April, 1966), 203.

it is necessary to recognize that there is a tremendous variation in the amount of power over political outcomes in the city which is in the hands of the members of the system itself. Even here, the urban polity may be viewed as a closed system, though the variation in the amount (significance) of locally exercised power would presumably condition the structure of power. Competition for power would be less where the stakes are low.

However, if the purpose is to explain political outcomes generally, and urban system outputs specifically, it is necessary to consider all the decision centers with power over the city. Even in the U.S. decision centers for specific matters and for specific cities are often located in the state or national government. One of the central problems of comparative urban research is to deal with the great variation among countries respecting centralization and decentralization of power to act in urban affairs. Some countries do not delegate significant authority to local government bodies. Others, like Brazil, provide broad independent authority for municipal government in law but not in reality. Brazil's federal constitution provides the forms for decentralized government at state and municipal levels in a pattern that many students of the subject would regard as ideal. One simple defect, however, reverses form and reality. Municipal governments have only the most meager financial resources.

It is crucial to deal with this particular variable, since it concerns the validity of political system analysis for urban government. Where the formal city is no more than an administrative district of the central government in fact, the urban "subsystem" is at best an unimportant factor in explaining urban political outcomes. In this case the analyst who seeks to focus on a specific urban polity has the alternative of redefining the urban system to include all the decision centers that affect outcomes in the locality. When he does this, he may find that much of his "system" in fact consists of elements of state and national institutions, and that these elements also constitute much of the "system" for other urban communities as well. The dilemma is that urban study becomes either insignificant or diffuse.[5]

---

[5] An interesting discussion of the problems of municipal and national system relationships which bears on this point, among many others, runs through Frank

Thus, it becomes crucial to measure real political autonomy. Despite legal norms large cities tend to have more autonomy than small ones. The problem is to find appropriate indicators of real autonomy. Traditionally formal-legal criteria have been employed.[6] An alternative approach has been explored using an index based on the percentage relationship between local and national public revenues and expenditures in forty-five nations.[7] The measurement of autonomy, or devolution, is not only of concern to the researcher, but also to the policy-maker. Frank Sherwood's study in these pages explores the problems encountered in implementing a policy of devolution, recognizing that formal devolution alone cannot be expected to produce real autonomy.

The third level of analysis concerns the behavior of the individual in urban settings. For this purpose some definition of what is "urban" is needed. This is rather easily provided by adopting some minimum standard of urbanity which is obviously non-rural, such as a minimum population size for urban centers of 50,000 with a density criterion.[8] The more serious problem is the isolation of cultural factors from "urban" factors. That is, the apparent effect of city size may disappear when one compares the inhabitant of a city of 20,000 in a highly urbanized country with many metropolitan areas, to the man who lives in a city of the same size which is one of a very few urban centers in a predominantly rural country.

These problems are compounded by the spatial alternatives open to the urban researcher. Here he faces a series of complex problems. The least of them is that in different countries data are

---

Sherwood, *Institutionalizing the Grass Roots in Brazil* (San Francisco: Chandler, 1967).

[6] For a discussion of this question see Frank P. Sherwood, "The Correlates of Decentralization: Interpretations, Speculations, Strategies" (unpublished paper presented to the CAG Urban Studies Seminar, University of North Carolina, August 1967), mimeo, pp. 1–10.

[7] Paulo Reis Vieira, "Toward a Theory of Decentralization: A Comparative View of Forty-Five Countries" (doctoral dissertation, University of Southern California, Los Angeles, 1967). This study is concerned with the correlates of decentralization.

[8] Robert Fried reports that in portions of Italy towns of 35,000 to 50,000 are essentially "rural," having peasant populations, "Urbanization and Italian Politics," *Journal of Politics*, XXIX (August, 1967), 511. See also Nathan Whetten, *Rural Mexico* (Chicago: University of Chicago Press, 1948), p. 524. Whetten says to be urban a Mexican town must be over 10,000 population.

collected on the basis of different definitions of what is urban. The core of the problem is that the area of urban settlement, the governmental boundary, and the area of the urban political community do not correspond. The governmental boundary may include much more or much less than the area of urban settlement. While the political community or system probably *tends* to conform to the governmental boundary, this can by no means be relied on. In some metropolitan areas formal boundaries are overlapping to an extent that they are very poor guides to the limits of the political system. In other areas such as Brazil, the political system is largely confined to the densely populated urban area, while the governmental boundary extends a considerable distance into a rural hinterland excluded from power. In this volume William and Judith Hanna report a study of two African towns, one in Nigeria and one in Uganda. In both cases the urban area was closely circled by the official town boundary while the area of primary political interaction extended well beyond into the territories of the clans from which the town dwellers came. In one case the political community was encompassed in a county, while in the other no formal boundary marked the area of interaction. Another problem is suggested by Fred Burke's study of African local systems. His category of "segmented local political systems" includes those in which authority is distributed without regard to specific spatial boundaries.[9]

The problem does not stop here, however. Even if we are able to isolate those communities where the governmental boundary and the political system conform to the "real" urban community, there is a serious additional problem. There are two definitions of "urban." One is that used above, which is defined by density and size of population. The other, usually referred to as "urbanism," reflects behaviors or "style of life." How valid is the assumption that an urbane style of life will be found in large, densely populated communities? However valid the assumption may have been during certain periods of history, or in certain countries, it is certainly not a universal pattern. When we broaden the context of urban studies to the world we find many exceptions. The persist-

[9] Fred G. Burke, *Local Goverment and Politics in Uganda* (Syracuse: Syracuse University Press, 1964), p. 239 *passim*.

ence of a "folk" culture in places like Rangoon; the existence of
constantly reinforced pockets of rural population resulting from
migration—especially in cities not experiencing industrial growth
—and strikingly different rates of assimilation in urban settings,
call into question the use of the size-density criterion.[10] If "urbanity" cannot be assumed in large cities, it would appear, "rurality"
cannot be assumed in the hinterland judging by the argument in
Guyot's contribution to this volume, to say nothing of the well
known "urbanity" of such rural districts as upper Westchester
County and similar suburban areas which ring many metropolitan
centers.[11]

These complexities suggest the fruitlessness of attempting to
seek out areas which conform to traditional criteria. Rather, it
seems appropriate to accept formal local government boundaries
for research purposes, and to recognize that *change* in the direction
of increasing density and scale, whatever the previous base, is the
crucial indicator of urbanization. Changing areas can be distinguished from static or declining ones. Even a process of de-urban-
ization is conceivable, though we could by no means conclude that
lowered residential density in a given space is necessarily the indicator of such a process. Lowered density can be found in such
places as industrial parks, urban renewal areas, and the like, where
the significant inference is that a change in urban land use is
occurring.

COMPARABILITY

We have just raised a question about the universal utility of
size-density criteria as a basis for selecting the unit of analysis for
urban political research. This implies what should now be made

[10] On the last point an enlightening analysis is Lyle W. Shannon and Magdaline
Shannon, "The Assimilation of Migrants to Cities: Anthropological and Sociological
Contributions," in Leo F. Schnore and Henry Fagin (eds.), *Urban Research and
Policy Planning* ("Urban Affairs Annual Reviews," Vol. I [Beverly Hills: Sage, 1967]).

[11] A detailed critique of the use of the rural-urban dichotomy is found in Philip
M. Hauser, "Observations on the Urban-Folk and Urban-Rural Dichotomies as
Forms of Western Ethnocentrism," in Philip M. Hauser and Leo F. Schnore (eds.),
The Study of Urbanization (New York: Wiley, 1965).

explicit. That is, we face a choice of assumptions about the comparability of urban communities. There are at least three alternatives.

We have questioned the first, but most prevalent assumption. This holds that there are certain universals that apply to urbanization. Cities are characterized by relatively greater size, density, and heterogeneity of the population. These factors lead to secularization, secondary relationships, segmentation of roles, and multiplication (or breaking down) of norms. Individual isolation increases. It is asserted that such effects are independent of industrialization or of culture.[12] The appeal of this analysis is very great. If we could assume all this, we could take the additional step of searching for the universal political and administrative techniques which would be effective in handling urban problems, given any specified ends.

The second assumption, in contrast to the first, is that there are no universals which hold true of urban communities, and that, therefore, there is no basis on which to compare them as a class. This position is more commonly implicit rather than explicit. However, it appears frequently enough as writers assert, for example, that comparisons are valid within the British Colonies, or within Spanish America, or within Western Europe, but that comparisons between these areas can produce nothing useful because each area exhibits an entirely different cultural syndrome which dominates political events, behaviors, and structures within that category. The same rejection of comparability may be based on grounds of governmental structure, with or without presuming that this, in turn, is a reflection of the broader cultural factors. Thus, it is commonly asserted that there is no basis for comparing large with small cities, cities in federal systems with cities in unitary systems, or industrial with trading cities, to pick at random.

We suspect that this second assumption arises from the efforts of researchers to justify their own particular needs to include and exclude, for very pragmatic reasons, some of which will be noted below. A third position has more appeal. If we neither assert nor deny the presence of universals, where do we begin? While the

12 Louis Wirth, "Urbanism as a Way of Life," *American Journal of Sociology,* XLIV (July, 1938), 1–24.

answer is not simple in practice, it is clear as a methodological concept. In the presence of a confusion of complex variables whose relationships are not known, we must somehow control most of the variables while focusing on the relationship between two, or a few of them. This is frustratingly difficult in the case of urban community comparisons. Given the notorious non-comparability of urban political community data due to differences in the kinds of data collected, the processing and availability of data, the methods of collection, the variation in ability and goals of the collectors, and the preservation practices, most research of a rigorously comparative kind requires that the researcher send his own staff into the field. As a result of the problems discussed above, he is able to achieve comparability by controlling variables through a careful selection of cities which are similar with respect to a number of variables. Fortunately there are a great many cities in the world. So the researcher, for example, might select for a study of leadership behavior only cities that have the following characteristics: heavy industry, a shipping (port) center, population of 500,000 to 700,000, 50 per cent of the population from a major ethnic group and the remainder equally divided among two other ethnic groups, federal system of national government, and a similar degree of autonomy. One might have to search the world to find a significant number of examples, and they might be scattered so widely that the research would be extremely expensive. Moreover, whatever uniformities should appear (recognizing the number of variables still uncontrolled using this particular universe) would apply only to this particular set of cities. Despite the operational difficulty, however, the ultimate reward would be cumulative, and, therefore, valuable. Whatever uniformities might appear from this approach could not be attributed to cultural factors, since culture would deliberately have been left uncontrolled.

Culture, however, is not a variable to be completely cast aside. A great variety of individual case studies explain apparently unique patterns of political behavior in cultural terms. In the final chapter Robert Alford provides us with an appropriate perspective with which to deal with these matters. He suggests that a specific series of events may not differ very much from one country to another, but that what we must look for is a variation in the *probability* that certain types of events or behaviors will occur. This probability, he suggests, will vary with structural and cultural factors. The notion that one negative example will disprove a hypothesis thus appears less useful than the strategy of discovering the incidence of certain types of events or situations in different urban communities, and then trying to discover what variables tend to correspond to different probabilities that such situations will be found.

We have argued, then, that comparability may be sought by controlling the type of urban polity through selection of similar city types in a variety of cultural or structural settings; or that it may be approached through observing the incidence of a given type or series of situation or event in a variety of cultural or structural settings. This observation is not intended to derogate research which controls both culture and structure as in the case of comparative studies within the U.S., for example. These provide us with valuable clues. If great variability occurs *within* cultures and structures, we would certainly expect the same among cultures. Where we observe uniformity within cultures, these may be sought between nations of similar historical background, then among nations of somewhat dissimilar background, and finally among nations of highly dissimilar background, until we observe the break in the pattern, or, more likely, the decreasing incidence of the behavior in question. Deil Wright's study of manager cities in the U.S. was deliberately included in this volume partly in order to observe in the same context the contrast in approaches.

The above remarks are addressed to general questions of *what* to compare. There are many additional very thorny questions of *how* to compare cross-nationally. How can we be sure that we have compared the same thing, given our particular research objectives? This has been dealt with at length in discussions of comparative political research. Here we will only discuss one particular problem of equivalence which is crucial in urban political studies, though it also appears in cross-national research generally. How may we identify and compare subgroups in the community? The core of the problem is that the subgroup structure of urban communities differs radically cross-nationally. Unlike such cases as political culture, leadership ideology, formal structure, and participation level, no models or typologies of subgroup structure have been developed which are suitable for comparing cross-nationally. The upper, middle, and lower class distinction is employed, but is of little value when it is the division within these groups, and sometimes transcending them, that is significant.

We have little difficulty listing and broadly classifying the kinds of interest groups. In the U.S. the list of associational groups relevant to politics is notorious. Institutional groups like the church, the army, the bureaucracy, exist in all countries. In the less developed and transitional countries ascriptive communal groups abound. The vast variety of these has made it difficult even to coin a term to encompass such variable elements as those suggested by the terms tribe, clan, race, status, religion, language, clect, *panelinha,* extended family, and others. James Coleman has made the point that the relative strengths and roles of subgroups of different kinds have a reciprocal dependence.

> The strength and tenacity of communal and similar groupings militates against the emergence of functionally specific groups as the foci of interest identification and expression. The fact that the latter are either nonexistent or undeveloped serves not only to perpetuate the former, but also to invite, if not to compel, institutional interest groups to assume a preponderant role.[13]

Thus, it is not useful simply to list the subgroups in the urban community, but rather we must identify the syndromes of interrelationship among groups which are displayed among urban communities.

The immediate research problem is illustrated by the techniques of power structure analysis developed in the United States. They tend to identify associational and institutional groups but not the less formal types. The Miller-Form technique, for example, employs an identification panel consisting of fourteen people, two each considered knowledgeable in the areas of mass communications, business, labor, welfare, education, government, and religion.[14] William Hanna notes that in his study of Umuahia and

---

[13] Gabriel Almond and James Coleman (eds.), *The Politics of the Developing Areas* (Princeton, N.J.: Princeton University Press, 1960), p. 548.

[14] William H. Form and Warren L. Sauer, *Community Influentials in a Middle-Sized City* (East Lansing: Institute for Community Development, Michigan State University, 1960).

Mbale such a panel would not have been relevant and could not be reproduced. Further, he suggests if each of these sectors had existed, it would not have been appropriate to use the same panel, because of the presence of other crucial groupings in the African communities which would have been left out.[15]

The problem is not only one of identifying the groups and their role in the political process, but also the vertical and horizontal linkages of the groups outside the community and how these linkages condition local political behavior. Thus, in the case of the *panelinha* as described by Anthony Leeds the linkage is vertical, going to the state and possibly national levels in a variety of areas of activity.[16] In the case of the African community the focal actor described by William and Judith Hanna has both vertical and horizontal linkages. This problem is only partially solved by concentrating on the group leader and his role. Role analysis would be effective if all the groups had a single discreet leader who was not involved in a leadership role in other groups. However, some of the groups noted above have a much more complex leadership structure than this.

Now we come to the rather presumptuous task of characterizing the research that students of comparative urban government have done. Rather than to present a catalogue and classification of all the studies in the fashion of an annotated bibliography, the intention is to represent five major themes around which the bulk of significant work clusters. This procedure runs the danger of disregarding entirely works which do not fit the scheme, and of underemphasizing major studies which exploit several of the themes. These costs will be paid in the interest of emphasizing the major contrasting approaches. In each area the substantive questions which seem the most important will be noted.

A dominant fact about the entire body of material is that in each category a shift has recently occurred in the research empha-

---

[15] Hanna, *op. cit.*, p. 7; see also a discussion of the general problem with relation to Latin-American urban power structure studies in Francine Rabinovitz, "Sound and Fury Signifying Nothing? A Review of Community Power Research in Latin America," *Urban Affairs Quarterly*, III (March, 1968), 111–22.

[16] Anthony Leeds, "Brazilian Careers and Social Structure: An Evolutionary Model and Case History," *American Anthropologist*, LXVI (December, 1964), 1321–45.

sis. Formerly, empirical work was theory poor while rich in descriptive detail. During the past decade theory has outrun empirical validation. A second trend has been a shift in interest from static situations to a concern with the processes of change. What appears below is a mixture which reflects past scholarship, contemporary research, and some models which remain to be detailed and tested in the future.[17]

The five substantive research problems are: (1) the effects of local government structure in metropolitan areas, (2) the urban and local government systems of nations, (3) problems of community integration, especially the roles of community elites, (4) the effects of ecological factors on local political systems, and (5) the effects of urban politics on the national polity.

FORMAL STRUCTURE IN METROPOLITAN AREAS

In 1965, Frank Smallwood noted that:

> Despite centuries of reliance upon local government institutions, neither England nor the United States has ever really developed a coherent theoretical framework in which to evaluate the effectiveness of such [local government] institutions, especially in terms of their future relevance to the newer challenges of urbanization that have come to characterize modern society.[18]

Having the good fortune of several centuries in which to create useful local government institutions in these countries, trial and error was sufficient to create highly viable structures. Latterly, tensions have risen in the industrial megalopoli, while metropoli

---

[17] The present writer expresses a great debt to the participants in the Conference on Comparative Research in Community Politics, University of Georgia, 1966 in the preparation of this section. The reader will find in the proceedings of this conference a more detailed commentary on many of the matters discussed here, particularly with reference to comparative studies in the United States. See Thomas R. Dye (ed.), *Comparative Research in Community Politics* (Athens: University of Georgia Press, 1967).

[18] *Greater London: The Politics of Metropolitan Reform* (Indianapolis: Bobbs-Merrill, 1965), p. 288.

of the developing world have succumbed to the worldwide trend toward metropolitanization. In these circumstances scholars have turned to the analysis of the metropolis as a problem of formal organization, as a problem in effective administration, and, most recently and tentatively, as a problem of systemic function.

The first of these approaches has until recently been investigated by searching for means of retaining the old relationship between the urban community and its governmental boundary—keeping the city limits at or beyond the limit of urbanization. The utility of this procedure was assumed for much of the last half century. The difficulty of achieving this objective in practice led to the study of a variety of modifications of the one-government concept allowing for cooperation, consolidation of single functions, and two-tier systems as alternatives. The first studies of comparative metropolitan government, other than seriatim descriptions of discreet situations, were inspired by the desire to discover the causes of success or, more frequently, failure of metropolitan governmental reform campaigns.[19] These studies employed such concepts as participants, group motivation, strategies, and stakes to explain the outcomes in particular cities. For the first time research focused on what did happen rather than what should happen. Only in 1963 was more than one case evaluated within a single book on a comparative basis; this was when Scott Greer used the same variables to consider the reform campaigns of St. Louis, Cleveland, and Miami.[20] Here he identifies nine gross variables and how they operated in each city.[21]

The next step on the road to the construction of empirical

[19] The most useful of these are: Edward Sofen, *The Miami Metropolitan Experiment* (Bloomington: Indiana University Press, 1964); Henry J. Schmandt, P. G. Steinbicker, and G. D. Wendel, *Metropolitan Reform in St. Louis: A Case Study* (New York: Holt, Rinehart & Winston, 1961); Frank Smallwood, *Greater London: The Politics of Metropolitan Reform* (Indianapolis: Bobbs-Merrill, 1965); Brett Hawkins, *Nashville Metro: The Politics of City-County Consolidation* (Nashville: Vanderbilt University Press, 1966); Henry J. Schmandt, *The Milwaukee Metropolitan Study Commission* (Bloomington: Indiana University Press, 1965); Christian Larsen et al., *Growth and Government in Sacramento* (Bloomington: Indiana University Press, 1965); and Winston W. Crouch and Beatrice Dinerman, *Southern California Metropolis: A Study in Development of Government for a Metropolitan Area* (Berkeley: University of California Press, 1963).

[20] Scott Greer, *Metropolitics: A Study of Political Culture* (New York: Wiley, 1963).

[21] *Ibid.*, p. 198.

propositions about metropolitan structure is to evaluate the effects of structural change. The discovery of indicators of such effects has been elusive. A pioneer step in this direction is reported in this volume by Dan Grant, who sought the perceptions of key informants in Miami, Nashville, and Toronto in order to judge the effects of the new metropolitan governments on eight questions central to reform campaigns. The eight central issues vary in the degree to which they can be empirically measured. Measurement, however, is more reliable than our ability to attribute change to the structural reform. Future steps might involve the study of a sufficient number of experimental situations to enable researchers to distinguish change due to structural reform from other sources of change.

The second area of comparative metropolitan studies is concerned less with structure as such than with the more immediate and increasingly pressing task of administering the functions of the metropolis. The most common approach to this subject has been the study of some particular governmental function through a case study of a decision or series of decisions.[22] Within the present decade, however, a new interest in comparing action on common metropolitan problems among a variety of the great cities of the world has become apparent.[23] The most notable product of this interest to date has been a series of studies conducted by the Institute of Public Administration and the United Nations. Data have been collected in thirteen major metropolitan areas including Calcutta, Casablanca, Davao, Karachi, Lagos, Leningrad, Lima, Lodz, Paris, Stockholm, Toronto, Valencia, and Zagreb. For the most part, data were collected in each of these urban regions on the basis of the same highly structured study guide. Some of the data are in quantitative form, and much more are not. The

[22] The most notable collections of metropolitan cases are Roscoe C. Martin *et al., Decisions in Syracuse* (Bloomington: Indiana University Press, 1961) and Deil Wright and Robert Mowitz, *Profile of a Metropolis* (Detroit: Wayne State University Press, 1962). Both compare a variety of decisions within a single metropolitan area.

[23] See the series edited by Franco Archibugi, *Inchiesta Sull' Organizzazione Administrativa De Alcune Grandi Metropoli Del Mondo* (Rome: Centro di Studi e Piani Economici, 1967). Among the cities covered in this study are Moscow, Paris, Toronto, Chicago, London, New York, Stockholm and Philadelphia.

crucial point is, however, that sufficient comparability has been achieved so that it is now possible for the first time to construct a set of propositions about comparative metropolitan administration to be subjected to empirical testing. The study has appeared in two forms: individual city monographs, and an analytical volume based on the individual field studies.[24] To the comparative urbanist the analytical volume is of great interest.[25] It consists chiefly of descriptive generalizations on a vast range of problems of urban administration both organizational and functional. Administrative "problems" are defined as "governmental and bureaucratic factors that limit the capability of the public sector . . . to respond to urban demands" for extension of basic services, the need for which is the result of rapid urbanization, and to do so at minimum costs while insuring that the physical growth enhances the urban environment and that appropriate economic development of the area occurs.[26] This represents a definition of urban administration consistent with the usual formally stated development goals of the communities themselves.

These manifest goals are used as the general criterion for assessing success of metropolitan administration. Conclusions are drawn respecting factors that interfere with goal achievement. Decision-making diffused among greater, rather than fewer, decision centers, for example, is presumed to lessen effective administration—a conclusion reminiscent of U.S. metropolitan studies. Perhaps the most striking conclusion is that national level policies, as represented in national plans, have important developmental implications for urban centers which have not been carefully assessed. Explicit national urbanism policies, moreover, have proven inefficient in achieving the goals of metropolitan administration. In sum, the work of Walsh and the Institute team takes

[24] The individual monographs include: Annmarie Hauck Walsh, *Urban Government for the Paris Region* (New York: Praeger, 1968); Babatunde A. Williams and Annmarie Hauck Walsh, *Urban Government for Metropolitan Lagos* (New York: Praeger, 1968); Eugen Pusic and Annmarie Hauck Walsh, *Urban Government for Zagreb, Yugoslavia* (New York: Praeger, 1968); Hans Calmfors, Francine F. Rabinovitz and Daniel Alesch, *Urban Government for Greater Stockholm* (New York: Praeger, 1968); David Cattell, *Leningrad: A Case Study of Soviet Urban Government* (New York: Praeger, 1968).

[25] Annmarie Hauck Walsh, *The Urban Challenge to Government: An International Comparison of Thirteen Cities* (New York: Praeger, 1969).

[26] *Ibid.*, p. 9.

initial, important but inconclusive steps both in the direction of empirical comparative analysis and of normative advice on the solution of perceived problems.

The study of metropolitan government is peculiarly devoid of rigorously empirical research on administrative problems. An important exception is a recent comparative study of metropolitan fiscal behavior by Campbell and Sacks.[27] A series of tax and expenditure variables are explained by use of a number of independent variables derived from census data. These patterns are compared among metropolitan areas and within metropolitan areas. The study is similar to work previously done in particular cities, or for particular categories of local or state governments. It is unique, however, in that it performs the complex task of treating metropolitan regions as units. In the process, some innovative analytical techniques are employed to resolve such problems as the differing patterns of state-local aid among the states, in order to achieve comparability among metropolitan areas. While the study is confined to the United States, some of these techniques are suggestive for cross-national comparisons where the same kind of dissimilarities are encountered.

A third focus to the study of comparative metropolitics is the "system" approach. This is not to imply that there is a single view of what the metropolitan "system" is. Three models of the system have been distinguished.[28] Victor Jones has suggested that the metropolitan system may resemble the arena of international politics and that local governments treat with each other as more or less independent sovereignties.[29] A second analogy compares the metropolitan region to an economic market. From this point of view each political unit supplies a different combination of services and levels of service from which the consumer may choose

[27] Alan K. Campbell and Seymour Sacks, *Metropolitan America: Fiscal Patterns and Governmental Systems* (New York: The Free Press, 1967).

[28] These are discussed in Henry J. Schmandt, "Toward Comparability in Metropolitan Research," in Thomas R. Dye (ed.), *Comparative Research in Community Politics* (Athens: University of Georgia Press, 1967), and Oliver P. Williams, "Life-Style Values and Political Decentralization in Metropolitan Areas," *Southwest Social Science Quarterly*, XLVIII (December, 1967), 299–301.

[29] Victor Jones, "The Organization of a Metropolitan Region," *University of Pennsylvania Law Review*, CV (February, 1957), 538–52. This idea is developed in Matthew Holden, "The Governance of the Metropolis as a Problem in Diplomacy," *Journal of Politics*, XXVI (August, 1964), 627–47.

when he selects a site for home or business.[30] The third "model" has no name, and perhaps its versions are different enough so that it should not be termed a "model" at all. In any event, there is a perceptible tendency to view the metropolitan system as holistic. Here the central concern is the integrative tissue which ties the whole system together. This approach has proven more easily operationalized than the others in political terms and a variety of social science concepts have been brought to bear. Life-style and socioeconomic distance have been employed in evaluating patterns of integration—an outgrowth of the studies of support and opposition to formal governmental integration efforts.[31] Of special interest and potential utility in cross-national comparisons is Oliver Williams' distinction between "life-style" and "system maintenance" functions. He contends that life-style functions, reflecting diverse value orientations, tend to be decentralized governmentally, while the system maintenance functions (e.g., utility and communications systems) reflect convergent values and interests and tend to become centralized.[32]

An entirely different approach to metropolitan integration has been developed by Karl Deutsch and his associate James V. Toscano. Toscano studied transaction flows in the Philadelphia metropolitan area as measured by such variables as residence-work locations and intergovernmental agreements to evaluate integration. He concludes that it is possible to develop measures which are comparable within and among U.S. and Canadian metropoli-

[30] See Charles Tiebout, "A Pure Theory of Local Expenditures," *The Journal of Political Economy*, LXIV (October, 1956), 416–24; Robert Warren, "A Municipal Services Market Model of Metropolitan Organization," *Journal of the American Institute of Planners*, XXX (August, 1964), 193–204; Vincent Ostrom, Charles Tiebout, and Robert Warren, "The Organization of Government in the Metropolitan Area: A Theoretical Inquiry," *American Political Science Review*, LV (December, 1961), 385–87. This model has been questioned by Wilbur R. Thompson, *A Preface to Urban Economics* (Baltimore: The Johns Hopkins Press, 1965), pp. 259–63.

[31] See especially Oliver P. Williams *et al.*, *Suburban Differences and Metropolitan Policies: A Philadelphia Story* (Philadelphia: University of Pennsylvania Press, 1965), chap. 9; and Brett Hawkins, "Life Style, Demographic Distance and Voter Support of City-County Consolidation," *Southwest Social Science Quarterly*, XLVIII (December,1967), 325–37.

[32] See Oliver Williams, "A Framework for Metropolitan Political Analysis," in Thomas Dye (ed.), *Comparative Research in Community Politics* (Athens: University of Georgia Press, 1967), and "Life-Style Values and Political Decentralization in Metropolitan Areas," *op. cit.*

tan areas.[33] The utility of the same measures in countries where technological levels are much lower is yet to be explored.

Complementing and extending the approaches to internal integration of metropolitan areas just discussed is the recent work of Harold Kaplan.[34] He applies the concepts of functional analysis to the metropolitan area for the first time. Two groups of system functions are identified: the adaptive, external, problem-solving function which adjusts the polity to its physical and social environment; and the integrative function which provides normative and non-normative internal integration for the system. These concepts are refined conceptually, but not operationalized in this study in a fashion which would make them immediately useful in cross-national metropolitan studies. However, this work is a superb example of the utility of a single case in the refinement of concepts of theoretical relevance, and in applying them to a metropolitan arena.

Kaplan discusses the conflict between the integrative and adaptive function and says that:

> Successful integrative performance is the securing of enough internal support and unity to provide for a continuity in the system's structure and to permit the system to meet environmental demands. Successful adaptation may be defined as the attraction of sufficient external support to make survival and the securing of internal support possible.[35]

The treatment is development oriented, and development is defined as "an increase in the level of a system's adaptive or integrative performance." [36] Differentiation and specialization are taken as the index of development. They increase the possibility of absorbing all the relevant messages from the environment, though they make agreement within the system more difficult. "The key to sustained development appears to be the creation of coordinating mechanisms that preserve much of the system's earlier unity without curbing the development of more complex structures." [37] The

[33] James V. Toscano, "Transaction Flow Analysis in Metropolitan Areas: Some Preliminary Explorations," in Philip E. Jacob and James V. Toscano (eds.), *The Integration of Political Communities* (Philadelphia: J. B. Lippincott, 1964).

[34] Harold Kaplan, *Urban Political Systems: A Functional Analysis of Metro Toronto* (New York: Columbia University Press, 1967).

[35] *Ibid.*, pp. 246–47.

[36] *Ibid.*, p. 247.

[37] *Ibid.*, p. 249.

ideas combined here are not new in themselves, reflecting Deutsch, LaPalombara and Eisenstadt among others. The application to metropolitan communities, however, is original. The Kaplan volume serves as a link between the internal integration of a metropolitan community and the relation of that community to its environment—i.e. to the national political system. The role of urban governments generally in the national system is a second major focus of the literature, to which we now turn.

LOCAL GOVERNMENT IN THE NATIONAL SYSTEM

Urban governments stand in a relationship to their national government (and the urban system to the national system) such that both produce significant impacts on the other. Perhaps unfortunately, however, scholars and others tend to view urban government either from the point of view of the national impacts on the local system or the reverse—the impacts of the local systems on the nation. Keeping in mind the reciprocal nature of intergovernmental relations, we will focus first on national impacts on local systems.

The bulk of what has been written on local government systems is descriptive of existing formal arrangements and divisions of power and activity between central and local authorities.[38] Some efforts have been made to devise classifications of these systems. For example, the UN report on *Decentralization for National and Local Development* employs a fourfold division based on the division of power between central and local governments: (1) services provided by local governments on a comprehensive basis; (2) some services provided by local governments, others provided by the

[38] The core of this literature is: United Nations Technical Assistance Program, *Decentralization for National and Local Development*, ST/TAO/M/19 (New York: United Nations, 1962); Henry Maddick, *Democracy, Decentralization and Development* (London: Asia Publishing House, 1963); Harold Alderfer, *Local Government in Developing Countries* (New York: McGraw-Hill, 1964); Samuel Humes and Eileen Martin, *The Structure of Local Governments Throughout the World* (The Hague: Martinus Nijhoff, 1961). In addition to these studies, there is a very large number of studies of local government systems in particular countries and regions.

central government or its districts; (3) central and local government authority parallel, resulting in predominance of centrally provided services due to inadequate local resources; and (4) most services directly provided by the central government. Insofar as they are intended to describe country patterns, such categories tend to de-emphasize the variations in real relationships which occur in the case of large cities with their larger resources, both financial and political.[39]

A contrasting approach to classification is that of Fred Burke, extracted from the African experience.[40] He classifies political systems rather than formal institutions, and uses the differing patterns of social connective tissue which tie the system together as the basis for classification. Thus, local systems are (1) predominantly segmented, based on kinship ties and not strongly tied to a particular geographical area; (2) predominantly spatial, based on the bond of occupying a common geographical space; and (3) predominantly functional, based on bonds of profession, class, interest, or other specialized function. One can see in this set of types the possibility that they may be related to different developmental stages on the road between traditionalism and modernity. The functional type Burke identifies as characteristically urban, where the tie to a common locality is weaker than that of functional roles in the society. Defining the local political system in this way suggests one explanation for the difficulty in transferring local space-oriented loyalties in a suburban community to the larger metropolitan "community." The essence of the latter is functional specialization, while the former is homogeneous and place oriented.

When we pass from descriptions of "systems" of local governments and their institutions, we find that the propositions about national impacts on urban and other local governments center around two critical questions: (1) the extent and character of governmental policy to control the settlement pattern on the land (the size and location of cities in urban terms), and (2) the extent

---

[39] A modified version of this classification is now being developed by the UN, and will include the additional dimension of the degree to which the local government pattern is integrated at the metropolitan level.

[40] Fred G. Burke, *Local Government and Politics in Uganda* (Syracuse: Syracuse University Press, 1964), pp. 239–46.

and character of autonomy to be exercised by urban governments.

National policy on urban location is discussed in two contexts. The initial stages of urbanization in an underdeveloped country are attributed almost universally to the impact of foreign influence. The impact is described in economic, technological, or administrative terms in varying mixtures.[41] Especially the capital city and regional capitals are seen as the outgrowth of the administrative needs of colonial governments. With the political elite assembling in the political capital two things appear to follow: the tendency to pour national resources into the capital city's physical development; and the development of the elite's financial interests through the capital, be it commercial expansion or later industrial expansion.

In the later and post colonial stages of development, the context is the urbanization policy of the nation itself. Pressures toward urban growth are clearly worldwide at the present juncture in history, however exogenous the initial stimuli may have been. Policies toward this growth have been directed toward slowing it, channeling it, and stimulating it. These may all appear at different times and places within as well as among countries. Political analysts have only begun to probe the significance and potential of policies of urban control. A few illustrations will suggest the range of considerations involved. India has concentrated on the development of villages, virtually disregarding such old British-built cities as Calcutta, Bombay, and Madras. This appears to be a slow-down strategy of making the rural society sufficiently attractive to prevent the urban migration. Britain and France have both tried measures intended to prevent further centralization of population around London and Paris through channeling of population to smaller urban centers. Eastern European countries, notably Poland, have well developed policies of urban decentralization intended to channel population to medium sized places.

[41] Among a host of examples the following are illustrative: Norton S. Ginsburg, "The Great City in Southeast Asia," *American Journal of Sociology,* LX (March, 1955), 455–62; Kenneth L. Little, "The West African Town: Its Social Base," *Diogenes,* XXIX (Spring, 1960), 16–31; Paul F. Cressey, "Urbanization in the Philippines," *Sociology and Social Research,* XLIV (July-August, 1960), 402–9; William F. Ogburn, "Technology and Cities: The Dilemma of the Modern Metropolis," *Sociological Quarterly,* I (July, 1960), 139–54.

On the other hand, some countries have attempted to increase urbanization as a method of increasing development, especially with reference to certain regions of the country. The Brazilian case is of interest. The original colonial capital city was Salvador, but in 1763 it was moved to Rio de Janeiro with an immediate effect on the development of the more southerly area. In 1960 the capital was again moved, this time to Brasilia in the interior for the purpose of developing the hinterland. Unlike Rio, Brasilia was a new town, as were two state capitals built for similar developmental purposes: Belo Horizonte, the present capital of Minas Gerais, and Goiânia, the present capital of Goias. An equally important, if less dramatic example is that of Japan where legislation changed the taxation and tenant-farmer relationships with the immediate effect of freeing the peasantry for the urban migration which followed.[42]

In developmental terms, the rationale for deliberate urbanization has been elaborated by John Friedmann, notably in terms of the Venezuelan and Chilean locales. Friedmann refers to urbanization at a faster rate than industrialization as "hyperurbanization." He urges hyperurbanization because of its alleged effect of stimulating modernization more rapidly.[43]

These overt forms of urbanization policy stand in marked contrast to the covert forms of which India may be an example. For the most part urbanization policies are discussed in terms of their general effects on development and/or modernization, or of the economic effects alone. The analysis of the political consequences of urbanization policies is virtually lacking. In the

---

[42] Eiichi Isomura, "The Problems of the City in Japan," *Confluence*, VII (Summer, 1958), 150–56.

[43] Friedmann's position has been developed in John Friedmann, *Regional Development Policy: A Case Study of Venezuela* (Cambridge: The M.I.T. Press, 1966); "The Strategy of Deliberate Urbanization" (Santiago, Chile: The Ford Foundation Urban and Regional Advisory Program in Chile, 1967), mimeo; and in John Friedmann and Tomas Lackington, "Hyperurbanization and National Development in Chile: Some Hypotheses," *Urban Affairs Quarterly*, II, No. 4 (June, 1967), 3–29; the contrary thesis that urbanization ahead of industrialization is a drag on development is stated by Philip M. Hauser, "The Social, Economic, and Technological Problems of Rapid Urbanization," in Bert F. Hoselitz and Wilbert E. Moore (eds.), *Industrialization and Society* (New York: UNESCO, 1963), p. 203; and in N. V. Sovany, *Urbanization and Urban India* (New York: Taplinger, 1966).

present volume James Guyot takes a step in the direction of filling this gap as he discusses an indirect form of urbanization policy which he calls "creeping urbanism." He not only identifies the effects of the policy on local communities in Malaya, but the unanticipated reactive effects on the national polity.

The second major focus of concern with national policies is the question of centralization *v.* devolution. The propositions in this area tend to be concerned with two questions. First, is rapid economic development dependent on central planning; and second, is central planning for development inconsistent with some or all of the elements of political development? This is not the place to evaluate the arguments pro and con. Gross indicators suggest that economic and political development are not negatively correlated on a cross-national basis. This seems to leave us free to enumerate the centralist tendencies which are conducive to development as well as the devolutionist tendencies toward the same end. When we do this we find that there are important considerations on both counts. The shortage of trained technicians; the greater glamor of the central government; the fact that the economy is integrated at the national, not the urban, level; the close relation of national to urban politics in countries with primate cities; the national government's relation to foreign sources of aid; the notion that hyperurbanization is so severe that only the central government can treat it (seen as an ailment) and similar considerations suggest the need for central governmental decision-making.

On the other hand, the arguments against central decision-making are even more familiar: political instability at the center vitiates the effectiveness and continuity of programs; there is a decision-making bottleneck at the top; the national elite is traditionalist as compared with the urban elite; local autonomy is requisite training for political development; and central administrators do not understand local conditions. The appropriate strategy cannot be settled by a debate as between these sorts of arguments. Major governmental efforts at devolution are to be observed in all three developmental worlds—the West, the Communist, and the uncommitted. The Anglo-Saxon pattern is familiar. The success of Yugoslavia is beyond doubt by their own standards. The most extensive evidence is to be found in the writings of Ursula Hicks dealing with the former British colonies. Her general position is that local autonomy is a positive element in economic development, and that the British policy of indirect rule (both direct and created varieties) was essentially developmental in its rationale, from the time of its originator, C. T. Metcalfe, British Resident at Delhi (1811–19).[44] Historical analysis is limited in its utility for deriving the conditions under which devolution achieves specified goals to the extent that modern conditions are not duplicates of historic situations. The rapidly changing technology makes duplication less and less likely. What is needed is empirical analysis of the contemporary dimensions of devolution, and this subject is virtually untouched.[45] Frank Sherwood moves in this direction in this volume, and sets forth conditions under which it is reasonable to assume devolution might reasonably be applied, giving attention particularly to the variables of industrialization, communication, and national unity. He then proceeds to develop the conceptual framework which he suggests as an aid in devising appropriate strategies for building strong local response systems.

COMMUNITY POLITICAL INTEGRATION

The comparative urbanists' concern with urban integration has taken disparate forms, and the studies referred to below have often not been approached under the label of integration. The term itself is of recent use in community studies, perhaps because of its vagueness. The analogies between integration of political communities of many sorts, from international to local, have recently spotlighted the utility of integration as an object of com-

---

[44] Ursula K. Hicks, *Development From Below* (Oxford: Clarendon Press, 1961), pp. 1–25.

[45] A pioneer study is Paulo Reis Vieira, *op. cit.*

munity study.[46] In general there are two ways of observing urban integration. One is to define it, as do Jacob and Teune, and then to determine to what extent the necessary indicators are present. The other is to assert that integrative performance is one of the necessary functions of the political community, and judge its presence in terms of how well that function is performed as measured by the results. As Harold Kaplan expresses this approach, "Successful integrative performance is the securing of enough internal support and unity to provide for a continuity in the system's structure and to permit the system to meet environmental demands." [47] Thus, if a system survives it is integrated, and degrees and bases of integration above the survival level are not part of the functional requisite even though they may have much to do with the course and quality of development.

Students of comparative urban integration have generally dealt with the subject from the perspective of political culture, the process of politicization, or role structures and relationships. Of these three concerns, urban political culture is the most recent to appear as such. An excellent discussion of the general concept of political culture with reference to urban communities is found in Alford and Scoble's recent study.[48] They distinguish three aspects of political culture including public norms, leadership orientations, and mass orientations. In their study of four Wisconsin cities they consider all three and conclude that in those cities there is no distinctive and integrated local political culture.[49] Almond and Verba in *The Civic Culture* deal only with mass orientations, and in terms of local government consider the relations between local autonomy, local structure, and orientations toward participation. They find that attitudes favoring participation in local affairs are found in countries where opportunities to participate also

[46] For a discussion of the nature of the concept see Philip E. Jacob and Henry Teune, "The Integrative Process: Guidelines for Analysis of the Bases of Political Community," in Philip E. Jacob and James V. Toscano (eds.), *The Integration of Political Communities* (Philadelphia: J. B. Lippincott, 1964).

[47] Kaplan, *op. cit.*, p. 25.

[48] Robert R. Alford and Harry M. Scoble, *Bureaucracy and Participation in Four Wisconsin Cities* (Chicago: Rand McNally, 1969), chap. 3.

[49] *Ibid.*, chap. 12. Harold Kaplan came to the same conclusion with regard to Toronto when he indicates that normative integration in that metropolitan area derives from Canadian normative integration rather than Toronto area norms. Kaplan, *op. cit.*, p. 17. Kaplan's method is quite unlike that of Alford and Scoble.

exist. Of their five countries, the most deviant case is Italy, where both participation norms and opportunity are very low.[50]

In contrast to Almond and Verba's approach, Agger, Goldrich, and Swanson deal with political culture in the sense of the political ideology of leaders. In the terms of Alford and Scoble, these are leadership orientations. Political ideology, as they view it, is composed of five variables: (1) conception of the community, (2) preferences as to who shall rule, (3) sense of socioeconomic class, (4) sense of cultural class, and (5) attitudes toward the legitimate method of allocating values.[51] Using the first two of these variables they develop a matrix which produces seven distinct ideologies which were actually discovered among leader groups in the four study communities. Additional ideologies were represented among groups which did not attain leadership status.[52] The methodology which operationalized the concepts of the study was relative to the findings along the chosen dimensions in the four study cities. A different population of research communities would probably have produced different classifications. Thus, in cross-national research the ideologies elicited in the U.S. might have collapsed into one or two. However, the findings of the study suggest, in contrast to the indications of Kaplan and Alford and Scoble, that local political cultures may in fact exist, at least along the dimension of leader attitudes. The real point is not that there are conflicting findings, but rather that different definitions, assumptions, and methodological approaches produce different cues as to the existence of distinct political cultures in different urban communities. Agger proposes to investigate the matter on a cross-national basis through use of the fourth of his components of leader ideology: "sense of cultural class."[53]

[50] Gabriel Almond and Sidney Verba, *The Civic Culture: Political Attitudes and Democracy in Five Nations* (Princeton, N.J.: Princeton University Press, 1963), chap. 6; see also chap. 7.

[51] Robert E. Agger, Daniel Goldrich, and Bert E. Swanson, *The Rulers and the Ruled: Political Power and Impotence in American Communities* (New York: Wiley, 1964), p. 19.

[52] *Ibid.,* p. 19. The names of the ideologies are orthodox conservatives, progressive conservatives, community conservationists, Jeffersonian conservatives, radical rightists, liberals, and supremacists.

[53] Robert E. Agger, "Proposal for an International Study of Citizen Attitudes Towards and Participation in Urban Policy Innovations at the Community Level," in Thomas R. Dye (ed.), *Comparative Research in Community Politics* (Athens: University of Georgia Press, 1967), pp. 71–90.

The studies noted above have dealt at length with urban political culture. A variety of propositions on the role of aspects of political culture in urban communities is scattered through the literature. A rather common statement asserts that ideology is more important as an explanatory variable in large than in small urban systems. Another widely stated is that large cities are more characterized by leftist (or radical) ideologies than small cities. Frank Sherwood has suggested that there is a systemic need for expectations of performance, in terms of rendering urban services, in order to produce tensions which in turn stimulate action on the part of governmental authorities.[54] This notion is in marked contrast to the general idea that greater stability is necessarily a prerequisite to development—either economic or political. Questions such as these cry for comparative research.

Political socialization is a neglected area in the study of urban community integration. It is clearly established that there are differential rates of integration of immigrants into the urban centers to which they migrate. Rural immigrants may collect in slums and undergo political socialization very slowly. Some studies show that kinship and communal ties are actually strengthened after movement into an urban ghetto in place of the assumption of urban political norms. Yet there has been little systematic study of the question. An important exception is the study of four settlements of rural immigrants, two each in Santiago, Chile and Lima, Peru.[55] The experience of each was carefully studied and the patterns of politicization were measured. The key finding revelant here was that the imposition of sanctions by governmental authorities had a marked negative effect on politicization, which is not necessarily a continuous process, but may be reversed by the imposition of sanctions under some circumstances. This suggests that while tension may be functional to the system under some circumstances, it may not be under other circumstances—at least from the point of view of political development.

The third approach to integration of the urban community

[54] Frank Sherwood, "Brazil's Municipalities: A Comparative View" (unpublished MS), p. 114.
[55] Daniel Goldrich, Raymond B. Pratt, and C. R. Schuller, *The Political Integration of Lower Class Urban Settlements* (St. Louis: Social Science Institute, Monograph Series, Washington University, 1967).

is concerned with elite roles and the relationships among various elites within the urban political system. The tradition of the "power structure" studies in the United States has been that of the case rather than the comparative study. However, in recent years a few comparative studies have appeared.[56] These studies have been more concerned with concepts like power, structure, and decision-making than with integration. Such concepts are of intrinsic interest in their own right, but for the most part they have not been cross-national in their applications, and they have been subjected to careful criticism in a number of other places, so they will not be reviewed here.[57] One leading student of community power structure has noted that, ". . . a reorientation of the entire community power field toward the comparative study of community structural characteristics which predispose com-

[56] The most extensive study is that of Agger, Goldrich, and Swanson, *op. cit.*, which compares two Oregon cities and two North Carolina cities; Robert Presthus compared two New York cities in *Men at the Top: A Study in Community Power* (New York: Oxford University Press, 1964); Atlanta has been studied at two different points in time by different scholars using similar methods: Floyd Hunter, *Community Power Structure* (Chapel Hill: University of North Carolina Press, 1953), and M. Kent Jennings, *Community Influentials: The Elites of Atlanta* (New York: The Free Press, 1964); Delbert Miller has studied Seattle; Bloomington, Indiana; Bristol, England; Cordoba, Argentina; and Lima, Peru and reported his findings in "Decision-Making Cliques in Community Power Structures: A Comparative Study of an American and an English City," *American Journal of Sociology*, LXIV (November, 1958), 299–310; "Industry and Community Power Structure: A Comparative Study of an American and an English City," *American Sociological Review*, XXIII (February, 1958), 9–15; "Town and Gown: The Power Structure of a University Town," *American Journal of Sociology*, LXVIII (January, 1963), 432–43; with James L. Dirksen, "The Identification of Visible, Concealed, and Symbolic Leaders in a Small Indiana City: A Replication of the Bonjean-Noland Study of Burlington, North Carolina," *Social Forces*, XLIII (October, 1964), 548–55; "Community Power Perspectives and Role Definitions of North American Executives in an Argentine Community," *Administrative Science Quarterly*, X (December, 1965), 364–80.

[57] Wallace S. Sayre and Nelson W. Polsby, "American Political Science and the Study of Urbanization," in Philip F. Hauser and Leo F. Schnore (eds.), *The Study of Urbanization* (New York: Wiley, 1965), pp. 127–35; Alford and Scoble, *op. cit.*, chap. 1, "The Comparative Study of Urban Politics"; Claire W. Gilbert, "Community Power Structure: A Study in the Sociology of Knowledge" (unpublished Ph.D. dissertation, Northwestern University, 1966); Claire W. Gilbert, "Some Trends in Community Politics: A Secondary Analysis of Power Structure Data from 166 Communities," *Southwestern Social Science Quarterly*, XLVIII (December, 1967), 373–81; Terry N. Clark, "The Concept of Power: Some Overemphasized and Underrecognized Dimensions," *Southwestern Social Science Quarterly*, XLVIII (December, 1967), 271–386, and commentaries on this paper in the same issue; Charles M. Bonjean and David M. Olson, "Community Leadership: Directions of Research," *Administrative Science Quarterly*, IX (December, 1964), 278–300.

munities toward different types of decision-making processes is becoming increasingly apparent."[58]

Elite roles, however, have not become the exclusive possession of the students of power. Several concepts of more direct application to the question of integration in an urban political community have been employed by William and Judith Hanna who studied two African towns, Umuahia, Nigeria and Mbale, Uganda. Their work, which is reported in this volume, was preceded by two earlier articles.[59] Here they developed the concept of the "middleman" who is a community influential who bridges the gap between the people of the ethnic enclave in which he lives, and the influentials of other communities within the urban place. He also bridges the vertical gap between his people and the center elite leaders who are national or regional leaders of power, wealth, and prestige. The middleman is thus viewed as participating in each of the three subsystems, which overlap and, therefore, the middleman is in a position to play a "linkage role" among the three systems. The middleman engages in "integrative transmissions" between the three subsystems, as well as "integrative manipulation" in order to optimize his status.

The significance of leader roles of these types derives from the fact that in the developing world the sharp break between the urban and the rural, even within the urban community itself, is an increasingly prevalent phenomenon with the continued rapid rural to urban migration. Insofar as this gap can be bridged through a blending of rural and urban through such roles as the middleman, a tension-reducing mechanism may be created. In African towns of medium size this blending process seems well established, as compared with Latin America, for example.

Some horizontal linkages identified by the Hannas include religion, occupation, and politics. Rural polyethnic politics, however, is projected into urban centers, but the presence of strangers

---

[58] Clark, *op. cit.*, p. 286; Clark's suggestion is exemplified by the excellent recent review of community power research in Latin America by Rabinovitz, *op. cit.*

[59] These are William John Hanna and Judith Lynne Hanna, "The City in Modern Africa," in Horace Miner (ed.), *The City in Modern Africa* (London: The Pall Mall Press, 1968), pp. 151–84; "The Integrative Role of Urban Africa's Middle-places and Middlemen," *Civilisations*, XVII (1967), 1–16.

who perform "buffering roles" tend to ease these conflicts. Authority and influence tend to be separated in such a fashion that the
influentials tend to dominate extramural and important decisions,
while the formal authorities of government make lesser categories
of decisions. From concepts such as these the way in which urban
African communities are integrated is developed by these authors
in the present volume.

The potentially close and mutually fruitful relation between
intranational and cross-national urban comparisons is demonstrated in Wright's study of the roles and role related behaviors
and perceptions of U.S. city managers in these pages. In focusing
on the pre-eminently integrative role of the U.S. city manager
he reveals vertical and horizontal linkages of a quite different sort
from those investigated by the Hannas. Casting his discussion in
terms familiar to the comparativist, he deals with formalism in
manager cities, the clash of universalist and particularist norms
as they appear in the public-regarding and private-regarding behaviors in American urban politics, and the effect of the administrative oriented citizenry as compared with the policy oriented
citizenry—perhaps a reflection of Almond and Verba's participant
and subject concepts. In these and other ways Wright lengthens
the dimensions of comparison from the small African town to
American cities of over 100,000 population. The comparison is
plausible.

ECOLOGY OF URBAN POLITICAL
SYSTEMS

During the past decade and a half students of comparative
urban politics have turned to a variety of ecological variables—
demographic, economic, political, and, occasionally, physical—in
an effort to explain political outcomes or more modestly to associate ecological with behavioral variations. With the exception of
some studies now in progress, the ecological approach has been employed chiefly in the United States. It has ranged from the compari-

son of wards or other subdivisions within a municipality, comparisons among cities within a single metropolitan area, to comparisons between cities and metropolitan areas.

Unfortunately, research on political ecology is greatly constrained by the necessity to employ census data rather poorly adapted to measurement of crucial political dimensions, supplemented by the available information on formal governmental structure. Consequently, there is a certain vagueness surrounding the question of what the variables really are which chosen indicators purport to measure. The magnitude of this problem has led some to the conclusion that in cross-national research in particular, as well as in U.S. research, it may prove necessary to collect through systematic field surveys the series of data designed more precisely to serve research needs.[60]

Perhaps the most prominent area of ecological research has been concerned with the correlates of urban tax and expenditure levels. The effort has been to consider expenditures as representing policies—outputs in system parlance—and ascertain what factors tend to explain variations in levels, and sometimes kinds, of expenditures. The correlation of political variables with such outputs has been relatively fruitless, and socioeconomic factors seem more useful. The latter approach has been taken within metropolitan areas in such studies as Wood's *1400 Governments* (New York), Sacks and Helmuth (Cleveland), and Hirsch (St. Louis).[61] Campbell and Sacks have taken a long additional step by comparing fiscal behavior in thirty-six U.S. metropolitan areas. Dependent variables were expenditures and taxes with the important distinction made between education and non-education expenditures. The great variability in patterns of educational financing

[60] In the United States this has given rise to an effort to establish a "permanent community sample" to collect comparable data in a sample of U.S. communities and over time. See Peter H. Rossi and Robert Crain, "The NORC Permanent Community Sample," in Thomas R. Dye (ed.), *Comparative Research in Community Politics* (Athens: University of Georgia Press, 1967), pp. 109–32. A related idea is the "urban observatory" which has been proposed in various contexts, usually with a more applied orientation.

[61] Robert Wood, *1400 Governments* (Cambridge: Harvard University Press, 1961); Seymour Sacks and William F. Helmuth, *Financing Government in a Metropolitan Area* (New York: The Free Press, 1961); Werner Z. Hirsch, "Expenditure Implications of Metropolitan Growth and Consolidation," *The Review of Economics and Statistics*, XLI (August, 1959), 232–41.

could thus be handled. Independent variables included income, state aid pattern, whether welfare is a state function, home ownership, and proportion of rural population outside the central cities. The metropolitan areas as a whole were studied as well as central city and suburban comparisons. Local government organization variables were introduced, but did not show any significant relationship to the fiscal variables.[62]

A study of the governments in the Philadelphia metropolitan area concerned itself with fiscal measures of policy, but in addition with other policy outputs such as land use.[63] The permanence of land use patterns, however, made this a measure of policy as of the time of development, introducing new ambiguities. Interlocal cooperation policies were explored, with the finding that similar social rank of communities was a positive factor in producing cooperative agreements. The thrust of the entire study is that while metropolitan differentiation produces some pressures for political integration, there are equally strong pressures tending toward the maintenance of policies of separatism.

Studies such as those noted above leave open the question of whether in fact variations observed are variations in policy, or merely in external constraints on policy-makers who have little choice in the matter. An effort to bring ecology to bear more directly on policy processes is represented by those studies which correlate ecological variables with voting behavior and with formal governmental structure. The voting studies have been comparative within metropolitan areas only, notably in St. Louis, Cleveland, and Nashville.[64] In several cases these have been supplemented with sample survey data. The ecology of local government structure has become the object of a considerable number of investigations, all comparative in nature. These show clearly

[62] Campbell and Sacks, *op. cit.*

[63] Williams *et al.*, *op. cit.*

[64] See Brett W. Hawkins, "Life-Style, Demographic Distance and Voter Support of City-County Consolidation, *op. cit.*; Walter C. Kaufman and Scott Greer, "Voting in a Metropolitan Community: An Application of Social Area Analysis," *Social Forces*, XXXVIII (March, 1960), 196–204; Richard A. Watson and John H. Romani, "Metropolitan Government for Metropolitan Cleveland: An Analysis of the Voting Record," *Midwest Journal of Political Science*, V (November, 1961), 365–90; James A. Norton, "Referenda Voting in a Metropolitan Area," *Western Political Quarterly*, XVI (March, 1963), 195–212.

that there are relationships between socioeconomic variables and structure of U.S. communities.[65] What these relationships mean is a matter of controversy. Banfield and Wilson have proposed that two distinct urban political cultures—the "public regarding" and the "private regarding"—exist in the United States, and that these are related to structures and policies in certain ways.[66] Wolfinger and Field studied 309 cities over 50,000 in population in the U.S. and concluded that the ecological conditions presumably associated with each culture or ethos did not in fact so correlate. A central factor in the ethos theory was form of government, and while this also did not correlate, Wolfinger and Field found that the variable of region did correlate with structure of city government. They speculated that the age of the city may have been the crucial factor explaining regional differences.[67] Lineberry and Fowler, on the other hand, attempted to use ecological variables and governmental structure to shed light on the same ethos theory, studying 200 U.S. cities over 50,000 population.[68] They concluded that the data were consistent with the ethos theory for the most part. Moreover, they concluded that while cities associated with each political ethic did not differ from each other significantly in terms of demographic variables, they did differ in behavior as indicated by policy outputs, measured chiefly through expenditure levels.

The one certain conclusion that can be drawn from the ecological studies is that structure, function, and culture of the urban political community are subtly and highly interdependent. We have made little progress toward a model that will comprehend these elements of the system, or a methodology to test the model. It is with the view of beginning to fulfill this need that Robert Alford in this volume offers his analysis of how cultural,

[65] See Henry Schmandt, "Toward Comparability in Metropolitan Research," *op. cit.*, pp. 30–38 for a detailed discussion of these studies.

[66] Edward Banfield and James Wilson, *City Politics* (Cambridge: Harvard University Press and The M.I.T. Press, 1963).

[67] Raymond Wolfinger and John O. Field, "Political Ethos and the Structure of City Government," *American Political Science Review*, LX (June, 1966), 306–26.

[68] Robert L. Lineberry and Edmund P. Fowler, "Reformism and Public Policies in American Cities," *American Political Science Review*, LI (September, 1967), 701–16.

structural, and situational factors have been used in comparative urban behavior and decision-making studies, and how environmental factors impinge on the same processes.[69]

URBAN POLITICS AND NATIONAL POLITICS

Propositions about the effects of urbanization on the national political system flow freely from the literature of national development. For the most part these generalizations do not reflect a concern for the effect of intra-urban-system politics as an input into national politics. Instead, broader generalizations tend to cluster around the following widely accepted process: urbanization is a worldwide trend in the developing nations. Urbanization inevitably produces a growing middle class between the old agrarian elite and the (usually landless) peasant. As the middle class increases in size it also increases in political influence, not because of its size as such, but because of certain characteristics of the middle class. These characteristics are pre-eminently its literacy and its tendency to participate in politics.

While these propositions are widely accepted, the consequences of politicization of an urban population are subject to some controversy. One line of commentary suggests that middle class politics tends to strengthen the traditional structure since the middle class identifies with the elite and seeks to share power for the purpose of climbing to the top.[70] The predominant view, however, tends in the other direction. It asserts that the political

[69] The present essay develops further the schema described in Robert Alford, "The Comparative Study of Urban Politics," in Leo F. Schnore and Henry Fagin, eds., *Urban Research and Policy Planning* ("Urban Affairs Annual Reviews," Vol. I [Beverly Hills: Sage, 1967]), pp. 263–302; and Alford and Scoble, *Bureaucratization and Mobilization in Urban Politics, op. cit.,* chap. 1.

[70] Claudio Veliz in *Obstacles to Change in Latin America* (London: Oxford University Press, 1965), p. 2 *passim* argues that the middle class, after being in power three or four decades in a number of countries, has in fact strengthened the traditional structure, perpetuated instability, and brought on economic stagnation in some cases; Celso Furtado in Claudio Veliz (ed.), *ibid.,* pp. 152–56 says that urbanization was not accompanied by political change in Brazil, having arisen in the context of the traditional agrarian elite system.

power of the middle class is exercised in behalf of political change and modernization.[71]

The prevalence of two distinct views of the matter offers the opportunity to consider whether both may not be valid. The most extensive consideration of the role of the middle class—or middle sectors—is that by John Johnson.[72] For Latin America Johnson traces, through historical analysis, the role of middle sectors in differing situations, times, and places. He notes Argentina does not fit the pattern of middle class political power, despite its advanced technology and large urban population. He begins to develop the theme that the middle sectors, variously composed in various countries and times, sometimes sought organized labor as an ally, while in other situations it sought an alliance with the elite. This approach is developed analytically by Luis Ratinoff who relates urban middle class political strategy to the relation between aspiration and satisfaction differentials.[73] Roughly, his model states that middle class movements begin by soliciting lower class support. In power, the middle class governments establish institutions sought by the labor groups such as social security institutes, educational systems, and labor ministries (staffed, of course, by the middle class). This expansion of the middle class allows it freedom from its labor allies, and as it relies on itself its impulse toward a downward distribution of power, prestige, and wealth declines. Insofar as this life history is typical, urban politics may be modernist or traditionalist depending on the phase of the cycle.

This effort to add analytical precision to historical analysis has its counterpart among those who would specify more exactly the process by which urbanization may lead to political power.

[71] See Daniel Lerner, *The Passing of Traditional Society: Modernizing the Middle East* (New York: The Free Press, 1964), pp. 57–66; Lucien Pye, "The Politics of Southeast Asia," in Gabriel A. Almond and James S. Coleman (eds.), *The Politics of Developing Areas* (Princeton, N.J.: Princeton University Press, 1960), pp. 100–1; Irving Louis Horowitz, *Urban Affairs Quarterly*, II (March, 1967), 5–31; Friedmann and Lackington, "Hyperurbanization and National Development in Chile," *op. cit.,* p. 9.

[72] John J. Johnson, *Political Change in Latin America: The Emergence of the Middle Sectors* (Stanford: Stanford University Press, 1958).

[73] Luis Ratinoff, "The New Urban Groups: The Middle Classes," in Seymour Martin Lipset and Aldo Solari (eds.), *Elites in Latin America* (New York: Oxford University Press, 1967), pp. 61–93.

Lerner specifies this process in general terms.[74] Urbanization causes, because it requires, literacy and the creation of mass media. These in turn result in increased participation. This causal model has been stated more explicitly with a statistical test suggesting that the causal chain is urbanization causing education (literacy), causing mass communications, causing democratic political development in the sense of participation.[75]

The Lerner thesis employs broad concepts: urbanization and modernization. In order to subject it to meaningful tests, these need to be refined. A large step in this direction is taken by Francine Rabinovitz in this volume. She distinguishes urbanization from urbanism on the one hand, and a number of dimensions of "political development" on the other. The latter include stability, participation, and institutional development. For each, appropriate indices are employed, as well as composite indicators of political development. The analysis suggests that the effects of urbanization and of urbanism may be quite selective in terms of different dimensions of political development.

This suggestion is consistent with some almost random clues in the recent literature that the effects of urbanization may not be unidirectional. Eleanor Main concluded that urbanization had differential effects as between Italy, West Germany, and the United States. Where the political culture was participant, urbanization tended to increase participation. Where, as in Italy, the political culture was non-participant, urbanization was associated with decreased participation.[76] Moreover, the variable "middle class" is in great need of further analysis in terms of its behavior in urban as well as national politics, as Johnson suspected. Kallman Silvert has noted the presence of both strong traditionalist and modernist attitudes among various urban groups.[77]

---

[74] Lerner, *op. cit.*, pp. 59–61.

[75] Donald J. McCrone and Charles F. Cnudde, "Toward a Communications Theory of Democratic Political Development: A Causal Model," *American Political Science Review*, LXI (March, 1967), 71–79.

[76] Eleanor Catherine Main, "The Impact of Urbanization: A Comparative Study of Urban and Non-Urban Political Attitudes and Behavior" (unpublished doctoral dissertation, University of North Carolina, 1966), p. 173 *passim*.

[77] Kalman Silvert, "Leaders, Followers, and Modernization in Latin America," in Roy C. Macridis and Bernard E. Brown (eds.), *Comparative Politics: Notes and Readings* (rev. ed.; Homewood, Ill.: Dorsey Press, 1964), pp. 651–55.

The unexplored agenda for research on urban political effects on national politics certainly includes further research on these subjects. In addition, totally unexplored areas include such questions as the dominance of particular cities in national politics, urban leadership as a component of national leadership, linkage roles between urban and national leadership, strategies of political influence by urban political groups, and most importantly, the role of industrial elites in urban and national politics.

CONCEPTS AND STRATEGIES OF COMPARATIVE URBAN RESEARCH

This brief review of the major areas of urban governmental research suggests a number of summary conclusions about the nature and problems of this research field. These are related primarily to concepts and strategy for research. The prime concepts are virtually by definition urbanization and urbanism. The first suffers from confusion as between the relative emphasis on average density *v.* focalization of the settlement pattern. Urbanism is ambiguous in that it is used to refer to a patterning of a way of life, but whether this way of life is a breaking down of the traditional social relationships into anonymity and anomie or a shift to "modern" attitudes and behaviors is a matter of the emphasis of the particular researcher.

Attention should be given to the additional question of the relation of urbanism to social mobilization which is at the core of so much current writing. This is an evident overlapping in the concepts which it would be useful to clarify. Deutsch defines social mobilization as "The process in which major clusters of old social, economic, and psychological commitments are eroded or broken and people become available for new patterns of socialization and behavior." [78] This comes very close to current usages of "urbanism."

---

[78] Karl W. Deutsch, "Social Mobilization and Political Development," in Harry Eckstein and David E. Apter (eds.), *Comparative Politics* (New York: The Free Press, 1963), p. 583.

These difficulties are compounded by differing assumptions about whether urbanization precedes and leads to urbanism or vice versa. The older notion is that urbanization itself is what produces urbanism. In the developing world of today, however, the causal relation sometimes appears to be reversed. New technology and new methods of communication can produce changed aspirations in rural populations which produce, or at least add to, the vast urban migrations so characteristic of the present day.

Perhaps equally crucial is the concept of devolution. The structure of this concept is sufficiently complex as to suggest further clarification. In essence, the concept involves the delegation of power from a central government to local governments, resulting in autonomy at the grass roots. A first problem is that governmental institutions, especially in metropolitan areas, appear to fall on a continuum rather than into two discreet groups.[79] At what point does a local entity cease to become an instrumentality of the central government and become an instrument of the locality in which it is situated? It is necessary to answer this question with precision before useful classifications of local government systems are possible. At that point it becomes relevant to inquire what the utility and consequences of devolution may be. Does it produce political participation and socialization but at the expense of developmental efficiency? Or is it in fact a more efficient road to development? These are central questions for the urbanist. A related concern is whether devolution tends to reduce the power of the center, or whether, in fact, devolution may even increase central potential to achieve modernization and ultimately stability, respect, and power. A marked contrast is noted between the view of the metropolitan problem in the U.S. and Brazil, for example. In the former the political engineers view the problem as how to achieve centralization, while in the latter the problem is perceived as how to decentralize and break the log jam of decision at the center.

In approaching these kinds of very central questions, several concepts promise to provide useful insights. One of these is role. In particular, because of the concern with the relation of system to subsystem, it is the boundary role or dual role that may be of use,

[79] Walsh, *The Urban Challenge to Government, op. cit.,* p. 157.

and a distinction must be made between these two. The role at the point at which two systems touch may perform a certain function, to be contrasted with the function of the actor whose role is central to two or even three subsystems, as in the case of the Hanna study. The whole question of overlapping and interpenetration of systems by means of role combinations is involved here. This overlapping is significant not only among formal roles, but also as among informal leadership roles, party positions, professional roles, communicator roles, broker roles, and so forth. The overlapping of roles seen as a vertical system of overlays is an unexplored area with a very few exceptions. With role-mapping performed, the correlation of these patterns with role recruitment patterns can provide a dynamic dimension to the analysis of urban system relationships. Since the evidence seems to indicate that administrative and political roles do in fact overlap, it would appear difficult to justify considering the political context of administration as a set of peripheral constraints within which professionalism may hold sway. Professionalism, under some circumstances, may prove just as contextual as politics, with the city manager system as a case in point.

The last comment suggests several concepts which seem relevant in exploring urban system relationships. One is role stress which we presume occurs whenever we find dual roles. Going beyond roles to the systems which they constitute, however, we are led in the direction of concepts of organization theory. System tension, system response, and the change capability of systems immediately come to mind. What are the system conditions which enhance change capability? What conditions maximize decision-making capacity? Answers to questions such as these would provide an approach to local government engineering—a matter which raises the question of research strategy.

Assumptions about how to approach research which is intended to be "useful," "practical," or "consumable" vary. Some would confine the search to eliciting answers to the question, "What works?" based on assumptions that the political context is not a variable to be manipulated. This view may be a necessary survival behavior for researchers who operate from within the system itself. Others, however, would not make assumptions about fixed variables. The real problem is how to insure that these two groups can communicate with each other. Among various efforts to describe an ideal-type research process, the following steps have been outlined: description, classification, explanation, verification, prediction, prescription, installation, and evaluation.[80] This list implies that the research process has as an ultimate objective to produce change in desired directions, though admittedly, it is possible to do research without this assumption. Given some such set of research steps, we do not have to assume that an individual researcher, planner, administrator, or politician should or is competent to engage in all of the steps in the process. Victor Jones has suggested a simple design to indicate what the relationships among the key participants are at various stages in the enterprise (see Figure 1). He suggests that description, classification, and explanation of phenomena are activities in which the researcher, planner, and politician-administrator are all involved, but to very different degrees. The researcher carries the heavy load at these preliminary stages. The planner is involved to a lesser degree, and the politician or administrative leader to a very slight extent. Verification and prediction are quite technical operations in which the researcher is heavily involved. The planner is also concerned at these stages since he will soon be the consumer and interpreter of the results. The politician-administrators are not involved, since these are purely technical operations. At the point of prescription the planner becomes heavily involved (as is the pharmacist in the medical analogy), and the politician-administrators are even more heavily involved (as is the physician). Installation is the province of the politicians and administrators. In the evaluation stage the politicians and administrators are again dominant since normative judgments are involved, but the planner is also concerned due to his need to communicate back to the researcher what the next problem to be solved may be. In general the planner performs the role of communicator between the researcher and the politician and administrator.

This little formulation is only illustrative, but perhaps suggests a way of dividing the effort in a set of closely interrelated

[80] Robert T. Daland, "A Strategy for Research in Comparative Urban Administration" (Bloomington, Indiana, CAG Occasional Papers; 1966).

activities. The fact that most research is not neatly performed in this series of integrated steps does not mean that it is inefficiently done. On the contrary, there may be advantages in disregarding the chronology in any immediate sense. What such a conception

Figure 1

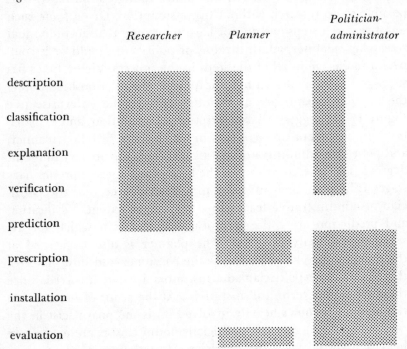

	Researcher	Planner	Politician-administrator
description			
classification			
explanation			
verification			
prediction			
prescription			
installation			
evaluation			

of the research enterprise does do is to provide a perspective that could help to give a focus to research of any particular kind, and thus to lead to an economy of effort. It also suggests the dangers, for example, in leaping from classification to prescription without some serious consideration of the intervening steps.

Keeping these steps in mind may remind the researcher of choices he might otherwise disregard. For example, when the researcher contemplates cases that have been described, he must choose whether to study deviant cases carefully for clues to new categories of classification (or new propositions), or on the other hand to disregard them in the search for a central tendency. With sufficient description and classification it becomes necessary to define an appropriate breaking point between rural and urban. Description tells us that this point varies from society to society. Similarly, major errors in prediction might be produced if the researcher failed to recognize that in some countries urban governments are essentially service oriented as to function, while in others they are primarily political in function. What variables are important? Is the distinction between election and appointment of the chief executive a crucial one? Must we assume that the study of urban government is the study of geographically bounded systems, systems with other kinds of boundaries, or for that matter unbounded systems?

The chapters which follow illustrate some of the ways in which these kinds of research concepts and strategies have been employed. It may be appropriate to close this introduction by stating firmly what is the most serious problem confronting cross-national urban research. Data are generally unavailable and non-comparable. While this may be a common plaint of the social scientist, the needs in urban governmental studies are monolithic. An early goal should be an international municipal and local yearbook which would break down existing data by urban units of government, and which would also contain new data not now available. Data collection should be done according to international standards set by the United Nations. An early effort should be the identification of data which are available, but not yet assembled in any central place. Only through moves such as these can comparative urban governmental research move forward in a significant way.

2/

Devolution as a Problem
of Organization Strategy

FRANK P. SHERWOOD

THIS PAPER IS CONCERNED with a classic problem of social
life: how to relate people to each other in such a way as to gain
the maximum benefits of cooperation and to minimize the costs of
dependent behavior. The special point of inquiry is the institutional role of the local government in the pattern of relationships
that comprise a national political system. On the one hand, the
nation-state desires to have each community engage actively in
the resolution of its problems; on the other, there is no enthusiasm
when such engagement creates dissonance in the system as a whole.

It is of some significance that this is a problem not at all
unique to governments. Yet the perspectives of organization theory
are quite often ignored by students of government.[1] The first part
of the chapter is, therefore, concerned with putting the problem
in the context of organization theory. A second part seeks to set
forth some of the conditions under which we might expect a
society to provide for more independent, autonomous behavior
at the local, subnational level. The third and final part suggests a
conceptual framework, the institution-building model, for the
examination of strategies for building strong local response systems.

[1] In fact, research on devolution-decentralization issues has been relatively
limited, as John Friedmann reported in the *CAG Newsletter*, V, No. 1 (November,
1967), 16. He wrote that the subject "has indeed been a stepchild among social
scientists."

LOCAL GOVERNMENT AND
ORGANIZATION THEORY

Role is generally defined to mean a set of behaviors; it is not synonymous with position. Thus, the examination of the role of local government involves more than the structure of reporting or authority relationships. The concept of role is more dynamic, in that it essentially calls for specification of the ways in which the unit will participate in a given system. Such a perspective raises many questions. How great are the interdependencies among roles? How can boundaries be drawn around roles? How is power to be shared among the roles, subsystems, and system? How are such power distributions to be reflected in terms of activities and resources?

Such questions are, of course, only illustrative. The critical point is that any analysis of the role of local government in a national system involves panoramic inquiry. It is not a narrow, structural question. The problem is one of organization strategy. Theoretically, a development-seeking nation is searching for an arrangement of roles that will enable it to meet its goals as expeditiously as possible. In this sense, the problem of organizing a polity is not in its general nature different from organizing for any other human purpose. In all cases, the strategy perspective forces us to ask questions about the system values to be sought, the allocation choices to be made, and the tactics to be utilized. Obviously, different strategy decisions will require different organizational responses.

In the literature of organization theory, the transaction with the environment is increasingly seen as crucial; the real test is how successful the organization is in working out this relationship. Are its outputs sufficiently used and valued by its clientele to attract new inputs of energy? Such a view of organization-environment relationships requires an emphasis on the points of contact between the two, the quality of the communication channels between boundary position and processor, the values that are observed in processing, the speed with which decisions get translated into outputs, and the extent to which such outputs are directed toward the most strategic clientele targets. In the United States we have been forced to the environmental view because of the rapid pace of change in our culture. Dingbats that are desired in 1968 may have no clientele by 1970; and the organization that assumes environmental stability will find survival very precarious.

With the worldwide move from the farm to the city, environmental considerations are becoming increasingly crucial in the study of local government. There is need for an organizational form which can take account of the diverse and typically pressing demands the city dweller makes on his government. Turkish commentators at a CENTO Symposium on the role of local government in national development told a familiar story, noting that the rate of urban growth since World War II was about double the country's annual population increase of 2.7 per cent. Furthermore, the direction of migration from rural areas was to the larger urban centers with more than 50,000 population. As a result, the housing shortage in Turkey's big cities has become very serious. Nearly half of the population of the capital city of Ankara lives in *gecekondus,* essentially shanties; in Istanbul the figure is put at 21 per cent. The Deputy Mayor of Ankara reported:

> . . . overt and disguised unemployment has become serious in the cities, and housing has become particularly acute. In Ankara alone there are 70,000 shanties in which 370,000 people live without any kind of municipal services. This figure represents 42 per cent of the capital's total population, while 53 per cent of this figure represents the newcomers from the villages. The extent of the problem needs no other elaboration.[2]

While it is obvious that no organization form is going to solve the truly awesome problems of urbanization, it is fair to suggest tests against which alternative organization strategies might be judged. For example, there is the basic problem of allocating scarce resources as between personal and public wants, as well as allocations among competing public needs. Can the organization

---

[2] Ali Cankaya, "The Growth of Cities and the Role of Local Administration," in Frederick T. Bent and Joise Lackland Shields, eds., *The Role of Local Government in National Development* (Ankara, Turkey: Central Treaty Organization, 1965), p. 142.

style do anything to increase the willingness to commit societal resources to the resolution of urban problems? Can it help to aggregate and process the urban community's interests in such a way as to make resource allocations as reflective as possible of norms and values? Finally, can the way in which these decisions are taken contribute to a commitment to the system as a whole? To put it more simply, we would like to identify an organization strategy that would make it easier for citizens to part with money for needed urban services, would make sure that the most essential urban needs were met first, and would cause people to feel that the system was operating in such a way as to give their interests and needs a fair hearing. Essentially, an organization strategy must be submitted to a test of function; and the particular emphasis given to an array of possible functions will differ according to the situation.

If we were to test organization strategy in the agricultural-rural context, would the criteria be the same as in the industrial-urban? Probably not in most cases. With much greater homogeneity, the rural area does not require its organization to maintain contacts with, and capabilities to process demands from, a great diversity of interests. A less monetized system requires less attention to the processes by which resources are allocated and more to the means by which citizens are induced to participate in immediately reliable and tangible community self-help projects. With rural development increasingly being seen as a means of reducing the push toward overurbanization, it is likely that an optimal organization strategy for the rural areas would place more value on mechanical efficiency. The question of allocation would be less important than seeing to it that the choices made were implemented. Mechanical efficiency also becomes a better test because the environment is presumably more stable.

The case of Iran seems particularly appropriate to the point that functional requirements within a nation may necessitate varying organization styles. One Iranian has written:

> In certain cities we feel acutely the pinch of overcrowding; whereas in a large number of smaller towns we suffer from the opposite problem, namely the scarcity of population. This is due to uncontrolled migration from the small towns to larger cities. There is some danger that more

and more small towns will become extinct. Therefore, each of the 13 provinces has its own problem of growth or lack of it and within each province every town and village finds itself affected by the movement of people to larger urban areas.[3]

Not only in Iran but elsewhere, governments have tended to treat both the large and the small as if their organization requirements were the same, though it is clear their environments are very different. Similarly with the literature in the field. Several of the most basic books have dealt with the local government as a closed system, seemingly removed from the environment to which it is expected to respond. Basically, the tendency to treat structure as if it were an independent variable unrelated to function and environment has been very destructive to any solid theorizing on organization strategies in the developing societies. The claim that local government (or decentralization) is equally desirable in the rural village, the small city, and the large city leaves little room for the care and rigor necessary in an approach to problems of this magnitude.

In short, the role of local government in national development cannot quickly be resolved by sweeping generalizations. Local governments are open systems, in the sense that their very purpose is to traffic with their environments. In most cases, structure is an outcome of function; and the relationship between the two must be the point of departure for any profound analysis of the organizational place of local government.

BASICS OF ORGANIZATION THEORY

Before proceeding to a more definitive consideration of the relationship between environment and local government, it is necessary to examine further certain assumptions about organizations. In the process, the key words commonly used to describe central-local relationships will also be considered.

---

[3] M. R. Sahbazian, "The Role of Local Government in Meeting Problems of Urban Growth," *ibid.*, p. 102.

• *Hierarchy and the Centralization-Decentralization Continuum*

Typically, the foundation of such analysis and proposition-alizing has been hierarchy, a pyramidal form by which power and authority are distributed among the members. The purest form of hierarchy results in the integration of all collective activity at the peak point of the pyramid. The occupant of this position is expected to have an overview, a rationality, and an omniscience that will enable him to test all behaviors against the interest of the collectivity. His principal function is that of allocating re-sources, rewards, penalties, and so forth. From his vantage point, he makes these allocations in terms of the goals and interests of the organization.

Such theory has led to the idea of a centralization-decentraliza-tion continuum, which is really an attempt to describe the power relationships among the various participants in the system. First, however, it is important to examine some of the assumptions of the continuum and to consider the extent to which they limit its usefulness and applicability. The continuum assumes that there is a certain quantum of power within an organization that can be distributed in differing ways; and it does not account for the fact, now rather well documented, that power is highly variable. The addition of power at one level of the hierarchy does not at all mean the automatic withdrawal of power at another.

There is also a question as to where the continuum begins and ends. If centralization means the consolidation of all power in the top position, the concept of organization is denied. As soon as another person participates in the action, the power relation-ship has changed; and therefore absolute centralization is impos-sible to achieve.

The other end of the continuum is even more troublesome. The line between "pure" decentralization *within* an organization and actual separation *from* the organization is very unclear. This conceptual problem is particularly important in the context of this chapter; if decentralization has no *inter*organizational dimen-sion, as I think it does not, it helps us little in understanding rela-tionships that are non-hierarchical in character.

In most uses of the term, "decentralization for development," both hierarchical and non-hierarchical assumptions are embraced. Maddick, for example, gives the following definitions:

> Decentralization—embracing both processes of deconcentration and devolution.
> Deconcentration—the delegation of authority adequate for the discharge of specified functions to staff of a central department who are situated outside the headquarters. (Hierarchical)
> Devolution—the legal conferring of powers to discharge specified or residual functions upon formally constituted local authorities. (Non-Hierarchical)[4]

Maddick's view (also expressed in other documents) raises the basic question of whether an organization concept which posits participation in a command system is fundamentally similar to that which posits separation and sufficient autonomy to behave independently of the larger system. In my opinion, the similarity is not that great; and many problems have arisen because we have not been willing to face the fact that one approach is fundamentally hierarchical, the other non-hierarchical.

In a classic work, Dahl and Lindblom have emphasized the differences between a system of integration whose control is achieved through hierarchical command and one whose integration is a result of spontaneous, autonomous behavior by participants.

> Hierarchy is a familiar, widespread and important social process for economizing. . . . Roughly, a hierarchical process of organization is one in which leaders exercise a very high degree of unilateral control over non-leaders (p. 227).

> . . . Control is always a direct relationship between two or more human beings. In loose language, A controls the responses of B if A's acts cause B to respond in a definite way. To put it in stricter and more cumbersome language: B is controlled by A to the extent that B's responses are dependent on A's acts in an immediate and direct functional relationship (p. 94).[5]

A variation of such direct, hierarchical control is what Dahl and Lindblom have called "manipulated field control," in which

---

[4] Henry Maddick, *Democracy, Decentralization and Development* (London: Asia Publishing House, 1963), p. 23.

[5] Robert A. Dahl and Charles E. Lindblom, *Politics, Economics and Welfare* (New York: Harper and Bros., 1953).

the hierarchical authority relationship is absent but in which other means of control are available—a category which seems to describe central-local relationships in many countries.

• Non-Hierarchical Concepts

While it is generally thought that such control mechanisms are about the only means by which system integration is to be achieved, there is in fact a tremendous range of system-oriented behavior that occurs without reference to power and dominance. In some cases, it is simply reciprocal. Lindblom has used the term, "partisan mutual adjustment," to describe the bargaining and accommodation that often occurs. In other cases, the behavior is more unilateral. The action of one person is taken without awareness of its indirect effect on another. The market, with its system of rules, is our prime example of integration without hierarchy.

In these considerations, the concept of autonomy, reflecting separation, is extremely important, as Dahl and Lindblom indicate:

> Controlled behavior may best be thought of as lying at one end of a continuum of which the other end is autonomous behavior. Autonomy is the absence of immediate and direct control. An individual's responses are autonomous or uncontrolled to the extent that no other people can bring about these responses in a definite way.[6]

At one time it may have seemed academic to argue the distinction between hierarchical and non-hierarchical forms of organization in the governmental sphere. However, the experience in Yugoslavia during the past fifteen years represents a particularly major and seemingly successful attempt to move toward non-hierarchical forms through the expansion of autonomy for local governments and for economic enterprises.[7]

[6] *Ibid.*, p. 96.

[7] The economic success of Yugoslavia has been well documented. As Albert Waterston has written: ". . . Few can claim the degree of success achieved by Yugoslavia in carrying out economic development plans." See his *Planning in Yugoslavia* (Washington: The Economic Development Institute, International Bank for Reconstruction and Development, 1962), p. 1. Of forty-five countries studied, we place Yugoslavia among the top ten in degree of autonomy granted local governments. For a quick structural view see *Decentralization for National and Local Development* (New York: United Nations Technical Assistance Programme, 1962), p. 226–43.

- *Decentralization and Devolution Defined*

It is obviously difficult to resolve the definitional and conceptual questions I have been raising. Slates can never be wiped clean; and the fact is that decentralization is such a common term that it cannot be ignored or excised from the language. It might be possible, however, to begin to apply more rigor to its definition. Its unidimensional character should be emphasized and its meaning restricted to the power relationship within a given hierarchical structure. Centralization is best defined as involving the concentration of power at the top of the pyramid and decentralization as indicating the dispersal of power throughout the structure. From this point of view, decentralization and deconcentration become synonymous; but it should be pointed out that organization theorists much more commonly use the former term.

Limiting the concept of decentralization to the hierarchical setting obviously requires the use of another word to describe the local government which is separated from the command system of the center. Devolution has been commonly used to define this type of power relationship; and there is no reason for seeking another word. However, it is important to keep in mind the basic argument that devolution in this context means the transfer of power to geographic units of local government that lie outside the formal command structure of the central government. It is not decentralization. Thus, devolution represents the concept of separateness, of diversity of structures within the political system as a whole. In summary, we have two words: decentralization to describe an *intra*organization pattern of power relationships and devolution to describe an *inter*organization pattern of power relationships.

- *The Core of Devolution: Autonomy*

Because it is based on system separateness, devolution inevitably implies autonomy, which is the freedom to behave outside the constraint of direct control. However, it does not necessarily foreclose the existence of universalistic rules within which such behaviors must occur. Knowledge of the rules, predictability as to their application, and calculability of the costs of an infraction are all necessary conditions of autonomy.

Autonomy also implies system integrity, in the sense that a system must have boundaries and therefore identity. To put it another way, there can be no autonomy if there are no boundaries. Further, the establishment of boundaries suggests a system wholeness. We assume that all the immediate interdependencies have been brought within the same system, making it possible for elements in the environment to treat the system as a totality and, therefore, to respect its boundaries. One of the problems of metropolitan organization in the United States is that such system integrity has seldom been achieved.

The idea of the local government as a system interacting with other systems in the nation demands recognition that the autonomy is the basis of devolution. Essentially this means that the local unit is self-contained, has generally agreed-upon functional and real limits of activity, and is in transaction with an environment to which it provides outputs and from which it receives inputs. As an autonomous unit, it will have its own capabilities to receive messages from the environment, to process those demands, and to direct its outputs toward the functions it seeks to fulfill.

CORRELATES OF DEVOLUTION

The extent of devolution varies greatly, of course, from nation to nation. There are formal-legal differences, as in the recognition of the local government in the national constitution, powers granted recognized local governments, the numbers of local governments, and the methods of selecting the leaders of local governments. The United States, for example, has over 90,000 units of local government, as contrasted with approximately 4,000 in Brazil. Informally, too, differences can be detected, as measured by the percentage of total government expenditures made at the local level.

To the obvious question of why the differences, I return to my early point that structure typically follows function. Devolution is an outcome of social forces operating on a particular national system; and to the extent possible, it would be desirable to know of any imperatives that universally tend to push a nation toward greater or lesser devolution. In other words, it would be useful to identify any environmental factors that seem commonly to correlate with given patterns of devolution. Such an analysis has not only academic significance; it can also provide useful guidelines for weighing the applicability of a strategy of devolution to a given society. It is interesting that virtually no research has been done on this question; indeed, there is some implication that the question need not be asked. Among the proponents of a larger local government role (i.e. devolution), there is an assumption of universal applicability. If it is good in one place, it is good in another. Though the circumstances may be temporarily different, the long run desirability of local government in all cases appears to be taken for granted.

In the well-publicized study by the United Nations on the role of local government in national development, it was said that, "The powers and functions to be allocated to local authorities will depend in part on the country's system of decentralization and can only be decided by individual governments in the light of all relevant factors previously mentioned." [8] Clearly such an enigmatic statement offers little help in identifying an organization strategy. Indeed, the impression is that devolution precedes function; once the structure has been established, it is time to ask what it will do.

Clearly, we are in need of much better data on what *has* happened in nations where devolution has been adopted as a strategy. Such inquiry involves all kinds of perils; difficulties of definition, reliability of data, and so forth. Yet it is quite apparent that our present loose, hypothetical statements can only be validated or rejected on the basis of research.

A preliminary effort in this direction has been made by Professor Paulo Reis Vieira, Deputy Director of the Brazilian

[8] United Nations, *op. cit.*, p. 25.

School of Public Administration (EBAP).[9] The purpose of his investigation was to examine the experience of forty-five countries, to plot their relative levels of devolution, and then to determine the extent to which certain factors in the environment seemed to associate with devolution. To be sure, such an undertaking requires a considerable bravado. Professor Vieira had limited funds, found data more inaccessible and/or unavailable than he imagined, and was constantly required to make interpretations that may have materially affected the quality of the findings.

The study covered countries for which relatively comparable information was available in the Los Angeles area. It was essentially a study of experience. That is, it was considered useful to hypothesize that those countries with the highest amount of devolution were those who had experienced the greatest functional need for it. Put another way, it was assumed that the continued existence of a devolved pattern of government was an organizational expression of a satisfactory state of affairs, in which the requirements of the system were being met. The point is important conceptually, inasmuch as no effort was made in the research to ascertain how, and in what degree, devolution was answering specified functional needs within a particular nation-state.

Briefly, the Vieira research computed a devolution score for each of the forty-five countries, based upon the ratio of local government revenues and expenditures to total government spending and receipts over a ten-year period (1953–63).[10] On this ground, Sweden was revealed as the country with the greatest devolution, followed by Norway, the United Kingdom, Switzerland, and the United States. (See Table 1.)

At least two basic questions can be raised about the validity of this ranking, though in fact the countries at the top of the Vieira list are generally regarded as having strong local governments. The first query deals with the definition of local government. No effort was made to establish a standard definition; the

[9] See Paulo Reis Vieira, "Toward a Theory of Decentralization: A Comparative View of Forty-Five Countries" (doctoral dissertation, University of Southern California, Los Angeles, 1967).

[10] In his work Professor Vieira used the word decentralization to describe the phenomenon of devolution; the research, however, is concerned with the role of local governments in the forty-five nations.

Table 1

DECENTRALIZATION SCORES FOR 45 COUNTRIES

Rank	Country	Decentralization on Score
1	Sweden	111
2	Norway	85
3	United Kingdom	81
4	Switzerland	78
5	United States	73
6	Denmark	68
7	Yugoslavia	66
8	China (Mainland)	62
9	New Zealand	61
10	Algeria	57
11	Belgium	55
12	Netherlands	55
13	Colombia	53
14	Ireland	50
15	Canada	48
16	Italy	47
17	Poland	44
18	Portugal	41
19	Japan	40
20	Spain	34
21	Brazil	33
22	Bulgaria	30
23	Syria	30
24	Jordan	29
25	Romania	28
26	Tanganyika	28
27	Iraq	25
28	Puerto Rico	24
29	Ghana	22
30	Israel	21
31	Barbados	18
32	Guatemala	17
33	Australia	16
34	Ceylon	16
35	Dominican Republic	16
36	El Salvador	16
37	Finland	16
38	India	16
39	Mexico	16
40	Morocco	16
41	Peru	16
42	Trinidad and Tobago	16
43	United Arab Republic	16
44	Venezuela	16
45	(South) Vietnam	16

SOURCE: Paulo Reis Vieira, *op. cit.*, p. 161.

data were taken as given by the governments involved. If a particular nation accounted for an expenditure as that of a local authority, it was so considered. The second problem involves the degree to which money reflects the actual state of devolution in a particular system. My contention is that the ability to acquire resources and dispose of them is central to autonomy. Ideally, it would have been helpful to develop measures of the percentage of revenues actually raised locally and of the number of personnel employed in local government activities. However, such data were not available; and the ranking, therefore, had to be built on a less-than-complete picture of local government resources.

While interesting, the devolution score of a nation is only of value if we can use it to reconstruct a better understanding of the functions the organization strategy was designed to serve. In countries like Sweden and the United States, of course, the strategies have evolved over a long period of time and on grounds that have seldom been articulated. Only today, as we seek to make modernization a far more contrived process, is it perhaps reasonable to talk about organization strategy and about choice.

Twelve environmental factors were studied to identify their association with devolution levels. In general, it appeared that the geographic-demographic factors in the environment (area of the country, population size, heterogeneity, density of settlement, and level of urbanization) did not have a strong association with the degree of devolution. On the other hand, economic-technological factors (levels of GNP, status as an industrial or agricultural society based on predominant mode of employment, and scale and character of communications network) did seem to be strongly associated with devolution.

In summary form, the following relationships were identified between the degree of devolution and the twelve independent variables:

Not Significant (at 5 per cent level)

(1) *Population.* No significant correlation (.11) was found between the population of a nation and degree of devolution.

(2) *Population Density.* No significant correlation (—.01) with the density of a nation.

(3) *Area*. No significant correlation (.11) with the physical area.

(4) *Urbanization*. No significant correlation (.25) with the percentage of urban population.

(5) *Public Consumption as per cent of GNP*. No significant correlation (.09) with the percentage of public expenditures in relation to the gross national product.

(6) *Constitutional Organization*. No significant correlation (−.04) with status as a federal system.

(7) *Ethnic Composition*. No significant correlation (.02) with heterogeneous population.

Significant

(8) *Age*. There was a correlation significant at the 2 per cent level (.35) with the age of a nation.

(9) *Gross National Product*. There was a correlation significant at the 5 per cent level (.28) with the size of the gross national product.

(10) *Communications*. There was a correlation significant at the 1 per cent level (.65) with the index of mass media.

(11) *Nature of Country*. There was a correlation significant at the 1 per cent level (.54) with status as an industrial nation.

(12) *Number of Local Units*. There was a correlation significant at the 5 per cent level (.29) with the number of local governments.

Thus, five of the twelve variables hypothesized to relate significantly to the degree of devolution stood the necessary statistical test that the relationship in the degree identified would not occur more than five times out of a hundred by chance.

The absence of a strong relationship between urbanization and devolution, of course, does not at all deny the significance of the urban problem; but it does suggest that urbanization in itself may not be as strong an argument for a strategy of devolution as has sometimes been suggested. A central government, in short, may be the better for urban services in some countries.

The very strong correlation between the economic-technological variables emphasizes the importance of separating the phenomenon of urbanization from industrialization; the level of industrialization may be the far more significant factor in weighting organization alternatives. Second, it seems clear that stresses in the hierarchical system tend to emerge when the goals of the organization become more complex. The industrialized nation, with its high technology and elaborate specialization, is very likely to experience the greater problems in resolving the conflicts complexity brings. Thus, the level of industrialization may be one test of the degree to which a nation needs to move toward a plurality of structures. Finally, the relationship of communications to devolution is most significant. The non-hierarchical system, involving reciprocating and cooperating interactions under independent entities, very likely requires more highly advanced communications technology. Knowledge of rules, awareness of penalties, and continuous updating of situational information are the bases for system integration in the non-hierarchical situation; they are relatively less important in the superior-subordinate pattern of hierarchy. Where communications capabilities are limited, it may therefore be quite unrealistic to consider devolution as a strategy in any but very long run terms.

Beyond his discovery of the significant association between devolution and economic-technological variables, Professor Vieira made two other findings that are significant.

The first tends to validate the generally-held position that diverse structures within a system can be tolerated only when the integrity of the system itself is not in question. That is, national unity seems to be a necessary precondition for devolution. He hypothesized that the older a nation was, the more likely that it had system integrity. Between the age of a nation and its level of devolution he discovered a correlation of .35, with a 2 per cent possibility that the association occurred by chance. It is, of course, true that the age of a nation is not always easy to calculate. Iran, for example, has had a very long national identity, but it has spent a good deal of its national history under at least *de facto* occupation. The two decades since World War II have involved major efforts to make the nation-state a reality. These limitations, however, only suggest the need for more empirical research in order to test the dependence of devolution as an organization strategy on the existence of national unity.

One other finding by Professor Vieira suggests the problem of circular causation. It asks whether structure must always follow function. In this instance, he discovered that the number of local government units showed a distinct association with the level of devolution (r = .29, significant at the 5 per cent level). This prompts the inevitable question. Which came first? The basic thrust of this chapter suggests that the local governments were products of functional needs in the system; but it is also apparent that the causal direction may be reversed. Organizations act on their environments, as well as being the recipients of environmental demands. To what extent have 90,000 local governments propelled the United States toward devolution?[11] Are there circumstances in which local governments can be used as a means of creating their own impetus toward devolution? Is there an irreducible minimum of environmental hospitality needed to provide at least a launching pad for such initiatives through structure? The question is a tantalizing one which runs through much of organization theory.

Reference to a specific situation, that of Brazil, may help to suggest the significance of expanding the work begun by Professor Vieira. Historically, the role of local government in the Brazilian political system has been modest. Indeed, Brazil was strongly centralist in its beginnings; and the creation of the federal system of government under the Constitution of 1891 was in fact more a borrowing of U.S. political institutions than an outgrowth of indigenous demands for autonomy. The Revolution of 1930, which brought Getúlio Vargas to the Presidency, reduced the powers of the states and represented a resurgence of the central power. Interestingly enough, however, it was during the Vargas dictatorship that the "municipalist" movement in Brazil began to gain strength. The short-lived 1934 Constitution was the first to recognize the municipal governments as an important element in the nation's political life; and the 1946 Constitution, adopted following the overthrow of Vargas, is often regarded as "munici-

[11] It might be added that the 90,000 units of local government represent only the iceberg of the structures that operate in the United States in support of devolution. A tremendous range of economic and social structures pushes in the same direction, in marked contrast to the situation in Iran. Morton Grodzins has written with insight on the ways in which these structures coalesce in his "Local Strength in the American Federal System," in Marian D. Irish, editor, *Continuing Crisis in American Politics* (Englewood Cliffs: Prentice-Hall, Spectrum Books, 1963), pp. 132–52.

palist" because of the heightened status given local government. The nation operated under the 1946 Constitution for about twenty years.

Since the 1934 Constitution, the cause of municipalism in Brazil has been proposed on a nationwide, global basis. That is, the strengthening of local institutions has been seen as a necessity throughout the country, despite the fact that there are tremendous differences in economic and social development in the north and in the south. The effort to follow a national strategy of devolution, despite the existence of such differences, makes the case of Brazil interesting.

The reasonably tight framework within which the individual states had to relate to their municipalities is suggested by the problem encountered when the old Federal District of Rio de Janeiro achieved statehood (as Guanabara) in 1960. Though it contained only .02 of one per cent of the land area of the nation and was heavily urbanized, the financing arrangements for municipalities in the Constitution virtually required the new state to establish local governments. Only an amendment to the Constitution in 1961 gave Guanabara freedom to make its own choice in the matter; and in 1963 the citizens voted overwhelmingly against establishing a local government structure.

The system of federal-municipal tax sharing, established in the 1946 Constitution, is also to be noted. This program, which enabled the municipalities to share in 10 per cent of federal income tax receipts, provided for an absolutely equal distribution of the monies regardless of size, role in the state, and so forth. Capital cities, typically the largest and growing the fastest, received nothing under the program.

These attempts to form a common mold of devolution, of course, encountered quite different environments in the north and south. For other research purposes, I have prepared indices of industrialization and urbanization, based on 1962 data, which suggest how markedly varied developments in Brazil have been. The state of São Paulo, which has been the scene of Brazil's industrial expansion, had an urbanization index of 48 and an industrialization index of 64; the southern state of Santa Catarina, largely regarded as rural-agricultural, still had an industrialization

index (19) equivalent to its level of urbanization (19). Cities in the
south of Brazil have grown, it appears, because of their functions
as finance and manufacturing centers. In contrast, the northeast
state of Pernambuco, whose capital is Brazil's third largest city,
had an urbanization index of 30 but an industrialization index of
only 18; the state of Bahia had the same level of urbanization as
Santa Catarina (19) but an industrialization index considerably
lower (8). At least until 1962, it appeared that the northern cities
were experiencing the same problems of urban growth as the
south; but it was not at all clear they were performing the same
economic, and perhaps social and political, functions.[12]

As might be expected in the highly diversified Brazilian context, the tax sharing program produced quite different results in
the north and in the south. In a state like São Paulo, it was of
relatively minor importance. On the other hand, in the north a
large number of municipalities derived virtually all their income
from the tax share. There was a seemingly unwarranted expansion
of the number of municipalities in several northern states simply
to secure a greater share of federal funds. It is also interesting that
a survey of more than 2,000 municipalities conducted in 1959
showed that only about 15 per cent of the northern cities had an
accounting officer, as contrasted with 95 per cent in the south;
that more than half the city councilmen in the south served without pay but only 10 per cent in the north did, and that salaries
for municipal work were only about half as high in the north as
in the south.[13]

In recent years the U.S. Aid Program in Brazil has devoted
fairly substantial resources to the development of municipalities
in the northeast; in doing so, there has been an implicit support
of devolution as an organization strategy. Indeed, to the extent
that efforts have been made to support urban development in the
northeast, energies have concentrated primarily on the municipalities. A major institution designed to provide technical assist-

[12] Details on this problem are contained in Frank Sherwood, *Institutionalizing
the Grass Roots in Brazil* (San Francisco: Chandler, 1967), pp. 17–30.
[13] The Brazilian Institute of Municipal Administration (IBAM) carried out a
truly monumental survey in 1959 that covered 96.6 per cent (2,340 of 2,423) of the
municipalities then existing. The results were reported in *Municipios do Brasil*
(Rio de Janeiro: Instituto Brasileiro de Administracao Municipal, 1960).

ance to the municipalities has, for example, been established with U.S. help in Recife.

One can ask what U.S. AID strategy ought to be in such a circumstance. Because the U.S. has been concerned about the development of the northeast and because the municipalities have been considered formally responsible for the provision of urban services, support of the municipalities was perhaps natural. Yet it appears that the north is the least appropriate place in Brazil to pursue a strategy of devolution. Given the economic-technological conditions, it might have been better to dismiss the municipalities as a viable unit and to concentrate assistance in urban development on the states and national government.

Though it may seem unnecessary to emphasize the point, the impact of the environment on patterns of devolution needs continually to be underscored. The work of Professor Vieira is noteworthy because it represents at least one attempt to provide empirical data on which to base a more profound discussion of the utility of a policy of devolution in a given situation. The Brazilian example simply gives further evidence of the need to recognize that a structure, in the last analysis, must be congruent with its environment. In Brazil the drive for uniformity ignored the very real differences in needs between the north and the south.

IMPLEMENTING A STRATEGY OF DEVOLUTION: A PROBLEM IN INSTITUTION-BUILDING

Assuming that the circumstances of a particular nation-state do dictate an organization strategy of devolution, with all its implications for autonomy and system separateness, the issue of implementation arises. Essentially, what is needed is a conceptual scheme which will account for variables critical to the enhancement of the role and status of local government. Yet the literature seems generally to have ignored the problem, or, what is worse, to advance propositions that are contradictory to the theory of devolution.

Maddick, for example, has commented that the Brazilian municipalities were never able to achieve the goals set for them by the municipalist Constitution of 1946 because they insisted too much upon autonomy. Such intransigence can be "disastrous" for development, he observed, continuing:

> All this results from the insistence on independence and the failure of authorities to cooperate between themselves. With no area organization, with no control and no guidance over local authorities being exercised by the central government . . . the major problem is—in what way can local governments be improved? [14]

He also labeled Brazil the "most extreme example encountered of local autonomy." [15] If that had been true, of course, logic would require us to regard Brazil as a highly devolved political system. According to the Vieira index, however, Brazil ranked twenty-first among the forty-five countries. The obvious point is that the actual role of local government in a system is defined by far more than a formal-legal statement in a constitution.

Furthermore, the nature of devolution must be kept clear. It involves autonomy and independence. A strategy of implementation therefore takes system separation as a goal. Ambivalence on this question—as in the resort to central "guidance"—can impose such constraints on local behavior that the motivational significance of the strategy is lost.

Devolution suggests the need to develop local governments as institutions. An institution in these terms is an organization which is perhaps most characterized by the feeling of the people in it and the elements around it that it has intrinsic importance. They believe in it, gain satisfactions from it, and would very likely do much to secure its survival. In short, the organization has value. While the view of an organization as having institutional qualities is not entirely new, it is a conceptual approach that has received relatively little attention.

The work of Philip Selznick, particularly his *Leadership in Administration* published in 1957, has undoubtedly been most instrumental in advancing the idea. He has written:

[14] Maddick, *op. cit.*, p. 243.
[15] *Ibid.*, p. 244.

. . . to "institutionalize" is to *infuse with value* beyond the technical requirements of the task at hand. The prizing of social machinery beyond its technical role is largely a reflection of the unique way in which it fulfills personal or group needs. Whenever individuals become attached to an organization or a way of doing things as persons rather than as technicians, the result is prizing of the device for its own sake.

The test of infusion with value is *expendability*. If an organization is merely an instrument, it will be readily altered or cast aside when a more efficient tool becomes available. Most organizations are thus expendable. When value infusion takes place, however, there is resistance to change. People feel a sense of personal loss; the "identity" of the group or community seems somehow to be violated; they bow to economic or technological considerations only reluctantly, with regret.[16]

Following the intellectual directions of Professor Selznick, four universities (Pittsburgh, Indiana, Michigan State, and Syracuse) associated several years ago to undertake joint studies of the institution-building process in developing countries.[17] A grant from the Ford Foundation made it possible to support research and to establish a headquarters at the University of Pittsburgh. Supported by funds from this program, two Brazilian professors and I have been able to study institution-building in two organizations in Brazil. One of these is the Brazilian Institute of Municipal Administration (IBAM), which was created in 1954 to provide technical assistance to the municipalities.[18]

The pursuit of these research interests led inevitably to closer examination of the municipalities themselves, as a basis for understanding the environment in which the Brazilian Institute operated and from which it sought legitimation and acceptance. The

[16] Philip Selznick, *Leadership in Administration* (Evanston, Ill., and White Plains, N.Y.: Row, Peterson, 1957), pp. 17–19.

[17] The framework of the institution-building model has been reported in various places. A good summary is in Milton J. Esman and Hans C. Blaise, *Institution-Building Research: The Guiding Concepts* (Pittsburgh: Research Headquarters, Inter-University Research Program in Institution Building, 1966), mimeo. See also Milton J. Esman and Fred C. Bruhns, "Institution Building in National Development—An Approach to Induced Social Change in Transitional Societies," in *Comparative Theories of Social Change* (Ann Arbor: Foundation for Research on Human Behavior, 1966), pp. 318–47.

[18] For a report of this institution-building study see Aluizio Loureiro Pinto "The Brazilian Institute of Municipal Administration (IBAM): A Case Study of Institution-Building in Brazil" (dissertation submitted in fulfillment of the Dr. of Public Administration requirement at the University of Southern California, 1967).

concern with institution building as a process logically led to the question: How institutionalized are Brazil's municipalities?

In *Institutionalizing the Grass Roots in Brazil,* I have tried to deal with this question.[19] Suffice to say here, my conclusion was that Brazil's municipalities did not achieve a substantial degree of institutionalization under the 1946 Constitution, and the 1967 Constitution will probably result in a net decline from previous levels.

The institution-building model developed by the Inter-University Consortium places major emphasis on the relationship of the organization to its environment, on the basic theory that insularity is impossible. It is not enough that the membership prizes an organization; elements in the environment must also have an investment in it. But environment as such is an amorphous concept. It is necessary to be more specific about the points of contact and the nature of the transaction.

Three organization-environment relations have been postulated in the institution-building model. There is an *enabling* transaction which links the organization to elements which have energies to export and which have the freedom to establish their direction. A second relationship has been termed *functional* in the model. These transactions primarily involve the targets of the organization's outputs, both psychic and material. They are, generally, the clientele of the organization. Finally, there are linkages that are *normative,* in the sense that they either support or oppose the goals for which the organization stands. Such normative transactions can, of course, be extremely strong or relatively weak. In addition, elements less directly in contact are regarded as *diffused.* It should be observed that these categories describe types of transactions, rather than units in the environment. As a result, one organization might have enabling and functional linkages with the organization under analysis.

This model directs greater attention to the way in which a local government relates to its environment. From where does the local government receive its inputs? On what grounds? With what values attached? With what intensity? Where are the outputs directed? In what quantity? With what effect for institutionaliza-

---

[19] Sherwood, *op. cit.,* see particularly chap. 4.

tion? What are the elements in the environment that support or oppose the local government? With what intensity? Under what circumstances? With what effect on the institutional quality of the local government?

In the last analysis, the transaction of the local government with its own community seems to be crucial. This is a perspective that is sometimes overlooked because of the assumption that everyone who votes is a member of the municipal organization. Particularly in terms of outputs, however, the clientele transaction is with the local citizenry. In other words, the functional linkage is immediately local. It is also probable that the local people form the most important normative linkage for the local government. Although other cities may also provide positive normative supports, it is likely that a major share of the linkages from outside the community will be negative. At various points in higher echelons, centralizing values will be held; and the extent to which the local government is prized by its community will be a basic factor in the defense of its boundaries and integrity.

Where the resources to support an organization come from only one point in the environment, a single decision can mean the survival or demise of the organization. When a municipality depends on a single source in the environment for its resources, as in the case of a central government, its potential for institutionalization is thereby reduced. Furthermore, it is not clear that elements in the environment that provide resources in a one-way enabling transaction really establish an exchange relationship which can result in their prizing a municipality. When a central government shares a tax with a local government, it receives no direct output. Benefits are only indirectly received, in many cases very indirectly. Under such circumstances, how much can the central government be expected to value the local?

If the municipality is to have enabling transactions with a large number of elements in the environment, the community clientele must be involved. In effect, the parties to the functional transactions also become parties of the enabling linkage; the concept of the citizen as subject *and* participant thus is central to the institutional development of the municipality.

When we consider the implementation of a strategy of devolution in institution-building terms, then, the community becomes the crucial factor in the environment of the local government. The community is obviously not of exclusive importance; but it does seem clear that the enabling, functional, and normative transactions must be of high volume and intensity with the community. That view seems not to have been fully appreciated by the municipalist makers of the 1946 Constitution in Brazil. They basically tried to build local government institutions by establishing (a) strong legal bulwarks against interference; and (b) a conduit through which money could flow from a point in the central government to the municipalities. It was not clear how the Brazilian municipalities, heretofore relatively unimportant in the political system, were to be valued either by the central government or by their local communities. The result was that the boundaries, so carefully drawn in the law, were never so inviolate. They were penetrated in many different ways. The money never appeared in the prescribed amounts; in some cases it never flowed from the center at all. Where institutionalization has occurred, as in the south of the country, the transaction with the community seemed to have made the difference.

While the orientation here has been on the environmental aspects of the institution-building model, five internal variables are also considered to be crucial to institutionalization: leadership, doctrine, programs, internal structure, and resources. These variables, it will be observed, tie quite directly to the linkages: resources to enabling transactions, programs to functional transactions, and doctrine to normative relationships. The structure of the organization, which obviously includes its leadership, is critical to the success of the transactions.

In this regard, leadership has appeared as the key variable in the institution-building studies thus far completed by the Inter-University Consortium. Ambiguous though the concept is, it does seem that human organizations require humans to set directions, to prod the membership, to symbolize the effort, and to serve as buffers against a hostile world outside. Sometimes these functions may be performed by various members of a leadership structure; in other cases they may fall to a single individual. In some of the most highly devolved nations, like Sweden and the U.K., there traditionally have been collective leadership structures. The same seems to be true of Yugoslavia. In Brazil, it could be argued that the problem has been in good part the concentration of leadership in a single individual. The mayor has been the central figure. If he works hard, is honest, and has public interest values, the government may do well. Since he cannot be re-elected, there is inevitably a successor; and the experience seems to have been that it is very hard to put two good mayors back to back.

In a few pages, it is difficult to do full justice to the institution-building model, particularly as it relates to strategies for devolution. The idea of the institution is closely related to the conceptualization of the local government as a "whole" system with sufficient independence and autonomy to discharge its full membership obligations in a larger system of governments. The stability of such a non-hierarchical patterning depends in considerable part on the extent to which the individual unit members are valued, both by the membership and by relevant elements in the environment. Where there is such prizing, we can generally be assured of continuity in the system as a whole, of a stability of relationships, and of observance of the boundaries and rules that give the system integrity.

In the achievement of institutional status for a local government, the analysis suggests that the critical transaction is with the immediate community. This is the point at which a major share of the activity must occur and from which we would expect the infusion of values in the local government to ensue. Here, again, the "whole" system is an important consideration; for the prizing of the local government will very likely depend on the degree to which a satisfactory exchange relationship has been established between the outputs directed to the environment and inputs sought from it.

SUMMARY

There are many forces operating in this increasingly interdependent world requiring organization strategies which provide for flexibility of response to changing environmental imperatives. Particularly in the urban areas, the community provides the basis for one level of system response. However, it must be understood that the ability to summon resources and to deal with problems in an adaptive-coping fashion demands freedom. This is not to suggest that freedom must be absolute; rules must be established in any system.

The essential idea of devolution is system separateness, in which local governments discharge obligations as part of a national political system and not as dependent elements of a central hierarchy. The concept of devolution is non-hierarchical in the sense that it posits a number of governments having a coordinate, system relationship with one another on an independent, reciprocating basis. Each, within geographic and functional boundaries established by the total system, enjoys autonomy. Particularly in recent years, devolution has been offered as a happy answer to problems of congestion at the center, red tape, and bureaucratic negativism. There has also been the persistent theme that the only "real" democracy can occur at the local level. In fact, conscious efforts to expand the role of local government do not seem to have been particularly successful; and one very likely reason is that few were really prepared to move in the non-hierarchical directions implicit in devolution.

Circumstances do, of course, differ from nation to nation; and the organization style of a particular country will be a function of the demands to which its governments must respond. Experience seems to support this statement. The levels of devolution in the forty-five countries studied by Professor Vieira were markedly different, both in terms of formal-legal provisions and in terms of more dynamic indicators, such as percentages of total government expenditures. Since we may assume that governments in the future will give increasing attention to the conscious manipulation of organizational patterns in the pursuit of societal goals, it becomes increasingly important to be more specific about the relationship between organization and environment. In revealing the strong correlation between economic-technological factors and devolution, the study of Professor Vieira suggests one important consideration to the policy-maker pondering the expansion of the local government role. It also emphasizes the need for more and better data on the basis of which to contrive organizational responses that will be congruent with requirements of the environment.

Finally, it must be recognized that a cordial environment does not in itself guarantee effective, adaptive local governments. In many societies, the economic-technological environment is changing with astonishing rapidity; and it may be in the national interest to move toward patterns of devolution. Yet the history of local government may have been one of privilege for a few, impoverishment, and inaction. Essentially, the problem is to give status to the local government and to cause it to be prized by its members and by its environment. Such a task demands a conceptual scheme that will focus on the variables critical to the success of such an effort. In this respect the concept of institution-building seems to have real utility. The model produced many insights into the reasons why the policy of devolution prescribed in the Brazilian Constitution of 1946 was never fully realized. Furthermore, the institution-building approach suggests that the prizing of local government must depend in large part upon the success with which it transacts with its own community. In the last analysis, these transactions help the local government to secure necessary supports, to avoid dependence on any single enabling element in its environment, and to fend off those forces in the environment which would destroy the boundaries making it a whole system.

The issues raised in this chapter, I believe, have scarcely been touched in the literature of comparative government and administration. Yet public policies do not wait. There is a very real, practical need for more research and generalizing on the limitations and the promises of devolution as an organization strategy.

3 /

Urban Development and Political Development in Latin America

FRANCINE F. RABINOVITZ

A RECENT SURVEY OF THE study of urbanization in political science states that one of the most neglected areas in this field
concerns the internal political consequences of urbanization. The
authors note that countries around the world in the process of restructuring their political and economic systems have, at the same
time, produced drastic changes in the distribution of the population within their nations. But, while political decisions promote
or retard urbanization, governments "seldom count the political
consequences of such decisions as heavily as consequences relating
to capital formation, economic development or international
prestige." [1]

It is the aim of this chapter to tap this neglected area by exploring the political consequences of urban development in one
region of the world, Latin America. The first section of the chapter describes some of the relationships generally posited between
urban phenomena and national political development, and the fit
of these general hypotheses to the Latin-American region. Next,

AUTHOR'S NOTE: I am indebted to the members of the summer seminar
and the 1967 CAG pro-seminar, as well as to Professor Alfred Clubok
of the University of Florida, for advice and to Mr. William Reynolds
for statistical work.

[1] Wallace Sayre and Nelson Polsby, "American Political Science and Urbanization," in Philip F. Hauser and Leo F. Schnore (eds.), The Study of Urbanization
(New York: Wiley, 1965), p. 145.

a method for the further analysis of the association between urban development and political development is presented. Finally, new hypotheses derived from this more systematic treatment of the relationship of urban development to political development in Latin America are presented.

POSITED RELATIONSHIPS BETWEEN URBAN AND NATIONAL DEVELOPMENT

What are the relationships generally posited between urban and national development, and how does the Latin-American experience fit them? While little work has been done on the relationship of urban to national politics, urbanization is assumed to function generally to promote national development. Urbanization is urban development defined as a physical and spatial agglomeration process. There is a predisposition to infer from the experiences of Western countries a linkage between urbanization and "modernizing" forces in society, economy, and polity. At least three types of associations have been identified on a worldwide basis.

First, a positive correlation exists between the degree to which a country is urbanized and its degree of economic development.[2] However, a straight line linkage of urbanization and industrialization is probably simplistic. A whole group of other economic attributes, including energy consumption, show higher correlations with urbanization than does industrialization.[3] In some countries or areas urbanization is neither a necessary nor a sufficient precon-

---

[2] Kingsley Davis and Hilda H. Golden, "Urbanization and the Development of Pre-Industrial Areas," *Economic Development and Cultural Change,* III (October, 1954), 6–26. The correlation between urbanization and industrialization here is +.86. See also Leonard Reissman, *The Urban Process* (New York: The Free Press, 1964), chap. VII; J. P. Gibbs and T. W. Martin, "Urbanization and Natural Resources," *American Sociological Review,* XXIII, No. 3 (1958), 266–77; Malcolm Rivkin, "Urbanization and National Development" (paper presented at Inter-Regional Seminar on Development Policies in Relation to Urbanization, Pittsburgh, 1967), mimeo.

[3] Leo F. Schnore, "The Statistical Measurement of Urbanization and Economic Development," *Land Economics,* XXXVII (August, 1961), 229–46.

dition for economic growth.[4] Under certain conditions urbanization may even slow down economic change.[5]

Second, a positive association exists between levels of urbanization and changes in the values and beliefs of societies. The host
of social characteristics commonly linked with urbanization is here
referred to as "urbanism." Increased levels of urbanization may
bring with them forces which mediate modern social ideas and
conditions to migrants. There is a high correlation between the
level of urbanization and literacy, the extent of higher education,
inhabitants per physician, and the per 1,000 population.[6] In this
relationship there is also often a basic antagonism between town
and country. The emergence of urban centers is said to produce a
cleavage between traditional, village-based persons and modern-
ized urban elites.[7] However, it is not at all clear that urbanization
per se destroys traditional cultures. The social characteristics associated with Western urban societies include the predominance
of secondary relationships, individualism, the propensity for
change and social mobility, anomie and social disorganization.[8]
But these are not always the traits toward which the residents of
recently formed urban areas, particularly the twentieth century
"preindustrial cities," are moving.[9]

[4] Eric E. Lampard, "The History of Cities in Economically Advanced Areas," *Economic Development and Cultural Change,* III (January, 1955), 81–136.

[5] Carl Bridenbaugh, *Cities in the Wilderness* (New York: Ronald Press, 1938) and *Cities in Revolt* (New York: Knopf, 1955).

[6] See for example Bruce M. Russett *et al., World Handbook of Political and Social Indicators* (New Haven: Yale University Press, 1964), pp. 295–97; United Nations, *Report on the World Social Situation* (New York: United Nations, 1961); Daniel Lerner, *The Passing of Traditional Society* (Glencoe, Ill.: The Free Press of Glenco, 1958); Gino Germani, "Urbanización, Secularización y Desarrollo Económico," *Revista Mexicana de Sociologiá,* XXI (Mayo-Agosto, 1963).

[7] Bert F. Hoselitz, "The Role of Cities in the Economic Growth of Under-developed Countries," *Journal of Political Economy,* LXI (June, 1953), 195–208. A fascinating type of rural-urban antagonism exists in Israel, where no ingrained peasant way of life was disrupted by urbanization, but an anti-urban ideology exists. See Bernard D. Weinryb, "The Impact of Urbanization in Israel," *Middle East Journal,* XI, No. 1 (Winter, 1957), 23–36.

[8] Louis Wirth, "Urbanism as a Way of Life," in P. K. Hatt and A. J. Reiss (eds.), *Cities and Society* (Glencoe, Ill.: The Free Press of Glencoe, 1957); Robert Redfield, *The Folk Culture of Yucatan* (Chicago: University of Chicago Press, 1940).

[9] Gideon Sjoberg, *The Pre-Industrial City* (Glencoe, Ill.: The Free Press of Glencoe, 1960); Robert Redfield and M. B. Singer, "The Cultural Role of the Cities," *Economic Development and Cultural Change,* III (October, 1954), 53–73;

A positive association has also been posited between urbanization and political development. For example, Lucian Pye, commenting on the political implications of urbanization for the political development process states that:

> Urbanization is a critical process in the development of the modern nation-state. Historically all complex and advanced civilizations have sprung from the city and in the contemporary world urban life is the dynamic basis for most of the activities and processes we associate with modernity. . . . Therefore any systematic effort to transform traditional societies into modern nations must envisage the development of cities and modern societies.[10]

Joseph LaPalombara reflects similar assumptions in stating that ". . . urbanization itself, whatever its causes, will necessarily bring some change in political culture. . . . New and different associative patterns are encouraged which will inevitably impinge on parochial and traditional values and attitudes." [11] Phillips Cutright, in his attempts to identify some of the correlates of national political development, found that the correlation of urbanization with political development was of the magnitude of .64. (The correlation of political development and communications was .80.) [12]

However, since urbanization is a profoundly disruptive process, in the social, economic and psychological spheres, it can also create tensions which disrupt stability and nation building. The "costs" of urbanization for political modernization include the ease which physical density lends to organization of extremist groups, the increasing contacts between different groups which may heighten tensions associated with regional differences, and the

Robert LeVine, "Political Socialization and Cultural Change," in Clifford Geertz (ed.), *Old Societies and New States* (New York: The Free Press, 1963), p. 60; John Gulick, "Old Values and New Institutions in a Lebanese Arab City," *Human Organization,* XXIV, No. 1 (Spring, 1965), 49–52.

[10] Lucian W. Pye, "The Political Implications of Urbanization and the Development Process," in *Social Problems of Development and Urbanization* (U.S. papers prepared for the UN Conference on the Application of Science and Technology for the Benefit of the Less Developed Areas, Vol. VII, Geneva, 1963), p. 84.

[11] Joseph LaPalombara, "Italy: Fragmentation, Isolation and Alienation," in Lucian Pye and Sidney Verba (eds.), *Political Culture and Political Development* (Princeton, N.J.: Princeton University Press, 1965), p. 326.

[12] Phillips Cutright, "National Political Development: Measurement and Analysis," *American Sociological Review,* XXVIII, No. 2 (April, 1963), 253–64. Seymour Martin Lipset, relying on ranks and means, also finds that urbanization is correlated with political democracy in *Political Man* (Garden City, N.Y.: Doubleday Anchor, 1963), pp. 37–38.

greater contact of relatively deprived city residents both with more privileged modes of life and with political ideologies focused on social justice.

The sequence followed by these processes is not entirely clear. The best known formulation has been provided by Daniel Lerner, who theorized that the process of "democratic political development" begins with urbanization and then moves through communications and industrialization phases toward the formation of a participant society:

> The secular evolution of a participant society appears to involve a regular sequence of three phases. Urbanization comes first, for cities alone have developed the complex of skills and resources which characterize the modern industrial economy. Within this urban matrix develop both of the attributes which distinguish the next two phases—literacy and media growth. There is a close reciprocal relationship between these, for the literate develop the media which in turn spread literacy. . . . Not until the third phase, when the elaborate technology of industrial development is fairly well advanced, does a society begin to produce newspapers, radio networks and motion pictures on a massive scale. . . . Out of this interaction develop those institutions of participation (e.g., voting) which we find in all advanced modern society.[13]

A causal model of this sequence indicates that political development is based on the spread of mass communications; urbanization effects political development mainly by increasing educational levels, which then increase mass communication.[14] It is also quite possible that some countries reverse the process, experiencing increases in mass communications on the basis of worldwide media spreading, which then generates urbanism.

Because there is so little accurate information about the dynamics of either urbanization or development in Latin America, existing studies seem both to support and contradict impressions gained from international analyses. Urbanization in Latin America is frequently linked qualitatively with improvements in the economy, the spread of modern sociocultural patterns, the rise of a politically moderate middle class, the growth of democratic prac-

[13] Lerner, *op. cit.*, p. 60.
[14] See Donald J. McCrone and Charles F. Cnudde, "Toward a Communications Theory of Democratic Political Development," *American Political Science Review*, LXI (March, 1967), 78; Raymond Tanter, "Toward a Theory of Political Development," *Midwest Journal of Political Science*, XI, No. 2 (May, 1967).

tices, and stability in politics and government.[15] An early quantitative study of all these variables in Latin America establishes Pearson correlations of —.91 between urbanization and economic underdevelopment, defined as persons employed in agriculture. The authors report a +.89 correlation between urbanization and "social development" as tapped by newspaper circulation. The correlation between urbanization and "the acceptance of democracy in culture and politics," measured by press freedom, is +.50.[16]

However, both qualitative and quantitative studies raise doubts about the easy acceptance of a linkage between urbanization and social, economic and political development in the Latin-American case. In the economic sphere, the most urbanized countries in Latin America have lower proportions of persons engaged in agriculture and higher gross products per capita than the least urbanized countries. The expansion in urban population has far outdistanced growth in manufacturing and modern industry within some countries. In Brazil, for example, traditional farming seems to have forced the expulsion of labor from rural areas before cities developed the industrial capacity to absorb it, particularly in the northeastern states.[17] Rapid urbanization has not

---

[15] See the association of urbanization and economic development in Pompeu Accioly Borges, "Graus de desenvolvimento na América Latina," *Desenvolvimento e Conjuntura* (Rio de Janeiro: Confederação Nacional da Industria, 1961); of urbanization and social development in Harley Browning, "Recent Trends in Latin American Urbanization," *Annals of the American Academy of Political and Social Science,* CCCXVI (March, 1958), 118; Julian Steward, "Analysis of Complex Contemporary Societies: Culture Patterns of Puerto Rico," in D. B. Heath and R. N. Adams (eds.), *Contemporary Culture and Societies of Latin America* (New York: Random House, 1965), p. 31; of urbanization and political development in John J. Johnson, *The Emergence of the Middle Sectors: Political Change in Latin America* (Stanford: Stanford University Press, 1958). The linking of urbanization and development in Latin America has also been noted and commented upon by Frank Bonilla, "The Urban Worker," in John J. Johnson (ed.), *Continuity and Change in Latin America* (Stanford: Stanford University Press, 1964), p. 186; Kenneth F. Johnson, "Urbanization and Political Change in Latin America" (unpublished Ph.D. dissertation, University of California at Los Angeles, 1963), p. 1; Luis Ratinoff, "The New Urban Groups," in S. M. Lipset and A. Solari (eds.), *Elites in Latin America* (New York: Oxford Press, 1967), pp. 61–93; and Alfred Stepan, "Political Development Theory: The Latin American Experience," *Journal of International Affairs,* XX, No. 2 (1966), 223–34.

[16] Paul Deutschmann and John T. McNelly, "Characteristics of Latin American Countries," *American Behavioral Scientist,* VIII (September, 1964), 25–29.

[17] Waldermiro Bazzanella, "Industrializaçao e Urbanizaçao no Brasil," *América Latina,* VI (January–March, 1963).

only failed to produce equally rapid economic expansion, but also generated some unhealthy economic effects. The urban emphasis on consumption is said to have retarded capital saving in Latin America and the urban expansion of tertiary activities has burdened the administrative budget of government while contributing little to national economic progress.[18]

The social impact of Latin-American urbanization in producing *urbanism,* the way of life usually associated with the spatial process, has only just begun to be analyzed in depth. Undoubtedly the rapid growth of cities in Latin America has contributed to the creation of new types of social structures, new centers of mass communication, and new institutions using individual merit as the stratification principle. Undoubtedly also, these changes have led to incongruence between rural, traditional, and urbanized, modern sectors in many countries in Latin America. In some areas the division between the cities and the interior is so great that writers refer "to the coexistence of two societies separated by centuries of distance." [19]

The division between urban and rural dwellers is clear-cut in regard to education, said to be the key product of urbanization which promotes development. In Latin America differentiations between educational levels seem to follow divisions between urban and rural areas. A high agricultural population is generally related to low numbers of teachers both within and between nations. While Brazil in the 1950s had highly developed educational systems in São Paulo and Rio, the per cent of matriculation in secondary education in relation to school age population was as limited in the northeast as in Haiti, the country with the most underdeveloped educational system among the Latin-American nations.[20] However, it is still unclear whether increased educational opportunities actually produce increased mobility or create new social values.[21]

[18] Denis Lambert, "Urbanization et développement economique en Emérique Latine," *Carvelle* (Université de Toulouse), III (1964), 266–74.

[19] Jacques Lambert, *Le Brasil. Structure sociale et institutions politiques* (Paris: Librarie Armand Colin, 1953), p. 313.

[20] Aldo Solari, "Secondary Education and Elite Development," in *Elites in Latin America, op. cit.,* p. 460–63; Frederick Harbison and Charles A. Myers, *Education, Manpower and Economic Growth* (New York: McGraw-Hill, 1964), pp. 45–48.

[21] See K. H. Silvert and Frank Bonilla, *Education and the Social Meaning of Development* (New York: American Universities Field Staff, 1961).

At the same time, in many cases we do not get in Latin-
American cities the patterns of disorganization incident to urban
living in Western urban models. Migration to Latin America tends
to occur heavily in communal groupings or invasions. Later migrants move alone to areas to which family has already moved.
This means that family life remains strong. Indeed, extended
family ties in cities often increase over those in rural areas. Thus,
among Latin-American migrants there seems to be less evidence
of impersonality, secularism, breakdown, cultural conflict with
rural styles or irreconcilable differences between generations than
Western experiences would lead us to expect.[22]

The relationships among urbanization, urbanism, and political development in Latin America are even less well understood
than the role of urbanization in fostering or impeding social and
economic change. In part, this seems to be because speculations
about urbanization, urbanism and the national polity often depend upon the previous adoption of one or the other of the
theories about urbanization and society or economy. The result is
that although urban development and national politics are commonly thought to be closely related, the details of the relationship
are obscure.

Following the customary hypotheses about the role of *urbanism* in development, one can find connections between changes in
values and life styles which result from the growth of cities and
the modernization of national politics. The linkage is complex in
the case of the traditional elites. The source of wealth is still often
the land, but the land now provides primary goods for national

[22] Case studies and surveys in Mexico, Brazil, Argentina, and Puerto Rico
support this view. See Oscar Lewis, "Urbanization without Breakdown: A Case
Study," *Scientific Monthly*, LXXV (July, 1952), 31–41; Fernando Henrique Cardoso,
Empresário Industrial e Desenvolvimento Economico (São Paulo: Difusão Européia
do Livro, 1964); Gino Germani, "Inquiry into the Social Effects of Urbanization in
a Working Class Sector of Greater Buenos Aires," in Philip Hauser, *Urbanization
in Latin America* (New York: International Documents Service, Columbia University
Press for UNESCO, 1961), pp. 206–33; Richard Morse, "Recent Research on Latin
American Urbanization: A Selective Survey with Commentary," *Latin American
Research Review*, I (Fall, 1965), esp. p. 41; Joseph Kahl, "Social Stratification and
Values in Metropoli and Provinces: Brazil and Mexico," *América Latina*, VIII
(January–March, 1965), 23–24; Joseph Kahl, "Urbanizacão e Mundancas Ocupacionais
no Brasil," *América Latina*, V (October–December, 1962), 28–29. Other studies are
cited in Alfred Stepan, *op. cit.*, p. 233 and Melvin M. Tumin, *Social Class and Social
Change in Puerto Rico* (Princeton, N.J.: Princeton University Press, 1961).

markets in large cities. Therefore, the landed capitalist becomes absorbed in the urban social and political systems and is forced to exchange traditional orientations toward control by terror and intimidation for more refined outlooks.[23] The linkage is even more pronounced in the case of the middle class. Urban development is said to bring about recognition of the middle sectors. They in turn lean toward creating an "open society, modern political organizations and a participant orientation." [24] Their existence also forces the traditionally powerful classes to engage in coalition politics for the first time.

The linkage of urban and political development is also apparent in regard to the urban low-income population. New settlements on the periphery of many Latin-American cities represent concentrated potential sources of votes and mass pressures. This visibility and concentration encourages new types of political organization, alongside trade unions and parties. These may take the form of mass support for "populist" political leaders who resemble American "boss" figures both in promising full employment through public works and supporting their appeals by distributing food, clothing and jobs. They may also take the form of association for defense against the authorities seeking to eradicate invasion shantytowns. While official agencies are quite obviously ambivalent about these, even such short lived local organizations typically are seen by some scholars as implying a stronger participant and political role for low-income groups.[25]

A variant on the customary linkage is provided by introducing the portion of the traditional Western view that emphasizes

[23] I. L. Horowitz, "Politics, Urbanization and Social Development in Latin America," *Urban Affairs Quarterly*, II (March, 1967); François Bourricaud, "Structure and Function of the Peruvian Oligarchy," in I. L. Horowitz (ed.), *Studies in Comparative International Development* (St. Louis: Social Science Institute at Washington University, 1966), II; Glaucio A. D. Soares, "The Political Sociology of Uneven Development in Brazil," in I. L. Horowitz (ed.), *Revolution in Brazil* (New York: E. P. Dutton, 1964), pp. 164–95.

[24] See Johnson, *The Emergence of the Middle Sectors, op. cit.*; and Ratinoff, *op. cit.*

[25] Morse, *op. cit.*, p. 56; Social Affairs Division of the UN ECLA, "Recent Changes in Urban and Rural Settlement Pattern in Latin America: Some Implications for Social Organization and Development" (paper presented at the Inter-Regional Seminar on Development Policies and Planning in Relation to Urbanization, Pittsburgh, 1966), mimeo, pp. 9–14.

the role of cities in altering values in the direction of alienation and estrangement. Following this model, it is possible to conclude that although urban growth in Latin America does change social values, the change exacerbates existing symptoms of national political instability. While in Brazil, Mexico and Peru the movement of peasants to urban centers has reduced revolutionary violence, in Argentina displaced peasants sought welfare in cities but did not find it. Their urban poverty generated frustration and anomie, manifested in the support of the Peronista movement. Similarly, it can be argued that middle class residents possess skills useful in "modern" societies, but in such abundance that some portions of the group get ahead at the expense of others with similar training. The dissatisfaction of the middle class expresses itself in the larger radical votes in big cities in election after election than in rural zones.[26] It is possible that such a reservoir of urban dissatisfaction contributes to the forces undermining political control so that opportunities for usurping power arise and are seized by armies or bureaucracies.[27]

Still another view of the association between urban and political development is derived from the evidence that the existence of cities in Latin America is not incompatible with retention of conformity to traditional or non-modern political ways. Although the city does seem to make migrants more aware of the existence of a central mechanism of political power that can be made responsive to group needs, patterns of reliance on family connections and protective relationships to obtain favors from the government are tenacious. The retention of personalism seems to be associated with the avoidance of specific service issues like housing and sanitation, although the direction of the relationship is an open question.[28] It is also noteworthy that voters in the biggest Latin-Amer-

[26] Evidence on Uruguay is cited in Aldo E. Solari, "Impacto político de las diferencias internas de los países en los grados e indices de modernización y desarrollo económico en América Latina," *América Latina*, VIII (January–March, 1965), 5–22; on Venezuela in John D. Martz, *Acción Democrática: Evolution of a Modern Political Party in Venezuela* (Princeton, N.J.: Princeton University Press, 1966); on Colombia and Mexico in K. Johnson, *op. cit.*

[27] Kenneth Johnson, "Causal Factors in Latin American Political Instability," *Western Political Quarterly*, XVII (September, 1964), 432–46.

[28] This view is taken by Frank Bonilla, *op. cit.* Examples of the tenacity of the rural style in city politics in campaigning among the *favelados* are also given in

ican cities, presumably the nation's most modern setting, frequently defeat "modern" parties in order to secure their present
advantages or win new favors.[29] Thus the tenacity of old patterns
in growing cities may have many possible consequences. On the one
hand it suggests that challenges to traditional elites will develop
only very slowly. On the other hand, it implies that the insecurity
of new groups, and hence the tendency to anomie and authoritarianism, may also be muted in Latin-American cities.

METHOD

Given the lack of standardization among the measures and
consequently among the posited relationships between urban and
political development in Latin America, a reassessment of the links
among urbanization, urbanism, urban politics, and national political development clearly constitutes a vital step in placing the study
of the consequences of urban development on a firm base. Ideally
we would want to develop a dynamic model of the link between
urban development and national political development by looking
at the relationship of urbanization, urbanism, and urban politics
at the individual, city, and national levels. This would indicate for
each level what configurations foster or impede particular types of
conditions or changes in the national political sphere.

Most of the theories about the relationships between urban
and political development focus on individual behavior or patterns of group activity in single cities, so there is a good basis for
beginning analysis here. However, most of the data available on
Latin-American urban and political development are national.
There is also strong theoretical justification for beginning analysis

---

Carlos Alberto de Medina, *A favela e o demagogo*, cited in Morse, *op. cit.*, p. 57;
Irving L. Horowitz, "Modern Argentina: The Politics of Power," *The Political
Quarterly*, III (October–December, 1959), 400–10; Horowitz, "Politics, Urbanization
and Social Development," *op. cit.*, p. 25; Bourricaud, "Lima en la Vida Política
Peruana," *op. cit.*

[29] This problem is discussed for Caracas, Venezuela by Frank Bonilla, "Review
Article on *Acción Democrática: Evolution of a Modern Political Party in Venezuela*
by John D. Martz," *Journal of Politics*, XXIX (February, 1967), 180–82.

with the national sphere. While in countries where urban politics are more autonomous, the overall national level of urbanization may not be an important factor, for Latin America national processes of all kinds are integrally and perhaps decisively related to urban actions.

Latin-American urban politics appears to be shaped by four factors which link it intimately with national politics: (1) Historically, Latin-American cities functioned primarily as centers of national political and economic life; (2) Although today some cities in some Latin-American countries are autonomous in form, in practice there is only limited autonomy from national dictates. This lack of autonomy is closely associated with the almost total absence of fiscal autonomy; (3) The Latin-American party system is geared to national concerns and not to local needs and interests; (4) Latin-American urban publics look to the nation and not the city to fulfill their needs.[30] Discussion of these four factors follows:

1. In the outlying regions of Latin America, independent rural settlements developed in the sixteenth and seventeenth centuries. Nucleated settlements of Indians predating the Spanish conquest also persisted. The cities of Latin America primarily served the crown. Urban institutions focused on "internal" functions were therefore weakly developed, as was the network of ties among cities within large areas. The crown's political and economic policies tended to insulate Latin-American cities and tie them individually to Lisbon and Seville.[31] The disregard of the city as an agent for the satisfaction of local needs was exacerbated by the fact that the municipality was the point of departure for settling the land, unlike the situation in the Western European city. Richard Morse states that:

> . . . it is clear that a significant sector of municipal society was composed not of townsmen, but of mere cohabitants whose horizons of hope or endeavor the city failed to contain. The city distributed status- and-fortune-seekers out to unexploited areas of economic promise with a

[30] The outlining of such factors was suggested to me by the work of Professor Donald Rosenthal, who has examined four factors present in American urban experience not likely to be present to the same extent in Asian urban political systems.

[31] Richard Morse, "Latin American Cities: Aspects of Function and Structure," *Comparative Studies in Society and History*, IV, No. 4 (July, 1962), 475, 478–79.

centrifugal effect that contrasts with the centripetalism of the late medieval town.[32]

Historically then, the *raison d'être* of Latin-American cities has been "external" rather than "internal."

2. Municipalities in Latin America took matters into their own hands while Spain was busy resisting Napoleon, and the movement toward independence from Spain was largely an urban affair. Today, however, although Brazil, Argentina, Mexico, and Venezuela have had nominally federal systems, most Latin-American nations have centralized governments in which municipalities are dependent on national governments. All powers not specifically granted to local units remain with the central government.[33]

It is possible to argue that the presence or absence of an autonomous sphere of politics at the urban level turns on the degree of *legal* autonomy of cities and municipalities in Latin America from the national government. Almost all the Latin American constitutions pay lip service to the principle of "municipal autonomy." Mexico, in its 1917 Constitution, even introduces the idea that the fundamental unit of the nation is the municipality and uses the free municipality as the basis of territorial division and political and administrative organization. However, in reality legal autonomy seems more a constant than a variable. In the same constitutions which grant freedom to urban units, regulations limiting the workings of municipal powers are set up so that the municipality ordinarily becomes an instrument of central power. Where this is not so, urban units are reduced to agencies lacking authority or finances to attend to the matters which constitutionally should be within their jurisdiction. Even in countries with

[32] Richard Morse, "Some Characteristics of Latin American Urban History," *American Historical Review*, LXVII, No. 2 (January, 1962), 329. Morse's work is particularly useful to the analyst focusing on urban political functions because it has been geared "not to exploring the historical origins of Latin American cities but to developing a functional theory clarifying the relation of the Latin American city to the settlement of the land and to the forms of economic production." *Ibid.*, p. 317.

[33] "Municipalities" in the Latin-American context refers to both urban and rural units. A good summary of the constitutional provisions effecting Latin-American municipalities in ten countries has been prepared by the Fundación para el Desarrollo, Caracas, Venezuela.

constitutional provisions for vigorous municipal government, the unequal distribution of tax resources makes genuine urban autonomy impossible.[34] In Brazil, where municipalities were until recently granted substantial powers to govern, not only fiscal limitations but the territorial instability of municipal units prevented cities from adequately fulfilling functions other than the maintenance of favorable political relations with state and national officials.[35] The upsurge of national planning institutions and programs may be causing the autonomy of the Latin-American municipality to shrink even further.

3. National party politics also thwarts the development of cities as instrumentalities for managing urban development. Latin-American political parties are geared to gaining control of national governments. Municipal elections are used to strengthen the national party, not to develop local leadership or services. A recent study of urban leadership in six Latin-American cities concludes that not only is the party primarily interested in national affairs, but that there is a tendency for local officials to see their personal advancement in national terms, not through success in governing the city.[36]

4. Finally, few demands are made on urban governments to perform "internal" functions, except insofar as cities are acting as agents in development programs produced by the national government. Many urban residents in Latin-American cities have no expectation that the urban political system can help them, and

[34] The situation is summarized in Banco Interamericano de Desarrollo, "El Financiamiento del Gobierno Local," *Reunión Sobre Financiamiento Municipal en Latinoamérica: Informe* (Washington: Inter-American Development Bank, 1966), pp. 22–31.

[35] Carr L. Donald, "Brazilian Local Self Government—Myth or Reality," *Western Political Quarterly*, XIII (December, 1960), 1043–55; "The Politics of Local Government Finance in Brazil," *Inter-American Economic Affairs*, XII (Summer, 1959), 21–37.

[36] Eagleton Institute of Politics, *Urban Leadership in Latin America: A Report to the U.S. AID* (New Brunswick, N.J.: Rutgers University Press, 1964). See also William V. D'Antonio and Richard Suter, "Primary Elections in a Mexican Municipio: New Trends in Mexico's Struggle toward Democracy," (South Bend, Ind.: Department of Sociology, Notre Dame, 1966), mimeo.

their loyalty to the urban community is faint.[37] Where demands
exist, there is relatively little organization for pressing these demands, beyond the level of quasi-familial social cells and local
associations in "slum" areas, which disband quickly as conditions
improve.[38]

Of course, none of these characteristics holds as an established
principle for all cities in Latin America. Even with our present
limited knowledge, many qualifications on the above statements
must be made. For example, in regard to the strong historical linkage of cities to the crown in Latin America it must be emphasized
that some medieval free city traditions do antecede national states
in Latin America, as they do in many Western nations. Richard
Morse states:

> New World settlers brought with them, to be sure, traditions of the
> medieval Iberian municipal community. These were standardized in
> Spanish and Portuguese legislation for the Indies on such matters as
> the municipal control of common lands, the corporate or guild structure
> of urban crafts, professions, and commerce, the election of town officials
> by property owners, and price control and regulation of commerce. It
> can even be argued that municipal autonomy showed renewed life in
> America at the very time it was being stifled on the peninsula. Much
> of this original vigor, however, was externally induced by the threat
> of Indian attack, by threats of foreign attack upon the coastal cities, by
> deprivation from famine or drought, and by geographical isolation. . . .
> As the external threats to survival were lifted, the disintegrative attraction
> of plain, mine and forest was asserted. This attraction was more damaging
> to the cohesion of urban society than was the surrender of municipal
> liberties to the nation states.[39]

In regard to the second point, i.e., that municipal autonomy
from national policies is generally quite limited, it must be added
that the practical application of the federal system, at least in
Mexico, makes some city governments more than mere adminis-

[37] See Frank Bonilla, "Rio's Favelas: The Rural Slum within the City,"
American Universities Field Staff Report, FB-1-61 (August, 1961).

[38] Many relevant sources are cited in Morse, "Recent Research on Latin American Urbanization," *op. cit.*, pp. 35–75. Field studies now being conducted are reported in Daniel Goldrich, Raymond Pratt, and C. R. Schuller, "The Political
Integration of Lower Class Urban Settlements in Chile and Peru" (paper prepared
for delivery at the 1966 Annual Meeting of the American Political Science Association, New York, September, 1966).

[39] Morse, "Latin American Urban History," *op. cit.*, p. 329.

trators of national programs. Many urban projects, rather than being determined at the national level, are initiated by the city.[40] Third, while party politics is nationally oriented, some countries, such as Brazil, have traditions of regional or local party structure.

Fourth, we must note that national power is so largely located in the big cities of Latin America that it can be argued that national politics is in some ways "urbanized," rather than urban politics being "nationalized." [41] Most Latin-American leaders come from cities. This is true not only of industrial and educational elites, but also of the Latin-American military[42] and even of leaders of peasant movements.[43] It may therefore be the case that issues and programs of interest to urban dwellers tend to come to the fore in politics as the major national issues treated by the government.

Despite these qualifications, it is difficult to view Latin-American cities except as subordinates in national systems. Therefore, in interpreting urban inputs and outputs, we must analyze not only the function in question but the influence on it of behavior which is national in political terms. The power of many

[40] Francine F. Rabinovitz, "Urban Development Decision-Making in the Mexican Federal District," in *Programs for Urban Development in Latin America* (Washington: U.S. Agency for International Development, 1965). A similar situation seems to exist in the Mexican states, particularly with respect to road building, according to Linda S. Mirin, "Public Investment in Aguascalientes" (unpublished Ph.D. dissertation, Harvard University, 1964).

[41] The issue was raised by George Blanksten, "Local Government in a Rising Technology: Problems and Prospects for Latin America" (paper presented at the 1964 Annual Meeting of the American Political Science Association, Chicago, September, 1964), p. 18. Blanksten concludes on the side of nationalization or internationalization of the political culture of large Latin-American cities, however. The idea that national politics may become "urbanized" is also a common proposition for U.S. affairs in the nineteen-twenties and thirties. See Charles E. Gilbert, "National Political Alignments and the Politics of Large Cities," *Political Science Quarterly*, LXXIX (March, 1964), 25–51.

[42] See for example, Irving Louis Horowitz, "The Military Elites," in *Elites in Latin America, op. cit.*, p. 160. Horowitz notes that the rural background of the Latin-American military is, at least for Argentina, largely a matter of the past. Argentine generals came from rural regions in the prewar years but by 1961 over half of them were born in Greater Buenos Aires, Entre Rios, Corrientes, or Córdoba. This is also true of the Peruvian navy, although less so of the Peruvian army. Ninety per cent of Peru's naval officers come from big cities, particularly Lima, according to Lyle N. McAlister, "Peru" (draft, 1967). Professional ties may, of course, be more important than origin in shaping the views of these officers.

[43] Anibal Quijano Obregón, "Contemporary Peasant Movements," *Elites in Latin America, ibid.*, p. 319.

urban officials turns on their effectiveness as brokers between the city and the central government.[44] The dependence of urban government on national systems also suggests that the major functions of urban politics in Latin America will be found in the national sphere. The city may be an agency that functions primarily to implement decisions made largely by the national government or, it may function primarily as a recruiting body for future national politicians, providing a point of entry for new leaders and a source of patronage to abet their rise. If cities are conceived and structured as agents of the national government, it is reasonable to hypothesize that a major impact of urban politics will be on functions pertaining to national development as well as to specifically urban inputs and outputs. This dependence implies that in predicting urban action or inaction there is a high probability that factors related to urban political systems will tend to drop out in relation to national factors. Hence, the justification for beginning to analyze the association of urban and political development at the national level.

The analysis which follows is an attempt to first identify some urban characteristics of twenty Latin-American nations on the basis of several indicators of urban development. Urban development used in this sense is a property of a country or region and not of one or several cities. The second objective is to determine whether there are significant statistical relationships among these indicators of "urban development" and of "political development." The question to be asked is: are different levels, trends or patterns of urbanization, urban service provision or urban growth associated with more or less modern, or even distinguishable, levels of national political development in Latin America?

[44] Following such a line of reasoning, Diego Lordello de Mello has suggested, for example, that the council-manager structure is inapplicable to Brazilian cities. City executives in Brazil are mainly important as influence wielders in state and national capitals, not as technically trained administrators. Diego Lordello de Mello, "The Chief Administrative Officer Plan and Its Applicability to Brazilian Municipalities" (unpublished M.S. thesis, University of Southern California, 1954), pp. 139–43. The argument is stated in Frank P. Sherwood, "Industrialization and Urbanization in Brazil" (paper presented at the Annual Meeting of the American Political Science Association, Chicago, 1964). See also Gary Hoskins, "Patterns of Power and Politics in a Venezuelan City: The Significance of San Cristobal's Development" (1966), mimeo, p. 19. Hoskins states that local power structure must be placed in the context of center-periphery relations for community development.

There are many things which such a limited analysis does not do. It does not give us firm confirmation about urban development as a cause of political development. Even where associations exist, both urban and political development may clearly be the result of a third or fourth factor which are related to both independently. The analysis does not tell us much about the association of social processes commonly linked with urban agglomeration and national politics. It is likely that in Latin America there are densely settled, "urban" areas without "urbanism" and both "urbanization" and "urbanism" without "urban self-government." This analysis also tells us little about what is occurring or is likely to occur within a particular city in a particular country, or in the life of a particular individual in a city. If the level of urbanization is closely associated with national electoral participation in Argentina, it need not necessarily be so in Mendoza or Córdoba. And, not all individuals in a city may go through the same kind of urbanization experience suggested by a linkage of levels of participation and level of urbanization for the nation at large. This analysis, focusing on urban development from a national perspective, is simply an initial effort which hopefully will stimulate more thorough analyses of urban development, focusing directly on urban politics, as soon as better data are available.

With these reservations and definitions in mind, the urban elements selected and the indicators used for them are:

(1) *Level of Urbanization*—Per cent of total population in cities of 20,000 or more, 20,000 to 100,000, over 100,000, according to latest census.[45]

(2) *Size of Cities*—Largest city as a per cent of total population, largest city as per cent of urban population, population in cities of

[45] Figures were derived from John Durand and César Peláez, "Patterns of Urbanization in Latin America," *Milbank Memorial Foundation Quarterly*, XLIII, No. 4, Part II (October, 1965), 166–96 and the *UN Demographic Yearbook*, 1964. Nine countries do not have post-1960 censuses whose figures are available. Here the 1950 figure was used. A major problem with the use and interpretation of these figures is that the criteria used in defining the limits of urban localities vary. Some countries use agglomerations without fixed boundaries. Some use localities under the jurisdiction of "urban" forms of government. The latter tends to understate the urban population.

The cards containing the raw data used here are held by the Latin American Data Bank of the University of Florida, Gainesville, Florida and may be obtained for re-use from that source.

100,000 or more as a per cent of urban population, according to latest census.[46]

(3) *Level of Urban Services*—Per cent of urban population with water connected to house, per cent of urban population with drainage connected to house, around 1960.[47]

(4) *Era of Urban Growth*—Period in which country became 25 per cent urbanized.[48]

The difficulties of translating the complex process of national political development, into adequate elements, no less simple, serviceable indicators are also enormous. While many authors have tried to define political development, there is little agreement on what constitutes the process or on what indicators best measure it. In addition, some studies mix referents for political development with social and economic variables including level of urbanization, making correlation of political with urban development artifactual. An added problem in the case of indices applicable to Latin America is that in many of the general systems for classifying development in a worldwide scheme, Latin-American countries fall into one category.

Rather than defending at length any particular set of elements and indices to measure each variable, many of the indicators used by other authors to rank or rate the political development of Latin-American nations have been assembled here. The elements of political development compiled and the indicators used for them are:

(1) *Electoral Participation*—Electoral participation as a percentage of total population; as a percentage of eligible population, around 1960.[49]

[46] Figures derived from Durand and Peláez, *ibid.*

[47] Figures derived from A. G. H. Dietz, M. Koth and J. Silva, *Housing in Latin America* (Cambridge: The M.I.T. Press, 1965), pp. 34, 242.

[48] Classification from Population Division, UN Bureau of Social Affairs, "Urbanization and Economic and Social Change" (paper presented at the Inter-Regional Seminar on Development Policies and Planning in Relation to Urbanization, University of Pittsburgh, October 24–November 7, 1966), pp. 45–47.

[49] Figures for electoral participation as a per cent of total population from Ivan Labelle and Adriana Estrada, *Latin America in Maps, Charts and Tables* (Cuernavaca: Center for Inter-Cultural Formation, 1963), p. 230, Russett *et al., op. cit.*, pp. 18–20. Figures for electoral participation as a per cent of eligible population from Christopher E. Baker, "Literacy as a Primary Determinant of Electoral Participation in Latin America" (unpublished M.A. thesis, University of Florida, 1966), Tables 13 and 14.

(2) *Representation*—Level of polyarchy, interest articulation by associational and non-associational groups and toleration of autonomous groups in politics,[50] and rating of "caudillismo."[51]

(3) *Constitutional Stability and Instability*—Mean years of constitutional government 1935–64,[52] deaths from group violence per population, 1960–62.[53]

(4) *Output*—Percentage increase in road construction (1954–62), electric power generation (1950–60), primary education (1950–60), per cent of total budget spent on social services (1960), per cent of central government expenditure spent on defense (1960).[54]

(5) *Executive and Legislative Institutional Development (1940–60)* [55]—Ranking by years ruled by a chief executive chosen in free elections, in which more than one party was represented in the legislature, in which a minority party held more than 30 per cent of seats,[56] and by effectiveness of legislature.[57]

[50] Arthur Banks and Robert Textor, *A Cross Polity Survey* (Cambridge: The M.I.T. Press, 1963), characteristics 101–3, 107–8, 115–7, 122–3.

[51] Merle Kling, "Taxes on the External Sector," *Midwest Journal of Political Science*, II (May, 1959), 127–50.

[52] Figures from Martin Needler, "Political Development and Social and Economic Development" (1966), mimeo, p. 10. The number of years each country is ruled constitutionally is computed by adding the years in at least six months of which the country was ruled by a chief executive chosen in more or less free elections and in which the government respected constitutional procedures and civil liberties and in which no extra constitutional changes of government occurred. A "strict" and a "loose" definition were used and their mean computed. Professor Needler explores the validity of this way of looking at "stability" and the question of to what extent Latin America's tendency toward "permanent instability" must be regarded as a "stable" method for governmental change in his forthcoming book, *Political Development in Latin America: Instability, Violence and Evolutionary Change.* I am indebted to Professor Needler for the opportunity to read the draft and make use of its orienting concepts and measures.

[53] Russett *et al., op. cit.*

[54] Charles W. Anderson, *Politics and Economic Change in Latin America* (Princeton, N.J.: D. Van Nostrand, 1967), pp. 334–36, 338, 344–45: Alfonso Gonzales, "Castro: Some Economic Benefits for Latin America" (paper delivered at the Southeastern Conference of Latin Americanists, Atlanta, 1967), mimeo.

[55] I was unable to find a suitable ranking of bureaucratic development. In available schemes, Latin-American nations fall into a single class. After the completion of this article the index of "administrative efficiency" compiled by Irma Adelman and Cynthia Taft Morris, *Society, Politics and Economic Development: A Quantitative Approach* (Baltimore: The Johns Hopkins Press, 1967), pp. 76–78, was called to my attention. While appearing too late for inclusion here, this index is now being added and analyzed. Schemes tapping cultural variations are also under separate consideration.

[56] Cutright, *op. cit.*, pp. 257–58.

[57] Banks and Textor, *op. cit.*, characteristics 174–7.

(6) *Party System*—Ranking by competitiveness, level of interest aggregation, extent of "personalismo." [58]

(7) *Military*—Rankings by political role and neutrality of the armed forces.[59]

Composite Indices

(1) *Fitzgibbon ratings* (1955–60)—A rank ordering of the political and social development of Latin-American nations by a panel of judges on criteria including education, standard of living, national cohesion, individual political dignity, absence of foreign domination, free press, free elections, free party organization, effective party opposition in the legislature, legislative scrutiny of executive, independent judiciary, public accountability of spending, production of vital social legislation, civilian supremacy, honest administration and intelligent local self-government.[60]

(2) *Coleman rating* (1960)—A grouping of Latin-American nations according to the level of competitiveness or authoritarianism, with the caveat that competitiveness, while an essential aspect of political modernity, is not a sufficient condition.[61]

(3) *Banks and Textor rating*—A grouping of Latin-American nations according to phase of development based on the degree to which the elites desire modernization, a break with agrarian institutions and creation of politically organized societies occurs, as well as the nature of rebellions.[62]

(4) *Lipset rating*—A grouping of Latin-American nations as Stable Dictatorships or Democracies and Unstable Dictatorships based on the presence or absence of a history of more or less free elections for most of the post-World War I period.[63]

[58] Banks and Textor, *ibid.*, characteristics 130–2, 156–8; Karl Schmitt and David Burks, *Evolution or Chaos: The Dynamics of Latin American Politics* (New York: Praeger, 1963), pp. 175–8.

[59] Edwin Lieuwen, *Arms and Politics in Latin America* (New York: Praeger, 1961), pp. 158–71; Banks and Textor, *ibid.*, characteristics, 184–6.

[60] Russell H. Fitzgibbon, "A Statistical Evaluation of Latin American Democracy," *Western Political Quarterly*, IX, No. 3 (September, 1956), 607–19 discusses the criteria. The 1955–60 rating is given in Russell Fitzgibbon and Kenneth Johnson, "Measurement of Latin American Political Change," *American Political Science Review*, LXI, No. 3 (September, 1961), 518.

[61] Gabriel Almond and James Coleman (eds.), *The Politics of the Developing Areas* (Princeton, N.J.: Princeton University Press, 1960), Table I, p. 534.

[62] Banks and Textor, *op. cit.*, characteristic 85.

[63] Lipset, *Political Man, op. cit.*, p. 32.

One problem is shared in both the conceptions of urban and of political development used. Both urban and political development may be so closely correlated with other kinds of social and economic development that separating the two out from the associated phenomena leads to overly simplistic judgments. On the urban side of the equation there are probably a host of traits shared by urban-industrial societies, some of which can be regarded as independent variables in respect to urbanization and others of which are consequences of urbanization.[64] Levels of social and economic development are also clearly related to levels of political development.[65] However, a comparison of the single processes should be undertaken without regard to related variables at this stage, for if we can specify the extent to which politically more developed nations differ from politically less developed nations in relation to type and degree of urbanization, we may then be in a better position to ascertain the manifold associations among a larger number of indicators of national and urban development.

The analysis is also limited by the quixotic state of statistics on Latin America. Problems arise in using data on urban areas in Latin America because definitions of urban places used in the censuses vary with respect to the levels of population concentration called "urban." In addition, some countries define the limits of urban localities by identifying urban aggregations forming demographic, social and economic units or metropolitan areas, while others rely on fixed administrative boundaries. The discussions that follow are based upon data from censuses taken in similar periods, with current data from censuses in 1960 or later, where possible, and follow the definitions recommended by the Population Division of the United Nations Bureau of Social Affairs.

The problems of using various statistics and ratings for political development and figures for participation or constitutional

[64] Schnore, "The Statistical Measurement of Urbanization and Economic Development," *op. cit.*

[65] A clear cut demonstration appears in Lipset, *Political Man, op. cit.*, pp. 27–63. The possibilities for separable consideration of political systems and socioeconomic factors have been argued by Gabriel Almond and G. Bingham Powell, *Comparative Politics* (Boston: Little, Brown, 1966), p. 309; and S. N. Eisenstadt, "Modernization and Conditions of Sustained Growth," *World Politics*, XVI, No. 4 (July, 1964), 576–94.

stability are less easily solved. Can we accept voting figures of 25.0 per cent of total population for Cuba in 1948 or 62.05 per cent of eligible population in 1954 as evidence of Cuban electoral "participation" knowing that ballot boxes were quite openly stuffed in the first year and only one candidate ran in the second? Is the existence of only three successful coups d'état from 1935 to 1964 in Venezuela an indication of acceptance, in comparison to Bolivia, Ecuador or Paraguay, when an undercurrent of violence existed in Venezuela during many of those years?

My conviction that the effort to assess the relationship between urban and political development in Latin America quantitatively is worthwhile rests on my judgment not that accurate measurement is now possible, but that it is necessary if we are ever to be able to analyze the world of Latin-American politics in a systematic and objective fashion. The emphasis here is not on data collection, but on the *introduction* of data to provide better answers to theoretical questions.[66]

RESEARCH FINDINGS

Several implications for political analysis can be drawn from the cross classification of the polities of Latin America by urban and political development. While the findings seem to support those observers who have linked urban development to political development, the deviations within this relationship must not be overlooked. Some indicators of urban development used here are associated with composite ratings of political development, electoral participation figures, the existence of stable chief executives

[66] Philippe C. Schmitter, "New Strategies for the Comparative Analysis of Latin American Politics" (paper prepared for delivery at the Latin American Studies Association Meeting, New York City, November, 1968) also makes a plea for the use of aggregate data in the study of Latin-American politics and discusses in detail some of the problems of reliability, availability, quality and validity which are merely touched on here. Other aggregate data studies which discuss the political impact of urbanization in Latin America include Raymond Tanter, "Toward a Theory of Political Development," *Midwest Journal of Political Science*, XI, No. 2 (May, 1967) and Lawrence Alschuler, "Political Participation and Urbanization in Mexico" (unpublished Ph.D. dissertation, Northwestern University, 1967).

and legislatures, and neutral military institutions. But these associations are contaminated by many deviations when the variables are closely analyzed.

• *Urban Development and Composite Ratings*
  of Political Development

According to the data at hand, the level and era of urbanization and the level of urban services in Latin America varies with the level of political development, insofar as political development is measured by the use of available composite indices. Table 1 indicates that, with the exceptions of Costa Rica and Cuba, there is a fit between era of urbanization and level of political development as defined around 1960 by both Coleman and Fitzgibbon. Countries 25 per cent urbanized prior to 1920 are those classed as "competitive" by Coleman or in the top four rankings by Fitzgibbon; countries achieving 25 per cent urbanization between 1920 and 1960 are in the middle of Fitzgibbon's scale and are primarily those classified as "semi-competitive" by Coleman, and those not yet 25 per cent urban by 1960 are also those classified as "authoritarian" by Coleman and in the last eight positions on Fitzgibbon's scale.

When era of urbanization is compared with the dichotomous political development rating schemes worked out by Banks and Lipset, the longest urbanized nations are also those regarded as most developed and the shortest urbanized those regarded as the least developed. Using these ratings, however, there is more variability among the countries which became 25 per cent urbanized between 1920 and 1960 and level of political development, and more disparity between the two schemes in classifying the eight to ten countries occupying the middle of the political development spectrum.

The level of urbanization in Latin-American nations varies directly with era of urbanization. The level of urbanization is also associated with the composite ratings of political development. If we divide Latin-American nations into three categories—the highly urbanized (47 per cent and over), the middle range (20–35

Table 1

SOME COMPOSITE RATINGS OF POLITICAL DEVELOPMENT
AND ERA OF URBANIZATION

Era of Urbanization	Political Development Rank (Fitzgibbon—1960)	Political Development Rating (Coleman—1960)
I. *25% by 1920*		
Argentina	4	Competitive
Chile	3	Competitive
Uruguay	1	Competitive
II. *25% betw. 1920–1960*		
Brazil	7	Competitive
Colombia	6	Semi-Competitive
Cuba	15	Authoritarian
Ecuador	10	Semi-Competitive
Mexico	5	Semi-Competitive
Panama	11	Semi-Competitive
Peru	9	Semi-Competitive
Venezuela	8	Authoritarian
III. *Under 25% in 1960*		
Bolivia	16	Authoritarian
Costa Rica	2	Competitive
Dom. Republic	18	Authoritarian
El Salvador	12	Authoritarian
Guatemala	13	Authoritarian
Haiti	19	Authoritarian
Honduras	14	Authoritarian
Nicaragua	17	Authoritarian
Paraguay	20	Authoritarian

per cent) and the least urbanized (under 20 per cent)—the categories predict Fitzgibbon's and Coleman's groupings in the three divisions with only two exceptions (Venezuela and Costa Rica) and also the extremes of the ratings by Banks and Lipset.

The indicators of urban services are associated with era and level of urbanization. These service levels are in turn linked with the composite ratings of political development, as indicated in Table 2.

The concept of the city as essentially a "modernizing" force is reinforced by the above observations. The countries which fall at the poles of the urbanization spectrum, like Argentina, Uruguay and Chile, or the Central American countries, excepting

Table 2

URBAN SERVICES AND POLITICAL DEVELOPMENT

Per Cent of Urban Pop. with Water Attached to House (1960)	Political Development Fitzgibbon (1960)	Per Cent of Urban Pop. with Drainage Attached to House (1960)
I. High (over 65%)		
Argentina	4	High
Chile	3	High
Colombia	6	High
Costa Rica	2	Medium (20–40%)
Mexico	5	——
Panama	11	——
Uruguay	1	High (over 40%)
II. Medium (40–65%)		
Brazil	7	——
Cuba	15	Medium
Dominican Republic	18	Low (under 20%)
Ecuador	10	High
El Salvador	12	——
Guatemala	13	Medium
Peru	9	High
Venezuela	8	Medium
III. Low (under 40%)		
Haiti	19	——
Honduras	14	Low
Nicaragua	17	Low
Paraguay	20	Medium

Costa Rica, show the most consistent relationship to political development. Countries with middle levels of urbanization show more variation, although tending also to fall somewhere in the middle range on various composite ratings of political development.

Despite the fact that the relation of political development defined by composite ratings and era and level of urbanization is positive and significant, extreme caution must be used in interpreting this finding. This becomes quite clear when we explore the relationship of specific aspects of political development to each other and to different measures of urban development.

In the first place, when we look at the association of political development indicators with one another, rather than with urban development, it appears that the term "political development," as employed in composite indices used here is a shorthand for constitutional stability in Latin America and for the creation of Western style executives and neutral armed forces. The political development ratings constructed by Banks, Coleman, Lipset and Fitzgibbon are closely correlated with each other and with the measures of executive stability devised by Cutright, national constitutional stability devised by Needler, and military role devised by Lieuwen. The composites are *not* closely associated with participation in elections, representation or output which maximizes social welfare policies.

This suggests that "political development" is defined for Latin America so heavily in terms of stable constitutional functioning that many of the characteristics associated with even the Western developed polity, such as the role of the individual as a political participant, and the value placed on individuals as beneficiaries of social policy, which often grows out of the dynamics of party competition when participation is widespread, tend to be down-graded.[67]

It also tends to support the views of many students of Latin America and other areas who have maintained that the concept of political development is an idealization of linear progress toward the conditions of Western politics and not a tracer of progress toward the attainment of whatever perhaps distinctive polity Latin-American countries may wish for themselves.[68] Since independent Latin America has generally been permanently unstable,[69] it is hard to draw any conclusion from such composite indicators of political development except that most of the Latin-American Republics are not developed. But, this is a function of the stability oriented definition latent in the composites.

In the second place, even in terms of this stability oriented model of Latin-American political development it is inaccurate

[67] See Martin Needler, *op. cit.*, chap. III.
[68] John Martz, "The Place of Latin America in the Study of Comparative Politics," *Journal of Politics*, XXVIII, No. 1 (February, 1966), 57–80. Joseph La-Palombara, "Theory and Practice in Development Administration" (CAG Occasional Papers, January, 1967).
[69] Anderson, "Toward a Theory of Latin American Politics," *op. cit.*; Merle Kling, "Toward a Theory of Power and Political Instability in Latin America," *Western Political Quarterly*, IX (March, 1959), 21–35.

to equate the "developed" polity with "urbanization" defined as the percentage of population in cities over 20,000 or over 100,000. Stability is closely associated with indicators of the level of urban service outputs in the system but not with growth rates and levels of population in cities. Participation in elections is closely related to era and level of urbanization but not to indicators of the level of urban services. Moreover, participation and stability are not closely associated with each other.[70] The import of this series of relationships is clearer if examined step by step.

• *Urbanization and Electoral Participation*

Let us first take up the phenomenon of electoral participation. It has been repeatedly maintained that in Latin America as a whole urbanization symbolizes the gap between the political and the apolitical population, meaning the enfranchised urbanite and the disenfranchised rural resident.[71] Pablo Gonzáles Casanova has observed that in Mexico the main facet of an urban-rural dichotomy is in electoral politics. The rural working class votes least; the poorest states are those where the least electoral opposition is registered.[72] Aldo E. Solari has argued that urbanization creates

[70] Exploration of the relationship of participation to stability in Latin America is beyond the scope of this chapter. However, it is interesting to note that a variety of views have been expressed about the linkage of participation to stability. Fred Riggs has made some effort to define the linkage, noting that at the outset we clearly recognize that the polity can founder both on the Scylla of political irresponsibility or be swamped by the Charybdis of administrative ineptness, "The Political Structures of Administrative Development" (CAG Occasional Papers, April, 1967), p. 75. Kalman Silvert and Gino Germani, "Politics, Social Structure and Military Intervention in Latin America," *European Journal of Sociology*, II (1961), 62–81, reprinted in Peter G. Snow, *Government and Politics in Latin America* (New York: Holt, Rinehart & Winston, 1967), pp. 299–318, state that high participation by voters is not a cause of instability but that it is an indicator of the level of functioning of "democracy and integration" in Latin America. Horowitz, *op. cit.*, maintains that high electoral participation is consonant with high stability, and low electoral participation and stability are inversely related in the middle stages of development, but devises an index of overall development by combining the two. Here the correlation between voting and mean stability is −.07 (total population) or −.38 (eligible population). Martin Needler deals with this relationship in detail in *Political Development in Latin America, op. cit.*
[71] Horowitz, "Politics, Urbanization and Social Development," *op. cit.*, p. 6.
[72] Pablo González Casanova, *La Democracia en México* (Mexico City: Era, 1965), pp. 107 ff.

high social mobilization in Uruguay, and the higher the social mobilization, the higher the political participation as measured by voting.[73]

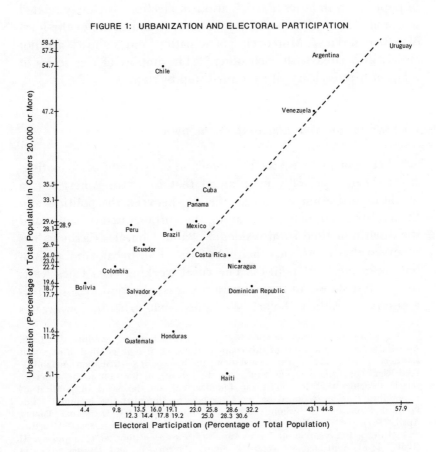

FIGURE 1: URBANIZATION AND ELECTORAL PARTICIPATION

The association of urbanization and electoral participation is confirmed if "urbanization" is defined as population in cities over 20,000 (r = .59) or over 100,000 (r = .53) as shown in Table 3. As shown in Figures 1 and 2, the association of electoral participa-

[73] Solari, "Impacto político de las diferenceias internas de los países en los grados e indicios de modernización y desarrollo económico," *op. cit.*

tion and urbanization is somewhat better explained by the size of the largest city (r = .71). But, it makes a considerable difference if we define "electoral participation" as voting in relation

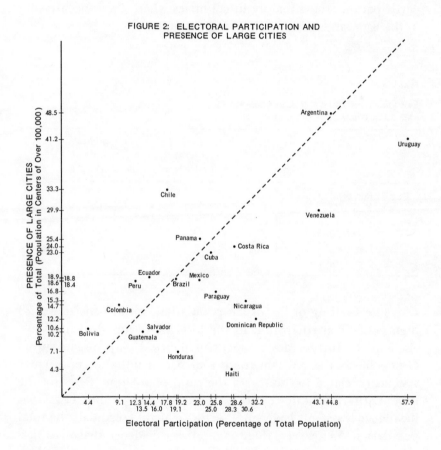

FIGURE 2: ELECTORAL PARTICIPATION AND
PRESENCE OF LARGE CITIES

to total population or to eligible population. The correlation of urbanization and voting participation disappears at all levels of urbanization if the eligible population figures are used, as indicated in Table 3.

Such discrepancies probably make electoral participation, insofar as it is at all related to particular levels of urbanization, assume some special traits which are not detected by the single indicators normally used. Urbanization may enfranchise many migrants from rural areas, bringing them into contact with political life perhaps for the first time. But, the enlargement of participation occurs mainly in countries where the concentration in the very largest city or cities is greatest.

Table 3

CORRELATION BETWEEN URBANIZATION
AND ELECTORAL PARTICIPATION (1960)

	Electoral vote as a per cent of total pop.	*Electoral vote as a per cent of eligible pop.*
Per cent in cities of over 20,000	.59	.16
Per cent in cities of over 100,000	.53	.20
Largest city as a per cent of total pop.	.71	.37

The swelling of the urban population, while associated with high political participation in the form of voting, does not show itself in the further development of political party organization. Others have observed that the prevalence of unstable, multiparty systems is related to the size of the rural population. Seven of the nine Latin-American countries listed by Banks and Textor as having such systems have rural sectors which exceed half the total population.[74] However, there is no direct evidence that urbanization is itself associated with the development of more modern parties. In the indices used here there are no significant associations between the measures of party system development and urbanization. The masses of rural peasants or artisans transplanted to Latin-American cities would seem to acquire some political significance as voters in the process. But, the transfer seems to be

[74] Banks and Textor, *op. cit.*, characteristics 152–5, cited by Horowitz, *op. cit.*, p. 15. The countries are Argentina and Venezuela.

separated from the expansion of organizational political party development.

• *Urbanization and Stability*

Now let us look at the indices of urban development and of constitutional stability. We are used to thinking that urban development produces an expansion in the politicization of the population and that this expansion is a critical factor in the prevention of revolutions because extremists find support primarily among the atomized sectors of the population.[75] The data here suggest, however, that while some expansion in political eligibility probably does take place in the large cities of Latin America, this may not drastically affect the stability of constitutionally derived state power.

As noted previously, the level of electoral participation is moderately associated with the level of urbanization and also with the size of the largest city as a per cent of total population. Constitutional stability as measured by Needler and also as rated by Banks and Textor is not associated with *any* of these factors. Stability is correlated with the urban indicators that measure the level of urban services. The percentage of urban population with water attached to the house is correlated at the .78 level (Pearson) with stability, and the percentage of urban population with drainage attached to the house at the .70 level (Pearson) with stability.

Ratings of the role of the military, and the development of Western style executive and legislative institutions are associated with urban service levels and stability, but not with urbanization or participation indices. In the nations designated by Lieuwen as having non-political armed forces, 75 per cent of the urban population has water; in countries with "transitional" army systems the average is 55 per cent; in countries with armed forces domination the average is 46 per cent. Similarly service levels are higher in

[75] William Kornhauser, *The Politics of Mass Society* (Glencoe, Ill.: The Free Press of Glencoe, 1959), p. 73; David Apter, *The Politics of Modernization* (Chicago: University of Chicago Press, 1965), pp. 453–58.

countries cited as having "neutral" armed forces by Banks and Textor than in those regarded as "interventive."

Level of urban services may be thought of as independent of level of urbanization, i.e., more dependent on national economic growth than on "urban" factors. In this regard it is interesting to note that urban service levels are not associated above the .30 level (Pearson) with any of the measures of "social output potential" examined for national services. To repeat, in the data presented the association is strong between *urban* services, political development indices and stability, but not between national and urban services, or national services and composite political development indices. It seems that "developed" polities in Latin America are *urban* mass consumption societies, but not necessarily nationally oriented toward social and physical welfare.

This finding should help to throw some light on the much debated hypothesis of "anomic urban agitation." It has been argued that "displaced peasants seek welfare and opportunity in great cities. Frustration of their expectations produces alienation and thus urbanization exacerbates existing symptoms of political instability." [76] But, there is also much evidence to support the view that the Latin-American urban migrant is unlikely to take his fate into his own hands through violence even when conditions are objectively quite miserable.[77] We have been wont to say that this passivity is a result of relative *increases* in environmental satisfaction perceived by migrants flowing into cities.[78] On a national level the data here indicate that high service levels are associated with stability and low service levels are associated with

[76] K. Johnson, "Latin American Political Instability," *op. cit.*, p. 439. This is also proposed in a general fashion in Almond and Coleman, *The Politics of the Developing Areas, op. cit.*, p. 537.

[77] The non-politicization of the lower class is discussed in Oscar Lewis, *La Vida* (New York: Random House, 1966), for Puerto Rico; Barrington Moore, "In the Life: A Review," *New York Review of Books*, June 15, 1967, p. 3; William Mangin, "Mental Health and Migration to Cities," *Contemporary Cultures and Societies of Latin America, op. cit.*, for Peru; Daniel Goldrich, "Toward the Comparative Study of Politicization in Latin America," *ibid.*, pp. 371–87, esp. p. 363.

[78] See Stepan, *op. cit.*, p. 231; and Wayne Cornelius, "Urbanization as an Agent in Latin American Political Instability: The Case of Mexico," *American Political Science Review* (forthcoming, 1969), for reviews of the literature on the importance of relative satisfaction among migrants, as the reason why agitation does not increase in cities.

national instability, however. Although developmental data rather than the cross-sectional data used here would be required to show it, it appears likely that while ideological and psychological factors play a role in assuring or undermining stability, they are keyed at some point to the real level of material services to urban residents.

There seem to be two separate urban processes occurring. The first process can be described as one of stabilizing national politics in Latin America which is associated mainly with service levels. The second is a process of making national politics more "participatory" through increasing the size of the electorate, which is associated with the level of urbanization. The two processes and the related urban phenomena, far from being identical, may not be closely associated. Their relationship is sketched below.

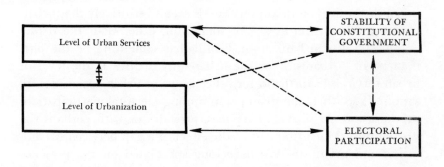

(The solid lines indicate likely strong correlations. The dotted lines indicate likely weak correlations. The cross hatched line indicates an intermediate level.)

CONCLUSIONS

The findings reported in many ways raise more questions than they answer. One set of intriguing possibilities has to do with the conceptualization of the disparate relationship among electoral participation and urbanization, stability and urban services, intepreted from the viewpoint of the political development variables. One might argue that the linkage of participation with urbanization but not with urban services is a product of the ruralization of Latin-American cities. Migrants from the countryside have arrived so recently that though an initial politicization, manifested in voting, has occurred, no network of relationships with politicians and bureaucrats controlling services has yet to be established. Alternatively it could be maintained that the disjunction is a function of the specialized role of electoral participation. If electoral participation is not an index of democratization but of the capacity of the government to mobilize the population when it wishes to do so, then the lack of association between electoral participation and services is not surprising, for voting need not have any relationship to felt pressure for better living conditions in the cities.

Other fascinating questions are raised in relation to the meaning of the indices on urban services. It seems intuitively that urban service levels are indicators of something other than the demographic level of urbanization. Could that something be the phenomena of "urbanism" or the urban way of life? Is the level of urban services a shorthand for other kinds of urban social mobilization? If so, then the disjunction among electoral participation, urbanization, stability and services, provides us with perhaps the first empirical measurement of the effect of a gap between urbanization and urbanism. We have long speculated on the presence of such differential effects but heretofore no measurable case has appeared.

The proportion of persons living in large cities around the world has often been used as a virtual synonym of political development. Because the last few decades have witnessed a more rapid pace of urbanization in Latin America than has been experienced before, expectation has been that there should also be a rapid advance in political development in the region. Such an assumption is quite misleading. Apparently we cannot determine the consequences of urban development for political development without estimating the costs and benefits of a whole variety of separable urban and political phenomena. Attention to the separate components of political development and of urban development suggests in fact that the kind of support different facets of urban development give to the building of different facets of political development may be quite selective.

4 /
Creeping Urbanism and
Political Development in Malaysia

JAMES F. GUYOT

THIS IS AN EMPIRICAL study and a speculative forecast of creeping urbanism in the rural development programs of the Malaysian government, and of the contribution this development could make to the general trend toward a more mature, or competitive, politics among the Malays.[1] It is part of a larger study

AUTHOR'S NOTE: This study is based on a year's field research in Malaysia during 1966–67 which was supported in part by grants from the Chancellor's Committee for Comparative and International Studies at UCLA and the Center for Southeast Asian Studies at the University of California, Berkeley. Most of the material on Federal Land Development Authority schemes was gathered while touring eleven of the sixty-six schemes then underway in different parts of the country. This was made possible and profitable through the kind assistance of FLDA headquarters and the managers of the schemes. To the Faculty of Economics and Administration of the University of Malaya the author is indebted for the opportunity to share field research experience and floor space during part of the Faculty's study of the Lenga land development scheme.

A return to Malaysia for several months in the summer of 1968 with supplemental sponsorship by the Southern Asian Institute of Columbia University provided a broader base of experience and considerable positive feedback in support of the speculations put forth here. It would be a delight for the author but tedious for the reader to name the academic and other individuals in Malaysia and outside who have contributed corrections to earlier versions of this chapter. Perhaps it will be sufficient to number them as thirteen.

[1] The political system discussed here is that of peninsular Malaya, now known officially as West Malaysia. The original Malaysia was formed in 1963 by the union

comparing political development and bureaucratic performance in Burma and Malaysia. The theme of that larger study is the collapse of the Burmese civil service under attack by a fiercely competitive, highly mobilized, and poorly disciplined political elite. By contrast, the Malaysian civil service has been generally supported by a well-tempered, congenial political class. Burma's postwar failures in economic development can be attributed in part to the collapse of its civil service while Malaysia's continuing progress is supported by the competence of the administrative system.

My forecast is the passing of the pastoral stage of politics among the Malays. In pastoral politics the Malay voter demands of government only that it exercise authority, maintain the Sultan, defend the faith, and curb the Chinese should they stray from the pursuit of money into the political realm. The passing of this stage will be facilitated by rural development programs in which rural folk are organized and urbanized in order to receive economic benefits more efficiently. A consequence of such organization will be the firm establishment of expectations and demands for further benefits and the conversion of local political organizations from vote delivering devices into competitive markets in which political commodities (votes and government benefits) are traded. Such competitive politics will probably reduce the highly centralized and responsible control of the party held by the current generation of leaders.[2] This more mature stage of politics will in turn place greater pressures of a less responsible sort on the civil service. Unless the civil service can adapt to the new political environment, its effectiveness will be seriously eroded, as has happened in other new nations.

This malevolent system is sketched out in Figure 1 below. Malaysia's quite competent civil service, energized by the postwar political elite, has been able to carry out a number of surprisingly

of Singapore and the Borneo territories of Sabah and Sarawak with the peninsular states of the Federation of Malaya. Singapore was ejected from Malaysia two years later. The Borneo territories which are now known as East Malaysia are part of the same nation but remain separated from West Malaysia in economic, social, and political time as well as by several hundred miles of water. Hence, their exclusion from this discussion.

[2] Samuel P. Huntington, "Political Development and Political Decay," *World Politics*, XVII, No. 3 (April, 1965), 386–430.

Figure 1

PASTORAL AND COMPETITIVE POLITICS IN THE MALAYSIAN SYSTEM

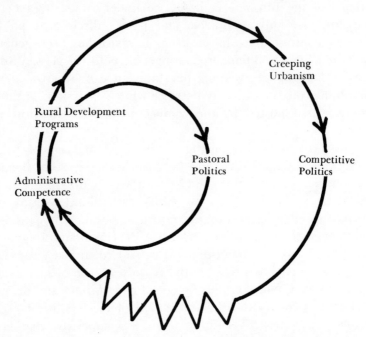

successful rural development programs.[3] The success of these programs (following the inner circle of arrows) has redounded to
the credit of the ruling party which continues to support the
success-producing administrative apparatus. The larger circle of
arrows, however, indicates some unanticipated long run consequences which may alter the system. Thus, the creeping urbanism
engendered by rural development may increase the competitive
nature of politics, resulting in an attack on a rationally functioning bureaucracy. Whether the bureaucracy can absorb such conflict and what consequences a reduction in administrative capacity
would have for the future success of rural development programs
are questions which carry us into a second run around the system,
an exercise which is beyond the scope of this chapter.

[3] Gayl D. Ness, *Bureaucracy and Rural Development in Malaysia: Study of
Complex Organization in Stimulating Economic Development in New States* (Berkeley: University of California Press, 1967).

For analysis of these processes I have chosen the rubber and oil palm schemes of the Federal Land Development Authority (FLDA), a program of providing "land for the landless" by opening new land to settlers under what is in effect a state managed plantation system. This program is peculiarly appropriate for several reasons: (1) as the most successful of government rural development efforts it has become the main thrust for future, greatly expanded programs; (2) because it is so successful and so intensively organized it is more likely to show a significant impact on other aspects of society; and (3) again, because of its success and intensive organization it is more open to observation by outsiders. The number of people directly affected by the program by 1967, ten years after independence, was relatively small, about 63,000 out of a rural population of four million. However, the direction of its current and future impact on politics corresponds with other, larger forces.[4]

I have left out of this analysis what may be considered the most important aspect of Malaysian politics, the communal conflict between Malays and Chinese. This was done because that constellation of problems has already been much analyzed and because Malaysia in its first ten years has coped with it more successfully than any reasonable political scientist could have expected. Any overall judgment of where Malaysian politics is going will have to include the communal element, yet it may be useful here to limit our concern to developments within the major arena of Malaysian politics, the Malay community.[5]

THE VARIETY OF URBAN PHENOMENA IN MALAYSIA

Malaysia is one of the more successfully developing countries of the underdeveloped world. In per capita measures of gross

---

[4] Some of the social changes attributed to FLDA schemes here are assessed as broad trends in Malay peasant society at large by M. G. Swift, "Economic Concentration and Malay Peasant Society," in M. Freedman (ed.), *Social Organization* (London: Cass, 1967), pp. 241–69.

[5] For a discussion of the communal character of Malaysian society see my "The Two Cultures and Malaysia's Development Revolution" (paper presented at the Association for Asian Studies, March, 1968), mimeo.

national product and educational output Malaysia ranks above all her Southeast Asian neighbors, with the exception of the recently separated island city state of Singapore.[6] As a further proof of modernity, and again excepting Singapore, Malaysia is the most urbanized nation in Southeast Asia, with about 21 per cent of her population in towns of over 20,000.[7] But like her wealth and education, Malaysia's cities are largely non-Malay phenomena. The Chinese, who comprise less than 40 per cent of the total population, outnumber Malays by more than three to one in cities of 20,000 and above. This shift in racial imbalance from city to countryside is shown in Figure 2. Chinese outnumber Malays in cities and towns of all sizes while Malays dominate the countryside. In the national calculus, however, the Chinese count for much less. Politics is predominantly a Malay game. This is because the Malays view themselves and were viewed before by their British masters as the true sons of the soil (*bumiputra*). The result has been a series of constitutional protections and "Malay privileges" as well as such practical political advantages as the drawing up of parliamentary constituencies with extra weight given to rural areas. More importantly, UMNO, the Malay branch of the ruling Alliance party plays the dominant role in all aspects of the party, except for finance. By contrast, MCA, the Chinese branch, has played the role of company union, guaranteeing the cooperation of the Chinese community after its most active political elements went underground in 1948. In consequence the major thrust of government programs since independence has been toward rural development with scant attention given to the cities where the mass of relatively disenfranchised Chinese congregate. Yet, if we leave the cities (defined in purely demographic terms as population agglomerations of 20,000 or more) there is still much to be seen that is urban, and that is politically relevant.

In the world at large, urbanization, industrialization, bureauc-

---

[6] Bruce M. Russett *et al., World Handbook of Political and Social Indicators* (New Haven: Yale University Press, 1964), pp. 155–57, 213–20; Frederick Harbison and Charles A. Myers (eds.), *Manpower and Education: Country Studies in Economic Development* (New York: McGraw-Hill, 1965), p. 326.

[7] Hamzah-Sendut, "Urbanization," in Wang Gungwu (ed.), *Malaysia: A Survey* (New York: Praeger, 1964), pp. 85, 86.

Creeping Urbanism and Political Development in Malaysia

Figure 2

ETHNIC IMBALANCE BY SIZE OF COMMUNITY

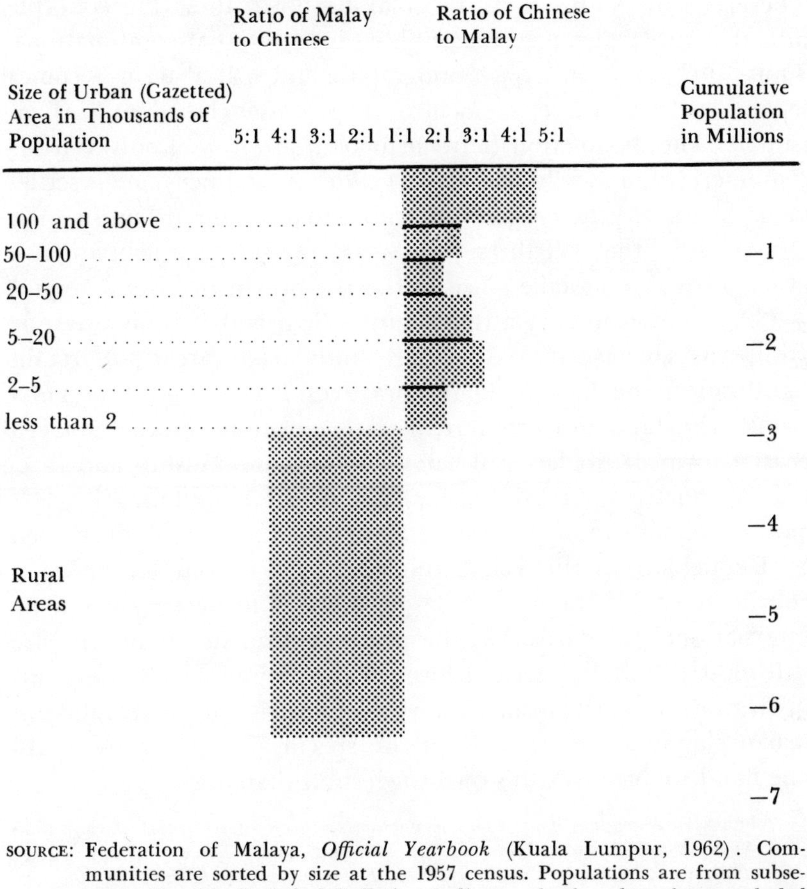

	Ratio of Malay to Chinese	Ratio of Chinese to Malay	
Size of Urban (Gazetted) Area in Thousands of Population	5:1 4:1 3:1 2:1	1:1 2:1 3:1 4:1 5:1	Cumulative Population in Millions

100 and above		
50–100		−1
20–50		
5–20		−2
2–5		
less than 2		−3
		−4
Rural Areas		−5
		−6
		−7

SOURCE: Federation of Malaya, *Official Yearbook* (Kuala Lumpur, 1962). Communities are sorted by size at the 1957 census. Populations are from subsequent Monthly Statistical Bulletins. Indians and others have been excluded from the computations.

ratization, and political mobilization appear as correlative processes. But in specific situations elements of one may appear without the full concurrence of the others.[8] Thus, in some societies forms of industrialization appear without all the attendant bureaucratic

[8] Neil J. Smelser, "Mechanisms of Change and Adjustment to Change," in Bert F. Hoselitz and Wilbert E. Moore (eds.), *Industrialization and Society* (The Hague: UNESCO, 1963), p. 33.

machinery, or outside of a strictly urban environment.[9] Similarly, political mobilization may take place far into the countryside. There is some value, then, in breaking down these big concepts into elements that can be reassembled into different combinations. Thus, "urbanization" as a demographic and spatial term becomes separable from those sociocultural processes labelled "urbanism."[10] The disjunction between urbanization, in Louis Wirth's characterization as a "relatively large, dense, and permanent settlement of socially heterogeneous individuals," and urbanism, the "way of life" that Wirth and his successors saw as a consequence of the former, may take place in the real world in several ways.[11]

A common finding at odds with Wirth is that individuals or groups which have moved spatially into urban areas still retain significant non-urban values and practices. Bruner finds that Toba Batak who hold modern bureaucratic positions in the modern coastal town of Medan still carry on the same kinship and ceremonial practices as their cousins back in the mountain villages.[12] Hauser demonstrates that the "folk-urban continuum" developed by Redfield from the Wirth model does not hold for cities in Southeast Asia.[13] Rangoon is large, dense, and heterogeneous by international standards, but the people within its boundaries are still mostly "folk." A second form of the disjunction between urbanization and urbanism as a way of life is the appearance of urban characteristics outside of the specifically urban areas. On one hand we have Wirth's own suggestion that,

[9] James C. Abegglen, *The Japanese Factory: Aspects of its Social Organization* (New York: Asia Publishing House, 1958); Manning Nash, "Some Notes on Village Industrialization in South and East Asia," *Economic Development and Cultural Change,* III, No. 3 (1955), 271.

[10] See the recent statements of this point of view by David Popenoe, "On the Meaning of 'Urban' in Urban Studies," *Urban Affairs Quarterly,* I, No. 1 (September, 1965), 17–33; and John Friedmann, "Two Concepts of Urbanization: A Comment," *Urban Affairs Quarterly,* I, No. 4 (June, 1966), 78–84.

[11] Louis Wirth, "Urbanism as a Way of Life," *American Journal of Sociology,* XLIV (July, 1938), 1–24; also in Louis Wirth, *Community Life and Social Policy* (Chicago: University of Chicago Press, 1965), pp. 110–32.

[12] Edward M. Bruner, "Urbanization and Ethnic Identity in North Sumatra," *American Anthropologist,* LXIII (1961), 508–21.

[13] Philip M. Hauser, "The Folk-Urban Ideal Types: B. Observations on the Urban-Rural Dichotomies as Forms of Western Ethnocentrism," in Philip M. Hauser and Leo F. Schnore (eds.), *The Study of Urbanization* (New York: Wiley, 1965), pp. 503–7.

while the locus of urbanism as a mode of life is, of course, to be found characteristically in places which fulfill the requirements we shall set up as a definition of the city, urbanism is not confined to such localities but is manifest in varying degrees wherever the influences of the city reach.[14]

Going yet farther afield, the anthropologists Sol Tax and Oscar Lewis find a goodly number of presumably urban social qualities imbedded down deep in village culture.[15]

In such circumstances it cannot be altogether illegitimate to describe some of the goings on in the Malaysian countryside as tendencies toward urbanism. Moreover, it seems particularly appropriate to use elements of the concept of urbanism to analyze events in the countryside if we conceive of each element as defining a dimension along which social practices may creep rather than as an open and shut category. In this way it becomes possible to range a series of communities, or one community at several points in time, along these dimensions and observe which elements of the total concept fit together. In situations of decreasing opportunity for the exercise of primary authority relations, is there an increase in the formality and autonomy of political organizations? Does the monetization of the household economy bring in its train a greater consciousness of one's own interests as conflicting with the interests of others? What happens to the aspiration level of the landless peasant who is showered with the benefits he is told are his birthright?

There are, then, two perspectives from which we will view the FLDA schemes in Malaysia: as urbanization (demographic); and as urbanism (a way of life). First we look at them as agglomerations which are somewhat larger, more meaningfully dense, and in some ways more (and in other ways less) heterogeneous than the *kampongs* (villages) from which the FLDA settlers have been recruited. Next we will try to draw a before-and-after picture of the social, governmental, economic, and communications experiences of these settlers to see what hints their comparative urbanism gives us about trends in politics among the rural Malays.

[14] Wirth, *op. cit.*, p. 115.
[15] Hauser, *op. cit.*

SPACE, RACE, AND NUMBERS
ON FLDA SCHEMES

By international standards Malaysia's land development schemes barely approach the size of the cities. For the sixty-one schemes in operation or planned by 1963–64 the average population per scheme works out to 1,980 persons. While this average figure is below the U.S. Census standard of 2,500 for an urban area, the wide variation in the size of individual schemes places a number of them above the U.S. minimum. For instance, the Kulai scheme in Johore contained, when filled up as of the spring of 1967, 368 families for a total population of 2,955 residing in one residential area. Schemes of similar size are found in Kelantan and Pahang. As an example of variations of size within one state, Table 1 presents the current and expected number of settlers in

Table 1

SIZE OF FLDA SCHEMES IN THE STATE OF TRENGGANU

Scheme	Settlers on Scheme as of February, 1967	Planned Number of Settlers All Phases	Estimated Total Population (No. of settlers times six)
Jerengau	Phase I 132	592	3,552
Belara	Phase I 55	257	1,542
Chalok	Phase I 162	442	2,652
	Phase II 220		
Bukit Badang	Phase I 0	530	3,180
Seberang Tayor	Phase I 90	217	1,302
Tenang Besut	Phase I 63	66	396

Total for six schemes 12,624
Average per scheme   2,104

SOURCE: Records available in the FLDA Regional Office, Kuala Trengganu, February, 1967.

the schemes at present underway in the state of Trengganu, an area of intense rural development activity as UMNO, the government party, battles continuously to maintain the control it wrested from an Islamic extremist party. Here three of the six schemes will meet the U.S. standard. Another fact to be noted from Table 1 is that migration of settlers onto the schemes takes place in phases of 200, 100, or fewer settlers at a time. Thus, the full impact of the size of the operation is not felt until the scheme is well established and underway. This is a conscious policy adopted in response to misfortunes that beset some of the earlier schemes when hundreds of settlers confronted thousands of acres of jungle in a frantic effort at instant development.

Density is a close collaborator with size in producing the demographic base for urbanism. In Malaysia large family size helps out so that, for instance, on the Kemmendore Land Development Scheme we have a population of 2,080 crowded into 380 homesites in a residential area of 220 acres. This produces a density of 6,050 per square mile. This figure would be higher on other schemes which also use the standard one quarter-acre house lot but have household sizes closer to the FLDA-wide average of 5.9. In density the schemes are well above the U.S. minimum standard of 2,500 per square mile and approach the average for central cities in the U.S., which is 8,000 per square mile.[16]

How does this all compare to the standard Malay *kampong,* or village? There are a number of diverse studies of recent and contemporary village life in Malaya which provide us with a base point for comparative calculations on a range of social variables.[17]

[16] Philip M. Hauser and Leo F. Schnore, *The Study of Urbanization* (New York: Wiley, 1965), pp. 9, 11.

[17] These begin with Raymond Firth's study of the social structure and economy of fishing communities: *Malay Fishermen: Their Peasant Economy* (2nd rev. ed.; London: Anchor, 1966), and proceed through geographical reports on seven different padi-growing areas by E. H. G. Dobby *et al.,* "Padi Landscapes of Malaya," *The Malayan Journal of Tropical Geography,* VI (October, 1955), whole volume; and X (June, 1957), whole volume; through a series of anthropological studies of particular communities or areas: M. G. Swift, *Malay Peasant Society in Jelebu* (London: Athlone Press, 1965); K. O. L. Burridge, "Rural Administration in Johore," *Journal of African Administration,* IX, No. 1 (1957), 29–36 (available in more extended form as *Fieldwork in Batu Pahat* (Singapore: University of Malaya Library); S. Husin Ali, *Social Stratification in Kampong Bagan: A Study of Class, Status, Conflict and Mobility in a Rural Malay Community* (Singapore: Malaysian Branch, Royal Asiatic Society, 1964); Peter J. Wilson, *A Malay Village and Malaysia: Social Values and Rural Development* (New Haven: Human Relations Area Files, 1967); and on to several recently completed but as yet unpublished field studies of politics, economics, and religion in Malay *kampongs.*

The *kampongs* pictured in these studies appear as small clusters of one hundred or fewer houses distributed unevenly through a *mukim* (township) which might have a population of several thousand. Some clumps of houses are compact, denser than the one quarter-acre house lots on FLDA schemes. More often the pattern is linear, following a road or stream. A government report recognized the significance of the difference in size between the standard FLDA scheme and the traditional *kampong*. The original plan drawn up for the Jengka Triangle, a massive project for distributing 50–60,000 landless persons over 150,000 acres of the Pahang jungle, recommended units of about 150 households, less than half the current size, in order to approximate the settler's previous environment. In terms of size and density alone we may place FLDA schemes closer to the urban end of a rural-urban continuum than we would place traditional Malay *kampongs*.

Judgments about heterogeneity as an urban attribute are much less quantifiable than those of size and density. Quite a lot depends on the social distance between the various groups as well as the relative size of minorities. Malaysia is, if anything, heterogeneous. It is a multiracial state attempting to create a multiracial society while most of the legal and natural subdivisions of that society are parcelled out into relatively homogeneous ethnic units. The elite cadre of the Malayan Civil Service is Malay at the ratio of about seven to one while the specialist services, with the exception of the police, range from 65 to 85 per cent non-Malay. The faculties at the University of Malaya range from 1 per cent Malay students in Engineering through 5 per cent in Science, 13 per cent in Medicine, 22 per cent in Agriculture, and 35 per cent in Economics, to an overwhelming majority in Malay studies. *De facto* residential segregation is rampant in the capital city and throughout the countryside.[18] While race is not the only relevant social variable, it generally turns out to be the most powerful as well as the most readily assessable one. Ironically, one geographer searching for a more powerful measure of social class in hopes of developing an alternative to race as an explanatory variable inad-

[18] T. G. McGee, "The Cultural Role of Cities: A Case Study of Kuala Lumpur," *Journal of Tropical Geography*, XVII (May, 1963), 178–96.

vertently demonstrated the importance of differences in dialect groups within the Chinese community.[19] The Malay *kampong* is typically an ethnically homogeneous unit, although within the *mukim* there may be occasional Chinese or Indian shopkeepers and laborers. A classic description is that given by Firth for three Kelantan fishing villages with a total population of about 2,000.

> The resident population consists of three elements. Most important are the local Malays, describing themselves as "people from here" (orang sini), that is, born in the area. . . . Of next importance are the non-local Malays, specified by their origin—Jelawat people, Tumpat people, "inland people" (orang darat), etc. In this category are a few Malays from Trengganu and from Patani in southern Siam, which has a Malay population closely allied to that in Kelantan. There were in all about five Malays from outside Kelantan and twenty from other areas in Kelantan as permanent residents. There were no Malays from the west coast living in the area.

> The third element in the area is non-Malay, mainly Indian and Chinese, and numbers about a score in all. . . . The Indians are Muslims and as such they are socially more acceptable than the Chinese. They all wear the Malay sarong . . . and speak tolerable Malay. They tend to congregate together, out of about ten in the census area two were married to Malay women and two others were living with Malay women. . . . Nearly all were shopkeepers. . . . The Chinese remain separate in most social affairs though some . . . have assimilated a great deal of Malay speech and customs. . . . One old man, however (said locally to be possibly a Japanese), did embrace Islam, mainly, it ap-

[19] W. Donald McTaggart, "The Grading of Social Areas in Georgetown, Penang," *Journal of Tropical Geography*, XXIII (December, 1966), 40–46. The author was puzzled by the finding that one of his two low status criterion groups scored higher on wealth indicators while the other scored higher on educational indicators of status. A ready explanation is available in the different proportions of Cantonese and Hokkein speakers in the two groups.

Ness, *op. cit.*, chap. 3, argues that Malayan society is becoming less plural and more national. To demonstrate this point he utilizes a variety of ingenious indices of ethnic concentration which show a slight decline from the 1947 census to the 1957 census. Such a trend may be truly taking place, but the impressive conclusion that follows from his evidence is that the change is slight and uneven. There are also some methodological problems in making such measurements. For instance, the greatest decline in ethnic concentration in the labor force occurs in government employment in the balance between Chinese and Indians. But for most social purposes the really important ethnic distinction is between Malays and non-Malays, both Chinese and Indian. From this perspective ethnic concentration in government service as Ness measures it has increased rather than decreased.

peared, in order to be able to marry a Malay woman. . . . The Chinese keep a couple of shops . . .[20]

This portrait is replicated in a west coast rubber growing area in the 1960s by Peter Wilson.[21] For a broader survey we can look at the seven padi districts in seven states studied by Dobby.[22] One was exclusively Malay, being on the east coast where many areas are Malay reservations in which no others can own land. Four of the other *mukims,* in Perak, Kedah, Negri Sembilan, and Perlis, were 82 per cent, 93 per cent, 94 per cent, and 95 per cent Malay. The other two *mukims* were ethnically split. One, which was within a mile of the largely Chinese port city of Malacca, was 52 per cent Chinese. Malay households were concentrated in two distinct areas of this *mukim* while the Chinese as such were evenly scattered but within themselves segregated as between Cantonese, Tiechius, and Hakkas. A similar pattern appeared in the *mukim* which was just a couple of miles from the Georgetown-Butterworth-Prai metropolitan complex in Penang.

In comparison to the *kampongs,* FLDA schemes might be considered more ethnically homogeneous since there are no Chinese shopkeepers. The settlers are almost totally Malay with the exception of two schemes, one in Malacca which was 38 per cent Chinese and the other, the multiracial showpiece Bilut Valley in Pahang, which included Chinese and Indians.[23] There were no Chinese on schemes in six of the nine states which had schemes going as of 1964. On the side of heterogeneity it should be noted that some of the schemes may mix local Malays with more recent Malay immigrants from Java to a greater extent than normally takes place in *kampongs.* Where such mixing does occur it is often encouraged administratively by, for instance, mixing the intake within each phase and by assigning house lots to each ethnic group in alternate order.

In economic and occupational terms the FLDA schemes are more homogeneous than were the settlers' native *kampongs* in that all settlers are supposed to be relatively landless. This con-

---

[20] Raymond Firth, *op. cit.,* 1946 ed., pp. 67–68.
[21] Wilson, *op. cit.*
[22] Dobby, *op. cit.*
[23] R. Wikkramatileke, "Variable Ethnic Attributes in Malayan Rural Land Development," *Pacific Viewpoint,* V, No. 1 (May, 1964), 35–50.

trasts to the disparities of rural land ownership turned up by
Dobby and S. Husin Ali.[24] An element of diversity might be introduced by the 20 per cent quota allotted to ex-service personnel
(army and police) in applications for places on the schemes. However, this quota seems rarely to have been filled, in part because
life on the scheme is rougher than the barracks life these ex-
servicemen have been used to. On the Kemmendore scheme
Wikkramatileke found that 25 out of 108 Malay settlers listed
their previous occupation as in the security forces.[25] None of the
100 Chinese so classified themselves. In Kampong Awah 13 of 125
in the first batch of settlers were identified as ex-servicemen and
this was true of 5 out of 88 on Ulu Jempol, but none of the 282
settlers in the state of Trengganu whose application forms were
inspected by the author indicated that they were ex-servicemen.
A range of rural occupations—padi farmer, rubber tapper, *kampong* laborer, fisherman—and several skilled occupations are
stated by prospective settlers on their application forms in a
pattern that seems little more heterogeneous than the pattern
normally found in the rural areas.[26]

   One other possible source of heterogeneity also turns up a
mixed finding. On some FLDA schemes settlers are brought together from over a wide area of the state or the nation while on
others they may come from a few local villages. Most states will
accept only settlers from within their own borders and the sequence of schemes coming on stream is matched by the circulation
of settler selection committees about different sections of the state.
One state, Pahang, which has a population density of only 23 per
square mile, will accept up to 50 per cent of its settlers from out
of state, a necessary liberality if it is to fill the huge Jengka Triangle scheme which, it is estimated, will increase the population
of the state by one-third.

   The conclusion we come to is that there is a perceptible and
most likely significant increase in the intensity and diversity of

[24] Dobby, 1955, *op. cit.* and S. Husin Ali, *op. cit.*

[25] Wikkramatileke, *op. cit.,* p. 41.

[26] A precise analysis of such statistics would not be meaningful, given the likely
distortions. Agricultural occupations are apt to be overstated since the point system
for settler selection gives preference to those with agricultural skills while members
of the settler selection committees are rarely able or inclined to ascertain whether a
particular candidate has indeed had such experience.

personal contacts confronting a settler removed from the traditional, small *kampong* to the somewhat larger, more significantly dense, and in some ways more heterogeneous scene of the FLDA land development scheme. Given this relative urbanization of FLDA settlers, let us now look at their comparatively urban way of life.

THE MALAY PEASANT FAMILY IN THE VILLAGE AND ON THE SCHEME

The family is the fundamental unit of Malay peasant society.[27] In its extended form, varying degrees of kin play well established and important roles. A network of mutual responsibilities serves the functions of social control and conflict resolution. If Abdul has been aggrieved by Ahmed, he does not accost his assailant openly but instead goes to Ahmed's *abang* (big brother) or some other responsible kin who transmits the complaint, administers the rebuke, or otherwise makes up for the transgression of the *adat,* or customary law. The extended family legitimates the important events in a man's life—circumcision and his first marriage. In this the degree of the extension is quite important: full participation of all the relevant kin is required to produce a full strength ceremony. The traditional family is extended also in the very thorough-going sense that children do not necessarily live with their biological parents but are occasionally adopted by near kin either to reduce the burden of support on the family of procreation or, more likely, to gratify the child-loving desires of an older couple or of senior kin whose children have grown up or who are otherwise childless. A final function of the extended family is to offer support in case of need. Thus, no man is really

---

[27] Common central characteristics of the peasant family appear in four separate studies: Rosemary Firth, *Housekeeping among Malay Peasants* (London: Athlone Press, 1943; rev. ed., 1966); Judith Djamour, *Malay Kinship and Marriage in Singapore* (London: University of London, Athlone Press, 1959); Peter J. Wilson, *op. cit.;* and M. G. Swift, *Malay Peasant Society in Jelebu, op. cit.* This last study is less representative of Malaya at large as it deals with the Minangkabau matrilineal kinship system peculiar to the state of Negri Sembilan.

poor as long as he has less poor kin nearby. Recourse to family is particularly important in the case of divorce, a well accepted practice of Californiamagnitude (throughout the states of Malaya and over the years the ratio of approximately one divorce for every two marriages seems to hold constant). In case of divorce, both partners return to their respective homes where their near relatives almost immediately begin negotiating new matches. All these activities of the traditional extended family run into obstacles on the FLDA scheme.

It is a common proposition of studies of rural-urban differences that the extended family is found on the farm while the urban family goes nuclear. On this dimension the FLDA family is clearly more urban than the *kampong* family. The major reason for this is that settlers are admitted to the scheme as a nuclear family with no guarantee that other relatives will also be admitted. More importantly in the long run, there is no provision for the accommodation of the children of settler families on the same scheme or nearby schemes. This focus on the nuclear family is evident in the age distribution of adult males. Taking a non-random sample of 800 heads of families accepted as settlers on schemes in Pahang and Trengganu, we find the peak decade made up of those twenty-five to thirty-four years old as of 1966. This decade accounts for 47 per cent of the adult males on the schemes in contrast to the 30 per cent of the adult male population of Malaysia which fell into this decade in the 1957 census. This age group is particularly favored by the point system used for settler selection in order to recruit men most able to carry on the hard labor of land development (for this they should not be too old), and most inclined to accept the responsibilities of the task (for this they should be married and not too young). This absence of adolescents, aunts and grandparents has created a series of little Levittowns in the jungle.

The road to Levittown has been paved by advances in public health which have raised the net reproduction rate amongst Malays at large and produced a secular trend toward a younger population of which 33 per cent were under ten years old at the 1957 census. In the middle 1960s a number of FLDA schemes were ahead of this trend. The point system of settler selection helps

here also since large families are favored. At Lenga about 40 per
cent of the population was under eleven while those under twelve
accounted for 54 per cent at Tenang and 50 per cent at Kulai.[28]
The phenomenon is widespread, as indicated by the average family size of 5.9 for settlers moving onto schemes in the early 1960s.
This is a far cry from the conditions Rosemary Firth found in her
Kelantan fishing villages in 1940 where the average size of the
peasant's family was 3.5 persons and "in no household is the
number of children very much more than that of able-bodied
adults." [29]

The shift from conventional to nuclear families brings consequences for other elements of the urban syndrome. Conflict
resolution passes from the extended family and its interlocking
larger community to the bureaucratic staff sent out by government
to maintain social control. The growing horde of children without grandparents heightens the need for such social services as
health and schools to keep them happy and occupied. In the economic sphere the accumulation and exchange of mutual obligations of a diffuse nature is displaced by the more modern practice
of posting on the headquarters building a list of those settlers in
arrears to the cooperative store. As regards the handling of divorce
among the settlers, there is no real information, although this, too,
would probably be one of the new burdens assumed by the
bureaucracy established to maintain social control on the scheme.

In discussing these changes in family life we should keep in
mind that the decline of the support and influence of the extended
family depends on the difficulty of communications between the
nuclear settler family and their place of origin. In Kampong New
Zealand, where most of the settlers had been drawn from the area
around Pekan, the royal capital of Pahang, the majority of them
took the seventy-five-mile bus trip "home" on weekends, no doubt
maintaining kinship obligations by bus just as did the Toba Batak
Bruner studied in Medan. But over time, as on other schemes,
the FLDA staff frowned on this practice with increasing effective-

[28] R. Wikkramatileke, "State Aided Rural Land Colonization in Malaya: An
Appraisal of the F.L.D.A. Program," *Annals of the Association of American
Geographers*, LV, No. 3 (September, 1965), 401; and personal communications.
[29] Rosemary Firth, *op. cit.*, 1966 ed., p. 11.

ness. Their doctrine was that all of the settler's life must be focused
on the scheme.

FACE TO FACE WITH BUREAUCRACY

Let us now look at the changing role of government as it
relates to FLDA settlers. Government to the urbanite means
bureaucracy while to the rural dweller in underdeveloped countries the government officer is a relatively rare sight. In this respect
Malaya was more urban than others since of all the British colonies
in Asia it was "more closely administered" and hence, say some
of the old colonial service officers, better administered.[30] The
countryside in Malaya was ruled by seventy district officers distributed over the peninsula while Burma, with about three times
the population and five times the area, got by with half that
number.[31]

Furthermore, administration in Malaya traditionally meant
the administration of Malays, leaving out of consideration the
large Chinese portion of the population who were governed largely
by their own leaders, with some control in later days by a small
branch of the civil service known as the Chinese Protectorate. The
district office had long been an important place to the rural Malay
because that was where events having to do with land took place
and land was important to the "sons of the soil." With the shift
in government policy toward a development goal following independence, the impact of the bureaucracy on the countryside escalated.[32] From a genteel concern with maintaining law and order,
collecting revenue, and administering justice, bureaucrats in the
countryside were jolted into a massive passion for building roads,

[30] Victor Purcell, *The Memoirs of a Malayan Official* (London: Casell, 1965).
[31] The disproportion continues into the post-independence period. In 1964
Malaya had approximately 47.2 civil servants in its "elite cadre" (MCS) for every
million of population, more than twice the ratio for Ceylon (19.7) and ten times
that for Burma (4.53) or the two larger ex-colonies, Pakistan (4.47) and India
(4.40). Adapted from Ralph Braibanti, "Concluding Observations," in Braibanti &
Associates, *Asian Bureaucratic Systems Emergent from the British Imperial Tradition* (Durham: Duke University Press, 1966), table 4, pp. 648–49.
[32] Ness, *op. cit.*

bridges, mosques, community halls, schools, and market stalls and
for promoting adult education, double cropping, and other community development activities. This effort reached down past the
district officer with his district development committee and engaged his *Penghulus,* the locally selected heads of *mukims,* who
in turn energized *kampong* development committees made up of
the *Ketua Kampong* (head of the village) and ten local worthies.
Great sums of money were available for acceptable projects and
their implementation was motivated by a "Red Book" planning
procedure and a military style "operations room" follow-up. The
Deputy Prime Minister, who is also Minister for Defense and
Rural Development, toured the districts making surprise inspections at district and *kampong* level with carrot and stick in hand.
For those who had done well, "spot grants" were available for
village wells, a foot-bridge across a stream, or wall-to-wall carpet-
ing for the mosque. Any civil servant who dragged his feet was
subject to public rebuke and possible curtailment of his normal
progress through the civil service ranks. Officers soon learned to
heed the command to go to the people.

Indeed, the visiting bureaucrat has become a common oc-
currence for the *kampong* dweller, but bureaucracy itself has become a day to day institution for the settler on a FLDA scheme.
His house is a numbered unit in an overall plan laid out by the
Department of Town and Country Planning following Kent
County concepts. His social life, or his work life, or both, is under
the direction of a *Ketua Blok* (block head) appointed by the manager of the scheme. This *Ketua* unlike the *Ketua Kampong* back
home carries few ties of family or tradition.

The role of the *Ketua Blok* varies from scheme to scheme.
Like the *Ketua Kampong* in the traditional setting he is usually
differentiated from his cohabitants in some social as well as
official sense. On the average he will be slightly older. He may
be distinguished by his previous occupation. On an established
scheme nineteen of the twenty-four *Ketuas* were former members
of the police, customs, or armed forces. On one new scheme, the
three *Ketuas Blok* were formerly a teacher, a policeman and a
soldier. Yet on a third scheme, again a new one, the three *Ketuas*
had been an odd job man, a casual laborer, and a *kampong* car-

penter. On some schemes there are *Ketuas* elected by the settlers for every ten houses to handle the social side of settler life. Another set of *Ketuas* work in the field, are appointed by the manager and perform only the functions of a straw boss. On other schemes *Ketuas* are appointed only for field supervision with the FLDA staff taking on the total role of social control. Or, again, one set of *Ketuas* may perform both roles, in which case they are most likely appointed rather than elected. Just as the *Ketua's* role and mode of appointment varies from scheme to scheme, so does his tenure. On one fairly troubled scheme the manager provided a list of *Ketuas* to the author on request, but explained that it was not very significant as they would probably be removed shortly (the same has happened to a number of managers on that scheme, too). No figures are available for the length of tenure of *Ketuas Kampong* in the traditional village, but the general impression is one of stronger community ties and stability of office.

Above the *Ketuas* are the first line of the FLDA bureaucracy, the field assistants, who were usually older men who had performed similar roles as employees of rubber estates. More recently this post has been filled by young men with some technical training who have the opportunity to become cadet managers and climb up the FLDA hierarchy. Scheme managers are a disparate lot, chosen with minimum concern for formal qualifications aside from a requisite level of technical competence, and promoted or demoted largely on the basis of the results they produce. Success in this role depends primarily on hard work, initiative, and honesty, much more so than in the more formally constituted and routine civil service posts such as that of a district officer or an officer in the Agricultural Service or other specialist services.[33]

FLDA's major concern with the settlers has been the problems of control. The natural orientation of FLDA's structure and personnel is toward economic and technical matters. As a result

[33] In a separate study the author is contrasting the role demands, recruitment criteria, and career lines of FLDA managers and regular members of the Malayan Civil Service. Here it is noteworthy that, taking the twenty-eight managers who have been employed by FLDA for five years or more, we can explain about 25 per cent of the variation in their current rank by knowing what rank they held five years ago. For a comparable group of 103 MCS officers, about 90 per cent of the variation in rank is explained by standing five years previously.

they have achieved a measure of economic and technical success, which is more than can be said of most land development programs around the world.[34] By centralizing the land development program and applying heavy doses of money and supervision FLDA succeeded where many of the earlier schemes, which had been initiated under state auspices and managed by district officers with the FLDA acting only as a lending agency, were on the road to failure.[35] Today those schemes which are behind schedule in bringing the rubber into production or which have particular problems with settler strikes are more apt to be the ones begun by states. A further contrast may be made to the Fringe Alienation Schemes, in theory a much more economical form of land development. In these, land on the fringe of established agricultural areas is allocated to *kampong* dwellers under modest supervision by the district officer. The almost universal failure of these projects (much of the young rubber is choked out by sheet *lallang* grass) can be attributed in great measure to the lightness of supervision.

To maximize supervision for technical and economic benefits, the FLDA has shifted over the years away from an early reliance on settler labor organized on the traditional principle of *gotong royong* (mutual self-help), and toward the allocation of more and more of the stages of development (clearing the jungle, burning, planting the cover crop and the main crop, bud-grafting and weeding) to contract labor while deferring the day when the settlers arrive to settle their land. Under this new system settlers may spend less than one year getting acquainted with their five- or six-year-old plants before they begin to tap them to bring in the harvest. On one mature oil palm scheme where the PWD had been behind schedule in constructing houses and bringing in piped water there were as yet no settlers. Chinese contract labor from a nearby town harvested the fruit for the first nine months. In this way the schemes have become more and more like the big

[34] Carl K. Eicher, "Transforming Traditional Agriculture in Southern Nigeria" (a paper delivered at the Annual Meeting of the African Studies Association, Bloomington, Indiana, October 26–29, 1966).

[35] Willard A. Hanna, "Cushioning and Conditioning the Pioneer: How Indigent Settlers Achieve Self Sufficiency," *American Universities Field Staff Reports Service*, Southeast Asia Series, XIII, No. 20, Malaysia (New York, 1965).

private estates, except that they do not have to deal with the National Union of Plantation Workers.

Small wonder then that managers often say, "my problems only began when the settlers came on the scheme." The flavor of these problems in the earlier days is given in a report of a Malay manager for the very first scheme:

> . . . the work of initiating the settlers to a life of discipline, orderliness, and healthy community living has proved the most challenging aspect. . . . To appreciate the extent of the problem it must be pointed out that settlers were extremely poor and had large families to support. Most were illiterate and had a complete distrust of any new technique. The majority were ignorant of jungle felling and clearing. . . . Physically, they were incapable of standing more than three hours of strenuous work a day. Through rigorous regimentation, training and practical education, carried out with as much understanding and sympathy as possible, the settlers have come . . . [to] behave like ordinary men and women in a civilized community.[36]

The political implications of this style of engagement of settlers with government are many and important, and will provide the substance of a later section of our analysis. It will also be useful to look at the purely economic elements of urbanism separately, as will be done shortly. Here we should consider the other ways in which government on the FLDA scheme is more urban than elsewhere in the countryside.

Government in urban areas not only presents a more bureaucratic face; it also produces more results. Urban levels of service are generally higher than rural levels. In Malaysia, government investment in rural development outshadows any concern it may have in city development, which is left primarily to private enterprise and the less politically potent Chinese and Indian minorities. Still, amongst Malays in the countryside, those on the FLDA schemes are getting more of the per capita pie than their more rural cousins. Estimates of government investment per settler range from Malayan $10,921 (one Malayan dollar equals about U.S. 33 cents) to Malayan $18,000 depending on what is counted

[36] Robert Ho, "Land Settlement Projects in Malaya: An Assessment of the Role of the Federal Land Development Authority," *Journal of Tropical Geography,* XX (June, 1965), 9.

and when.[37] The services provided include adequate housing (800 square feet of floor space on the earlier schemes, 1,200 on the later ones); chlorinated and fluoridated water; a cooperative store; a mosque calibrated to the size of the scheme; a community hall; resident or itinerant medical personnel; and a subsidized bus line to the nearest large town. The result of receiving such open-handed benefits on the aspiration levels of those who had up to the point of joining the scheme accumulated the least of almost any segment of society are quite predictable. One group of settlers who conceived of their admission to a scheme as evidence that they were chosen people refused to accept the standard model of mosque the PWD planned to build for them, asking instead for the next larger model, which was intended for larger schemes. In the end their complaint came to naught because the FLDA formula was supported by the Minister for Rural Development. As the structure of political power becomes more localized, the settlers are more likely to win.

ECONOMIC RELATIONS

A close correlate of most other rural-urban differences is the proportion of the labor force engaged in agriculture. Often this is a more available and more valid indicator of the rural or urban character of a particular area than other measures.[38] Isn't it particularly perverse then to speak of agricultural development as engendering urbanism? The answer is that we are speaking in relative terms and plantation agriculture as an industrial form of organization carries with it more elements of urbanism than does peasant agriculture. This shift from peasant to plantation agri-

[37] *The Rocket* (Organ of the Democratic Action party), No. 1965, December, 1966, p. 7.
[38] Sorokin argues that "the principle criterion of the rural society or population is [agricultural] occupation." Pitirim A. Sorokin and Carle C. Zimmerman, *Principles of Rural-Urban Sociology* (New York: Henry Holt, 1929), pp. 15, 16. For an intriguing paradox of agriculture as an occupation and the city as a legal form applied to open spaces within a metropolitan area see Winston W. Crouch *et al.*, *Agricultural Cities: Paradoxes in Politics of a Metropolis* (Department of Political Science, University of California at Los Angeles, 1964).

culture is precisely the transformation that many of the FLDA settlers have undergone. This transformation entails three major changes in the economic life of the settler; (1) an increase in labor discipline; (2) increased monetization; and (3) the experience or at least the expectation of increased wealth.

Let us take the last one first as it is the central rationale for the whole FLDA effort, symbolized in the Authority's motto and the title of its policy statement "no need to be poor." The object was to open up land to the landless in order to develop the productive resources of the nation and raise the level of income of one of the poorest segments of society. Not all settlers were really landless. Those with holdings of up to two acres were allowed under the rules, and some with larger holdings could also come in since a complete check of the records by the settler selection committee would have been impossible and impolitic. Nor were all settlers necessarily poor. On occasion a scheme may contain a state senator or assemblyman or the owner of a Mercedes-Benz pirate taxi. However, by and large they were people who as of reaching middle age had accumulated little and thus were characterized by one official, who had formerly been a school teacher, as "social drop-outs." To these people FLDA presents three forms of wealth and one form of debt.

The most important form of wealth is the ownership of eight to ten acres of rubber or oil palm land, some orchard, and a house and lot. When settlers who complained about the hard life on the schemes were asked why they did not leave, the answer was that they held on to the hope of coming into possession of valuable land, a strong incentive in any peasant society. The second form of wealth is an expected income when the rubber matures of M$350 to M$400 per month, which is about four to six times the average for rural Malay households in the late 1950s.[39] An income of M$600 or so might be expected on oil palm schemes. The third is a subsistence allowance of M$50 to M$70 per month while the land is being developed, declining as settler income from his land increases. All of these benefits are conditional. The size

---

[39] E. K. Fisk, "Features of the Rural Economy," in T. H. Silcock and E. K. Fisk (eds.), *The Political Economy of Independent Malaya: A Case-Study in Development* (Berkeley: University of California Press, 1963), pp. 166–67.

of the subsistence allowance depends on the amount of work on the scheme that is available from month to month. The income is expected, not actual, subject to a certain decline in the world price of rubber, and on the oil palm schemes to an uncertain allocation of costs and profits. Title to the land is not clear; it cannot be sold or subdivided among one's heirs. In addition, there is the possibility of a settler being ejected from the scheme for disciplinary reasons. The conditional character of these sources of wealth moves the settler away from the category of nature's nobleman and over toward that of industrial employee, a shift in the urban direction which we may expect to locate him at a different point in the political arena from the *kampong* bound peasant.

The one form of debt accumulated by the settler is an obligation to FLDA for the costs of developing the land once it returns an income. These costs include the subsistence allowance previously paid to the settler for work on his land, the costs of contract labor on that land, the expenses of the PWD in erecting his house and installing water, and, in some circumstances, the expenses of the administration, all at 7 per cent interest per annum. What is the settler's attitude toward this debt? Much will depend on his previous experience with creditors, in most cases Chinese middleman monopolist-monopsonists.[40] Malay padi planters and fishermen are typically entangled in a diffuse net of debts and personal obligations to local middlemen who play the combined role of supplier-purchaser-moneylender and to others with whom they work or play, or share some other social tie.[41] This is less true of those with a low capital, constant income occupation such as rubber small-holders or mixed farmers.[42] The repayment of these debts is rarely a conclusive act. With the middleman the padi planter runs a system of revolving credit on purchases of staples

[40] Clifton Wharton, Jr., "Marketing, Merchandising and Moneylending: A Note on Middleman Monopsony in Malaya," *Malayan Economic Review*, VII, No. 2 (October, 1962), 24–44.

[41] Raymond Firth, *Malay Fisherman*.

[42] M. G. Swift, "Capital Saving and Credit in a Malay Peasant Economy," in Raymond Firth and B. S. Yamey, *Capital, Saving and Credit in Peasant Societies: Studies from Asia, Oceania and the Caribbean and Middle America* (Chicago: Aldine, 1964).

and small luxuries in the shop guaranteed by the middleman's first option of purchasing his rice. With his friends most loans become, sooner or later, either small acts of charity or the breaking point of friendship. It seems reasonable to suspect that a similarly casual attitude toward economic obligations prevailed among those settlers who were *kampong* laborers or occasional labor on rubber holdings. By contrast, the settler's debt to FLDA is explicit and large. The incentive to avoid full repayment is consequently great. The extent of actual repayment may become, as it has in other countries, an important political question. Much will depend on perceptions of success and comparative benefits as between settlers and the rest of society, and among settlers on different schemes.

One of the great labors in building Communism in the Soviet Union was the adjustment of the Russian peasant to the labor discipline required in an industrialized society. A similar transformation must take place in the settler coming onto the FLDA scheme. Except for the very small proportion who served with the police or army, the settler's previous job history has been a casual one. Even where he did work on a rubber estate it was more likely as an occasionally employed weeder rather than a daily tapper. On the scheme the settlers fall out for roll call at 6 A.M. six days a week.

In the earlier days settlers were allotted their own plots to clear and cultivate. The results were catastrophic. Standards of clearing and culture varied widely, with sheet *lallang* rampant in one man's stand a threat to his neighbors as well as a drag on the progress of the scheme as a whole. As a remedy, groups of settlers were assigned to a particular area from which each settler's own plot would be drawn by lot on reaching maturity. Another area in which organizational learning led to tighter control was in the distribution of subsistence allowances. Initially paid out to every settler on a monthly basis, they were next doled out at the rate of M$2.90 per day for every settler who showed up at reveille and was still in the field at quitting time. Later, standards were further tightened when norms were set for particular kinds of work and payment was prorated on fulfillment. Today some kinds of work, such as digging ditches or harvesting oil palm fruits, is paid for on a piecework basis. Theoretically, all forms of subsidy will end when the settler gets title to his own plot of mature rubber, but still the sheet rubber is supposed to be sold through the FLDA organization so that FLDA can reclaim a portion of its debt on each day's run. The result is a certain amount of smuggling out of the scheme—little children running through the jungle with unsmoked sheets or women walking out the gate in a false pregnant pose. In the case of oil palm, control will continue indefinitely since harvesting must be synchronized over a large area in order to get the plucked fruits to a mill within twenty-four hours of picking. The political consequence of such control and labor discipline is the same as with other aspects of industrialization: conflicting interests are defined and sharpened; the "class enemy" (management) is readily identified.

A third change in the settler's economic relations is the increasing monetization of his work and home life.[43] This is evident in the kinds of calculations used in determining his family allowance for the month and in his credit balance at the cooperative store. Making purchases off the scheme is frowned upon, especially when the prices are lower, and often quite difficult since credit is not readily available. The settler's earnings for the month go first to clear his account at the cooperative store, with little left over for obligations incurred on the open market.

It is characteristic of the accompanying shift in perceptions that one settler, much disgruntled over how his monthly allowance was disappearing in explicit and exhaustive fashion, grumbled that before, on the *kampong* "rice was free" but now he had to pay for it. Perhaps equally important in quantifying the settler's perception of his place in the universe is the flood of information

---

[43] The Malay peasant economy at large is characterized by Swift, "Capital Saving . . .", *op. cit.,* as a developed monetary economy with a long standing awareness of commercial concepts, even for exchanges that do not actually involve money. Wharton has shown that in Province Wellesley (one of the most modern areas) rubber smallholders behave like very rational economic men. These characterizations are less true for the "social drop-outs" who are recruited to FLDA schemes, so that a transition to greater monetization does indeed take place for them. Clifton Wharton, Jr., "Malay Rice and Rubber Smallholders: Economic Man Revisited" (paper read at the Spring 1966 Meeting of the Association for Asian Studies, New York).

about how much the government is doing for the FLDA settler in particular and the rural population in general. This campaign is intended by the government as a general support building activity. By equipping rural folk with concepts for comparing their condition with what it used to be the government is also preparing them to compare with the positions attained by others and with the aspiration level generated within themselves, a not necessarily intended consequence.

COMMUNICATIONS

Increased size, density, and heterogeneity heighten social contact and the sense of contrast. That is the simple physical explanation for many of the social differences between urbanism and the country life. In this way Daniel Lerner can weave urbanization into his theory of modernization as increasing communication.[44] For our purposes it will be well to distinguish between (a) the extent of contact or communication and (b) the form that contact takes—whether it is contrasting or simply more of the same. This is important because when we consider the political consequences of a change in the character of communications experiences we will want to distinguish between the extent of political participation and the form of that participation, that is, whether it is competitive or not.

A clear before-and-after picture of the settler's performance as a social communicator would be difficult to draw with the data at hand although again, we may be able to estimate change by comparing his current condition with what is known about the conditions in *kampongs* in general and the settler's likely position within that setting.[45] In attempting to measure the extent of in-

[44] Daniel Lerner, *The Passing of Traditional Society* (Glencoe, Ill.: The Free Press of Glencoe, 1958), pp. 43–75.
[45] Some good comparative data on literacy, mail and magazine readership, and radio ownership may soon be available from the government's family planning survey of a large random sample of pregnable women.

volvement in a communications net we can expect that settlers will receive more mail on the scheme than they did back home simply because there is now a need to write in order to carry on at least a portion of the communications that went by word of mouth before. We may also expect that they may be more readily organized into adult education classes for purposes of improving their literacy. We do know that their children can be more easily herded into schools at the primary level since schools are available on all schemes and in closer proximity to residences than in the scattered *kampongs*. In addition, various scheme managers have taken a special interest in promoting the education of the children (even in one case imposing an illegal tax to pay for transportation to schools outside of the scheme) from a conviction that the only real hope for improvement lies with the next generation. Travel beyond the borders of the scheme is available by means of a subsidized bus line. The mass media are more available to the extent that a secure or rising income increases the likelihood of owning a transistor radio, as many do. Newspaper readership, as elsewhere, is higher where there is a convenient central gathering place—a barber shop on one scheme. In addition, the settler on the scheme is linked into the FLDA network of announcements, circulars, and meetings organized as platforms for local or higher level officials.

The form of contacts the settler has with the outside world is more likely to be contrasting and comparative than the kind of communications he engaged in before arriving on the scheme. As was suggested in the section on monetization, the settlers are being equipped with concepts that facilitate the making of a variety of comparisons. There are several bases for comparison and contrast between FLDA schemes, and the FLDA communications network facilitates this. Comparisons are made by the FLDA staff, which at the manager and assistant level has a high rate of circulation among schemes. Usually the purpose of these comparisons is to urge the settlers who lag to emulate those who are doing better. This is the explicit purpose of a Stakhanovite style newssheet which is widely distributed on the schemes.

Comparisons raise questions of "fairness" or "equal treatment." Here a major distinction between rubber and oil palm schemes appears. By and large oil palm produces about twice the income per acre that rubber does. Furthermore, oil palm comes to maturity more rapidly than rubber, in about three to four years in comparison to rubber's six to seven years. For these reasons many rubber estates in Malaysia, even some owned by the Dunlop tire company, are cutting down their rubber and replanting with oil palm. A larger portion of the more recent FLDA schemes are oil palm, but not all land which will support rubber is suitable for the palm. By some oversight in planning, the size of settler's plots on oil palm schemes is the same as on rubber, hence they have the potential for about twice the income.

Consider the possibilities of the following situation. Gedangsa is a rubber scheme and Sungei Dusun a new palm oil scheme about five miles distant. There is considerable contact between the two because the settlers on Sungei Dusun are mostly Javanese and disinclined to put wives to work as contract labor. Therefore, much of the contract work on Sungei Dusun is done by wives and dependents of Gedangsa settlers. In addition, settlers from each scheme may avail themselves of the fifteen mile bus trip to Tanjong Malim on the main trunk road. In fall 1967 Sungei Dusun began harvesting its first crop of oil palm while the Gedangsa settler had to wait another year to start tapping, by which time he had accumulated an even larger subsistence debt. One might expect the Gedangsa settler to sense a legitimate economic complaint when he meets the Sungei Dusun man in Tanjong Malin buying a transistor radio which he himself cannot yet afford. There have already been some complaints and inter-scheme conflict. Interviews with settlers on a number of schemes indicate that there is considerable awareness of the benefits available elsewhere: for instance, who has the 800 square foot house rather than the 1,200 square foot model, or whether five or ten houses have to share the same water outlet. The important and as yet unascertainable question is whether now, and in the future, comparisons will focus more on differences between schemes or on differences between the before and after conditions of the settlers themselves. The FLDA staff and rural development movies make much of the latter contrast, but we may expect settlers to become increasingly aware of the former.

THE PASTORAL STAGE OF POLITICS AMONG THE MALAYS

To understand the impact which creeping urbanism in the countryside may have on politics in Malaysia we must first sketch the character of the political game as it is currently played. The current stage of the game may be characterized as "pastoral" or "preadolescent" because it engages primarily the rural electorate, which plays the role of an obedient child accepting guidance from an ascriptive superior rather than that of a flaming youth pursuing an ideological goal or a mature and calculating adult who backs the man who can get him the most.

Looking first at the pastoral element we are confronted with the paradox of a high level of political participation independent of and in some ways in opposition to, the Lerner thesis of modernization, that urbanization leads to increased communication which in turn creates increased political participation.[46] The Malay community in Malaysia, which is highly rural, is also highly mobilized to participate in politics. In 1959, 81 per cent of the Malay population twenty-one and over was registered to vote in state and federal elections.[47]

[46] It should be noted that Lerner, *op. cit.*, p. 60 provides evidence only for a correlation of these characteristics, not for a phasing of the processes, which is a speculative element in his theory.

[47] The overall voting turnout, which includes the relatively less mobilized Chinese and Indian communities, was only 54.6 per cent of the population twenty and above at the 1957 census Federation of Malaya, *Official Yearbook* (Kuala Lumpur, 1962), II, 68 and Table 8. We can estimate the per cent of the eligible population actually voting in each community by pro-rating the overall percentage on the basis of a "racial breakdown of the electorate" made by the Elections Commission in 1959 (T. G. McGee, "The Malayan Elections of 1959: A Study in Electoral Geography," *Journal of Tropical Geography*, XVI [October, 1962], 99) and assuming an equal rate of fall-off from registration to voting in each community. The results of this calculation are that 62 per cent of the Malays of voting age voted compared to 50.8 per cent of the Chinese and 35.4 per cent of the Indians. By 1964 a much larger proportion of the total population was registered to vote (with much of this increase coming in the Chinese community) and a slightly

This high rate of participation may well be a reflection of
the tightness of the traditional Malay community. All males are
expected to turn out at the mosque for Friday prayers and all
voters are expected to turn out at the polls on election day.
Similarly, membership in UMNO, the dominant Malay party, is
widespread. While there is not much room for more participation,
there is a chance for a change in the character of that participation, from pastoral to competitive.

So far, competition within the Malay community has been
minimal. UMNO began its electoral career as an alliance with a
Chinese party that swamped the opposition with 80 per cent of
the valid votes cast, winning fifty-one of the fifty-two seats in the
election of 1955. In the 1959 parliamentary elections a serious
challenge was mounted by the PMIP, an extremist communal
party, but its strength was confined to the relatively traditionalist
states of Kelantan and Trengganu.

By means of clever political manipulation in Trengganu the
strength of the PMIP was further reduced in the 1964 parliamentary elections. The political struggle currently going on in Kelantan has taken on aspects of God versus Mammon, with federal
money confronting local magic.[48] The relation of politics to administration in these two states may foreshadow developments
elsewhere were political competition among Malays to become
more widespread.

---

larger proportion of registered voters voted, R. K. Vasil, "The 1964 General Elections in Malaya," *International Studies*, VII, No. 1 (July, 1965), 57, 61. Whether
or not our inferred ethnic differential in the percentage of the eligible population
actually voting carried over into the 1964 election cannot be clearly calculated. An
analysis of the turnout of registered voters by constituency showed only a slightly
higher turnout in predominantly Malay constituencies than in predominantly non-
Malay constituencies, K. J. Ratnam and T. S. Milne, *The Malayan Parliamentary
Election of 1964* (Singapore: University of Malaya Press, 1967), p. 399. However,
such a calculation takes no account of any ethnic differential in the percentage of
eligible citizens who are registered in the first place.

[48] An example of this is the bye election campaign in Kelantan, part of which
was reported in the Ministry of Information's *Warta Malaysia*, III, No. 32 (August
19, 1967), 5.

> The Assistant Minister of National and Rural Development, Enche Sulaiman
> bin Bulon, told the people of Pasir Mas Hulu constituency that it was now the
> time for them to decide wisely whether to continue living in poverty under
> the PMIP rule or to share the prosperity of other States under the Alliance
> rule. . . . The Assistant Minister was speaking at Kampong Lubok Itek . . .
> where he made an on-the-spot grant of $3,000 for construction of a gotong
> royong mosque and a bridge . . .

Within UMNO itself overt competition is also kept to a minimum. The main issues over which controversy is apt to arise are communal ones, such as the recent National Language Bill which made Malay the sole official language but left too many loopholes, by which the government may tolerate the use of English or Chinese by other races, to please some significant Malay extremists within the party. The continuing relative racial harmony is founded on a high level agreement between UMNO top leadership and the MCA, to suppress public controversy of a communal character which often originates in local branch meetings of the constituent parties. In pursuance of this end party discipline within UMNO required the expulsion of one of the members of the central executive committee for connivance in opposition to the language bill. A measure of internal party stability is the fact that during its first ten years of ruling independent Malaysia, the alliance cabinet lost only two out of the six Malay charter members and one later arrival while adding seven more Malays to the expanding club. The first to go was an Agriculture Minister expelled in an honest to goodness fight; he wanted to wipe out the middlemen dealing in rice. An Education Minister was let go reluctantly after the opposition parties caught him in a clear case of corruption and his counter suit for libel failed in court. In the spring of 1967 the Home Minister announced that he would retire within a few months for reasons of health. No policy clash or personality liability can be clearly attached to his going since en route he was scheduled to be acting Prime Minister. Such elite cohesion is based on a number of shared characteristics and shared experiences and a sincere devotion to the trusted and kindly Prime Minister, Tunku Abdul Rahman. At the state level there has been more movement. In four of the nine peninsular states, which have been controlled by UMNO during the decade, the *Menteri Besar* (Chief Minister) has been replaced at the instigation of UMNO Central. This has also happened to both of the *Menteris Besar* selected in the two Borneo states since their adherence to Malaysia four years ago.

Throughout, there has been a highly cooperative relation between the political elite and the administrative class. Primarily this is a result of the gradualness of Malaysia's political develop-

ment. There was no revolutionary break with the past touched off
by war and the Japanese occupation as in Indonesia, Burma and
Vietnam. Political leaders and local bureaucrats continued to be
recruited from one and the same class, sharing ties of birth, education, and experience. In fact, the bureaucracy has been the
major recruiting ground for the political elite.[49] This cozy relationship is capped off by the Deputy Prime Minister, Tun Razak,
who is also Minister for Defense and for Rural and National
Development. Razak is the model of the instrumental leader run-
ning in tandem with an expressive leader, the Tunku.[50] With
Razak, himself a committed bureaucrat, as the pivot between
party and bureaucracy, the goals of rational performance were
supported rather than eroded by the transition from administrative
government in the colonial period to political government in the
independent period.

THE COMING COMPETITIVENESS: DEVELOPMENT OR DECAY?

In the beginning we suggested that the pastoral stage of
politics would pass and that the FLDA, and more significantly,
the rural development program in general for which the FLDA
serves as an advanced model, would play a role in its passing. To
put the argument in perspective such a development should be
related to the more general discussion of political development
which currently animates the discipline of political science. Much
of the current discussion has been handily summarized and fundamentally challenged in Samuel P. Huntington's perceptive article,
"Political Development and Political Decay." Huntington's main
point is that while the quest for understanding has thrown up a
wide variety of variables associated or entangled with something
called "modernization," the "characteristic . . . which is most
frequently emphasized, however, is mobilization, or *participa-*

[49] Robert O. Tilman, *Bureaucratic Transition in Malaya* (Durham: Duke
University Press, 1964).
[50] Ness, *op. cit.*, p. 242.

tion." [51] Too little attention is paid, he fears, to the process of *institutionalization*, which is necessary if increased participation is to lead to positive development rather than to decay. Politics in Malaysia today is highly participative, and in the Malay sector, finely institutionalized. Our speculation is that the creep of urbanism as we have seen it manifested on land development schemes will bring about changes in the form of political participation and alter the institutions of politics in such ways as to encourage developments which Huntington would label decay.

What are these changes? Using the conventional language we would say that in the Malay political system at large there appears to be a movement "forward" from diffuse to specific definitions of the political role, from ascriptive to achievement criteria for political role performance, and "backward" from universalistic to particularistic goals in the issues at stake in elections. Speaking plainly, the politicians have become concerned more with pork barrel and constituent services than with such great national issues as gaining national independence or keeping the Chinese in their place. Jean Grossholtz (in a personal communication, 1967) finds such a trend evident in an examination of legislative debates over the years.[52] Presumably politicians are evaluated and supported by their constituents less in terms of their piety or personality and more in terms of what they can do for them. As Gayl Ness has amply demonstrated, UMNO has developed an efficient political machine for arousing localist demands for government benefits.[53] To date this machine is still under the control of the administration down through the hierarchy from state development officer to district officer to *Penghulu* to *Ketua Kampong*. It has been a strong arm of the federal government acting in opposition controlled areas. Can both central and administrative control of this machine continue in the face of the social changes it brings about?

So far the administration has exercised an increasingly strong

[51] Huntington, *op. cit.,* p. 388.

[52] Both Professor Grossholtz and another Malaysia specialist, James C. Scott have pointed out to the author that the "economic" interests referred to here have a communal character as well since the constant justification for preferential benefits for Malays is the need to give them a leg up in economic competition with the Chinese.

[53] Ness, *op. cit.,* pp. 206–11, 240–44.

arm on the FLDA schemes, too. In the early days when the schemes were largely state affairs local politics played a large role in selecting settlers and settling disputes between settlers and managers. UMNO branches were openly established on a number of schemes. Then Tun Razak cracked down on scheme politics. It ran counter to his goals of output and efficiency. Settlers could belong to political parties, but they would have to organize outside of the scheme. Politicians who wanted to come on the scheme to talk with settlers must first notify the manager. When an UMNO divisional chairman was sacked from a scheme for stirring up the settlers, his appeal through the UMNO hierarchy was decided at the top by Razak, who supported the FLDA. It would not be accurate to describe relations between FLDA local staff and local politicians as open warfare: on some occasions the manager can make use of politicians to help him control the settlers. But the strength of the local staff is altogether dependent upon the amount of support received from above, at the level where politics and administration merge in one man. Were politics among the Malays to become more competitive, as it is in the state of Trengganu, then political pressure on the administration must increase. Thus, the oldest FLDA scheme in Trengganu is plagued by political factions among the settlers while the management is demoralized by interference on the part of state level politicians, who must be given relatively free rein since, as one high UMNO figure explained, "there are PMIP members on that scheme."

There are great potential sources of support for more competitive politics in the FLDA schemes and, to a lesser extent, in the rural development program at large. Issues become increasingly available as the schemes mature and settlers come more and more into their own, cultivating their own gardens, comparing their near and distant neighbors' gardens, and calculating the income foregone as debt repayment. The kind of manager who has been successful in the technical and economic stages of land development may be less successful in the later stages of social development.[54] Not only do schemes provide issues; they are an organizational base for a new politics. Schemes are not randomly

[54] This is similar to the changing role of the city manager in the U.S.

distributed about the countryside but concentrated in particular areas where suitable land is available or where local political conditions may have required them. The state of Pahang, for instance, will increase its population by one-third with the completion of the Jengka Triangle project. The political consequences of such an organized influx must give local politicians pause for planning.

One crucial question is, who will be the next generation of national political leaders, and will they be able to maintain the cohesive, and hence responsible character of the party? The Tunku has been retiring gracefully since before the 1964 elections, turning over more and more of the control of affairs to his announced successor, Tun Razak. It is symptomatic that during much of the budget session of parliament in the spring of 1967 he was down in Singapore helping direct a movie based on a play he had written about an ancestor of his who was a vampire king some 700 years ago. Tunku Abdul Rahman is a unifying force across the ethnic communities and within the Malay community. His successor has fewer resources to draw on in his task and has so far shown less political savvy about the correct handling of contradictions within the party. Much of the cohesion of the current political ruling class was shaped in the rooms they shared in the Inns of Court in London following World War II. No such shared experience animates the lower levels of the party. If the next generation of political leadership comes from the men below, the rural schoolteachers with their roots in the constituencies, rather than some more centrally selected group, such as the higher civil service or other University of Malaya graduates, then the cohesive institution that is UMNO may dissolve into localism.[55]

A second question is whether the next generation of FLDA managers, or for that matter, the next generation of higher civil servants in general, will learn to deal wisely with politicians. The current inclination is either to avoid politicians or to fight them under the protection of big brother. If the day comes when the party has to maintain its electoral support by competition within the Malay community, distributing benefits in exchange for votes, which is quite explicitly the case in the states of Trengganu and

---

[55] Another, more complicated alternative would be the cooptation of local leaders who are then infused with the ethos of the existing elite.

Kelantan, then top political support of lower level bureaucrats becomes exceedingly difficult.

In Burma district administration dissolved before the on-slaught of locally based, undisciplined politicians.[56] Malaysia will probably not follow the Burma road for a variety of reasons, but the tendency is there and bears watching as rural development brings urbanism to the countryside.

[56] James F. Guyot, "Bureaucratic Transformation in Burma," in Ralph Braibanti and Associates, *Asian Bureaucratic Systems Emergent From the British Imperial Tradition* (Durham: Duke University Press, 1966), pp. 354–443.

5/

Polyethnicity and Political Integration in Umuahia and Mbale

WILLIAM JOHN HANNA
JUDITH LYNNE HANNA

THE POPULATIONS of such loci of immigration as New York City and Lagos Municipality have historically included members of a number of relatively distinct ethnic groups. In the mid-twentieth century, polyethnic agglomerations have emerged throughout the world because of the enormous increase in geographic mobility and the failure of urban areas to become assimilated unities. Our objective in this report is to contribute to an understanding of how such agglomerations "hang together." To this end, we shall describe the structure of political integration which existed in two polyethnic urban-centered communities, Umuahia in what was at the time of our research the Eastern Region of Nigeria (since seceded as the Republic of Biafra) and Mbale in southeastern Uganda.

AUTHOR'S NOTE: The 1963 research upon which this report is based was supported by a Ford Foundation grant administered by the African Studies Center and Office of International Programs, Michigan State University. Data processing and analyses, greatly facilitated by University of North Carolina equipment and computer programmer William Reynolds, were supported by funds of the Comparative Administration Group/Comparative Urban Studies Group's Summer Seminar. We also wish to thank members of the Seminar for their stimulating comments. A full report of our 1963 research, *Leadership and Politics in Urban Africa* (Chicago: Rand McNally) is forthcoming.

POLYETHNICITY AND INTEGRATION

Two central concepts in this chapter are "polyethnicity" and "integration." The former term is suggested by Riggs's "poly-communal" in his model of the prismatic society[1] and used to designate a population which is at least moderately participant but only slightly assimilated. The characteristics of such societies have been of increasing concern to social scientists. In 1937 Hancock described "communalism" as "the phenomenon of collision or tension between several communities coexisting on a single territory."[2] Shortly thereafter, when introducing the concept of the "plural society," Furnivall wrote: "In its political aspect a plural society resembles a confederation of allied provinces. . . . But it differs from a confederation in that the constituent elements are not segregated each within its own territorial limits."[3] In a polyethnic community, (a) ethnic group membership shapes political perspectives and practices and (b) there is at least some institutional duplication based upon ethnic group membership. Thus, polyethnicity is viewed as a variable rather than an attribute, and the plural society is an extreme case.

According to our conceptualization, there are two interrelated kinds of integration: of practices and of perspectives. (This duality has roots in the mainstreams of social thought, including Tonnies' *Gemeinschaft* and *Gesellschaft,* and Durkheim's mechanic and organic solidarity.) Basically, the integration of practices implies cooperative interaction; it is typically described by such terms as common effort, collective action, and mutual facilitation.[4] Thus,

---

[1] Fred W. Riggs, *Administration in Developing Countries: The Theory of Prismatic Society* (Boston: Houghton Mifflin, 1964).

[2] W. K. Hancock, *Survey of British Commonwealth Affairs* (London: Oxford University Press, 1937), I, p. 430.

[3] J. S. Furnivall, *Netherlands India* (Cambridge: The University Press, 1939), p. 447.

[4] Under some circumstances, conflict can also contribute to integration. Holzner writes: "We do not look upon a society as an ongoing system where one component meshes with another, but we see it as an arena of conflict which defines for the various subsystems certain positions of power" (Burbart Holzner, "The Concept 'Integration' in Sociological Theory," *Sociological Quarterly,* VIII, No. 1 [1967], 60).

Kaplan writes about the integrative process in terms of a "common framework providing for the common pursuit of at least some goals and the common implementation of at least some policies." [5] Jacob and Teune state that "the essence of the integrative relationship is . . . collective action to promote mutual interests." [6] And Deutsch writes about "the shift from mutual inhibition to mutual facilitation of the fundamental efforts." [7]

Each of the above quotations links practices to perspectives. For as Williams has pointed out,

> Integration is more than a balance-of-power situation or a symbiotic interdependence. Modern sociology seeks to find this something else by investigating the extent and kind of common value orientations in a social system. A basic postulate is that the integration of a society can be defined in terms of the sharing of common prescriptions and proscriptions for conduct, belief, valuation.[8]

This directs attention to what political scientists have termed "political perspectives," or somewhat more narrowly, "political culture." Perspectives include identifications, preferences, and beliefs. In a recent volume devoted to the study of the third component of perspectives, Verba writes: "As we use the term 'political culture' it refers to the system of beliefs about patterns of political interaction and political institutions. It refers not to what is happening in the world of politics, but what people believe about those happenings." [9]

The proper study of political polyethnicity and integration requires that attention be given both to the practices and to the

---

Simmel, Coser, and others have explored such integration-related serendipity of conflict as the development of mutual knowledge, the acceptance of common rules, the development of common interests in objects, and the initiation of other types of interaction.

[5] Morton Kaplan, *System and Process in International Politics* (New York: Wiley, 1957), p. 98.

[6] Philip E. Jacob and Henry Teune, "The Integrative Process: Guidelines for Analysis of the Bases of Political Community," in Philip E. Jacob and James V. Toscano (eds.), *The Integration of Political Communities* (Philadelphia: J. B. Lippincott, 1964), p. 5.

[7] Karl W. Deutsch, "Integration and the Social System: Implications of Functional Analysis," in Jacob and Toscano, *op. cit.*, p. 183.

[8] Robin Williams, *American Society; A Sociological Interpretation* (1st ed.; New York: Knopf, 1951), p. 517.

[9] Sidney Verba, "Comparative Political Culture," in Lucian W. Pye and Sidney Verba (eds.), *Political Culture and Political Development* (Princeton, N.J.: Princeton University Press, 1965), p. 510.

perspectives of those within the unit of analysis. Although these two manifestations of an actor's involvement are clearly inter-related, they display a (variable) degree of independence. Both polyethnicity and integration should themselves be considered variables rather than attributes. A community might be rated as more-or-less polyethnic, as well as more-or-less integrated. Of course, no evaluative preference is herein placed upon one or another rating.

In 1963 our examination of practices was largely confined to impressions gained from non-random participant and non-participant observation. We were, for instance, able to attend a number of political meetings at which apparently important decisions were made; this gave us the opportunity to see who attended, who was active, who tried to influence whom, and so forth. Quantitative data on practices are for the most part based upon answers to several questions included in an interview schedule administered to reputed local influentials, identified local officials, and sampled adults. (Although respondents' statements about remembered actions may not have high validity, our limited validity checks were encouraging.)

Our 1963 examination of perspectives was primarily based upon the same interviews with influentials, officials, and sampled adults. But by contrast, many perspective-evoking questions were included. (The responses themselves are analyzed as perspectives.) For purposes of analysis, the codes of responses were grouped into eighteen (and for influentials and officials, nineteen) sets. Most concern beliefs about what is taking place in community politics, and preferences about what should take place. The sets are (1) general spheres of most important community problems, e.g., political, economic, environmental, (2) points of problems' impact, (3) specific community problems, (4) specific community political problems, (5) general causes of problems, (6) general groups responsible for problems, (7) political actors responsible for problems, (8) general solutions to problems, (9) political solutions to problems, (10) agents of solutions, (11) actions currently being taken to solve problems, and the actors involved, (12) degree of consideration that should be given to various categories of actors in deciding community issues, (13) bases of community influence,

(14) general spheres of hopes and fears concerning the future of the community, (15) points of impact for hopes and fears, (16) specific hopes and fears, (17) specific political hopes and fears, (18) general spheres of community concern, and (19) types of influential community associations and organizations.[10]

UMUAHIA AND MBALE

Both research settings include a town center plus surrounding periurban areas which are interactionally and culturally linked with the town.[11] The decision to employ such a geosocial unit of analysis was based upon previous research indicating that in most parts of Africa there are close social, political, economic, and cultural links between towns and their surrounding areas, plus our own preliminary observations substantiating the existence of such links in our two research settings.

Umuahia and Mbale share a number of similar features, including characteristics of the indigenous people, modern political development, and urban functions, location, and size. Indeed, these similarities viewed from afar contributed to our choice of research sites because we wanted to hold as many "gross" factors as possible "constant."

Approximately 99 per cent of the residents of Umuahia are members of the Ibo tribe, the predominant people in the area which formerly constituted the Eastern Region of Nigeria. With the exception of several subgroups located outside the Umuahia area, the Ibos have traditionally had a segmentary political system and "there is strong evidence of a cultural emphasis upon in-

[10] Our methods of research are further elaborated in William John Hanna, "Image-Making in Field Research: Some Tactical and Ethical Problems of Research in Tropical Africa," *American Behavioral Scientist*, IX, No. 1 (1965), 15–20; "The Cross-Cultural Study of Local Politics," *Civilisations*, XVI (1966), 81–96; and with Judith Lynne Hanna, "The Problem of Ethnicity and Factionalism in African Survey Research," *Public Opinion Quarterly*, XXX, No. 2 (Summer, 1966), 290–94.

[11] "Umuahia" is both the name of the urban-centered community's encompassing province and the town's former official and unofficial name (in 1963 it was officially known as Umuahia-Ibeku); "Mbale" is the name of the urban center. We usually use these names to refer to communities composed of urban and periurban areas, but in neither research setting is this always the practice of local residents.

dividual achievement affecting rank status." [12] Although the indigenes of the Mbale area are divided into four tribes, the Bagisu of Bugisu District and the Teso, Banyuli, and Bagwere of Bukedi District (other major tribes in more distant parts of Bukedi include Samia-Bagwe and Japadhola; the District's people are collectively called Bakedi), in general they share the Ibo's characteristics of political segmentation and individual achievement. Perhaps one useful indicator of the similarities among Umuahia and Mbale indigenes is that they were both perceived by British administrators to be troublesome and difficult to handle, in contrast to the collaborative peoples found in some other parts of Nigeria and Uganda.

The areas where Umuahia and Mbale are now located were both brought under British control at the turn of the century. Pacification expeditions were made to the former area in 1901–2 and again in 1904; the principal military pacification activity in the Mbale area occurred in 1901. Missionaries and administrators soon arrived in both places as they began to assume the characteristics of nascent towns.

Important political benchmarks for Umuahia and Mbale took place approximately sixty years after the Europeans' first sustained presence, Nigeria becoming independent in October, 1960, and Uganda's transfer of sovereignty following two years later. In 1963 the two research settings' formal structures of local governance were quite similar. In both Nigeria and Uganda, one ministry was devoted to the affairs of local government and its local representative was a District Officer (called District Commissioner in Uganda). Local councils largely constituted on the basis of popular elections operated under the district officers but also had direct communication channels to the ministry. Subordinate local councils operated in the periurban areas of both communities. Figures 1 and 2 outline the formal governmental relationships operative in 1963.

Since our research was completed, Nigeria fell to military rule, the Eastern Region seceded to become Biafra, and a military conflict between Nigeria and Biafra began. Uganda's post-1963

---

[12] James S. Coleman, *Nigeria: Background to Nationalism* (Berkeley: University of California Press, 1958), p. 28.

Figure 1

STRUCTURE OF LOCAL GOVERNMENT IN UMUAHIA

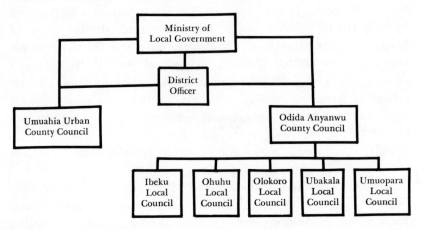

history has only been less eventful by comparison: the central government subdued a kingdom by force, the constitution was

Figure 2

STRUCTURE OF LOCAL GOVERNMENT IN MBALE

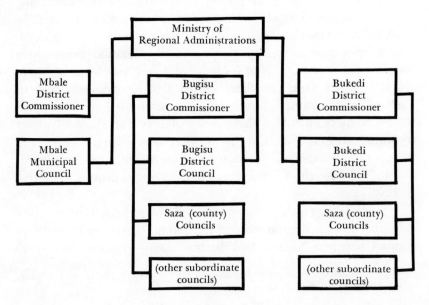

abrogated by fiat, and in general much greater power has been assumed by the center. The elected councils in both areas have been suspended; centrally appointed administrators now constitute Umuahia's formal local government and in Mbale administrators and councilors were appointed by the central government.

Both Umuahia and Mbale are administrative, agricultural, and transportation centers. The towns are sites for their own urban government, as well as the headquarters of the surrounding districts and the provinces in which they are located. Umuahia is surrounded by Odida Anyanwu County, but the county headquarters is located in town to avoid the problems which would attend selecting one clan's land over another's for the site. Mbale is completely surrounded by Bugisu District, but Bukedi District is only a mile away. The peoples of both districts located their headquarters in Mbale as symbols of their rights to the town, which they had been competitively asserting for several decades. Provincial headquarters were relatively recent acquisitions of both towns, Umuahia becoming the administrative site of Owerri Province in 1947 (and later on, after boundary changes, Umuahia Province) and Mbale becoming the Eastern Province's administrative headquarters in 1954.

Umuahia and Mbale are both rich agricultural areas. The former is a center of oil palm production whereas Mbale has extensive cotton and coffee crops. Palm trees are indigenous to Nigeria, but both cotton and coffee were introduced to Uganda by the British (the former in 1909, the latter in 1912–13) to provide cash crops.

Rail and automobile roads have been of considerable importance in the histories of both Umuahia and Mbale. The railroad from Port Harcourt to the north reached Umuahia in 1913, marking its emergence as a town by bringing European traders and foreign African settlers to the area and channeling produce through it. Extension of the rail line to Enugu and the Northern Region and development of a road network centering on Umuahia further increased the town's importance. By 1945, Umuahia was the largest cattle-trading and distribution area in the Eastern Region. Mbale's economic development was significant even before a rail line reached the town in 1931. Around the turn of the century, the area served as a clearing point for ivory caravans working the northern part of Uganda; a bazaar was flourishing by 1903; and later the town was the focus of collection, processing and transshipment for cotton, coffee, hides, and skins. As railhead for three decades, the town's local business and commerce was considerably enhanced. Primary roads leading to Mbale from Soroti to the north, Palisa to the west, and Sebei to the east further contributed to its economic expansion.

By 1963, both towns had undergone moderate industrial development. A ceramics plant and a brewery had been sited at Umuahia and Mbale's industries included oil and soap factories, maize mills, and a coffee curing works. Both were import towns for the surrounding countryside—loci of wholesaling and retailing. They each had first class hotel facilities, a large modern hospital, sports clubs, and a score of doctors and lawyers. In 1963 Umuahia township had approximately 20,000 residents within its eight square miles and the entire Umuahia community had a population of approximately 100,000. (Since the 1963 census was viewed by Nigeria's regions as a means of increasing political representation and consequent economic allocations rather than an objective tally of people, its reports for Umuahia, 28,844 and 118,016, respectively, must be questioned.) In population and size, these figures are approximately double their 1952 equivalents. The most recent census in Uganda, in 1959, placed the population of Mbale Municipality at 13,269 and the entire community's at 106,701. By 1963, we estimate that there were approximately 20,000 and 120,000 residents, respectively.

Despite these similarities, Umuahia and Mbale are in several important respects strikingly different kinds of communities. Umuahia is clearly an African town: the population is over 99 per cent African (historically, the percentage never dropped below 90), all political influentials and economic dominants are African, and the area's very character manifests the influence of indigenous people. Employing such indicators, the Municipality of Mbale was not African in 1963. About one-third of the urban population was Asian (there were also more than 200 Europeans in residence) and the Asians constituted a majority of the town's influentials and all its economic dominants. There was only one African ratepayer in Mbale (he was not an indigene) and only one African businessman of any stature. The prevalence of dukas and saris contributed to the non-African character of the town. Even in the periurban area, non-African influence was felt, especially in the economic sphere but also in politics because of the working relationship between some rural African politicians and prominent town-dwelling Asians.

This qualitative difference between Umuahia and Mbale has been both cause and effect of contrasting histories of urban governance. For almost half a century Africans indigenous to the Umuahia area have held positions of authority in the local government structure, although Europeans maintained close supervision and filled the most senior positions until the advent of self-government in the mid-1950s. Stranger Africans were not represented in local government until about the same time. Actually, the body with policy-making authority for the town was for many years the Ibeku Clan Council, this clan having traditionally owned the land upon which the town is built. As the non-Ibeku living in town increased in number, they began to agitate for representation and eventual separation from the Clan Council's hegemony; pressure groups composed of strangers and non-Ibeku indigenes, with the announced aim of township autonomy, were formed in the 1940s. Political party activity began at about the same time. It was not until April, 1955, however, that the Umuahia-Ibeku Urban District Council was established. Continuing vigorous politics in and around Umuahia perhaps partly explains the ascension of Umuahia indigenes to positions of national prominence; Michael Okpara was Premier of eastern Nigeria and Johnson Aguyi-Ironsi was Supreme Military Commander of Nigeria.

Africans in the Mbale area were far less politicized than those in Umuahia, and in the municipality itself their political activity was minimal. (Party activity began a decade later than in Umuahia.) Africans living in the town of Mbale were, until fairly recently, considered for purposes of local government to belong to one of the district councils responsible for the periurban areas, because the town was predominantly non-African. By 1954, two additional local government structures were formed: the Mbale District Council which had responsibility for Africans not belonging to Bugisu or Bukedi Districts and the Town Council which was responsible for Asians and Europeans. Both councils were composed of government appointees chosen to represent major population segments. It was only in 1962, when the town achieved the status of a municipality, that the two authorities were consolidated and a system of elections was established that over time would replace all appointed councilors with those elected by residents. In 1963 Asians and Europeans were still occupying most senior administrative posts in municipal government. The system of governance in Mbale's periurban areas also involved a number of stranger "middlemen" between the central authority and rank-and-file African citizens. Members of the Baganda tribe served as "agents" or "advisers" during the first three decades of this century, gradually being replaced by indigenous chiefs. Burke writes: " 'Indirect rule' in its original sense was replaced by an indirect style of indirect rule." [13]

The historical development of government and politics in the Mbale area is reflected in a lower level of political awareness and participation among rank-and-file Africans, as well as Asians, compared with their counterparts in Umuahia. We asked respondents in both community samples who they thought were the most influential people in local affairs. In Umuahia 9 per cent of the respondents said that they did not know, but in Mbale the figure was 31 per cent. Participation in elections was also greater in Umuahia.

POLYETHNICITY AND INTEGRATION: 1963

Evidence obtained during our field research suggests that in both Umuahia and Mbale, patterns of political practices maintained sufficient continuity and boundary maintenance that it is appropriate to term each community a "political system." Each system, in turn, appears to be composed of several distinct primary

[13] Fred G. Burke, *Local Government and Politics in Uganda* (Syracuse: Syracuse University Press, 1964), p. 34.

subsystems (with coterminous cultures) so intercoupled that the output of one acts as an input for the other. These subunits (subsystems plus their cultures) are of three types: ethnic, locality, and interlevel. Each local polity contains several large ethnic subunits, one locality subunit, and one interlevel (local-regional/national) subunit. A simple hierarchical schematic is presented in Figure 3. As can be seen, the structure resembles the patterns of formal institutions of governance shown in Figures 1 and 2 (above).

Figure 3

GENERALIZED POLITICAL STRUCTURE

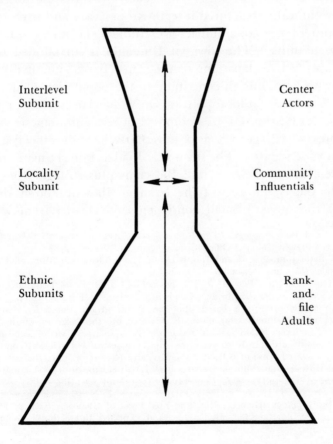

Interlevel Subunit	Center Actors
Locality Subunit	Community Influentials
Ethnic Subunits	Rank-and-file Adults

• *Ethnic Subunits*

Many urban and periurban residents in Black Africa think of themselves, in relationship to the town or wider community, "as 'strangers' having no civil responsibilities, rather than as citizens having rights and duties in the town." [14] One of our Mbale respondents put it this way: "People don't have much civil sense. They don't think of themselves as of Mbale." [15] Residents of most African urban-centered communities are divided "by traditional attitudes as well as by language, custom and religion [and thus a] town can have no single system of social norms." [16] This low degree of civility and norm homogeneity permits the prevalence of polyethnically structured integrative practices and perspectives.

Both of the communities we studied encompass numerous ethnic subunits.[17] The town of Umuahia is surrounded by the territories of five clans: one of the clans (Ibeku) nominally owns the town's land, but all contribute to the population of the town and are involved in local politics. Only one clan has any apparent historic unity; the rest are composed of semiautonomous villages or groups of villages which only recently have developed a sense of clan-wide identity. The town was divided into six main groups, the members of the five local Ibo clans plus stranger Ibos from outside the community. (The stranger Ibos are often divided among themselves.) Small contingents of Yoruba from western

---

[14] K. A. Busia, *Sociology: Report on a Social Survey of Sekondi-Takoradi* (London: Great Britain Colonial Office, Crown Agents, 1950), pp. 82–83.

[15] William John Hanna and Judith Lynne Hanna, Research Notes on Umuahia and Mbale (1963, unpublished).

[16] Kenneth Little, *West African Urbanization: A Study of Voluntary Associations in Social Change* (Cambridge: Cambridge University Press, 1965), p. 86.

[17] An ethnic subunit is based upon an ethnic group, the latter denoting a collection of individuals who mutually identify on the basis of origin and/or culture. The term "group" itself specifies "(1) the largest set of two or more individuals who are jointly characterized by (2) a network of relevant communications, (3) a shared sense of collective identity, and (4) one or more shared goal dispositions with associated normative strength." David Horton Smith, "A Parsimonious Definition of 'Group': Toward Conceptual Clarity and Scientific Utility," *Sociological Inquiry*, XXXVII, No. 2 (1967), 141; see also S. F. Nadel, *The Foundations of Social Anthropology* (Glencoe, Ill.: The Free Press of Glencoe, 1951), p. 146, who emphasizes regular, specific, predictable, and expected interactions among members of groups.

Nigeria and Hausa from northern Nigeria were also in the town.

Mbale is surrounded by Bugisu District and is only one mile from the Bukedi District boundary. The former District includes members of the Bagisu tribe; the latter, three proximate tribes. Also in the periurban area are the Baganda who, under the leadership of General Semei Kakunguru, were sent by the British in the late nineteenth century to pacify and rule the people near what is now Mbale. The British gave the General twenty square miles of land for his efforts and many of the invaders remained. Their holdings and presence are a continuing source of irritation to the indigenous Africans. Within Mbale Municipality all the above groups are represented to some degree, and there are two other relatively large groups (excluding the Europeans): Kenyan Africans and Asians from India, Pakistan, and Goa. Most of the Kenyans are laborers who, according to some informants, are harder working than the indigenous Africans who can easily return to their *shambas* (farms) for subsistence and cash crop income. The Asians are divided into Hindu groups (Patels, Lohanas, Sikhs, Jains, and others), Muslims (split into Sunni, Shia, and Ismaili sects), and a small contingent of Catholic Goans. Thus, one can say that in the Mbale area there are approximately eight main ethnic groups.

To study the nature of political perspectives, we asked respondents a series of questions about local influence, hopes and fears about the future, and so forth. Dividing respondents on the basis of their ethnic group membership, we then established a "homogeneity index" for each set of response codes for each group based upon the uniformity of the group members' responses. (All codes were dichotomized.) The highest index score, 50, indicates that all group members answered each item in a set in the same way. The score on an item is calculated by taking the absolute value of the difference between the per cent of respondents giving one alternative answer and from it subtracting 50. Thus, if 85 per cent of the members of a group answered "no," the homogeneity score on the item would be 85 minus 50, or 35. Similarly, if 10 per cent of the members answered "no," the score would be the absolute value of 10 minus 50, or 40.

The ethnic group homogeneity indices for Umuahia and Mbale are shown in Tables 1 and 2. Since the calculation of indices is not theoretically based, the meaning of a number best emerges from comparison. Looking first at the homogeneity of Umuahia ethnic groups, the interethnic range of the average set is found to be from 38.39 to 40.85. Five of the six index numbers

Table 1

HOMOGENEITY INDICES FOR MAIN UMUAHIA ETHNIC GROUPS

| | | | Ethnic Group | | | | |
Item Set	Ibeku	Ohuhu	Olokoro	Ubakala	Umu- opara	Other Ibos	All respondents in probability sample
1	28.95	39.29	36.81	34.69	33.52	34.03	33.93
2	35.71	42.86	44.51	37.76	36.81	39.92	35.84
3	44.14	43.29	43.63	45.92	44.29	44.79	44.31
4	45.79	48.50	49.23	49.29	46.92	47.65	47.77
5	38.19	34.03	39.42	33.04	36.54	34.38	33.76
6	49.07	50.00	50.00	50.00	48.72	50.00	49.69
7	40.00	46.67	43.85	48.57	47.69	44.12	44.86
8	33.33	35.00	37.91	35.71	37.91	32.35	33.78
9	45.00	49.00	48.46	48.57	49.23	47.06	47.75
10	41.67	43.50	48.46	42.14	40.00	40.59	41.89
11	43.43	40.00	40.91	40.26	41.61	45.19	40.91
12	26.90	13.54	9.23	12.86	17.69	17.95	16.60
13	30.75	41.50	27.05	30.91	31.54	33.90	31.08
14	31.95	39.29	34.62	34.69	39.01	33.19	33.16
15	42.48	41.43	46.70	37.76	37.91	40.76	38.52
16	42.78	40.57	36.81	39.18	34.18	43.95	39.21
17	41.58	49.00	40.00	45.71	37.69	48.24	44.11
18	29.37	37.86	37.91	36.73	36.81	32.35	34.04
$\bar{x}$	38.39	40.85	39.75	39.09	38.78	39.47	38.40

are higher than the one for the Umuahia area as a whole, which is 38.40. The exception is provided by members of the Ibeku Clan, who are sharply divided into pro- and antigovernment factions.

A similar picture emerges from an examination of the homogeneity of political perspectives in Mbale. The interethnic range of the average index numbers for ethnic groups in this area is from 37.53 to 40.33 and for the area as a whole it is 37.56. The one ethnic group whose homogeneity index drops below the area figure is the Bakedi. The probable explanation for this exception is that "Bakedi" includes all the people whose traditional homes are in what is now Bukedi District; five tribes have their homes in this area, three proximate to Mbale Municipality. (The number of Bakedi respondents was too small to divide meaningfully into component tribal groups for the purposes of this comparison.)

Table 2

HOMOGENEITY INDICES FOR MAIN MBALE ETHNIC GROUPS

			Ethnic Group			
Item Set	*Bagisu Africans*	*Bakedi Africans*	*Stranger Africans*	*Hindu Asians*	*Muslim Asians*	*All respondents in probability sample*
1	35.71	33.07	35.71	44.05	35.71	34.83
2	36.19	36.24	35.71	38.10	34.62	35.27
3	45.40	44.71	45.82	47.14	45.38	45.33
4	46.90	44.07	46.92	45.83	46.92	45.21
5	35.36	32.51	35.23	37.50	31.73	32.98
6	46.53	44.70	50.00	47.22	48.61	46.95
7	45.30	44.73	46.36	47.50	46.03	45.65
8	34.07	33.01	38.01	34.52	32.51	33.82
9	45.99	44.76	45.38	44.17	45.13	45.14
10	41.62	37.46	40.77	39.17	44.29	38.64
11	41.67	41.34	41.61	40.91	41.67	41.57
12	28.77	17.82	25.93	24.03	26.92	14.60
13	38.26	36.11	28.75	34.17	23.85	32.11
14	23.40	26.72	32.14	39.29	33.52	26.39
15	41.13	42.06	41.67	41.67	46.70	40.38
16	42.61	40.90	41.43	39.05	35.93	40.50
17	45.52	42.59	44.17	45.83	42.31	44.00
18	34.05	32.74	36.67	35.71	33.88	32.71
$\bar{x}$	39.36	37.53	39.57	40.33	38.65	37.56

An analysis of the differences between ethnic group perspectives further substantiates the ethnic subunit conception. The responses of sampled members of each ethnic group were compared on each of 217 items and the difference of means test was used to judge statistical significance. At the .01 level, chance would produce between two and three significant differences. However, as Tables 3 and 4 show, chance was surpassed on almost every intergroup comparison. In Umuahia the average number

Table 3

ETHNIC GROUP DIFFERENCES IN UMUAHIA INDICATED
BY CONTRASTING RESPONSE PATTERNS

Group Comparison		*Items significant at .01 level*
Ibeku	—Ohuhu	16
"	—Olokoro	6
"	—Ubakala	6
"	—Umuopara	15
"	—Other Ibos	2
Ohuhu	—Olokoro	15
"	—Ubakala	3
"	—Umuopara	10
"	—Other Ibos	5
Olokoro	—Ubakala	3
"	—Umuopara	2
"	—Other Ibos	11
Ubakala	—Umuopara	5
"	—Other Ibos	1
Umuopara	—Other Ibos	12

	Σ	$\bar{x}$
Ibeku	45	9
Ohuhu	49	9.8
Olokoro	37	7.4
Ubakala	18	3.6
Umuopara	44	8.8
Other Ibos	31	6.2
$\bar{x}$		7.47

of differences significant at the .01 level was 7.47; in Mbale the average number was 7.40 counting all pairs and 9.17 counting interracial pairs only.

Tables 1–4 demonstrate that ethnic membership influences political perspectives in both research communities. They also indicate that intra-ethnic homogeneity and interethnic contrasts are both slightly greater in Umuahia. However, the Mbale contrasts are high when linked to race: intraracial differences are considerably smaller than are the interracial.

Most of our knowledge about interacting practices comes from impressions gained during participant and non-participant observation. However, several relevant questions were included

Table 4

ETHNIC GROUP DIFFERENCES IN MBALE INDICATED
BY CONTRASTING RESPONSE PATTERNS

Group Comparison		*Items significant at .01 level*
Bagisu	—Bakedi	5
"	—Other Africans	6
"	—Hindu	11
"	—Muslim	19
Bakedi	—Other Africans	1
"	—Hindu	10
"	—Muslim	3
Other Africans	—Hindu	7
"	—Muslim	5
Hindu	—Muslim	7
		Σ $\bar{x}$
	Bagisu	41 10.25
	Bakedi	19 4.75
	Other Africans	19 4.75
	Hindu	35 8.75
	Muslim	34 8.50
$\bar{x}$		7.40
	African group—African group (3)	11 3.67
	African group—Asian group (6)	55 9.17
	Asian group—Asian group (1)	7 7.00

in our interview schedule to further explore interactions. Taken as a whole, our evidence indicates that (a) interactions are significantly more frequent among co-ethnics than between members of different ethnic groups; (b) interethnic interactions are considerably more common among elites than among rank-and-file community residents; and (c) when ethnic lines are crossed by the rank-and-file, the interactions are usually formal, such as in market transactions and visits to bureaucrats.

The pattern of political interactions is suggested by sampled adults' answers to the question, "When you want to learn something about the problems of (Umuahia/Mbale) and what is being done to solve them, whom do you ask?" Table 5 shows that co-ethnics were most often designated as the source of advice, espe-

Table 5

POLITICAL ADVICE IS MOST OFTEN SOUGHT FROM CO-ETHNICS

Respondent's Advisor	Umuahia		Mbale	
	N	%	N	%
Non–co-ethnic	3	3	17	18
Ethnic membership of advisor unrecorded	14	15	10	10
Co-ethnic	65	68	27	28
No advisor	14	15	43	45
	96	101	97	101

cially among those interviewed in Umuahia. The comparatively
large number of non–co-ethnics who are consulted in Mbale, added
to the "no advisor" responses, which appear to indicate a lack of
political involvement, serve to differentiate again between the
two research communities; political activities appear to be more
frequent and more ethnically structured in Umuahia. Another
difference is reflected in the frequency distributions of named
advisors: a wider scatter was obtained from respondents in Mbale.
Thus, there was a wider dispersion of ethnic advisory activities.

Patterns of interaction are further indicated by the associational life of Umuahia's and Mbale's residents. The organizations
of greatest importance to rank-and-file residents are either ethnic-
wide (but not multi-ethnic) in membership or based upon sub-
ethnic ties, e.g., a clan young men's association or a village welfare
association. In Riggs's terms, these associations are "clects." [18]
Busia's comments are again in point:

> Tribal associations may be a hindrance to the development of a sense of
> civic responsibility by the "strangers" resident in the town, but they pro-
> vide a means whereby people of similar interests are brought into social
> relationships; and more important still, through arbitration, and the con-
> trol they exercise over their members, they are potent factors for the
> maintenance of law and order within the town. In this sense they form
> part of the governmental institutions of the Municipality.[19]

Such ethnic associations are quite influential in the politics of
both of our research communities. As one respondent put it, "The

[18] Riggs, *op. cit.*, p. 171.
[19] K. A. Busia, "Social Survey of Sekondi-Takoradi," in International African
Institute (ed.), *Social Implications of Industrialization and Urbanization in Africa
South of the Sahara* (Paris: UNESCO, 1956), p. 75.

greatest organizations for solving problems are the [home] and clan unions—the cultural organizations. They were the greatest weapons against the British. Once a decision is made by them it is carried out. No power can force them to go back." [20]

Such associational development contributes to a polyethnic structure of political life. Coleman notes: "Organizational affiliations and informal relations provide the chain which links different members of the community together; if these affiliations are confined mostly within ethnic groups, or economic strata, or religious groups, and fail to tie these groups to one another, the lines of cleavage are already set." [21]

Polyethnicity in Umuahia and Mbale is also manifested in non-political ways. One is a tendency toward ethnic residential clustering. The most obvious clusters occur in Mbale, where Europeans, Asians, and Africans each form relatively homogeneous neighborhoods—although by 1963 some of the exclusivity was breaking down as a result of independence and the Africanization of offices which had the perquisites of subsidized housing. But beyond such obvious racial clustering, neighborhoods not part of government housing estates (where dwelling assignments were allocated on a first-come basis) were far from random in ethnic composition; and within dwelling compounds and single dwelling units most residents chose to live with co-ethnics. The trend over time, however, appeared to conform with Forde's developmental view:

In the early stages of settlement new populations with substantial ethnic homogeneity often developed an esprit de corps of which constructive

[20] Hanna and Hanna, *op. cit.*, 1963, p. 100.
[21] James S. Coleman, *Community Conflict* (Glencoe, Ill.: The Free Press of Glencoe, 1957), p. 22. The importance of ethnic organizations was increased, at least relatively, by the weakness of political parties. Chapman's observation, based upon research in Mbaise, also applies to Umuahia and Mbale:

The local organization of the party remained weak. Some areas of the Eastern Region exhibited characteristics of a "no-party state" instead of a one party political system. Since structural weaknesses did not really injure the party's electoral prospects, leaders never bothered building up strong branches. The weakness of the party strengthened the position of other organizations in the political process, particularly the ethnic unions. Branches sometimes operated as holding companies for ethnic unions or as fiefs of prominent individuals . . ." (Audrey Ruth Chapman, "The Relationship Between the NCNC and the Ethnic Unions in Mbaise, Eastern Nigeria" [paper read at the Annual Meeting of the African Studies Association, New York, 1967], mimeo, pp. 1–2).

use could be made in administration, social welfare, etc. But with growing differentiation of occupation, incomes and education in all too frequent conditions of unsatisfactory housing, social cohesion appeared to be
poorly maintained.[22]

Another manifestation of ethnic solidarity occurs in the division of labor. Two spheres of activity display obvious ethnic skew:
less prestigious occupations such as night soil collector and prosti-
tute, and industries with nepotistic hiring practices. It was reported, for instance, that the manager of one of Umuahia's major
industries rarely hired a person who was not his co-ethnic and
never hired someone from a particular rival clan. In Mbale retail
trade has until recently been the exclusive preserve of Asians and
within this group some contrasting occupational patterns appeared to exist between Hindus and Muslims. However, pressure
from Africans—political more than economic—has begun to
change Mbale's division of labor.

Since most co-ethnics tend to have similar perspectives and to
interact with each other more than they do with people of different ethnic groups, it is useful to view the urban-centered community as comprised of a heterogeneous town center, a number of
"ethnic enclaves," and several ethnic homelands. (See Figure 4.)
The African homelands of most Umuahia and Mbale ethnic
groups are located in these towns' periurban areas, but some are
many miles distant (e.g., the Hausa of Umuahia and the Baganda
of Mbale); and the Asians of Mbale have ties with homelands in
Asia (e.g., the Goans with Goa and the Patel Hindus with Gu-
jerat).

The integrative importance of ethnic enclaves in immigrant
America at the turn of the century has been widely recognized by
scholars and popular writers alike, but equivalent enclaves in
Black Africa have not been seen as clearly in terms of their integrative function. Yet in Africa, as elsewhere, "ethnic enclaves
make it possible for an African used to the ways of the countryside
to live in town and yet avoid highly disruptive environments by
providing a milieu for relatively slow and selective assimilation." [23]

[22] Daryll Forde, "Introductory Survey," in International African Institute,
op. cit., p. 42.
[23] William John Hanna and Judith Lynne Hanna, "The Integrative Role of
Urban Africa's Middleplaces and Middlemen," *Civilisations*, XVII, No. 1 (1967), 18.

Figure 4

POLYETHNIC URBAN-CENTERED COMMUNITIES

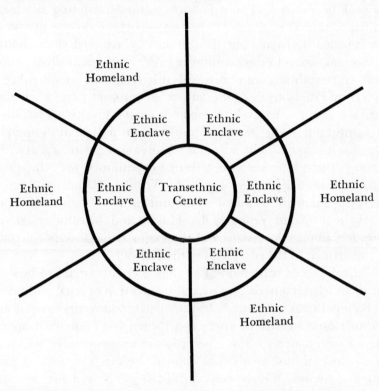

External interventions are minimal, pattern maintenance is relatively high, and adaptive potential is also high. "The immigrant,"
Banton argues, "is absorbed into the urban system, not by a process of individual change in line with the melting-pot conception
of assimilation, but through his membership in a local group of
people drawn from his own tribe." [24]

Three qualifications should be stated concerning the ethnic
subunits which have been discussed. For one, they are all to some
extent internally differentiated and factionally divided. This pattern is characterized by the comment of a prominent Umuahia
resident from one of the more faction-ridden ethnic groups: "We

[24] Michael P. Banton, "Social Alignment and Identity in a West African City,"
in Hilda Kuper (ed.), *Urbanization and Migration in West Africa* (Berkeley: University of California Press, 1965), p. 147.

have a lot of confusions in the villages—everyone wants to be at
the top. And so disunity reigns. Where there is a battle, the illiter-
ates will be enticed. There is such misunderstanding between
families within the village." [25] In this report we do not examine
such internal divisions, but they should be assumed throughout.

Second, not all ethnic subunits in Umuahia and Mbale constitute a "terminal community" as this term has usefully been
defined by Emerson, i.e., "the largest community that, when the
chips are down, effectively commands men's loyalty, overriding
the claims both of the lesser communities within it and those that
cut across it or potentially enfold it within a still greater society." [26]
Although there is no absolute terminal community, for "chips are
down" situationally, tribes (i.e., Ibo, Yoruba, Hausa, etc.) most
closely approximate terminal communities in Umuahia, whereas
in Mbale it would probably be Hindu and Muslim religious
groupings among the Asians and the major tribal groups (including the artificial "Bakedi") among the Africans.

Third, ethnic subsystems, like the other subsystems to be discussed, are characterized by a partial bifurcation of legal authority
and sociopolitical influence.[27] In each periurban component of an
African ethnic subsystem, there is a formal local council responsible for such matters as the supervision of village markets and the
maintenance of bush roads. The councils neither employ staff nor
receive grant-aid. (Other responsibilities of governance are assumed by the county or district government and by ethnic associations.) More influential, and encompassing township and periurban components, is an informal network comprising the most
influential members of the relevant ethnic group (a few of whom
are members of their local, county, and/or district councils). Some
influentials base their sociopolitical influence upon traditional
authority, some upon occupational, educational, economic, or
other extra-political success, and others' upon shrewd politicking.

[25] Hanna and Hanna, *op. cit.*, 1963, p. 62.
[26] Rupert Emerson, *From Empire to Nation: The Rise to Self-Assertion of Asian
and African Peoples* (Cambridge: Harvard University Press, 1960), pp. 95–96.
[27] For an extended discussion of bifurcation, see William John Hanna, "The
Relationship between Legal Authority and Sociopolitical Influence in Urban
Africa," *The Government of African Cities* (Lincoln: Lincoln University Press,
1968) pp. 89–95.

• *Locality Subunit*

There are two "cosmopolitan" subunits in each of our research settings, the locality and the interlevel. The former, largely composed of key local residents, operates at the community level and is interethnic in content; the latter links key local residents with national and/or regional power centers. Because we did not interview leaders at the center, our evidence concerning the nature of these subunits pertains primarily to the former. (The subsection to follow will describe the interlevel subunit because, although many relevant data are lacking, it must be understood in order to comprehend the totality of Umuahia's and Mbale's politics.)

Participants in the locality subunit do not have relatively homogeneous political perspectives and their political practices do not form a highly cohesive subsystem. To compare homogeneity, we calculated the index number of three categories of locality participants: influentials (those identified by reputational and decisional methods as relatively influential in their community); prominents (those identified by positional methods as holding high politically relevant offices, excluding influential prominents); and elites (influentials and prominents combined). Table 6 indicates that, in Umuahia, locality homogeneity is slightly less than ethnic homogeneity, whereas in Mbale, it is considerably less. The comparatively low level of Mbale locality homogeneity

Table 6

IBO HOMOGENEITY IN UMUAHIA AND AFRICAN-ASIAN
HETEROGENEITY IN MBALE

	Homogeneity Index	
Categoric group	*Umuahia*	*Mbale*
Influentials	37.14	31.25
Prominents	37.84	36.88
Elites	37.25	33.28
Sampled Adults	38.40	37.56
Average ethnic group	39.39	39.09

is probably a reflection of the politicized biculture which encompasses both Africans and Asians, in contrast with the pervasive Ibo culture of Umuahia.

Interethnic and community comparisons provide three additional vantage points. (1) There is a significant gap between the political perspectives of influentials (or any other elite category) and those of the sampled adults (most of whom were members of the "rank-and-file"). In Umuahia the differences of thirty response items were significant at the .01 level and in Mbale the number was fifty-five. (See Figure 5.) (2) Comparing the political perspec-

Figure 5

PERSPECTIVES CONVERGENCE AND DIVERGENCE AMONG UMUAHIA AND MBALE RESPONDENTS

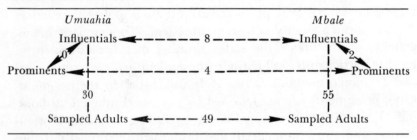

Figures indicate number of item differences significant at .01 level.

tives of the two communities' influentials, prominents, and adult samples, eight item differences between influentials and four between prominents reach the .01 level of significance, whereas forty-nine item differences reach this level for the sampled adults in the two communities. (3) Comparing the perspectives of influentials and prominents within each community, there is no item which yields a significant contrast based upon Umuahia responses, and for Mbale only two items reach the .01 level.

These patterns of political perspectives suggest a "cosmopolitan" orientation on the part of members of the two communities' elites. The convergence of perspectives between influentials and prominents within each community, influentials in the two communities, and prominents in the two communities, is striking when compared with the gap between elite and sampled adults' perspectives as well as the one between adult perspectives of the two communities. Thus, members of urban African elites appear to share a common cosmopolitan political outlook on the affairs of their respective communities. On the other hand, there does not appear to be a transurban common culture of workers, farmers, and other community residents. At the latter level, ethnic perspectives predominate.

Locality subsystems are not highly cohesive.

> A major problem in the civic integration of new states is the quickening of "primordial attachments" based on ties of blood, race, language, region, religion or custom. These attachments give rise to separatist, irredentist or factional groupings whose claims to recognition and autonomy cut across the claims of civic unity.[28]

An Umuahia respondent said essentially the same thing: "Now with development, it is worse than when people were primitive. With education, the people cannot extend their love beyond their family."[29]

Such divisiveness prevented political parties, labor unions, religious organizations, and other potential unifiers from being politically effective across ethnic groups. As a result, formal councils of officeholders and informal situational cliques of influentials appear to have been the principal transethnic political integrative structures in both Umuahia and Mbale.

Jacobson's 1965–66 study of social networks in Mbale provides additional evidence of the existence of a locality subunit restricted largely to key local residents. He concludes that "the [African] elite's social system in Mbale is a single system which has a common culture and which overrides ethnic differences among the elite. . . . Despite sub-divisions, elite Africans, in contrast to the non-elite, are linked into a single multi-ethnic elite friendship network."[30] However, his data show that even friendship

[28] Charles E. Woodhouse and Henry J. Tobias, "Primordial Ties and the Political Process in Pre-Revolutionary Russia: The Case of the Jewish Bund," *Comparative Studies in Society and History*, VIII, No. 3 (April, 1966), 331.

[29] Hanna and Hanna, *op. cit.*, 1963, p. 37.

[30] David Ellis Jacobson, "Social Order Among Urban Africans: A Study of Elite Africans in Mbale, Uganda" (doctoral dissertation, University of Rochester, 1967), p. vii. The author does not, unfortunately, study the division between Africans and non-Africans (the most important "ethnic" difference in Mbale).

patterns among Africans are to some extent influenced by ethnic-ity. A comparison of actual patterns of co-ethnic or other ethnic friendship choices with those generated by an assumption of randomness for the groups in his study sample (see Table 7) re-

Table 7

ETHNIC FRIENDSHIP CHOICES OF MALE AFRICAN ELITES
WITHIN CENTRAL GOVERNMENT

Ethnic Group	Number of Respondents	Own Group Observed	Own Group Expected	Other Group Observed	Other Group Expected	Total Choices
Ganda	18	16	10.0	20	26.0	36
Teso	13	9	4.0	12	17.0	21
West	7	8	2.0	12	18.0	20
Samya	4	1	0.4	5	5.6	0
Soga	3	1	0.4	8	8.6	9
Gisu	4	0	0.3	5	4.7	5
Dama	2	1	0.2	6	6.8	7
Kedi	3	1	0.3	5	5.7	6
North	6	3	0.8	7	9.2	10
Total	60	40	18.4	80	101.6	120

SOURCE: David Ellis Jacobson, "Social Order Among Urban Africans: A Study of Elite Africans in Mbale, Uganda" (Unpublished doctoral dissertation, University of Rochester, 1967), p. 156.

veal, for the three largest groups, contrasts significant at the .05, .01, and .001 levels (these are our figures employing the Chi-square test with 1 df.).

Thus, the locality subunit serves to link the peaks of ethnic hierarchies so that a more "cosmopolitan" culture emerges and at least a moderate degree of interethnic coordination is made possible. Figure 6 portrays this conception.

Obviously not all participants in the locality subsystems were equally powerful in local affairs. In Umuahia the Regional Premier, whose home was in the area, had the greatest influence. However, being concerned with international, national, and regional affairs as well as those of his home area, his locally based lieutenant (a co-ethnic) was in an immediate sense the most powerful man in Umuahia. One prominent resident described this man as "the eye of the premier here." [31] In Mbale the most powerful resident was the mayor of the municipality. His power apparently derived from his ability to work successfully with center Africans, local Africans, and local Asians. A prominent resident put it this way: "Our Mayor is first. He's such a nice person. He helps in everything. He can compromise. Although we don't al-

Figure 6

LOCALITY SUBUNIT

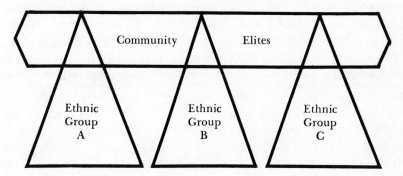

ways have his views, we would still obey." [32] These two men, the lieutenant and the mayor, were most instrumental in shaping the integration of practices in their respective localities.

   The locality subsystem has two parallel networks. One is formal and comprises such authoritative offices and institutions as the town clerk and the urban and county (or district) councils. The second locality subsystem network is informal but probably more powerful. Comprising the influential members of the constituent ethnic groups, it might be referred to as a clique or set of cliques (no negative connotation is implied by this term) with specific membership situationally determined. Concerning the distribution of power between council and cliques, one Mbale resident articulated the consensus in both localities: "A fair amount of decisions are made outside the council. Few councilors

[31] Hanna and Hanna, *op. cit.*, 1963, p. 135.
[32] *Ibid.*, p. 451.

make decisions." [33] Here is a somewhat more detailed description, as told by an Mbale Asian: "We're settling problems outside council. The night before the council there is a meeting at the house of ———. Privately, we call the Africans first; they are new, they must understand." [34]

Although formal authority and sociopolitical influence were in part bifurcated in the locality subsystems of both Umuahia and Mbale, the type of bifurcation was somewhat different. In our conceptualization, two kinds of bifurcation are possible: between actors and within actors. In the former, the positions of formal authority are held by different persons than are the positions of sociopolitical influence; in the latter, authoritative and influential positions are distinct, but they are held by the same persons. Thus, between-actor bifurcation calls attention to the emasculated or "front" legislature, on the one hand, and powerful behind-the-scenes politicians, on the other. Within-actor bifurcation distinguishes a single actor's public rituals from his private decision-making. In Umuahia between-actor bifurcation was high in the sense that many community influentials did not actively participate in the formal institutions of local government; the overlap of authorities and influentials was greater in Mbale. In terms of within-actor bifurcation, the influential authorities in both areas

Table 8

EVALUATIONS OF COUNCILORS

Evaluation	Umuahia	Mbale
Positive	13%*	54%
Mixed	37	25
Negative	50	21
N's	(90)	(72)

* "Don't knows" and "no answers" have been excluded from percentaging.

tended to make decisions outside the formal government structure. The contrasting types of bifurcation in Umuahia and Mbale

[33] *Ibid.*, p. 557.
[34] *Ibid.*, p. 440.

are reflected in the attitudes of sampled adults toward the local councils. The relatively weak council and councilors of Umuahia evoke a considerably more negative evaluation than do their Mbale counterparts. The figures are presented in Table 8.

• *Interlevel Subunit*

The interlevel subunit links local elites (most of whom are ethnic group leaders as well as members of the locality subunit) with the power center of the larger territorial political system. It does not include rank-and-file local residents because the preponderance of center-local interactions does not directly permeate to the rank-and-file level. Political communications, for instance, are transmitted (usually after modification for local consumption) by ethnic leaders.

Reference to Umuahia's center primarily means Enugu, capital of the former Eastern Region of Nigeria, and secondarily Lagos, the federal capital; for Mbale, it means Kampala and Entebbe, twin seats of the national government. Of course, these are political centers rather than physical locations.

It is not customary to include center actors in an analysis of a "local" political system, but we have done so here because of the obviously incomplete picture of locally relevant politics that would otherwise result. Other scholars have come to the same conclusion. As an example, Hassinger concludes on the basis of studies of rural America: "To understand what is happening in rural areas we must take into account the decisions of centralized agencies and their bureaucratic organization. . . . This should include the informal and the formal structuring of these organizations as well as their articulation with local systems." [35]

There is little evidence available on the degree of homogeneity among the political perspectives held by those in the interlevel subunit. However, we estimate that homogeneity is relatively high because of the demonstrated cosmopolitan perspectives of locality participants (plus the presumed cosmopolitan perspectives

[35] Edward Hassinger, "Social Relations Between Centralized and Local Social Systems," *Rural Sociology*, XXVI (1961), 358.

of center actors) and the inferred confluence of perspectives which takes place among persons who have to deal with each other regularly in order to manage the political affairs of an urban-centered community. In addition, we have content analyzed samples of speeches given by Dr. M. I. Okpara, in 1963 Premier of Eastern Nigeria, and Dr. M. Obote, in 1963 Prime Minister of Uganda, finding many similarities between their political perspectives and the consensus political perspectives of elites in Umuahia and Mbale, respectively.

We were able to observe directly many of the interactions which took place between center leaders and local elites. In Umuahia, for instance, most of the men whom we identified as community influentials actually went to the capital when an issue of importance arose, and Dr. Okpara would visit Umuahia periodically, calling many influentials in for meetings to make sure that local affairs were being conducted as well as possible. A similar pattern was found in Mbale, where several key men communicated frequently with government ministers, either in person or by telephone. And every few months, Dr. Obote would visit Mbale to talk with the mayor and other selected leaders.

There appeared to be two parallel, in part overlapping, networks encompassed in the interlevel subsystem. One, the network of formal authority, included the offices and institutions of territorial and local governance, e.g., territorial ministers, provincial commissioners, district officers, and town councilors. Formal interlevel communications traveled up and down this network. The second network was extra-governmental but apparently more influential. It comprised the leading political actors at the center and local influentials. Some locally prominent people were in both networks and others were not. In general, between-actor bifurcation was high in Umuahia; many community influentials did not actively participate in the formal interlevel institutions. The overlap of authority and influence was greater in Mbale, but within-actor bifurcation was high in that a distinction was often made between public ratifying authority and informal sociopolitical decision-making.

As in most countries, the territorial centers were considerably more powerful than were their local counterparts (economic control was a key factor). However, there was a somewhat greater willingness on the part of Uganda's leaders to permit decentralization. One indication of this is the different perception local prominents have of the distribution of power between center and local government. In Umuahia the center is on the average perceived to be more powerful, whereas in Mbale it is local government. Typical of the comments of elites in Umuahia is the following: "We local people in the town don't have a say. It's decided in Enugu and then made known in the press." [36] In Mbale, on the other hand, center intervention appears to have been more selective. "Leaders at the center come in only when something goes wrong," said one prominent businessman. "Interference [also] depends upon the type of problem." [37] The news in 1966 that Dr. Obote's center government suspended the Mbale Municipal Council and took direct charge of the local government dramatizes that final power and authority remain with the center.

Because of the center's predominance of power, some coordination of locality affairs is effected by center leadership. Thus, in a sense, the interlevel subunit contributes to the integration of the locality subunit. This is especially true in Mbale where the degree of locality integration between Africans and Asians is not high. Much coordination there results from the interlevel relations between local Asians and center Africans, on the one hand, and local Africans and center Africans, on the other. The direct channel to the center to which the locally "subordinate" Africans have access tends to equalize some relationships at the local level. This pattern is diagrammed in Figure 7.

In 1963, African leaders at the center appeared happy to work with the Asian leaders of Mbale. The latter were stabilizing influences, sources of money for African politicians, and teachers of nascent African businessmen. But the demands of young African politicians have to be met and African businessmen are developing individually or through cooperatives with government support. As a result, Asians are rapidly losing their influence in the community at large. There are at least four factors which explain why Asians were at all influential: Mbale was in an interim period

[36] Hanna and Hanna, *op. cit.*, 1963, p. 32.
[37] *Ibid.*, p. 430.

Figure 7

MBALE INTERLEVEL SYSTEM

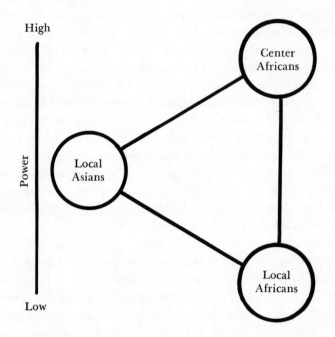

between European and African rule, the town center was an Asian home but only an African dormitory (restrictive urban housing regulations kept many Africans from establishing themselves in a meaningful way in the town), and some Africans did not have sufficient education or experience to cope with many urban problems.

COMMUNITY INFLUENTIALS AS SYSTEM INTEGRATORS

A variety of actors undoubtedly contributed to the integration (and disintegration) of Umuahia's and Mbale's political systems. It is our conclusion, however, that those who made the most important contribution were the community influentials. These individuals, fourteen each in Umuahia and Mbale, were identified by developing an influence index from responses to questions administered to a panel of knowledgeables, a set of reputed influentials, and a probability sample of adult residents.

Three caveats must precede our discussion. First, we do not imply that the integration which occurs constitutes a manifest function from the point of view of the community influentials; at least for a number of these men, it would probably be appropriate to classify their integrative contribution as a latent consequence of their activities. Second, exclusion of other actors' and factors' contributions to integration does not imply that they do not also contribute, but only that we have chosen this emphasis. Third, although we employ the terms "influentials" and "community influentials," there is no implication of the existence of a ruling elite which concerns itself with all issues and is uniformly dominant. Rather, these are the men who, according to our research findings, are relatively influential on a relatively large number of important issues. Their individual involvement is situational and far from uniform.

Virtually all community influentials participate actively in the ethnic, locality, and interlevel subsystems. For this reason, they are essential links among the subsystems, occupying "linkage positions." Loomis writes: "Systemic linkage may be defined as the process whereby one or more of the elements of at least two social systems is articulated in such a manner that the two systems in some ways and on some occasions may be viewed as a single unit." [38] The linkage that is performed by Umuahia's and Mbale's community influentials is schematically illustrated in Figure 8.

Linkage density should be viewed in variable terms. Two subunits or sets of individuals can be linked at one or many points; holding quantity and quality of interactions constant, linkage density increases as the number of points decreases. The limiting and middle types might usefully be referred to as diffracted, prismatic, and fused linkage. Figure 9 visually presents the three types of relationships.

Two questions in our interviews provide indications of the linkage density which existed in Umuahia and Mbale at the time

[38] Charles P. Loomis, *Social Systems* (Princeton, N.J.: D. Van Nostrand, 1960), p. 32.

Figure 8

COMMUNITY INFLUENTIAL AS INTER-SUBSYSTEM INTEGRATOR

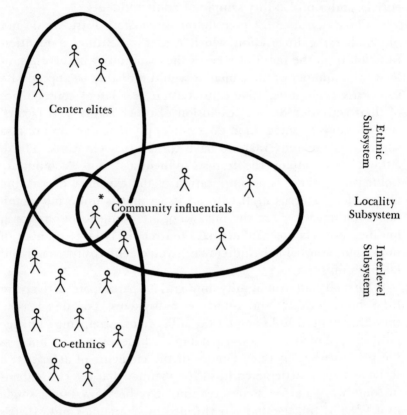

Center elites

Ethnic
Subsystem

Community influentials

Locality
Subsystem

Interlevel
Subsystem

Co-ethnics

NOTE: This schematic is drawn from the point of view of the locus community influential (asterisked). Each influential would have a similar schematic of subsystem participation.

of our field research. One asked respondents to name the most influential person in the urban-centered polity, and another asked them to name the person they go to for advice about a local problem. Summary results for the major ethnic groups are presented in Table 9.

The replies concerning influentials and advisors suggest that sampled residents of Umuahia may have had a greater awareness of the actual distribution of influence in their community, as judged by their more frequent mention of community influentials,

Figure 9

VERTICAL POLITICAL LINKAGE MODELS

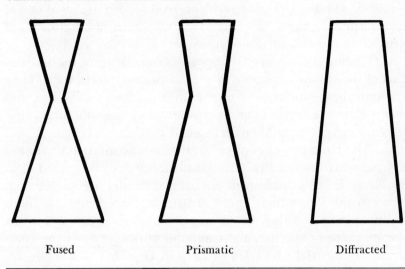

| Fused | Prismatic | Diffracted |

Table 9

ETHNIC GROUP CORRESPONDENCE
INFLUENTIALS AND ADVISORS OF SAMPLED ADULTS
IN UMUAHIA AND MBALE

Community and Group	Influentials	Advisors
Umuahia		
Ibeku	*Co-ethnic;* * co-ethnic	*Co-ethnic;* co-ethnic
Ohuhu	*Co-ethnic; co-ethnic*	*Co-ethnic; co-ethnic*
Olokoro	*Co-ethnic; Premier*	*Co-ethnic;* co-ethnic
Ubakala	*Premier; co-ethnic*	Co-ethnic; co-ethnic
Umuopara	*Co-ethnic; co-ethnic*	Co-ethnic; co-ethnic
Other Ibos	*Premier; Opposition leader*	Co-ethnic; co-ethnic
Mbale		
Muslim	*Mayor;* co-ethnic	Co-ethnic; Town clerk
Hindu	*Co-ethnic; co-ethnic*	*Co-ethnic; co-ethnic*
Bakedi	*Co-ethnic; co-ethnic*	Town clerk; D. C.
Other Africans	*Mayor;* non–co-ethnic	*Co-ethnic;* co-ethnic
Bagisu	Co-ethnic; *co-ethnic*	D. C.; *Town official*

* Italics indicate that the person is, according to rank order, reputed to be a community influential. The Mbale resident called "town official" (he is also a co-ethnic in Group IV) is a Muganda who was Chief of the Mbale African Local Government from 1954 until 1962 when that government was integrated with the general town administration. Since 1962, he has been the official advisor on African affairs to the town's government.

but at the same time they were more ethnically bound when seeking advice about local public affairs. Thus, it can tentatively be concluded that Umuahia residents tend toward the fused model of interunit linkages, whereas Mbale residents more closely approximate the diffracted model.

Community influentials appear to contribute to the integration of the system as a whole in at least two important ways. They transmit the perspectives of one subunit's culture to another, and manipulate the practices and perspectives of one subunit so that they are more compatible with those of another.

"The basic processes of political modernization and national development," writes Pye, "can be advantageously conceived of as problems in communication . . . the generally recognized gap between the Westernized, more urbanized leaders and the more tradition-bound, village-based masses . . . represents a flaw in the structure of the national communications." [39] It is the community influential who filled this gap in Umuahia and Mbale. (A dense flow of communications through the influential suggests that relatively few people have an above average impact on the integrative process.) In Senegal, Barker has observed a similar situation:

> Both in implementing policies related to development and in taking action to manage feedback and political input, the government has no recourse but to work through intermediaries who are or who become part of the local political situation. The position of these intermediaries —both spokesmen for local interests and government agents—as transmitters of action and information cannot be understood without reference to their place in the local political subsystem.[40]

Manipulating involves making the practices and perspectives of one subunit more compatible with those of another (or several other) subunits. Community influentials, as a general rule, have political and personal vested interests in making the subunits compatible with each other. Politically, survival may depend upon arranging activities and shaping opinions so that negative sanctions are not directed toward them by co-ethnics, fellow locality

[39] Lucian W. Pye, "Introduction," in Lucian W. Pye (ed.), *Communications and Political Development* (Princeton, N.J.: Princeton University Press, 1963), p. 9.
[40] Jonathan S. Barker, "Political Integration and Elite Recruitment in an Arrondissement of the Saloum Region in Senegal" (paper read at the Annual Meeting of the African Studies Association, Bloomington, 1966), mimeo, p. 5.

elites, or center actors. At the personal level, we assume that "the existence of dissonance in a person leads to a process of social communication by which he attempts to reduce the dissonance." [41]

Some research in Africa and elsewhere suggests that linkage positions are inherently stressful for their occupants. Fallers, for instance, while recognizing that an occupant helps "to maintain some unity and stability in the system," [42] concludes that "whichever way he jumps, he will be punished, both by his own remorse at having contravened values which are part of his personality, and by sanctions applied by others." [43]

However, this view fails to take five factors into account. (1) All linkage positions are not the same. As we have indicated earlier, they range from the fused to the diffracted. Thus, it becomes an empirical question as to the relationship between felt role conflict intensity and linkage density. (2) Most apparent conflicts are not stressful because the relevant subunits do not come into contact with each other. For instance, when an influential returns to his rural home, he may undergo a change in his perspectives and practices rather than a conflict between modernity and tradition. "Because they operate for the most part in different spheres of his social life, the African in the towns is able to handle the various sets without obvious difficulty." [44] (3) When conflicts arise, they can often be easily resolved. Thus, the influential who wants to entertain "cosmopolitan" guests but has a "traditional" urban home may either entertain in a hotel or take a new "sophisticated" wife and send the other one back to his rural home. (4) Many apparent conflicts are "buffered" by intermediary positions between the extremes. For example, an African is not often faced with the overlapping—and thus conflicting—demands of a cosmopolitan superordinate and a traditional chief; even if the ideal type superordinate and chief exist, there are probably men who stand between the superordinate and the African, and between

---

[41] Leon Festinger, *A Theory of Cognitive Dissonance* (Evanston, Ill.: Row, Peterson, 1957), p. 204.

[42] Lloyd Fallers, "The Predicament of the Modern African Chief: An Instance from Uganda," *American Anthropologist*, LVII (1955), 301.

[43] *Ibid.*, p. 302.

[44] A. L. Epstein, *Politics in an Urban African Community* (Manchester, England: Manchester University Press, 1958), p. 46.

the chief and the African, who tend to mediate the extreme positions. (5) Finally, it is sometimes the case that a conflict ascribed to a situation by the analyst is not perceived to be a conflict by the individual African, and therefore it is not troubling to him. There is empirical evidence to suggest that, faced with the superordinate/chief situation described above, many Africans (or others) would not realize that alternative demands were being made. This occurs either because the extremes have been buffered or because the individual selectively perceives and is not negatively sanctioned for his pattern of perception.[45]

When role conflicts are stressful, it is possible under some circumstances for a linkage position occupant to partially disrupt role relationships. For example, a community influential might break relationships with fellow influentials while retaining relationships with center leaders and co-ethnics. Actually, the focal actor and those audiences not connected with the major role appear to have a shared interest in developing alternative linkage points which, if they do not reduce objective role conflict, at least reduce negative sanctions and subjective role conflict. However, the option to disrupt partially is not often available for, as Merton points out, "the role-set is not so much a matter of personal choice as a matter of the social structure in which the status is embedded." [46]

When a role-set cannot be altered to the satisfaction of the occupant, withdrawal is sometimes chosen as a means of coping. Merton notes that "the option is apt to be that of the status-occupant removing himself from the status rather than that of removing the role-set, or an appreciable part of it, from the status. Typically, the individual goes, and the social structure remains." [47]

We do not have systematic data on degrees of role conflict and patterns of conflict resolution.[47a] However, comments by respond-

[45] For a discussion of buffering, selective perception, and other aspects of role conflict resolution in an African setting, see Alvin Magid, "District Councillorship in an African Society: A Study in Role" (doctoral dissertation, Michigan State University, 1965).

[46] Robert K. Merton, *Social Theory and Social Structure* (Glencoe, Ill.: The Free Press of Glencoe, 1957), p. 378.

[47] *Ibid.*, p. 379.

[47a] See Magid, *op. cit.*, for a study of role conflict and resolution in a rural African setting.

ents suggest that conflict was not often perceived as being high, and that at least some of the community influentials who withdrew from positions of formal authority were actually disrupting some role relationships in order to minimize role conflict.

CONCLUSION

The polyethnic and integrative patterns which emerge from research in Umuahia and Mbale appear to fit the same general model—i.e., including ethnic, locality, and interlevel subunits, and linkage positions occupied by local influentials. Yet the two communities display marked differences, such as Umuahia's sharper delineation among the perspectives of major ethnic groups' members and Mbale's less restricted linkages between ethnic and cosmopolitan subunits. The model's potential flexibility leads us to think that, with further development (e.g., all elements stated in variable language), it may be applicable to a wide variety of communities in Africa and elsewhere, at one point in time and over time.

Recognition that most urban-centered communities may closely fit the model has, we think, relevance to the solution of practical problems of local governance in the contemporary world, and to the monitoring of change. The development of government institutions which take community polyethnicity into consideration, such as the decentralized school system recently proposed for the City of New York,[48] may in the long run minimize inter-ethnic strains and promote constructive actions of ethnic and community-wide self-interest.

Research in Africa, the United States, and elsewhere has shown that ethnicity often stimulates competitiveness rather than hostility and violence,[49] keeps the class structure open, and absorbs some of the hostility that otherwise might be directed toward frail

---

[48] See Mayor's Advisory Panel on Decentralization of the New York City Schools, *Reconnection for Learning: A Community School System for New York City* (New York, 1967).

[49] Max Gluckman, *Custom and Conflict in Africa* (Glencoe, Ill.: The Free Press of Glencoe, 1959), pp. 1–26.

authority structures.[50] Noel has found that in-group pride (but not chauvinism) is positively correlated with attitudes and behavior favorable to integration. One manifestation, according to Noel, is a greater willingness of those with in-group pride to participate in civic politics.[51] This relates to Almond and Verba's observation that, "precisely because the development of a subject culture in England stopped short of destroying local and parochial structures and cultures, these could become available at a later time and in modified form as an influence network that could relate Britons as competent citizens to their government." [52]

The contemporary disintegrative crises in polyethnic urban-centered communities require massive research efforts to improve understanding and conceptualize policy alternatives, perhaps to be followed by the development of new institutions of local governance. It is our hope that the exploratory research we conducted in two African communities during 1963 will in some small way contribute to the integration which in so many areas has achieved high citizen priority in the latter half of the twentieth century.

---

[50] Immanuel Wallerstein, "Ethnicity and National Integration in West Africa," *Cahiers d'Etudes Africaines*, III (1960), 134–37.

[51] Donald L. Noel, "Minority Group Identification and Societal Integration," (paper read at the Annual Meeting of the American Sociological Association, Miami Beach, 1966), mimeo.

[52] Gabriel Almond and Sidney Verba, *The Civic Culture* (Princeton, N.J.: Princeton University Press, 1963), p. 25. Chapman writes that in Eastern Nigeria,

> the activities of [ethnic] unions generally increased the capabilities of the political system, particularly on the local level. Unions often performed functions that other political and administrative structures were not able to undertake. . . . Through the operation of the unions a rapprochement occurred between elements of the traditional social structure and the modern political and administrative system. . . . By providing a link between the local community and the regional political system the unions helped to make the modern political and administrative structures relevant and meaningful tor their members" (Audrey Ruth Chapman, "Political Development in Eastern Nigeria: The Role of the Ethnic Unions," *Dissertation Abstracts*, XXVIII, No. 4 [1967], 1321B).

6/

The City Manager
as a
Development Administrator

DEIL S. WRIGHT

THIS CHAPTER PRESENTS and discusses selected data from a survey of city managers in forty-five of the fifty-five manager-governed cities in the United States with a population in excess of 100,000. An effort will be made to relate the results of this survey to some of the themes prominent in the literature on cross-cultural comparative urban development. In what general ways is a study of U.S. city managers pertinent to the study of comparative urban administration and politics?

First, the worldwide trend toward urbanization, frequently but not always accompanied by increasing urbanism, suggests a parallel and the relevance for looking at politico-administrative dimensions in medium to large-size urban places.[1] Greater and greater population agglomerations appear inevitable in the face of the world's population explosion. Increasing size, scale, and intensity in urbanized areas appear to have important and reciprocal (or at least symbiotic) relationships with the non-urbanized hinterland. James Guyot has identified the penetration of urbanism into non-urbanized areas in Malaysia and the Hannas have

[1] David Popenoe, "On The Meaning of Urban in Urban Studies," *Urban Affairs Quarterly*, I, No. 1 (September, 1965), 65–82. See also John Friedman, "Two Concepts of Urbanization: A Comment," *Urban Affairs Quarterly*, I, No. 4 (June, 1966), 78–84.

shown the close ties between like ethnics in the cities and the rural areas in Africa.[2]

Second, our focus on council-manager cities in the U.S. is closely tied to a policy or developmental orientation. City managers are generally noted for their active, promotional, developmental outlook. To what extent this emphasis is a function of personality and professionalization in contrast to situation and structure is not clear. Empirical evidence does show quite consistently, however, that the council-manager plan is used most frequently in those U.S. cities and suburbs that are growing most rapidly.[3] The ecological setting, then, puts the formal plan and the city manager in a dynamic, change-conducive setting with an impetus, if not a compulsiveness, to respond.

Third, a focus on local government is consonant with resurgent interest in the role of local government in facilitating economic, social, and political development. Frank Sherwood has dealt extensively with the difficulties of "institutionalizing the grass roots" in Brazil.[4] Harry Friedman and Henry Hart have considered the role of local government in Pakistan and India, respectively.[5]

A fourth way in which this focus on city managers may have

[2] James F. Guyot, "Creeping Urbanism and Political Development in Malaysia," chap. 4 in this volume; William John Hanna and Judith Lynne Hanna, "The Political Structure of Urban-Centered African Communities," in Horace Miner (ed.), *The City in Modern Africa* (New York: Praeger, 1968), pp. 151–84. See also by the same authors, "The Integrative Roll of Urban Africa's Middleplaces and Middlemen," *Civilizations,* XVII (1967), 1–16.

[3] John H. Kessel, "Governmental Structure and Political Environment: A Statistical Note about American Cities," *American Political Science Review,* LXVI, No. 3 (September, 1962), 615–20; Leo Schnore and Robert R. Alford, "Forms of Government and Socioeconomic Characteristics of Suburbs," *Administrative Science Quarterly,* VIII, No. 1 (June, 1963), 1–17; and Robert R. Alford and Harry M. Scoble, "Political and Socioeconomic Characteristics of Cities," in *The Municipal Yearbook, 1965* (Chicago: International City Managers' Association, 1965), pp. 82–97.

[4] Frank P. Sherwood, "Devolution as a Problem of Organization Strategy," chap. 2 in this volume and *Institutionalizing the Grass Roots in Brazil: A Study in Comparative Local Government* (San Francisco: Chandler, 1967).

[5] Harry J. Friedman, "Administrative Role in Local Governments" (CAG Occasional Papers; Bloomington, Indiana, December, 1966); Henry Hart, "The Village and Development Administration" (CAG Occasional Papers; Bloomington, Indiana, December, 1966). For references to other materials on the subject of local government and development administration see Allan A. Spitz and Edward W. Weidner, *Development Administration: An Annotated Bibliography* (Honolulu: East-West Center Press, University of Hawaii, 1963).

relevance for comparative as well as developmental administration is in its underlying orientation toward political structures and behavior. This essay is not theoretically conceived nor is it intended to support or refute any arguments surrounding the debate over structural-functional analysis. The analysis does, however, select the council-manager form of government as its defined sphere of interest and the behavior, perceptions, and relationships of its chief executive as the specific empirical foci. The result is an orientation toward and an emphasis on structures that probably is most compatible with Fred Riggs's recent thinking on this problem.[6]

While the chapter eschews an elaborate or rigorous theoretical perspective, it is guided by and organized according to a conceptual scheme that may be outlined briefly as follows:

(A) *Developmental Politics*
   (1) partisanship
   (2) group participation
   (3) mass media and communication

(B) *Developmental Roles of the Executive*
   (1) management
   (2) policy
   (3) political

(C) *Developmental Policies*
   (1) efficiency
   (2) ethnographic
   (3) economic

The operational meaning given to each of the terms in the above scheme will be indicated in the course of the discussion. We should recognize in passing, however, the ease with which the outline could be recast into a simplified systems approach. The section on developmental politics could be viewed as the input side, including both demands and supports. The executive roles might be viewed as a portion of the conversion mechanisms and

---

[6] Fred W. Riggs, "The Political Structures of Administrative Development: Some Tentative Formulation" (CAG Occasional Papers; Bloomington, Indiana, April, 1967); and by the same author, "Structure and Function: A Dialectical Approach" (paper prepared for the 1967 Annual Meeting of the American Political Science Association, Chicago, September 5–9, 1967).

processes whereby the outputs, developmental policies, are determined. We will not adopt the terms and conventions of systems analysis but the rough parallel should provide sufficient initial orientation for the reader to grasp our future direction.

The council-manager plan of government is a structural form indigenous to the United States. Since its inception early in the twentieth century the form has spread rapidly in the U.S. and is now used in nearly 1,300 cities over 5,000 population. Its international dimension is indicated by the more than 2,000 cities using the plan in Canada, Finland, Ireland, Norway, Sweden, and West Germany.[7] An estimated 50,000,000 persons live in communities governed by this arrangement involving the complex collaboration between a popularly elected council and an appointed professional administrator. It is not necessary to describe the plan's formal characteristics or its much-debated pros and cons. The literature on these subjects is voluminous.[8] For present purposes the following appear to be prominent features deserving note:

(1) the plan developed from the ethos of a reform movement; support for it has had and still retains a high moral content;

(2) it appeals in theory and in practice to broad societal values, in this instance, entrepreneurial-based norms of economy and efficiency;

(3) its historic emphasis has been on the distributional or output side of the political system—the enforcement of regulations and the provision of governmental goods and services;

(4) it functions in a bureaucratized manner, with emphasis on explicit, rational, means-end responses to stimuli;

(5) in theory and largely in practice it telescopes or collapses relationships between popularly elected legislative officials and the bureaucracy into a single authoritative channel, the city manager (chief executive);

(6) its chief executives have become a mobile, professionalized

---

[7] *The Municipal Yearbook, 1967* (Chicago: International City Managers' Association, 1967), pp. 87–90.

[8] A useful bibliography is, David A. Booth, *Council-Manager Government, 1940–64: An Annotated Bibliography* (East Lansing: International City Managers' Association and The Institute for Community Development and Services, Michigan State University, 1965).

corps of manpower whose politico-administrative skills are valued by other levels of government and by private industry.

Other pertinent aspects of the plan will become evident in the remaining portions of the discussion.

The empirical data for this chapter are drawn from a larger body of information collected through a mail questionnaire survey in the summer and fall of 1965.[9] Of the fifty-five council-manager cities with a population in excess of 100,000, forty-five returned usable responses. Factual portions of the questionnaire were designed to be completed by administrative aides to the manager. Approximately one-third of the survey instrument was directed exclusively to the city manager. It requested information on his behavior, opinions, perceptions, and expectations. These latter data are central to this discussion of the city manager as a development administrator.

DEVELOPMENTAL POLITICS IN COUNCIL-MANAGER CITIES

Little or no justification need be offered for attentiveness to the ecology of administration.[10] The political context associated with council-manager government is of special relevance because of the plan's explicit aim to eliminate "politics" from the local scene. Witness the following statement of the reputed originator of the plan, Richard S. Childs:

> Politics went out of the window when Dayton's first city manager blew in and, after a single splutter, the local wings of the political parties ceased to function in municipal elections, either visibly or covertly. A

[9] The official sponsors of the survey were the International City Managers' Association and the Institute of Public Affairs at the University of Iowa. Full responsibility for the research design, execution, analysis and interpretations rests with the author and a colleague, Professor Robert P. Boynton of the University of Iowa. In addition to the present use of these data a summary descriptive monograph is currently in preparation.

[10] John Gaus, *Reflections on the Study of Public Administration* (Tuscaloosa: University of Alabama Press, 1947); Fred W. Riggs, *The Ecology of Administration* (London: Asia Publishing House. 1961).

self-renewing group of responsible and respected citizens finds and sponsors candidates and its leadership suffices to prevent scatteration [sic] of the good government vote.[11]

Politics meant partisanship to the early reformers and backers of the plan.[12]

How has local partisanship fared in the face of continued two-party contention for posts at other levels of government? Explicit partisanship is present in only a small proportion of the large council-manager cities. Only 13 per cent of the forty-five reporting cities indicated that ballots for council elections carried partisan designations. The figure nationally for council-manager cities over 5,000 is 16 per cent, considerably lower than the 51 per cent for cities governed under the mayor-council plan and the 39 per cent for those under the commission form of government.[13]

By probing beyond the dominance of official nonpartisanship we discovered a rather substantial departure between appearance and reality. Our informants, the city managers, were asked to judge whether the party affiliations of council and mayoral candidates were generally known and also the interest and involvement of political party organizations in local elections. (See Table 1.) Some informal partisanship is present in nearly half or more of the cities. The discrepancy between the announced or official patterns of behavior and the actual or real activities pursued has been characterized as *formalism* by Fred Riggs.[14] But the designation or identification of the discrepancy provides us only a starting point. To evaluate the phenomenon further we need to identify the degree of discrepancy by various groups and segments of the society, and the relationship of the formalism to other variables in the political and administrative setting.

[11] Richard S. Childs, *Civic Victory: The Story of an Unfinished Revolution*, (New York: Harper, 1952), p. 148.

[12] For an insightful and critical appraisal of Childs' philosophy in relation to the council-manager plan see John Porter East, *Council-Manager Government: The Political Thought of Its Founder, Richard S. Childs* (Chapel Hill: University of North Carolina Press, 1965). Also see Childs' rejoinder in "Critique of a Critique," *National Civic Review*, LIV, No. 8 (September, 1965), pp. 454–55.

[13] *The Municipal Yearbook, 1967, op. cit.*, pp. 108.

[14] Fred W. Riggs, *Administration in Developing Countries: The Theory of Prismatic Society* (Boston: Houghton Mifflin, 1964), pp. 15–19. We might also note that the reporting of the degree of partisan participation in manager cities by the city manager is subject to bias in the direction of minimizing the probable partisan participation.

Table 1

PARTISAN POLITICAL PATTERNS IN U.S.
COUNCIL-MANAGER CITIES OVER 100,000

	Percentages (N = 45)
Partisan elections for city council	13
Party affiliation of the mayor generally known	71
Party organizations actively interested in mayoral elections	60
Party affiliations of council candidates generally known	53
Party organizations actively interested in council elections	47
Type of involvement of parties:	
screen candidates	16
public endorsement	27
active campaigning	29
party leaders participate	31

Examples may be given briefly. Differences of 35 to 50 percentage points between official and unofficial partisanship are probably not large and create few tensions when we consider: (1) that a highly knowledgeable respondent is the judge, (2) that differences between the prescribed and the practiced may approach 100 per cent in some or many circumstances, and (3) that the discrepancy approaches zero when we compare formal partisanship (13 per cent) with the normal party function of nomination. Screen candidates appear in only 16 per cent of the cities. Analysis of the formalism dimension as an independent variable revealed few close associations with other political, policy, or administrative variables. In short, while some formalism is present in the political setting of manager cities, it appears to be relatively small and not overlapping with other political and non-political characteristics.

The presence of moderate partisanship in manager cities should not surprise us. It slightly mutes criticisms from political scientists who contend that the manager plan makes for sterile politics and acts as a depressant on voter participation and leader responsibility.[15] Bypassing questions of association and causation

[15] Oliver P. Williams and Charles R. Adrian, *Four Cities: A Study in Comparative Policy Making* (Philadelphia: University of Pennsylvania Press, 1963); Charles R. Adrian, "Leadership and Decision-Making in Manager Cities: A Study of Three Communities," *Public Administration Review*, XVIII, No. 3 (Summer, 1958), 208–13. An analysis of the impact of governmental structure (as well as other variables) on

we instead raise a more general problem: What is the overall complexion of group participation in city politics?

The categories for characterizing the complexion of group
involvement are threefold, one of which, partisanship, has already
been mentioned. The other two correspond directly with the political ethos categories that Wilson and Banfield term "public-regardingness" and "private-regardingness." [16] These concepts refer to
motivational and perceptual outlooks of participants in local politics. The former is described as being disposed to favor and make
choices on rather abstract conceptions of "the public interest" or
universal as opposed to particularistic criteria. This outlook is
found most widely distributed in middle and upper income
groups. "Private-regardingness" applies to persons whose participation in politics has a greater orientation toward self-interest, narrowly conceived. These two political ethics are best described by
Banfield and Wilson in their own terms:

> Although logically all of these cleavages—between the haves and
> have-nots, the suburbanites and the central city, the natives and the
> immigrants, and the major political parties—are separate and often
> cross-cutting, there is a tendency for them to coalesce into two opposed
> patterns. These patterns reflect two conceptions of the public interest
> that are widely held. The first, which derives from the middle-class
> ethos, favors what the municipal reform movement has always defined
> as "good government"—namely efficiency, impartiality, honesty, plan-
> ning, strong executives, no favoritism, model legal codes, and strict en-
> forcement of laws against gambling and vice. The other conception of
> the public interest (one never explicitly formulated as such, but one
> all the same) derives from the "immigrant ethos." This is the conception
> of those people who identify with the ward or neighborhood rather than
> the city "as a whole," who look to politicians for "help" and "favors,"
> who regard gambling and vice as, at worst, necessary evils, and who are
> far less interested in the efficiency, impartiality, and honesty of local

---

voter turnout in cities over 25,000 indicates that the mean turnout (per cent of
registrants voting) in council-manager cities was 41 per cent compared to 57 per
cent in nonmanager cities: Robert R. Alford and Eugene C. Lee, "Voting Turnout
in American Cities," *American Political Science Review*, LXII, No. 3 (September,
1968), pp. 796–813. Results consistent with this finding also appear in Eugene C.
Lee, "City Elections: A Statistical Profile, *The Municipal Year Book, 1963* (Chicago:
International City Managers' Association, 1963), pp. 74–84.

[16] James Q. Wilson, "Planning and Politics: Citizen Participation in Urban
Renewal," *Journal of The American Institute of Planners*, XXIX, No. 4 (November,
1963), 242–49; James Q. Wilson and Edward C. Banfield, "Public-Regardingness as a
Value Premise in Voting Behavior," *American Political Science Review*, LVIII, No.
4 (December, 1964), 876–87.

government than in its readiness to confer material benefits of one sort or another upon them.[17]

Wilson and Banfield analyzed voting behavior in several cities' referenda and found that many voters voted against their own self-interest.[18] They concluded that a measure of public-regarding-ness was an underlying explanatory concept for this behavior and that income level and type ethnic identification were important contributors to a greater or lesser degree of public-regardingness.

Our survey of council-manager cities could not consider voting behavior of the populace directly. We did attempt to recognize the public-regarding dimension through the medium of group participation in council elections and bond referenda. Table 2 furnishes findings on the extent and character of group participation in the survey cities according to the public-private political ethics.

Roughly one-third to one-half of the cities report various types of public-regarding groups involved in elections and referenda. About 80 per cent of the cities have at least one of the three public-regarding groups active in local civic affairs. There is no dearth of group involvement on the private-regarding side. Most notable is the frequency of labor union involvement in these cities. To some extent labor's participation is probably a surrogate for more partisanship on the local scene. Labor union connection with the Democratic party in urban areas is well known and documented.[19] Labor activism also suggests the potential greater polarization of issues among the private-regarding groups, e.g., Chamber of Commerce vs. Unions. This coincides with Lincoln Smith's contention that social class, status, and stratification are more

[17] Edward C. Banfield and James Q. Wilson, *City Politics* (Cambridge: Harvard University Press and The M.I.T. Press, 1963), p. 46.

[18] Wilson and Banfield, *op. cit.*; for a critique of the Wilson and Banfield thesis concerning public-regardingness see Raymond E. Wolfinger and John Osgood Field, "Political Ethos and the Structure of City Government," *American Political Science Review*, LX, No. 2 (June, 1966), 306–26; and also the exchange under "Communications to The Editor," LX (December, 1966), 998–1000.

[19] Nicholas A. Masters, "The Politics of Union Endorsement of Candidates in the Detroit Area," *Midwest Journal of Political Science*, I, No. 2 (August, 1957), 136–50; Nicholas A. Masters and Deil S. Wright, "Trends and Variations in the Two-Party Vote: The Case of Michigan," *American Political Science Review*, LII, No. 4 (December, 1958), 1078–90; Harold L. Sheppard and Nicholas A. Masters, "The Political Attitudes and Preferences of Union Members: The Case of the Detroit Auto Workers," *American Political Science Review*, LIII, No. 2 (June, 1959), 437–47.

Table 2

PARTICIPATION BY SELECTED GROUPS IN COUNCIL-MANAGER CITIES OVER 100,000

	Council Elections		Local Bond Referenda		
	Frequency of Involvement: Often or Occasionally	*Type of Involvement: Financial or Active Campaigning*	*Involvement and Position Taken*		*Type of Involvement: Financial or Active Campaigning*
			For	*Against*	
		(Percentages; *N* = 45)			
Public-Regarding Groups					
Good Government Association	33	27	24	—	20
League of Women Voters	31	4	47	—	27
Council-Manager Association	18	11	7	—	4
Private-Regarding Groups					
Labor Unions	78	47	42	2	24
Neighborhood Associations	56	22	29	7	25
Chamber of Commerce	42	4	73	4	44
Taxpayers' Organization	36	15	18	18	24
Racial Groups	4	4	—	—	—

sharply delineated in local communities than elsewhere in U.S. society.[20] If this is the case, then estimates of who benefits and who loses in local affairs are more clearly perceived by the active citizenry. But presence of a formal politico-administrative structure such as the council-manager plan may moderate or shift the civic agenda and the public's focus away from the real and/or perceived cleavages.[21]

The involvement of "public interest" groups indicates the distinctive impact of efforts to elevate the level of local elections above special interest and political party considerations. These groups also reflect the reform legacy present in the origins of the manager plan. Participation of special interest groups such as chambers of commerce, taxpayers' associations, and labor unions attest to the legitimacy of parochial interests in articulating their concerns at the local level. In addition, the active role played by parties, despite the preponderance of formal nonpartisanship, furnishes an alternative and somewhat subordinated means of interest aggregation. The party's non-ideological and instrumental role filters citizen and candidate considerations through a traditional but somewhat tarnished (locally) political mechanism.

We have identified the active presence of three political group orientations in most of these council-manager cities: public, private, and partisan. From the standpoint of political development and comparative analysis we can observe *at the electoral input level* what Pye has termed "separating the partisan and the nonpartisan in politics." [22] Pye referred to this problem as "one prime issue which rests at the heart of nation-building in most new countries. This is the issue of the management of diversity and

---

[20] Lincoln Smith, "The Manager System and Collectivism," *American Journal of Economics and Sociology,* XXIV, No. 1 (January, 1965), 21–38.

[21] Lineberry and Fowler find that in "reformed" cities, i.e., those with the council-manager form of government, there is reduced "responsiveness" to socioeconomic cleavages in the population. That is, compared with cities with other forms of government the association between tax efforts and expenditure efforts in relationship to social cleavage and heterogeneity variables, the correlations are higher in the unreformed or mayor-council governed cities than in the reformed cities that are governed by the council-manager plan. Robert L. Lineberry and Edmund P. Fowler, "Reformism and Public Policies in American Cities," *American Political Science Review,* LXI, No. 3 (September, 1967), 701–16.

[22] Lucian W. Pye, *Aspects of Political Development* (Boston: Little, Brown, 1966), p. 23.

unity, more specifically the need to relate the parochial and the universal." [23] One difficulty associated with the pervasive partisan or private coloring to politics in developing countries is the crisis it poses for leaders, compelling them to overcompensate in claiming the absolute primacy of universal or public interests over particular, parochial, and partisan interests. Leaders feel impelled to suppress or inhibit expressions or threats to universalistic standards as they see them.

In these cities we observe the presence and clash of universal, particular, and partisan positions in the campaign and voting arenas. Leadership, whether mayor, manager, city council, or all these collectively, is therefore absolved from laying sole and unique claim to the public (city) interest. These data document the legitimacy and institutionalization of particular, partisan, and universal interests. We cannot claim that council-manager cities have an exclusive claim in this respect. But they do reveal for purposes of illustration and analysis a core area of concern in dealing with development issues, the contingent and reciprocal relationship between pluralistic politics and governmental forms.

Communications generally and mass media in particular, have been recognized for their important role in political development.[24] Our survey was incapable of exploring communication processes. We did obtain, however, estimates of the involvement, quality of coverage, and influence of the mass media on city matters. The data we gathered relate only tangentially to many issues raised in political development literature, e.g., the structure of communication processes, objectivity of the mass media, the roles of media professionals, and the relation of mass communications to socialization. Our results from some questions posed do permit the brief exploration of one analogous issue (see Table 3).

That the mass media are relevant for and involved in politics is taken as an axiom. Our results, while disclosing substantial involvement, are perhaps as noteworthy for the fact that they do not reveal uniform or invariably high involvement. This suggests the "semi-politicized" character of the mass media and offers a coun-

[23] *Ibid., idem.*
[24] *Ibid.*, chap. VIII; and Pye (ed.), *Communications and Political Development* (Princeton, N.J.: Princeton University Press, 1963).

Table 3

THE MASS MEDIA IN U.S. COUNCIL-MANAGER
CITIES OVER 100,000

	Type of Media		
	Press	Radio	Television
		(percentages)	
Existence of the Medium Covering City Affairs	100	96	80
Often or Occasionally Involved in Council Elections	80	44	44
Public Endorsement of Council Candidates	78	30	28
Involved in Local Bond Referenda	87	75	80
Quality of Coverage: Rated as "excellent" by City Manager	51	28	31
Media Influence: Rated as "highly influential" by City Manager	51	2	8
N =	45	43	36

terpoint to findings concerning the near total immersion of mass
media in politics in developing areas.[25] The meshing of mass media with politics dilutes, if not destroys, an image that in some
degree is deemed necessary for developmental purposes, namely,
the appearance of objective and detached channels of information.

Some substitute measures of detachment are presented in city
managers' evaluation of the quality of media coverage. Coverage
is rated "excellent" in only about half of the cities for newspapers
and drops below one-third for radio and television. Furthermore,
the managers' perception of the media's influence on city issues in
no way corresponds to a seamless web of relations connecting politics and mass communication channels.

It is more than incidentally interesting to see the managers'
different views of the three media. The press stands out as the more
politicized member of the triumvirate. It is more involved, the
quality of its coverage is rated excellent in more cities, and it is
identified as highly influential in over half the cities. The proportions are in sharp contrast to those for the electronic media.

The managers' contrasting perspectives and evaluations of

[25] Pye, *Aspects of Political Development, op. cit.,* and also *Communications and
Political Development, op. cit.*

the three mass media furnish some insights into a major problem of development currently facing U.S. cities: civil unrest, disorders, and riots. It would be interesting, but beyond the scope of this chapter to explore the parallel concrete and analytic problems presented by developing nations and the "depressed" sectors of our rural areas and urban complexes. The six crises of political development described by Pye—identity, legitimacy, distribution, penetration, participation, and integration—would furnish exemplary starting points. All present greater or lesser degrees of crisis conditions to which our political institutions are expected to respond. Cities are currently confronted with substantial population segments that lack (but are finding) political identity, question the legitimacy of constituted authority, react negatively to the distribution of public benefits and burdens, fail to find effective channels for participation, and reject the nature and extent of public penetration into their daily lives, e.g., the police and social workers.

The mass media are important instruments in dealing with these crises but the results reported in Table 3 raise serious questions about media patterns and development in U.S. cities. The press is clearly closest to and for many purposes functions as an active part of local government. Norton Long has offered succinct observations on the press's public interest and public agenda-setting roles.

> Despite the built-in incapacity of newspapers to exercise serious governing responsibility for their territories, they are for the most part the only institutions with a long-term general territorial interest. In default of a territorial political party or other institution that accepts responsibility for the formulation of a general civic agenda the newspaper is the one game that by virtue of its public and its conventions partly fills the vacuum.[26]

In contrast to the daily press's role and relationship to established authorities is its small and slight impact on ghetto areas. A recent study reported that only 14 per cent of the households in a ghetto area subscribed to a daily newspaper.[27] The press simply does not reach the ghetto and city managers or other local leaders are

---

[26] Norton E. Long, "The Local Community as an Ecology of Games," *American Journal of Sociology*, LXIV, No. 3 (November, 1958), 260-61.

[27] *New York Times*, October 13, 1967, p. 26.

greatly mistaken if they assume that newspapers, where the bulk of political mass communication appears, are transmitting to all relevant publics.

The least politicized media, radio and television, exist to entertain in a way that newspapers do not. Local news, the core content of the press, is put in a restrictive format by radio and television and when the latter media do feature local concerns, they are cast in the most dramatic form with all the sense of immediacy that the instantaneous media can convey. The consequences of these contrasts for political leadership and for development are significant when seen in the context of the following considerations.

First, the electronic media are the chief channels of mass communication to the politically and socially alienated low-income groups. In his study of the Watts (Los Angeles) riots Robert Conot reports, for example, that to a ghetto family, "TV sets aren't considered negotiables. They are necessities." [28] Second, these channels are least used for conveying information about city activities and programs. Third, the power of instantaneous communication can serve as an inciting and exacerbating influence on the spread of rioting. Note the following invitation of a television cameraman to a Negro youth during the preriot stage of the Watts conflagration: "Hey, kid! Throw a rock! Throw one! I haven't seen you do anything yet!" [29] Fourth, the identified detachment and non-politicized nature of these two media reduce the political claims on them or constraints they feel in reporting on community affairs.[30]

Recent disorders, media behavior, and these data raise the

[28] Robert Conot, *Rivers of Blood, Years of Darkness* (New York: Bantam Books, 1967), p. 77.

[29] *Ibid.*, p. 51.

[30] Contrast the roles of radio and television with the following episode concerning the role of the press in one city. A city hall reporter-sleuth found that a local bank was uniformly rejecting loan applications from low-income ethnic areas but was consistently referring them to a certain local finance company. The finance company, charging usurious rates and getting its clients "hooked" on interest, had a covert partner, the recently elected city mayor. A vice-president of the bank making the initial referrals also happened to be a brother-in-law of the mayor. Armed with iron-clad information and supporting evidence, the publisher of the local daily newspaper confronted the mayor in private with the sordid story. The publisher extracted from the errant executive a firm promise to "shape up" and to work for the city's best interest (as seen by the publisher) in return for the publisher not exposing the politically damaging information.

opposite question to that posed by media roles in developing countries. The mass media may be too politicized and non-objective elsewhere in the world but in U.S. "developing areas" we might well query whether certain media are not too detached, insensitively objective, and insufficiently politicized. It is not our point to urge particular strategies for bridging the gap between the media, the masses, and the leadership of city government.[31] Whatever strategy or policy is pursued, it is necessary to take into account the roles that are played by the city executive in relation to developmental concerns generally.

DEVELOPMENTAL ROLES OF CITY MANAGERS

The behavior of city managers is posited as being fully and exhaustively characterized by three role categories: managerial, policy, and political. Any one manager's actions and relationships are a composite of these roles, although at this preliminary stage of dealing with the data we will confine our attention primarily to marginal distributions.

Our analysis is limited in at least three important respects. First, we are restricted by the strong structural-descriptive nature of the data. Second, the more dynamic and interactive aspects are limited to self-perceptions of these roles by the manager. Third, we do not have data on role expectations by relevant persons in the manager's role set.[32] The only role "norms" available are the general and somewhat shifting views of advocates and critics of the council-manager plan.

Our choice in focusing on the roles of the manager derives from an important formal and presumed behavioral condition. The council-manager form of government purportedly attempts to draw a clear line between and to set in sharpest apposition an

[31] Robert Paul Boynton and Deil S. Wright, "Is Anybody Up There Listening?" *Public Management*, L, No. 3 (March, 1968), 57–61; and also an unpublished paper by the same authors, "The Media, the Masses, and Urban Management."

[32] Robert L. Kahn *et al.*, *Organizational Stress: Studies in Role Conflict and Ambiguity* (New York: Wiley, 1964), pp. 13–14.

elected legislative body and an administrative bureaucracy. Interposed between this confrontation of the legislative body with the bureaucracy is the position of the city manager. While he is normally called an executive, this conventional designation fails to convey the variety, complexity, and paradoxes present in his position. The manager appears to be a powerful professional but a weak political leader. He seems dependent on the council for policy direction through their absolute control over his tenure. Yet the council often appears to take its cues from the manager on policy matters.

The manager plan juxtaposes a rational structure that is (or intends to be) administration within a larger irrational matrix represented by the pressures of political change. The interface among these forces of relative stability and dynamic change is supplied by the city manager. His role telescopes into a single position conflicting public demands, varied social strains, and shifting community tensions. His total role is analogous to a large transformer in an electric supply system; he regulates the current flow and alters the voltage. In addition he may even supply additional power and change the amperage on his own initiative.

• *Managerial Role*

From a purely descriptive standpoint what are the most representative features of the manager's managerial role? The figures in Table 4 provide indicators of the presence or absence of certain administrative characteristics in the sample cities.

The capacity of the manager to control the bureaucracy is linked to his abilities to secure information, allocate resources, and impose sanctions (or grant rewards). It is apparent from the tabled percentages under the staffing and budgeting categories that the bulk of these cities offer managers ample opportunities for asserting their influence on the bureaucracy. For example, in less than 10 per cent of the cities are there two or more agencies whose budgets are *not* reviewed and revised by the managers. These data suggest the limited presence of three features of financial administration identified by Fred Riggs as present in prismatic societies:

Table 4

MANAGEMENT ROLES OF CITY MANAGERS IN U.S.
COUNCIL-MANAGER CITIES OVER 100,000

	Percentages *(N = 45)*
Staffing	
Manager's office has professional staff	84
(Median staff size: 2 professionals)	
Professional budgeting staff	78
(Median number: 3)	
Six or more agency heads *not* appointed by the city manager	38
(Median number not appointed by manager: 4)	
Budgeting	
Two or more agencies that do not submit their budgets to the manager for review	9
City manager attends budget review sessions	69
Use of general policy guidelines to agencies for developing budget estimates	73
Budget process largely one of independent (non-programmed) decision-making	27
Budget process about equally balanced between making independent decisions and formalizing prior decisions	60
Reporting	
System of administrative performance reporting	62
Hold regular policy review sessions	49
Intervenors	
Elective official having most contact with administrative officials:	
mayor	33
councilman	7
no one stands out	53
Mayor has professional staff	51
Mayor has a limited role in:	
budgeting	22
appointment of agency heads	16
City council members attend budget review sessions	16

bureaucratistic allocations, engrossed (earmarked) revenues, and corners.[33] More importantly, they establish the limited effect of these autonomous influences at the administrative review level,

[33] Fred W. Riggs, *Administration in Developing Countries, op. cit.*, pp. 303–12. For illustrations of the existence of some degree of "Corners" in two U.S. cities and of city managers' efforts to contend with them see: Edwin O. Stene, "Seven Letters: A Case in Public Management," *Public Administration Review*, XVII, No. 2 (Spring, 1957), 83–90; and Ruth McQuown, William R. Hamilton, and Michael P. Schneider, *The Political Restructuring of a Community* (Gainesville: Public Administration Clearing Service, University of Florida, 1964).

one step prior to legislative consideration. In this respect the manager plan appears to be the most differentiated structure of several governmental forms employed in a diffracted society. It represents political development; although some see it as eufunctional, others view it as dysfunctional.[34]

The budget process, when institutionalized, is a means of achieving two interrelated managerial goals: (1) rationalization of means with objectives and (2) a mechanism of control over the attainment of the objectives. Budgeting is institutionalized in large manager cities; nearly four-fifths of them have separately designated staff to handle budget review and execution. The remaining cities use special personnel on a part-time basis to assist in the more routine aspects of budgeting. These city administrative systems, then, fall in Fred Riggs's category of complex bureaucracies, i.e., where multiplicity of command is widely institutionalized.[35]

To what extent is budgeting a process of independent decision-making as contrasted with the formalization of prior arrangements and agreements? To the extent that the former description applies, budgeting emphasizes the structured, deliberate, and *de novo* review of choices in the resource allocation process. The degree to which the latter dominates reduces the significance of the budget process and shifts attention to decision arenas elsewhere in the policy process. Of course, we might anticipate that neither emphasis would be complete and total for all possible fiscal choices. We were simply searching for the predominance of one pattern more than the other and found the dominance of *de novo* decision-making in 27 per cent of the cases. In 60 per cent of the cases the managers thought their budget processes were about evenly divided between the two patterns. These results suggest the presence of a hidden and antecedent dimension of budgeting, one which, if validated, would tend to downgrade the presumed critical significance of choice-making in the budget process itself.

[34] Marion J. Levy, Jr., *The Structure of Society* (Princeton, N.J.: Princeton University Press, 1952).

[35] Fred W. Riggs, "The Political Structures of Administrative Development," *op. cit.*, pp. 15–21.

It is interesting to speculate on possible similarities to cities with complex bureaucracies in developing countries. On the one hand, we might anticipate a heavy weighting toward the formalization side, attesting to the pervasive influence of politics in the administrative process.[36] Alternatively, we might suspect that under a highly polarized political situation, or where a single political leader dominates, budget review might function as the prime choice mechanism. These observations suggest hypotheses for testing that might put the local budget process at either of the two extremes in developing nations, rather than concentrated near the mean as in U.S. cities.

Additional aspects of budget decision-making deserve comment. The hallmark of a development-oriented focus in administration is a disposition to change. Our data on budgeting underscore the openness toward change in these cities, although the directions of the change remain unspecified. Nearly three-fourths of the managers report the use of general policy guidelines in budget preparation, opening the way for subordinate initiative in proposing changes. Furthermore, in an additional 16 per cent of the cities the manager indicated he used "few or no guidelines," allowing for the maximum amount of open-ended budgeting.

A curious contrast arises. Financial administration in the sala model of the prismatic society lacks central direction, is characterized by autonomous structures, and contains rigidities obstructing development. In the differentiated administrative model in a diffracted society, the existing differentiation opens the door to greater change. The paradox is that "developed" structures appear to be more capable of further and more rapid development. The explanatory and mathematical model best fitting such developmental patterns would appear to be discontinuous and multiplicative.

A final observation on the budget process draws on organi-

[36] See for example the exchange of views and controversy surrounding the introduction of performance budgeting in the Philippines. Malcolm B. Parsons, "Performance Budgeting in the Philippines," *Public Administration Review*, XVII, No. 3 (Summer, 1957), 173–79; responses appearing in the same journal are to be found in XVIII, No. 1 (Winter, 1958), 43–51; and XVIII, No. 2 (Spring, 1958), 129–32.

zation theory in relation to change processes. We have already identified the extent to which managers view the budget process as one involving primarily independent decision-making (27 per cent) or being about equally balanced between *de novo* choice and the ratification of antecedent decisions made external to the budget process (60 per cent). We think the appropriate and direct conceptual description for this *de novo* decision behavior is what March and Simon call non-programmed decision-making.[37] It also forms the decision base for planning and innovation within administration. The striking feature of our data is that in nearly 90 per cent of these cities budgeting contains a heavy loading of non-programmed decision-making. Despite recent literature and research emphasizing the marginal or incremental character of budgeting we hypothesize that in relative terms, it is less programmed and less incremental in these cities than in the localities of developing nations.[38]

Despite central administrative control accompanied by openness to change, the organizational structures and relational patterns in council-manager cities are not perfect models of monoliths. In a substantial proportion of the cities (38 per cent) the manager does not have appointive authority over several (six or more) department heads. Furthermore, there are both formal and informal means by which mayors and councilmen may become involved with administration—as "intervenors."

The most important intervenor is the mayor. Where the mayor is both popularly elected and has professional staff to assist him he tends to intervene far more in administration than when these structural features are absent. Although particular structural features induce greater mayoral intervention in administration this does not appear to produce a threat or a competitive relationship between the manager and the mayor. In other words, the joint involvement is not a zero-sum game. What Lucian Pye has referred to as the "prior role of administration" could be amended

[37] James G. March and Herbert A. Simon, *Organizations* (New York: Wiley, 1958), esp. chap. 7.

[38] Aaron Wildavsky, *Politics of the Budgetary Process* (Boston: Little, Brown, 1964); Thomas J. Anton, *The Politics of State Expenditure in Illinois* (Urbana: University of Illinois Press, 1966).

to include the pervasiveness of administration in the cities under review.[39]

• *Policy Role*

City managers exercise preponderant authority in the sphere of administration. In what ways and to what extent do managers

Table 5

POLICY ROLES OF CITY MANAGERS IN U.S.
COUNCIL-MANAGER CITIES OVER 100,000

	Percentages ($N = 45$)
Manager responsible for setting city council agenda	69
Less than one-third of policy questions put on council agenda are there at the initiative of someone other than city manager	65
Council aware of original departmental requests as well as manager's recommendations	85
Department or agency heads appear before council on budget matters	53
Three or more program areas examined by council in detail at budget sessions (median number: 3)	62
Two or more program areas in which council discussed basic policy matters at budget sessions (median number: 2)	47
Daily contact by manager:	
mayor	67
councilmen	7
Mayor plays predominant role in:	
proposing policies	20
developing support for policies in council	31
Mayor:	
sets council agenda: formally*	9
sets council agenda: informally**	13
makes policy recommendations to council: formally*	13
makes policy recommendations to council: informally**	40

* has official legal responsibility.
** exercises an important informal role.

assert themselves in policy roles? Some suggestive findings on this issue appear in Table 5. A reminder is perhaps necessary to recall

[39] Pye, *Aspects of Political Development, op. cit.*, p. 14.

that this role is conceptualized in terms of relationships with the city council and the mayor. We explored in some depth two specific aspects of manager-council relationships: the agenda-setting and budget review functions.

The ability to fix the agenda of issues brought before a legislative body is an important gatekeeper function. Sitting athwart the massive information system that constitutes the city bureaucracy the city manager filters the flow of administrative reality and communicates his perceptions of this world to the council.[40] His control over the items included on the council agenda in more than two-thirds of the cities is one indicator of his capacity to fix the boundaries of legislative concerns. But the manager's boundary-defining capabilities are by no means absolute. In about one-third of these cities one-third of the policy questions put before the council are there at the initiative of someone other than the manager. But the obverse proportions (two-thirds of the policy questions in two-thirds of the cities) do clearly establish the manager as the dominant policy initiator in most manager cities.

Corroboration of these findings on the manager's role in policy formulation comes from a separate survey of city managers in all U.S. cities. Of the more than 1,000 managers who responded, 86 per cent agreed with the statement: "On most occasions, the city manager, whether he likes it or not, must lead the council," and 58 per cent concurred with the contention that, "The successful city manager is the major policy formulator for his city government." [41]

With the manager assuming predominance in policy initiative, how does the council respond? Taking the budget as major mechanism for the expression of policy choices, we looked at selected aspects of council budget review.

Procedurally, we inquired about council awareness of original departmental requests before the manager revised and/or reduced them. We also asked if department heads explained and defended their departmental requests (and manager's recommendations) directly to the council. The rationale for these questions was the

<hr/>

[40] See March and Simon, *op. cit.*, pp. 164–66 for a discussion of the "Absorption of Uncertainty."

[41] Robert Paul Boynton, *Code: The City Manager and His Profession* (Iowa City: Institute of Public Affairs, University of Iowa), pp. 48, 50.

attempt to locate possible opinion alternatives and communication channels to the council other than those through the city manager. Indicators on two aspects of manager-council relationships were sought: (1) the potential for council exploration of policy alternatives beyond those regularly delineated by the manager,[42] and (2) some gauge of the power of lower participants in an organizational system.[43]

On the substantive side, we posed questions of how much detailed review the council afforded the manager's budget and how much of this review involved policy questions. We aimed at obtaining direct responses on the extent to which policy matters are explored in the council's budget review.

The results (Table 5) suggest that procedurally there is considerable opportunity for the council to examine policy questions and exploit possible differences of opinion. When actual review occurred, however, the council did not exercise its policy prerogatives extensively. It reviewed a median of three programs in detail and a median of two that raised basic policy matters. In about half the cities the councils raised policy questions in two or more program areas; in one-third of the cities no policy issues were raised during the budget review.

These findings further document the dominance of the manager in his administrative role and also lay bare the charge that the manager employs the budget as a means for manipulating the council into following his policy preferences. Three important qualifications suggest that the council performs something more than a ratifying or gadfly role in policy matters. First, we have already noted that budgeting is to some extent the servant of

[42] David A. Booth, "Are Elected Mayors a Threat to Managers?" *Administrative Science Quarterly*, XII, No. 4 (March, 1968), 572–89. Booth's survey of managers in small cities (2,500–10,000) found that approximately three fourths of the managers followed what he termed a "traditional" course of action in presenting major alternatives to the council. This consisted of presenting several rather than one recommendation to the council with supporting data and indicating the particular solution that the manager favors. Robert Paul Boynton's survey indicates that a slightly higher percentage (84) of the city managers follow the practice of outlining several alternative courses of action with the manager recommending the single alternative which to him appears best or most feasible. Boynton, *op. cit.,* p. 50.

[43] David Mechanic, "Sources of Power of Lower Participants in Complex Organizations," in William W. Cooper, Harold J. Leavitt, and Maynard W. Shelly II (eds.), *New Perspectives in Organization Research* (New York: Wiley, 1964), pp. 136–49.

policy made outside the routine of the budget process—all budgeting may be policy but all policy is not budgeting. Second, budgeting is incremental, even though a major part of it may be non-programmed. Its incremental character, particularly during the period between shift-points or discontinuities, is not likely to produce such significant changes so as to draw the attention, concern, and in-depth exploration by the council.[44] Third, the law of anticipated reactions applies. The manager's budget may not be altered an iota or reviewed in depth because he has accurately guessed council sentiments. Of course, the gaming can become rather sophisticated, as witnessed by the following comment by a manager who operated in a strongly partisan city: "In an election year, no matter who has a council majority, I always add on an extra percentage on the budget as insurance—for them and me; it's insurance for them at the ballot box because they can cut more and it's insurance for me in operating the programs next year!"

The city manager is occasionally compelled to share his policy role with the mayor. Whether such a sharing does or does not exist, the presence of a person officially designated as mayor requires some normalized relationship between the manager and the mayor and additionally, between the mayor and the council. In most cities the mayor clearly serves as the chief and regular channel through whom the manager initiates policy input and receives feedback in the form of wider political intelligence (Table 5). In less than one-third of the cities, however, can the manager count on the mayor for predominance in proposing policies or working hard to develop support among councilmen for a policy.

One explanation for the mayor's limited policy role is his weak formal position. Only in a very small number of cities is the mayor given, for example, formal legal responsibility for setting the council agenda or making policy recommendations to the legislative body. On an informal basis the mayor performs the recommendatory function in a substantially greater proportion

[44] Otto A. Davis, M.A.H. Dempster, and Aaron Wildavsky, "A Theory of the Budgetary Process," *American Political Science Review*, LX, No. 3 (September, 1966), 529–47.

(40 per cent) of the cities, although he is "predominant" in proposing policies in only 20 per cent.

An examination of the mayor's policy role in relation to his method of election revealed a positive association between the mayor's exercise of policy leadership and his popular election. This finding is somewhat at variance with a recent study of small council-manager cities. The conclusion drawn from that survey was that popular election of the mayor did not constitute a "threat" to managers in their policy leadership roles.[45] Our results suggest the opposite conclusion, that manager-mayor relations in the policy sphere tend toward a zero-sum game. The more initiative exercised by one, the less exercised by the other. Whether these contrasting results are a function of size or some other variables remains to be explored.[45a] At present, the city manager is the more predominant policy figure in most of these large cities. The mayor's role seems to be one that requires only lateral clearance before the manager initiates and builds support for policies.

• *Political Role*

The political role of the city manager has usually been expressed in popular parlance as "community leadership." We divided this general concept into two major dimensions and developed operational measures of managerial relationships external to the city government as an organizational system. The two dimensions were: (1) horizontal and (2) vertical.[46] Horizontal

[45] David A. Booth, "Are Elected Mayors a Threat to Managers?" *op. cit.*, p. 589. For results contrary to those of Booth and consistent with those indicated here see Williams and Adrian, *op. cit.*, p. 297, and Gladys M. Kammerer, "Role Diversity of City Managers," *Administrative Science Quarterly*, VIII, No. 4, (March, 1964), pp. 421–442.

[45a] Subsequent analysis of these data as well as a reexamination of the Kammerer and Booth studies cast considerable doubt on the accuracy of the competitive or zero-sum relationship between the manager and the mayor. In other words, the Booth findings and interpretations appear more valid and consistent with a closer analysis of these large city data. See Robert Paul Boynton and Deil S. Wright, "Policy Formation in Large Council-Manager Cities: Manager-Mayor Relationships," paper prepared for delivery at the Midwest Conference of Political Scientists, Ann Arbor, Michigan, April 24–26, 1969.

[46] Usage of these two terms is identical to that employed by Roland Warren, *The Community in America* (Chicago: Rand McNally, 1963). See also John Walton,

relationships are those lateral and boundary-spanning exchanges involving the manager in contacts with non-governmental groups and individuals within the city. Vertical relationships are those in which the manager has contacts with persons from superordinate levels of government, namely, officials of state and national governments. From the standpoint of organization theory these relationships fall within the scope of interorganizational analysis.[47] In more conventional but researchably imprecise terms the dimensions could be called: (1) manager-community relations, and (2) intergovernmental relations.

Our first interest was to explore communication channels from the city manager outward. To what extent do administrative officials in general and the manager in particular speak to groups on important and controversial issues? How notable a community figure is the manager through the mass media? Despite the limits of our research instrument and focus, we also sought data on where political information is located and how it is channeled to the manager.

The findings on community communication establish the city administration and the manager as involved participants in horizontal relationships in a substantial proportion of cities (Table 6). Active participation by the manager in speaking to groups occurs in more than three-fourths of the cities. In 40 per cent of the cities he is judged to be the most quoted city official in the local media. The mayor appears as the featured municipal officer in less than one-third of the cities.

"The Vertical Axis of Community Organization and the Structure of Power," *Southwestern Social Science Quarterly*, XLVIII, No. 3 (December, 1967), 353–68; and in the same issue, Roland L. Warren, "A Note on Walton's Analysis of Power Structure and Vertical Ties," pp. 369–72.

[47] Eugene Litwak and Lydia F. Hylton, "Interorganizational Analysis: A Hypothesis on Coordinating Agencies," *Administrative Science Quarterly*, VI, No. 4 (March, 1962), 385–420; Sol Levine and Paul E. White, "Exchange as a Conceptual Framework for the Study of Interorganizational Relationships," *Administrative Science Quarterly*, V, No. 4 (March, 1961), 583–601; Sol Levine, Paul White, and Benjamin D. Paul, "Community Interorganizational Problems in Providing Medical Care and Social Services," *American Journal of Public Health*, LIII, No. 8 (August, 1963), 1183–95; Burton R. Clark, "Interorganizational Patterns in Education," *Administrative Science Quarterly*, X, No. 2 (September, 1965), 224–37; Roland L. Warren, "The Interaction of Community Decision Organizations: Some Basic Concepts and Needed Research," *Social Science Review*, XLI (September, 1967), 261–70; and Roland L. Warren, "The Interorganizational Field as a Focus of Investigation," *Administrative Science Quarterly*, XII, No. 3 (December, 1967), 395–420.

Table 6

POLITICAL ROLES OF CITY MANAGERS IN U.S.
COUNCIL-MANAGER CITIES OVER 100,000

	Percentages (N = 45)
Horizontal Relationships	
City has a policy of encouraging administrative officials to give talks on important city programs	82
Manager speaks on controversial issues before groups, associations, etc.	76
Manager is the most quoted city official in local media	40
Mayor is the most quoted city official in local media	29
Manager holds formal press conferences	27
Major political leader is community is:	
mayor	16
person outside city government	49
no single person stands out	31
Official with closest contact to local political party leaders:	
mayor	27
manager	2
councilman	18
no single person stands out	44
Elective official most often consulted by manager on political issues:	
mayor	56
councilman	2
no one stands out	42
Manager's estimate of advice and information on political issues:	
fully informed	33
moderately informed	53
Vertical Relationships	
State government:	
Frequency of contact: more often than monthly	24
Uncooperative officials	12
Limited or no results	24
National government:	
Frequency of contact: more often than monthly	14
Uncooperative	6
Limited or no results	12
City officials having most contact with	
Elected local officials: mayor	53
manager	16
Appointed local officials: manager	71
Elected state officials: mayor	33
manager	31
Appointed state officials: manager	53
National elected officials: mayor	51
manager	18
National administrative officials: manager	49

The role of the manager all but disappears, however, when we examine the locus, transmission, and receipt of political intelligence within the city. The city manager identifies political leadership as located in no single person or else outside city government in all but 16 per cent of the cities. In nearly half of the cities the mayor or a councilman provide the chief means of contact with whatever political leadership exists. The mayor in a majority of cities, however, clearly emerges as the main channel for the manager to obtain political intelligence. Finally, managers in all but a few cities are reasonably well informed by the readings they obtain on political affairs.

The responding managers defined for themselves what constituted "full" or "moderate" information levels on political issues. This subjective measure, although unavoidable, is nevertheless an indicator of the confidence the manager enjoys in pressing for various policies. The manager's assessment of his awareness about the political pulse of the community may be objectively in error. But the assurance he enjoys in proceeding on a supposedly well informed basis is as important to the policy initiatives he takes as it is to the eventual policy outcomes.

It would be interesting to compare judgments of information adequacy among administrators in developing nations. The possibility appears deceptively simple, but at least three cross-cultural variables would require measurement and partialling. One would be a measure of expected information levels prior to governmental action. A second would be the time span or longitudinal expectations of the official regarding the long range–short range consequences of the action under consideration. A third difficult hurdle would be the locating of comparable decisions with respect to significance and function.

Two general and interrelated conclusions follow from this discussion of the horizontal political roles of the city manager. First, the manager plays an active and self-assured role in initiating politically relevant communications to the community. In this respect he seems to perform an outward-oriented "linking pin" role between the city as an organization and its larger community environment.[48] The reverse flow of information from the com-

[48] Rensis Likert, *New Patterns of Management* (New York: McGraw-Hill, 1961).

munity to city government, however, is not directly or extensively channeled to the manager. These comments bear indirectly on a question of considerable currency: What is the representational role of administrative officials? [49] From these data on city managers we suggest that in their horizontal (community or external) relationships administrators are advocates or representatives of the city (and its policies) to the public. But these managers are highly restricted in the extent to which they can lay claim to privileged intelligence about the preferred sentiments of the community at large. The city manager is a prominent representative *of* the city to politically aware and active segments of the community. His political role is narrowly circumscribed when analyzed in terms of speaking *for* a composite of community interests on policy matters.

Beyond the local community lie a variety of contacts that have been described as vertical or intergovernmental. [50] Our primary focus was on the interactions between cities and the state and national governments. We also attempted to identify selective patterns of intergovernmental contact by type of official.

The frequency and character of the city manager's contacts with state and national governments are identified under vertical relationships in Table 6. Contacts with the state government lay claim to managerial time at least once a month in about one-fourth of the cities. In about half that proportion of the cities the manager finds state officials not cooperative while the proportion of managers expressing disappointment over the payoffs from

[49] J. Donald Kingsley, *Representative Bureaucracy* (Yellow Springs, Ohio: Antioch Press, 1944); Norton Long, "Bureaucracy and Constitutionalism," *American Political Science Review*, XLVI, No. 3 (September, 1952), 808–18; Herbert Kaufman, "Emerging Conflicts in the Doctrines of Public Administration," *American Political Science Review*, L, No. 4 (December, 1956), 1057–73; Robert S. Friedman, Bernard W. Klein, and John H. Romani, "Administrative Agencies and the Publics They Serve," *Public Administration Review*, XXVI, No. 3 (September, 1966), 192–204; V. Subramaniam, "Representative Bureaucracy: A Re-assessment." *American Political Science Review*, LXI, No. 4 (December, 1967), 1010–19; and Frederick C. Mosher, *Democracy and the Public Service* (New York: Oxford University Press, 1968), pp. 10–14.

[50] William Anderson, *Intergovernmental Relations in Review* (Minneapolis: University of Minnesota Press, 1960). See also Commission on Intergovernmental Relations, *Report to the President for Transmittal to Congress* (Washington: U.S. Government Printing Office, 1955), and the reports of the permanent Advisory Commission on Intergovernmental Relations (Washington: U.S. Government Printing Office, 1959–68).

state-local contacts approaches one-fourth. The mere frequency of contact, of course, is not a valid indicator of significance. We were unable to obtain qualitative judgments on the overall importance of intergovernmental contacts but we did request the manager to indicate the three "most important and crucial" programs on which the city had contacts with the state or national governments. The programs mentioned most frequently as the subjects of these state contacts were highways, legal authorizations, and finances. The program areas mentioned as the primary basis of national-local contacts were urban renewal, welfare, and highways. These program designations attest to the general importance of these vertical relationships. It has also been contended, with some apparent accuracy, that the professionalized administrative capabilities of the city manager make him more adept in learning about and obtaining external financial support for local programs.[51]

A comparison of the proportions on the contact, cooperativeness, and result measures between national and state jurisdictions reveals an almost exact doubling of each proportion for the state over the national responses. Twice as many city managers experienced monthly contacts, uncooperative officials, and unsatisfactory results in their dealings with state governments than in their dealings with the national government. The differences jibe with a large number of observations and documented findings noting that large cities in the U.S. are better represented and obtain a more sympathetic hearing from the national government than from their respective state governments.[52]

The legal dominance of the state government over its cities and local jurisdictions is a well established fact. The opportunity to bypass the states through political and administrative channels, however, is an indicator of the slack, looseness, and relative openness of the U.S. multijurisdictional system.[53] From a developmental standpoint the existence of at least two viable superordinate jurisdictions affords the local unit an opportunity to engage in coali-

---

[51] Morton Grodzins, *The American System: A New View of Government in the United States* (Chicago: Rand McNally, 1966).

[52] *Ibid.*, Roscoe C. Martin, *The Cities and the Federal System* (New York: Atherton, 1965).

[53] William Anderson, *The Nation and the States, Rivals or Partners?* (Minneapolis: University of Minnesota Press, 1955).

tion-oriented behavior that is unavailable in a two-person (or two-jurisdiction) setting. The foundations for and explanation of such coalition behavior have been considered obliquely by several scholars.[54] Among the explanatory factors mentioned as supportive of the multijurisdictional coalition-based system are legal guarantees, political processes, fiscal independence, and administrative autonomy. There are also some articulate arguments which contend that in place of coalition behavior, which springs from an assumed underlying theme of interjurisdictional conflict, the modal pattern of intergovernmental behavior is cooperative rather than competitive.[55]

Whether dominated by cooperation or competition, it appears that vertical contacts by city officials are specialized according to the type of superordinate official to be contacted. The mayor usually runs interference where another elected official is contacted. This happens in a majority of cities when other elected local and national officials are approached. In only a plurality of cities (33 per cent) is the mayor the primary contact person in dealings with elected state officials.

A partial indicator of the city manager's important vertical role is his prominence in contacts with these elected state officials in 31 per cent of the cities. Where administrators in other juris-

[54] William H. Riker, *Federalism: Origin, Operation, Significance* (Boston: Little, Brown, 1964); Richard A. Musgrave (ed.), *Essays in Fiscal Federalism* (Washington: The Brookings Institution, 1965); Harry N. Scheiber, *The Condition of American Federalism: an Historian's View*, (U.S. Senate, Sub-Committee on Intergovernmental Relations [Committee Print], 89th Congress, 2nd Session, October 15, 1966); Edward Weidner, *Intergovernmental Relations as Seen by Public Officials* (Minneapolis: University of Minnesota Press, 1960); Deil S. Wright, *Federal Grants-In-Aid: Perspectives and Alternatives* (Washington, D.C.: American Enterprise Institute, 1968); and Paul N. Ylvisaker, "Some Criteria For a Proper Areal Division of Governmental Powers," in Arthur Maass (ed.), *Area and Power: A Theory of Local Government* (Glencoe, Ill.: The Free Press of Glencoe, 1959), pp. 18–37. It should be noted that the dominant theme underlying all of the aforementioned analyses is one of essential conflict and competition among the several jurisdictions in their intergovernmental contacts and relationships.

[55] Morton Grodzins, "The Federal System," in *Goals for Americans, Report of the President's Commission on National Goals* (Englewood Cliffs, N.J.: Prentice-Hall, 1960), pp. 265–82; Jane Perry Clark, *The Rise of a New Federalism* (New York: Columbia University Press, 1938); Daniel J. Elazar, *The American Partnership: Intergovernmental in the Nineteenth Century United States* (Chicago: University of Chicago Press, 1962); and Jacob Cohen and Morton Grodzins, "How Much Economic Sharing In American Federalism?" *American Political Science Review*, LVII, No. 1 (March, 1963), 5–23.

dictions are concerned the manager holds sway in nearly three-fourths of the cities on interlocal contacts and in about half the cities for state and national administrators. In short, the city manager serves as the prominent agent in fulfilling the vertical political role for council-manager cities.

• *Cognitive Role Perceptions*

Each manager was asked to judge how he perceived his involvement in, commitment to, and results from his behavior in each of the three role spheres. The manager was asked to rank the three roles—management, policy, and political—according to: (1) the amount of time spent on each, (2) his personal preference among the role behaviors, and (3) the extent to which each role activity contributed to successful performance. Summaries of the responses according to first-choice rankings among the roles are presented in Table 7.

A majority of managers see themselves operating chiefly as administrators and a near majority (46 per cent) rank this role as first choice in expressing their preference among the management, policy, and political roles. Only a plurality (37 per cent) ranks management first in its contribution to successful job performance. About one-third of the managers rank the political role (community leadership) highest in contributing to job accomplishment.

Several possible interpretations and explanations could be placed on these findings. First, at the community level, the results may reflect the different styles of leadership required by varying community characteristics and political structure patterns. Subsequent analysis of the data relating these role perceptions to city economic, social, and political characteristics may shed some light on this speculation.

Second, these cognitive perceptions may be related to psychological configurations of the manager's personality, decision styles developed from prior experience, and general achievement orientations and motivations. Measures of these characteristics such as those developed by McClelland, Atkinson, and others

Table 7

PERCEIVED ROLES OF CITY MANAGERS IN U.S.
COUNCIL-MANAGER CITIES OVER 100,000

	Management (Administrative Activities)	Policy (Council Relations)	Political (Community Leadership)
	(percentages ranking each activity first; $N = 45$)		
Involvement (Time consumed)	60	21	16
Commitment (Personal preference)	46	26	19
Results (Contributes most to job performance)	37	22	33

would be highly desirable.[56] We would expect, for example, that in terms of motivations these city managers would rank highest on achievement scores, followed successively by scores on power and affiliation measures.[57]

A third interpretation of the manager's cognitive role perceptions bases them on mass orientations and expectations about local government. It argues that the dominant popular conception of the activities of local government are administrative in character. An articulation of this thesis appears in Harry Friedman's CAG paper on local officials' roles in Pakistani rural development.[58] He suggests that executives' roles are conditioned in important ways by the dominance of administrative-oriented citizens. An administrative-oriented citizenry is contrasted with a policy-oriented citizenry. The latter perceives the relevance of government in terms of broad social issues and goal setting as opposed to limited, marginal choices perceived and weighed by adminis-

[56] David C. McClelland *et al., The Achievement Motive* (New York: Appleton-Century-Crofts, 1953); David C. McClelland, *The Achieving Society* (Princeton, N.J.: Princeton University Press, 1961); John W. Atkinson and Norman T. Feather (eds.), *A Theory of Achievement Motivation* (New York: Wiley, 1966).

[57] See James F. Guyot, "Government Bureaucrats *Are* Different," *Public Administration Review*, XXII, No. 4 (December, 1962), 195–202; and Rufus P. Browning, "The Interaction of Personality and Political System in the Decisions to Run for Office: Some Data and a Simulation Technique" (paper prepared for the Annual Meeting of the Midwest Conference of Political Scientists, Purdue University, Lafayette, Indiana, April 27–29, 1967).

[58] Harry J. Friedman, *op. cit.,* pp. 11–15.

trative-oriented persons. Access to public decision-making processes is sought by policy-oriented citizens in a variety of participational ways, through parties, pressure groups, etc. The administrative-oriented citizen channels his approach to government in a unidimensional manner, directly to an administrative agency. While this typology is suggestive and probably worthy of further elaboration, the linkages between popular perceptions (including responses to governmental action) and executive roles seem too tenuous at our present state of theory-building and empirical research. Greater benefits are likely to accrue, as this chapter implies, from attention to the political structures through which policies are developed and roles defined.

However explained, the fact remains that most of these city managers perceive the dominance of the administrative role in their organizational life. There are, however, significant proportions oriented to the policy role and a smaller proportion emphasizing the community political role. Further analysis of these data should allow us to identify how much role congruence exists across each behavior segment—involvement, commitment, and achievement. If we find a high degree of congruence across these activity areas then we will have taken an important first step in isolating managers by one of three dominant role orientations: (1) the professional administrator, (2) the policy executive, and (3) the community leader.

DEVELOPMENT POLICIES

Critical problems of community development stem not only from objective needs and external events but also from leaders' perceptions of these needs and the appropriate responses to a variety of demands. The abstract idea of needs was unmanageable for both substantive and methodological reasons. We approached the question of policy needs and responses by identifying three general policy "fields." These fields were based on pervasive themes in local governmental activities during the past two decades. We considered some of the recent literature on the categorization of policy outputs and found no classification scheme fully satisfactory although Parsons' person-object dichotomy did furnish a starting point.[59]

Parsons' two categories divide public policies along a basic cleavage in developmental politics. That split is the bricks and mortar complex versus the person–social benefits syndrome. The former puts emphasis on highways, urban renewal, public buildings, and a variety of other tangible and visible products of government activity. The person-oriented policy field not only includes ameliorating individual hardships through direct personal benefits and fostering the development of human resources but, in the present context of urban tensions, it also encompasses policies aimed at reducing intergroup conflicts by negotiation, bargaining, and mutual adjustment.

We refer to the first or tangible-output field as policies concerned with "efficiency." The second or human-oriented sector we have labeled as the "ethnographic" policy field. The concept of efficiency as used here requires little elaboration or justification. The term is employed in a narrow and restricted sense similar if not identical to the usage of turn-of-the-century municipal reformers.[60] Use of "ethnographic" may seem slightly strained but it conveys two important elements: (1) pertaining to man or mankind, and (2) graphing, characterizing, or interrelating the

[59] Parsons distinguishes the two types of policies and organizations according to the "materials" worked on, i.e., whether they are physical objects or people. The former identifies as production and the latter as service type organizations and policies. See Talcott Parsons, *Structure and Process in Modern Societies* (New York: The Free Press, 1960), pp. 21–22. See also Theodore J. Lowi, "American Business, Public Policy, Case Studies and Political Theory," *World Politics*, XVI (July, 1964), 677–715; Lewis A. Froman, Jr., "Categorization of Policy Contents" (paper prepared for a conference on the Study of Policy Content and Its Relevance for the Study of Politics Sponsored by the Committee on Governmental and Legal Processes of the Social Science Research Council, Princeton, New Jersey, June 15–17, 1966); and Lewis A. Froman, Jr., "An Analysis of Public Policies in Cities," *Journal of Politics*, XXIX, No. 1 (February, 1967), 94–108.

[60] For a value-based analysis and critique of the reformers' concepts of economy and efficiency see Dwight Waldo, *The Administrative State* (New York: Ronald Press, 1948). The physical focus of the term "efficiency" as used here connotes the engineering-oriented outputs of paving streets, constructing bridges, etc. The engineering background of many city managers has fostered a strong push toward programs and policies directed toward "efficiency" in the ends-oriented sense employed here, not in the means-oriented sense such as that employed by Herbert Simon, see *Administrative Behavior* (2nd ed.; New York: Macmillan, 1957).

ethnic and cultural differences among groups of men. The former focuses on the human or person-oriented aspects of public policies. The latter suggests the process of identifying and classifying people as a basis for formulating, enacting, and executing policies.

A third policy field was added to take account of particularly strong pressures to promote economic growth, an improved tax base, etc., through the attraction of industry and various other community "assets." This "economic" policy field reached full stride in U.S. cities during the 1950s and continues, apparently unabated. It reflects Riggs's comment in discussing financial administration that "In a diffracted system, a good slice of the government's budget is devoted to the promotion of commercial development." [61]

Physical facilities, or "municipal plant" as these have sometimes been called, have been historically the primary job of local and urban governments. The person-oriented social problems dimension has not been a major responsibility of cities but its intergroup tension component has recently escalated to the top of the municipal agenda. From a temporal standpoint, then, these policy fields—efficiency, economic, and ethnographic—constitute, respectively, traditional, modernizing, and emergent phases in the historical development of U.S. cities.

To explore development policies we employed a battery of questions aimed at tapping the manager's views in each field. Two types of questions were posed. The first asked for the manager's estimate about the extent of the challenge or problems posed in each policy field. The second type sought an estimate from the manager of the role he thought he should play in each field. This normative role question presented four different contexts in which the manager might choose a preferred role.

The results of our soundings are provided in Table 8. The responses to needs in the three fields present few surprises to close observers of urban politics and council-manager government. We might have expected the "edifice complex" to be more fully met than was actually the case. Concern over unmet problems in the efficiency field was expressed by about half the managers. A slightly higher proportion reported the need for attention to

[61] Fred W. Riggs, *Administration and Developing Countries, op. cit.,* p. 305.

ethnographic policies while the largest segment (58 per cent) indicated economic policies are not adequate.

Table 8

CITY MANAGERS POLICY ORIENTATIONS IN U.S.
COUNCIL MANAGER-CITIES OVER 100,000

	Policy Field		
	Efficiency (Physical Facilities)	*Ethnographic (Human and Intergroup Relations)*	*Economic (Industrial and Commercial Growth)*
	(percentages; $N = 45$)		
Extent of challenge or problem			
Not a problem	—	4	2
Fully or most met	49	38	38
Fully or most unmet	49	53	58
Manager should play a "predominant role" in:			
Proposing policies	40	4	11
Developing support in council	47	11	18
Developing support among the public	13	2	4
Leading and maintaining support	27	7	11
Manager should play a "prominent but not predominant role" in:			
Proposing policies	56	73	58
Developing support in council	44	67	56
Developing support among the public	58	51	47
Leading and maintaining support	53	51	51

Over one-third of these managers appear satisfied with ethnographic policies in their cities. In relation to the challenges to civil order and the aspirations for human welfare neither this proportion nor the unmeasured intensity of concern seems appropriate to meet the needs in this policy field. These responses, however, were gathered in 1965. The results might be considerably different if more recent responses were available.

The roles that managers think they should play in the policy fields exhibit noticeable variations. The two sets of tabled percentages indicate the proportions of managers who thought they should occupy a "predominant" or a "prominent" position in each of the role settings. Few inhibitions are present among managers concerning their forthright roles in promoting policies in the efficiency field. Some hesitancy does appear when it involves predominance in securing public support. Greater reluctance to assume predominance in any role context prevails in the ethnographic and economic policy fields. This is offset to some extent by substantial managerial willingness to operate in a prominent way in these two fields, whether as initiators, support builders, or public leaders.

These results clearly cannot be pushed very far. They confirm, as do unreported findings on managerial accomplishments and estimates of community needs, that physical plant and basic public services—efficiency policies—are prime concerns of these large-city managers. An additional undisclosed dimension was their strong orientation toward administrative forms—reorganization, administrative improvement, etc. The image of an efficiency expert or a "machine-model" administrator, however, is not the significant feature of our data on these managers.[62] The results on policy fields as well as the findings on the multiple roles of the managers stretch and distort the simplistic notions of the city manager as either the expedient executor of the council's will or the domineering dictator of public policy.

SUMMARY AND CONCLUDING OBSERVATIONS

A few years ago an article appeared with the title, "The Manager *Is* a Politician." [63] What we have delineated and discussed in this chapter is the idea that a city manager in a large U.S. city is *more* than a politician. He is more because he finds it necessary to engage in concrete behaviors that represent three analytically distinct roles, making his total role an amalgam of administrative,

[62] The "Machine Model" reference is drawn from March and Simon, *op. cit.*
[63] Karl A. Bosworth, "The Manager *Is* a Politician," *Public Administration Review*, XVIII, No. 3 (Summer, 1958), 216–22.

policy, and political action patterns. The largest element in his total role is administrative behavior. Here he is nearly the exclusive focal point for interface relations between the legislature and the bureaucracy. He is virtually unchallenged in his administrative capacity. He exercises predominant influence in the policy formulation and support building sphere, contingent to a considerable extent on the initiative of the mayor. Finally, the manager does operate prominently in various political roles both within and outside the community. Perhaps the most descriptive sense in which the manager of a large city might be termed a politician is in his personal ability to balance and render compatible these three diverse roles. This, of course, is using the term "politician" to mean achieving a workable balance among role behaviors—a broad academic concept rather than a concrete behavioral one. Indicative of the strains in adjusting to these diverse role demands is the near unanimous agreement (90 per cent) of city managers that their position is a "high-tension" occupation.[64]

The telescoping of diverse role behaviors in the position and person of the manager is the result of structural arrangements that both reduce as well as sharpen the gap between uncertainty and change characterized by the legislature and the stability and rationality featured in the municipal bureaucracy. It becomes the city manager's task to bridge this gap while at the same time recognizing the structural and behavioral distinctiveness of these larger forces. Two important elements aid the manager in achieving successful bridging behavior. The first is the existence of professional norms, a code of ethics. The code legitimizes his wide ranging behavior and lends psychological assurance in the context of high tensions. The second positive feature is career mobility. The availability of managerial positions in other cities (or aternative openings) allows city managers to exit more or less gracefully from positions where role balancing has become untenable. His career mobility gives the manager an important asset. If he so chooses, the manager can personalize and politicize his position in a city.[65] He may do this at the risk of his job but not

[64] Boynton, *op. cit.*, p. 45.

[65] One city manager in Iowa did this dramatically a few years ago. After repeated frustrations and energy expended in trying to work through and around a do-

necessarily at the risk of his career. As March and Simon have suggested, risk is related to the availability of external opportunities.[66] The way is opened for the manager to attempt new or creative ways of defining bureaucratic-legislative relationships. These circumstances undoubtedly contribute to the manager's image of being a significant change agent in a community, while at the same time ordering and rationalizing the change. In short, he epitomizes a development administrator.

The primacy and pervasiveness of administration in these council-manager cities pose several issues that can only be raised, not resolved. One such issue is that raised by Udy in the form of an hypothesis: "the greater the amount of pressure exerted on the organization from the social setting, the greater the emphasis on administration." [67] A critical factor, of course, is how one defines and operationalizes "pressure" and also what constitutes the relevant social setting. Lucian Pye succinctly summarized the pressure toward nation-building around the globe under the rubric of "world culture." He says:

> It [world culture] is based upon a secular rather than a sacred view of human relations, a rational outlook, an acceptance of the substance and spirit of the scientific approach, a vigorous application of expanding technology, an industrialized organization of production, and a generally humanistic and popularistic set of values for political life.[68]

This characterization of pressures operative on nations around the globe seems equally applicable to cities in the U.S. except that the pressures appear to be heightened in the American context. This would account for the great emphasis on administration in the surveyed cities. What remains to be confirmed are whether the administrative emphasis is greater in these manager cities than in other U.S. cities and how these intracountry variations compare on an internation basis.

The formal structures of council-manager government in the U.S. both reflect and reinforce the emphasis on administration.

---

nothing mayor, the manager delivered an ultimatum to the remaining members of the council. "Either he goes or I go," said the manager. The mayor resigned!

[66] March and Simon, *op. cit.*, chap. 4.

[67] Stanley H. Udy, Jr., "The Comparative Analysis of Organizations," in James G. March (ed.), *Handbook of Organizations* (Chicago: Rand McNally, 1965), p. 690.

[68] Lucian W. Pye, *Aspects of Political Development, op. cit.*, p. 10.

They reflect a Western culture that is activist and receptive to change. At the same time they reinforce the pressures to reduce (rationalize) the uncertainty components present in the pursuit of change. The city manager is charged with the paradoxical tasks of inducing change and reducing uncertainty. The manager's strong achievement orientations produce an evident commitment to deliberate, directed change. But there appears to be little in the theory and practice of the manager plan that allows for non-directed and spontaneous change as a prime force in development. External self-initiated forces for change are producing new pressures by various participational means, e.g., riots and boycotts as well as lobbying and voting. The management of tensions and demands arising from this new phase of popular politics confronts the structural and behavioral patterns of the council-manager plan with perhaps their most serious challenge.

Closely connected with the participational challenge or crisis is the viewpoint of the new entrants to the political process. Much evidence could be marshalled to show that the submerged and emergent segments in U.S. cities do not see political structures as neutral and impartial parts of the governing process. The views of organization theorists and other academics that organizations represent "the mobilization of bias" have permeated large segments of the populace through direct negative experiences rather than intellective processes. Herbert Simon recently pointed to the non-neutral character of public organizations. Neutrality has been replaced, he argues, not only with recognized bias but, more importantly, with *predictable* bias.[69] Simon does not deal with the problem of who perceives this neutrality nor does he deal directly with different dimensions that bureaucratic neutrality (or non-neutrality) may take, e.g., neutral in the partisan political sense, neutral in the sense of being impartial in policy outlook, and neutral in the sense of treating clients and others impartially and impersonally. Public administrators and most of the citizenry might agree that local bureaucracies are neutral in the first sense and not neutral in the second sense. But officials and various

[69] Herbert A. Simon, "The Changing Theory and Changing Practice of Public Administration," in Ithiel de Sola Pool (ed.), *Contemporary Political Science: Toward Empirical Theory* (New York: McGraw-Hill, 1967), pp. 86–120.

portions of the public are often at odds over whether neutrality prevails in the third sense.

An additional prominent issue surrounding the development process also arises from the structural and administrative emphasis of the council-manager plan. Gideon Sjoberg has contended that development is associated with the existence of authoritarian political structures joined with charismatic leadership.[70] These features, he contends, are accompanied by a style of politics that is impelled to dramatize and overemphasize political obligations as an ideology fostering development. The difficulty of mobilizing a body politic toward developmental goals, goals that fall within Apter's category of "consummatory" values,[71] leads Sjoberg to conclude, epigrammatically, that a devil, not a god is required for development. The relation of this theorizing to U.S. council-manager cities might seem remote. The important parallel lies in the domain of political structure; the contrasts are present in political style and developmental goals.

Of the diverse structural forms used in the United States the council-manager plan is the one most criticized for the concentration of great power in few hands. Cries of "dictatorship" by citizens in some manager cities are reflected in more sophisticated and less pejorative terms in academic literature. The strength of the local bureaucracy, the pervasiveness of administration, and the prominence of the city manager all point in the direction of powerful political structures more concerned with outputs than inputs. The style of politics and the nature of goals pursued in council-manager cities offer sharp contrasts with those delineated by Sjoberg. Manager cities are distinctive for the fact that they do *not* produce charismatic leaders. One of the major criticisms of the plan, especially in large cities, is that it does not produce evocative leadership.[72] Neither is there an apparent or uniform

---

[70] Gideon Sjoberg, "Political Structure, Ideology, and Economic Development," (paper prepared for the Carnegie Faculty Seminar on Political and Administrative Development, Department of Government, Indiana University, 1963).

[71] David E. Apter, *The Politics of Modernization* (Chicago: University of Chicago Press, 1965).

[72] The exchange between Wallace Sayre and John Bebout some years ago reviewed most of the arguments. See Wallace S. Sayre, "The General Manager Idea for Large Cities," *Public Administration Review*, XIV, No. 4 (Autumn, 1954), 253–58; John E. Bebout, "Management for Large Cities," *Public Administration Review*,

stress on political obligation. Furthermore, the configuration of groups involved suggests a pluralistic pattern of politics and the goals of development (e.g., developmental policies) are more instrumental than they are ultimate, terminal, or consummatory.

There are at least three reasons why centralized decision-making should produce more effective system response.[73] First, concentration of power should push the focus of action toward administrative arenas where bureaucratic expertise rather than patronage, partisanship, and personalism are applied to problems. Second, a centralized structure should be able to act more expeditiously because fewer participants are involved in approving a course of action. Third, centralization should insulate decision-makers from disruptive and tendentious elements. Despite the logic behind these reasons, there appears to be only fragmentary evidence supporting the basic proposition. Crain and Rosenthal found that U.S. cities were more likely to adopt fluoridation of water if cities had the council-manager or strong mayor plan than some weaker executive structure.[74] The same authors also found that manager-governed cities were more prepared to withstand the community divisiveness engendered by the water fluoridation than other cities. The degree of immunity from intense pressures was further enhanced by the relative professionalization of the city managers.[75] Findings presented by Zisk, Eulau, and Prewitt tend to confirm the structure-performance association in a left-

---

XV, No. 3 (Summer, 1955), 188–95. In some respects the several roles fulfilled by the city manager represent a collapsed behavior pattern more characteristic of a position in a fused society, as described by Fred Riggs. On the other hand, we must recognize that the total societal context falls within Riggs's diffracted category. The position of the city manager represents a fusion of roles that in other cities and in previous times were more differentiated. Criticisms of the manager plan seem to be taken chiefly on the grounds of role fusion. They also stem from concerns that even if the managerial, policy, and political roles can be fused, e.g., in the strong mayor, the manager plan gives priority to the first of these roles whereas preference and emphasis should be given to the latter ones. This argument is joined most directly in the debates of the relative merits of the manager plan for large cities.

[73] Robert L. Crain and Donald B. Rosenthal, "Community Status as a Dimension of Local Decision-Making," *American Journal of Sociology*, XXXII (December, 1967), 970–84.

[74] *Ibid.*

[75] Donald B. Rosenthal and Robert L. Crain, "Executive Leadership and Community Innovation: The Fluoridation Experience," *Urban Affairs Quarterly*, I, No. 3 (March, 1966), 39–57.

handed way. They conclude that where policy-makers tend to spend time mediating group conflicts they do so at the "expense of achieving efficient and practical solutions for community problems and the system may fail to adapt itself to a changing environment." [76]

The foregoing discussion leads to one question and one qualification. The question, as exemplified by the case of council-manager cities, is whether development hinges more on certain political structures than on particular styles of politics and goals sought. Whatever the requisites for development our theorizing needs to take account of the interrelationships between structure, behavior, and values.

The prominent and pertinent qualification pervading the entire discussion of comparative development is the microcosm we have selected for analysis. Not only have we focused on local executives but we have considered them in only one structural context. We do not know, other than speculatively and impressionistically, how much variation exists within U.S. local government. We have assumed that in council-manager government we have captured the developmental thrust in the U.S. in its sharpest and purest form. This may not be the case. Acceptance of Fred Riggs's argument concerning local government and circular causation would lessen the significance of this qualification. Riggs sees local government as interacting with the environment to reinforce the already dominant tendencies in a nation; local administration is a cause as well as a consequence of ecological conditions and there is relatively little intranation variability in local development tendencies.[77]

In conclusion we might observe that the United States of America has staked a claim to world leadership not only on the ideology of democracy but also on the grounds that we have developed the kinds of political structures that can effectively operationalize, or at least approximate, our national goals in governmental practice. Partly because we were "the first new nation,"

[76] Betty H. Zisk, Heinz Eulau, and Kenneth Prewitt, "City Councilmen and the Group Struggle: A Typology of Role Orientations," *Journal of Politics*, XXVII, No. 3 (August, 1965), 645.

[77] Fred W. Riggs, *Administration in Developing Countries, op. cit.,* chap. 12.

partly because of our economic and material successes, and for many other reasons, some of our political structures—federalism, popularly elected executives, representative legislatures, and local institutions—have been adopted and/or adapted by other nations. In fact, of course, the push underlying political development around the globe has been generated from far broader and more complex circumstances than "Yankee ingenuity." For many years political structures were seen as independent variables through which both political progress and political analysis might be advanced. A powerful and proper reaction to the structural emphasis carried the day but we are now beginning to rethink whether we did not throw the baby out with the bath. Simultaneously, the rethinking and reanalysis of our own political system indicates that its political development is in many ways analogous to and as complex as the problems of development in the Third World.

7 |

Political Access Under Metropolitan
Government: A Comparative Study
of Perceptions by Knowledgeables

DANIEL R. GRANT

IN THE MANY POST-MORTEM analyses of unsuccessful efforts
to achieve some kind of area-wide metropolitan government, one
of the most frequently mentioned reasons for defeat is the voter's
fear of loss of easy political access to local officials. Opponents of
proposals for metropolitan government commonly charge that the
new "super-government" would be less accessible to the average
citizen. The charge is made as it relates to all sections of the metropolitan area—core city, suburbs, and rural fringe, and undoubtedly has an equally strong emotional appeal to Negroes, wealthy
suburbanites, and farmers. It is said to be one of the most un-
beatable political issues facing those who campaign for metropolitan reorganization.

Many examples can be cited in the literature of political
science of implicit and explicit predictions of the effects of metropolitan government on political access of particular groups.
Edward C. Banfield has stated that "Metropolitan government
would mean the transfer of power over the central cities from
the largely lower-class Negro and Catholic elements who live in
them to the largely middle-class white and Protestant elements

AUTHOR'S NOTE: The author is indebted to the Ford Foundation and
the Vanderbilt University Research Council for grants in support of
research on which this chapter is based.

who live in the suburbs." [1] Ostrom, Tiebout, and Warren did not specifically predict loss of political access, but strongly imply it as they attack some of the assumptions of reformers who propose "gargantua" or consolidated government for the metropolis:

> . . . gargantua, with its single dominant center of decision-making, is apt to become victim of the complexity of its own hierarchical or bureaucratic structure. Its complex channels of communication may make its administration unresponsive to many of the more localized public interests in the community. The costs of maintaining control in gargantua's public services may be so great that its production of public goods becomes grossly inefficient. Gargantua, as a result, may become insensitive and clumsy in meeting the demands of local citizens for the public goods required in their daily life. Two or three years may be required to secure street or sidewalk improvements, even where local residents bear the cost of the improvement. Modifications in traffic control at a local intersection may take an unconscionable amount of time. Some decision-makers will be more successful in pursuing their interests than others. The lack of effective organization for these others may result in policies with highly predictable biases. Bureaucratic unresponsiveness in gargantua may produce frustration and cynicism on the part of the local citizen who finds no point of access for remedying local problems of a public character. The citizen may not have access to sufficient information to render an informed judgment at the polls. Lack of effective communication in the large public organization may indeed lead to the eclipse of the public and to the blight of the community.[2]

Charles Adrian attributes such a prediction to metropolitan citizens, especially suburbanites, in explaining their fear of metropolitan government:

> One of the greatest fears of the metropolitanite today is that he will lose access to, or influence over, government at all levels. He is confronted with a sense of alienation, or feeling that no matter what he does, his actions will not influence decisions which are important to him. Proposals for metropolitan-wide government add fuel to his anxieties. Incipient alienation is to be seen, in addition to attitudes toward core city government, in the belief that the suburbanite fight is a losing one—that eventually their area will become part of the core city or of a metropolitan super-government. . . .[3]

[1] Edward C. Banfield, "The Politics of Metropolitan Area Organization," *Midwest Journal of Political Science,* I (May, 1957), 87.

[2] Vincent Ostrom, Charles M. Tiebout, and Robert Warren, "The Organization of Government in Metropolitan Areas: A Theoretical Inquiry," *American Political Science Review,* LV (December, 1961), 837.

[3] Charles R. Adrian, "Public Attitudes and Metropolitan Decision Making," in Thomas R. Dye and Brett W. Hawkins (eds.), *Politics in the Metropolis* (Columbus, Ohio: Charles E. Merrill, 1967), p. 462.

Victor Jones has discussed the opposite side of the coin with respect to political access, implying that fragmentation and confusion of local governments in the metropolis may be a greater deterrent to political access than the bigness of metropolitan government:

> Citizens cannot understand or control the formulation and administration of governmental policies in a complex urban community when responsibility is divided among many independent and overlapping units. The task imposed, for instance, upon a citizen of Chicago who is supposed to hold responsible a multitude of high and low officials in nearly a dozen separate governments is an impossible one.[4]

Because so few metropolitan areas have adopted comprehensive area-wide government, the vast majority of published studies on the subject of "metropolitics" have dealt with the nature of the metro-rejection process rather than with actual effects of adopting metro. An increasing number of studies of the experience of the metro systems in Toronto, Miami, and Nashville have been initiated and a few have been published,[5] but none is comparative in nature and none has focused on the question of political access. This chapter seeks to compare pre-metro and post-metro political access in the Toronto, Miami, and Nashville areas, using data from a larger study of perceptions by knowledgeables.

Limitations of time and resources made it impossible to interview population samples in each of the three areas, and led to the alternative approach of interviewing a selected panel of "most knowledgeable" observers in each city, chosen by a uniform

---

[4] Victor Jones, *Metropolitan Government* (Chicago: University of Chicago Press, 1942), p. 83.

[5] See for example Harold Kaplan, *Urban Political Systems: A Functional Analysis of Metro Toronto* (New York: Columbia University Press, 1967); Frank Smallwood, *Metro Toronto: A Decade Later* (Toronto: Bureau of Municipal Research, 1963); John Grumm, *Metropolitan Area Government: The Toronto Experience* ("Governmental Research Series No. 19" [Lawrence: University of Kansas Publications, 1959]); Edward Sofen, *The Miami Metropolitan Experiment* ("Metropolitan Action Studies No. 2" [Bloomington: Indiana University Press, 1963]); David A. Booth, *Metropolitics: The Nashville Consolidation* (East Lansing: Institute for Community Development and Services, Michigan State University, 1963); and Brett W. Hawkins, *Nashville Metro: The Politics of City-County Consolidation* (Nashville: Vanderbilt University Press, 1966). The Miami and Nashville studies have dealt primarily, if not entirely, with the politics of adopting and establishing metropolitan government.

method and asked the same set of questions about their perceptions of the effects of adoption of metro.[6] Some of the more obvious limitations of this kind of study should be borne in mind: it is a study of their expressed *perceptions* of effects, which are not necessarily the same thing as actual effects; it is often very difficult to distinguish between changes uniquely related to the adoption of area-wide government and other kinds of change which have also occurred; it is difficult to know the effect of the interviewee's personal biases toward metro on his expressed perceptions; and in 1966—when the interviews were conducted—it was still too early to appraise many of the effects of Nashville's metro (adopted in 1962), though perhaps not too early in the case of Miami (adopted in 1957), or Toronto (adopted in 1953).

Before considering the findings on political access under metro governments it is important to give a brief picture of the three systems as adopted. Each followed a different approach to the common goal of area-wide policy formation and administration. Toronto's is a metropolitan federation of cities—originally thirteen cities when established in 1953 but consolidated to six in 1967 (five boroughs plus the city of Toronto). The upper level

[6] An effort was made to select the "knowledgeables" in each of the three cities in the same way in order to give greater comparability and meaning to the patterns of answers both in the aggregate and for the three cities compared. This was done by means of a structured "ballot" mailed first to five obviously knowledgeable persons in each city, with the request to "name the three persons you consider to be the most knowledgeable or best informed in the affairs of local government," in each of the following fourteen categories: political leaders, newspapermen, business and professional leaders, college professors, metro councilmen, metro administrative officials, labor leaders, Negroes or other ethnic minorities, active opponents of the original adoption of metro, active supporters of the original adoption of metro, persons most critical of metro today, persons most in support of metro today, persons you consider as probably best qualified to evaluate objectively the overall results of adopting metro, and other informed observers not included in the above categories. After a tabulation of the returned ballots, a ballot was sent to the person named most frequently in each category. After determining that twenty was the maximum number of persons that could be interviewed in the available time in each city, it was decided to attempt to interview at least one and no more than two of the persons receiving the most "votes" in each category. In all three cities fifty-six persons were interviewed, seventeen in Toronto, nineteen in Miami, and twenty in Nashville, and the goal of at least one in each category and no more than two, was achieved. Admittedly, this method is subject to some of the same criticisms made against Floyd Hunter's method of "electing" the community power structure by reputational balloting (in his *Community Power Structure* [Chapel Hill: University of North Carolina Press, 1953]), but some of these arguments are not really applicable in this situation.

of the federation is given responsibility for a considerable number of area-wide functions, with certain others being reserved for the local units. Since 1957 metropolitan Miami has had a two-tier form of government but it is not a federation of cities, technically speaking, because almost one-half of the population lives in unincorporated portions served directly by Dade County Metro. Although the twenty-seven cities under Dade County continue to perform a large number of functions—many of them alleged to be "properly area-wide" by advocates of consolidation—the charter actually gives Metro the power to take over such functions if they fall below an adequate standard of performance. Nashville has a single metropolitan government for the entire city and county area of 533 square miles that was achieved by consolidating the city of Nashville with Davidson County in 1962. The single government has two service areas with two different tax rates, one for an expandable urban services area of some 75 square miles, and the other for the total area including the urban core. Six suburban cities, performing only very limited functions, were permitted to remain in existence outside the urban services district, but their residents are otherwise under the jurisdiction of the metropolitan government in the same manner as all others.

In attempting to discover what informed observers of the three metropolitan areas think has happened to political access, if anything, as a result of adopting metropolitan government, an effort was made to use as clear and simple a definition of the term as possible. The fifty-six interviewees (seventeen in Toronto, nineteen in Miami, and twenty in Nashville), were asked, first as an open-end question and later as a fixed-alternative question, whether the adoption of metro had had any effect on the ability of "some groups of people to get an attentive hearing from responsible officials when they feel they have a problem." For the second question they were handed a list of seven categories of people and asked to rate the effect of the adoption of metro, using a five-point scale, on their ability to get an attentive hearing from the responsible officials.

Without the benefit of the list of groups the interviewees answered in rather general terms, but a comfortable plurality (44 per cent) believed that political access had actually been made

Table 1

EFFECT OF METRO ON THE POLITICAL ACCESS OF VARIOUS GROUPS
OF CITIZENS TO RESPONSIBLE OFFICIALS, AS PERCEIVED
BY KNOWLEDGEABLES

	Toronto	Miami	Nashville	Total
Access is easier	1	8	14	23
Access is harder	5	5	4	14
No effect, or mixed effects	10	3	2	15
Total answering	16	16	20	52

easier rather than harder, by the adoption of metro. (See Table 1.)
The rest of the interviewees were almost equally divided between
those saying metro had had little or no effect on political access
(29 per cent) and those who believed it had made political access
more difficult (27 per cent). Doubtless, proponents of metro will
want to interpret these figures in terms of the majority of 73 per
cent who deny that political access has been made more difficult
by the adoption of metro. Conversely, opponents of metro can
cite the majority of 56 per cent who deny that political access is
easier because of metro. In balance, proponents of metro will find
more comfort than opponents will in these figures because they
do tend to undercut one of the major anti-metro arguments. Although a significant number of observers reported that political
access is actually easier under metro, it would seem to be a "moral
victory" for proponents if there has been no evidence of significant
change in political access.[7]

[7] An effort was made to see whether the interviewees' expressed perceptions of
effect on political access were merely a reflection of their original support for, or
opposition to, metro. Toronto's interviewees included six opponents, six supporters,
and five neutrals or persons not there at the time of adoption, and the pattern of
answers was not significantly different among the three groups. In Miami, where
sixteen of the nineteen interviewees claimed to be original supporters, only one-
half of these believed access is easier, indicating no automatic bias in their perceptions. In some respects one's *original* position concerning metro in Miami seems
to have little contemporary relevance. Two Miami interviewees who were not
present at the time of adoption, and the one original opponent said access is harder.
Only three of the twenty Nashville interviewees said they originally opposed metro,
and two of these said access is harder, with one saying it is easier. This is hardly
enough to justify firm conclusions, but it provides some support for the charge that
Nashville opponents are inclined to see a less favorable impact of metro and proponents are inclined to see a more favorable impact. In the light of other survey
data (see footnote 8), the writer believes any effects of such bias are not serious.

SLIGHTLY MORE DIFFICULT
ACCESS IN TORONTO

When the interviewees' answers are compared in their three separate city groups in Table 1, three different patterns emerge. At the risk of oversimplifying the patterns, it can be reported that Toronto interviewees lean slightly toward saying that access is harder; Miami interviewees lean slightly toward saying that access is easier; and Nashville interviewees lean heavily toward saying that access is easier. Only one Toronto interviewee thought political access had been made easier. Two-thirds of the others thought Toronto's metro had had no effect or mixed effects on political access, and one-third expressed the opinion that access was made more difficult. Miami interviewees were more affirmative on the matter of political access, with one-half stating that metro had made it easier, but a considerable number (almost one-third) thought metro had made it harder and the rest felt there had been no significant change in Miami. According to 70 per cent of the Nashville interviewees, metro has very clearly improved political access, with only 20 per cent stating that access is more difficult and 10 per cent indicating no significant change.

The reasons given by those Toronto interviewees who believe that political access is more difficult under metro relate in part to the structural arrangement of the federated government, and in part to the nature of the major functions allocated to the higher level of government. Since no metro councilmen or officials *as such* are elected directly by the people, some interviewees felt that it made them harder to reach or talk to. Since the metro councilmen serve as elective officers of the city they represent, one contended that "their wearing two hats makes it very hard to pin them down—too easy for them to pass the buck." Several pointed out that the tasks assigned to the metro government were predominantly massive public works responsibilities which tended to encourage an image of metro as a "non-political construction company." Some thought that this made it perfectly proper that metro should be less accessible to the public and various interest groups, while the cities continued to be more accessible to interest groups at the "grass roots level."

Indicative of the comparative isolation of the Toronto Metro Council from direct pressure from interest groups is the following quotation from one interviewee:

> We discouraged delegations from coming to Metro Council. We didn't want delegations and pressure groups coming down to tell us how to run the bloody show. They would never come down unless they wanted to get in the way. One group tried to block the sewage plant, but now it's no problem. Nobody notices the treatment plant; there's no odor and it's not even visible to the residents. Such groups have no business coming to the Metro Council. The place for delegations is in the local municipality. The pressure should be applied at the local council level; then let their representative act for them at the Metro level. This may be contrary to democracy in a sense, but you just can't allow them to get before the Metropolitan Council. They're not welcome.

Other Toronto interviewees acknowledged this aloofness of the Metro Council, in varying degrees, but contended either that the selected functions being performed by metro are not so much the kind that attract groups desiring a hearing, or that any reduction in political access is simply a result of population growth and change in the area rather than being related to the metro form of government. As one person expressed it, "The things which people want to appear as delegations about are mainly municipal functions—property matters, zoning, parks, welfare, etc. But Bill 81 [the 1966 reorganization legislation] will undoubtedly involve Metro more and more directly with the people."

SLIGHTLY EASIER ACCESS IN MIAMI-DADE

Miami interviewees appear to have been strongly influenced in their answer to the question on political access by comparisons with the pre-metro county government, with the new metro government coming off much better in the comparison. Three principal reasons were given for the opinion that political access has been made easier by metro. Several described the old county commission's meetings as "star chamber" proceedings by its five members, a "closed-group kind of situation," with only monthly meetings, no formal agenda, and public hearings discouraged. The metro commission has nine members, meets every two weeks with a formal agenda, and interviewees reported frequent public hearings. Some pointed out that metro was adopted in conjunction with a county home rule amendment to Florida's constitution, which "moved our decision-making center from Tallahassee back to Dade County." Technically speaking, county home rule could have been adopted without adopting a novel form of metropolitan government, but the two seemed to be as one in the minds of most interviewees and they considered it to be relevant to changes in political access. One other cause cited for increased political access in metropolitan Miami is the "improved calibre of employees." As one expressed it, "Metro's unique and exotic character has attracted better officials at both the county and city level, and these people have an improved quality of openness to all people without discrimination."

The smaller number of Miami-Dade interviewees who felt that political access had been made more difficult focused primarily on the bigger bureaucracy brought about by metro and the red tape and delays said to result from it. One compared unfavorably the time required for getting building permits and inspections by metro and by one of the suburban cities, the latter said to give "one-day service in nine out of ten cases." Another simply said, "It is taking government too far away from the people. As conceived it would have been a wonderful thing." The view of the three who felt that metro had not changed political access one way or the other seemed to be that the great population growth in Miami and Dade County made it impossible to attribute any changes to metro government as such.

EASIER ACCESS PERCEIVED IN NASHVILLE

Far more than in the other two cities, the Nashville interviewees (70 per cent) believed political access was made easier by metro, and many of their reasons related specifically to the structural change inherent in city-county consolidation. Several stated that because there is only one government "it helps the people know who the responsible official is and eliminates the old city-county buck-passing." Another said "two governments made it harder to exert effective pressure, but now it is generally easier." Several pointed to the large metropolitan council, with thirty-five of the forty-one being elected from single-member districts, as being far more accessible to the citizens than was the old county governing body, and no less accessible than the former city council. The equal size of the councilmanic districts caused one interviewee to say, "Metro brought in one-man-one-vote to Davidson County long before it came to any other city or county in Tennessee. This improved political access." Two interviewees mentioned the creation of a division of information and complaints in the mayor's office as a means of improved public access under metro.

The 20 per cent who thought Nashville Metro had made political access more difficult were not in agreement on a single reason for this opinion, but they mentioned such things as the dilution of core city voters' political power by merging with the suburbs, the weakening of rural voters' influence by merging into a thoroughly urbanized government, and the construction of a governmental structure in which only one political faction could be in power at any given time. The 10 per cent who believed there had been no change simply indicated a confidence that "wise politicians will provide the necessary political access, whatever the governmental system."

POLITICAL ACCESS IN DIFFERENT GEOGRAPHIC AREAS

Interviewees were asked specifically about the effect of adopting metro on political access by residents of four different geographic areas—the central city, incorporated suburban cities, unincorporated suburban cities, and rural areas. The question was: "Assuming they feel they have a legitimate problem, how would you rate the effect of the adoption of Metro on their ability to get an attentive hearing from the responsible officials?" The aggregate answers for all three metropolitan areas, shown in Table 2, indi-

Table 2

EFFECT OF ADOPTION OF METRO ON POLITICAL ACCESS OF CITIZENS, ACCORDING TO THEIR PLACE OF RESIDENCE

Place of Residence	Rating	Toronto	Miami	Nashville	Total
Central city	Much easier	—	1	1	2 ⎫ 23
	Somewhat easier	2	9	10	21 ⎭
	No change	5	4	6	15
	Somewhat harder	8	2	3	13 ⎫ 15
	Much harder	—	2	—	2 ⎭
	Total answering	15	18	20	53
Incorporated subur-ban cities	Much easier	—	1	1	2 ⎫ 24
	Somewhat easier	4	7	11	22 ⎭
	No change	3	4	8	15
	Somewhat harder	8	3	—	11 ⎫ 14
	Much harder	—	3	—	3 ⎭
	Total answering	15	18	20	53
Unincorporated suburban areas	Much easier	—*	2	2	4 ⎫ 22
	Somewhat easier	—	8	10	18 ⎭
	No change	—	3	8	11
	Somewhat harder	—	3	—	3 ⎫ 6
	Much harder	—	3	—	3 ⎭
	Total answering	—	19	20	39
Rural areas	Much easier	—	1	2	3 ⎫ 17
	Somewhat easier	—	7	7	14 ⎭
	No change	4	2	10	16
	Somewhat harder	8	5	1	14 ⎫ 18
	Much harder	—	4	—	4 ⎭
	Total answering	12	19	20	51

* There are no unincorporated suburbs in Metropolitan Toronto.

cate that informed observers believe that residents of unincorporated suburban areas were affected most favorably, and residents of rural areas were affected least favorably by metropolitan government. Actually, the pattern of answers for the central city and

incorporated suburban cities is much more similar to that for the
unincorporated suburban areas than it might seem at first glance,
because there are no unincorporated suburbs in the Toronto
area and the question was, therefore, inapplicable there. In the
case of each of the four areas of residence a comfortable majority
of the interviewees expressed the opinion that political access
had not been made more difficult by the adoption of metro, that
is, it had been made easier or had not changed. More than 84
per cent felt this was true in the unincorporated suburban areas,
as did 74 per cent for the incorporated suburban cities, 72 per
cent for the central city, and 65 per cent in the case of rural areas.
Thus, even the rural residents who were adjudged to be least
favorably affected by Metro, were said by only 35 per cent to
have poorer political access.

The separate patterns of perceived political access in each
of the three metropolitan areas, based on the four geographic
variables in Table 2, do not differ significantly from the patterns
found in Table 1. Toronto interviewees consistently rated the
effects of metro on political access less favorably than did Miami
and Nashville interviewees. Over one-half of those answering
thought that Toronto metro had caused political access, both inside the central city and in the suburbs, to be "somewhat harder."
Four Toronto interviewees thought access was "somewhat easier"
in the suburbs because of metro, while only two thought so for the
core city.

Miami interviewees' perceptions of metro's effect on access
in the four different areas of the county might be compared
roughly as follows: central city—somewhat easier; unincorporated
suburbs—slightly easier; incorporated suburbs—almost no change,
but leaning toward easier; rural areas—almost no change, but
leaning toward harder. Nashville interviewees' perceptions of
changes in political access are more heavily on the easier side,
with "somewhat easier" being the most common rating in all
cases except for rural areas. One-half of the interviewees thought
there had been no change in political access in rural areas of
Davidson County, but only one of the others thought access had
been made harder for the rural residents. Three Nashville interviewees thought metro had made political access by central city

residents "somewhat harder," but no one thought access was harder for residents of suburbs, whether incorporated or unincorporated.

A recent study of the impact of metro on the rural portion of Davidson County includes findings of an opinion survey of voters in the non-urbanized area and is, therefore, of special relevance to this chapter.[8] In response to the question, "Who gave you the most attention, your Magistrates (before Metro) or your Councilman (under Metro)?", the interviewees answered in the following manner:

Magistrates	30.9%
Councilman	31.9%
No difference	37.2%

In one sense it indicates a clear "stand off" in opinion, yet 69.1 per cent of the voters are denying the hypothesis that metro reduces the individual attention received by them. Responses were even more favorable to a second question, "How do you feel about the effect of Metro on your personal ability to get an attentive hearing (from the responsible officials when you feel a problem exists in the community)?" Their answers were as follows:

Metro made it easier	50.0%
Metro brought no change	30.0%
Metro made it harder	20.0%

Thus, 80 per cent of Nashville's rural fringe voters deny that metro has made political access more difficult.

In summary, for the three metropolitan areas, the geographic variable in metro's effect on political access seems to have some significance with respect to rural areas, but very little significance with respect to core city and suburban differences. There is no evidence in the interview data to support a hypothesis that metro has a significantly different effect on political access to responsible officials by residents of the core city as opposed to suburban residents. There is some indication in the Toronto and Miami interview data, though of dubious significance, that political access in

[8] Robert E. McArthur, "The Impact of Metropolitan Government on the Rural-Urban Fringe: The Nashville-Davidson County Experience" (Unpublished Ph.D. dissertation, Vanderbilt University, 1967), pp. 233–38.

the rural areas is more negatively affected than in urban and suburban areas, but even this difference is not found in the Nashville data.

POLITICAL ACCESS BY NEGROES, OR OTHER ETHNIC MINORITY

One of the most surprising results of the interviews is the pattern of answers given concerning impact on the political access of Negroes or other ethnic minority groups. In interpreting the answers it is important to remember the statistical picture of ethnic minorities in the three areas. Miami-Dade estimates of minority-group population at the time of metro's adoption indicated there were approximately 140,000 Negroes (close to 15 per cent of the total), and 85,000 persons of Latin-American birth (over 10 per cent of the total). Not quite one-half of the Negroes resided within the city of Miami. The Nashville-Davidson County Negro minority accounted for 19.1 per cent of the population in 1960. Negro residence was predominantly inside the city of Nashville, accounting for 37.4 per cent of the city's population but only 5.3 per cent of the population outside the city. Although Toronto has experienced a heavy influx of immigrants from eastern and central Europe since the 1953 adoption of metro, the pre-metro ethnic structure was unusually homogeneous and Anglo-Saxon. The number of Negroes in Toronto is negligible.

The combined totals for all three cities, shown in Table 3, indicate that political access by Negro or other ethnic minority groups was thought to be more favorably affected by metro than any other group mentioned. Almost 82 per cent thought they either had easier access because of metro or that there had been no change. The bulk of these "votes" came from Miami and Nashville interviewees who were convinced that metro had made Negro political access easier—79 per cent in Miami and 70 per cent in Nashville. This is the only case in which the Miami interviewees gave even higher "political-access ratings" than the Nashville interviewees.

Table 3

EFFECT OF ADOPTION OF METRO ON POLITICAL ACCESS
BY NEGROES OR OTHER ETHNIC MINORITY

	Toronto	Miami	Nashville	Total	
Much easier	—	7	2	9	} 30
Somewhat easier	1	8	12	21	
No change	7	2	4	13	
Somewhat harder	5	1	2	8	} 9
Much harder	—	1	—	1	
Total answering	13	19	20	52	

The reasons given for these ratings are especially significant because most of the interviewees indicated an awareness of the difficulty of distinguishing between metro-related changes in Negro political access and those growing out of the civil rights movement and related social and political changes affecting the Southern Negro. Most seemed also to be familiar with the common allegation that the adoption of metropolitan government will dilute the political influence of core city minority groups by merging them with the populous suburbs. Miami interviewees leaned heavily on the role of increased professionalism of Dade County Metro employees as a cause of easier access for Negroes. More than one suggested that "professionalism does not discriminate; it is more open in matters of race." Another put it in terms of Negroes having easier access to the more urban-minded types under metro than to the old rural-type politician of the pre-metro county government. The one Negro interviewee in Miami expressed the opinion that political access by Negroes had been made "somewhat easier" by the adoption of metro.

Nashville interviewees expressed the same conclusion as Miami interviewees—that Negro political access was easier because of metro—but stressed two different explanations rather than the effect of professionalism. Mentioned most often was the elimination of split responsibility between the separate governments of Nashville and Davidson County. Knowing whom to see and the ability to focus pressure on that one place without easy buck passing was said to have helped achieve racial progress and harmony, including the creation of a human relations commis-

sion. Mentioned almost as frequently was the role of the thirty-
five single-member districts in providing easy access to metropolitan councilmen. When asked about any change in Negro political
access, several interviewees stopped to add up the number of
Negro members of the metro council (five) and compare this with
the old city council (three out of thirty) and the old county governing body (none out of fifty-five). Their conclusion was that,
because of careful attention to their interests by the charter draft-
ers, Negro political access in Nashville had actually improved.
Two of the Nashville interviewees were Negroes and one said
political access by Negroes was made "much easier" while the
other, who originally opposed metro, said "somewhat easier."

Toronto interviewees did not give a significantly different
pattern of answers with respect to ethnic minorities than to any
other group, and made it clear that they believed Toronto is
atypical in its ethnic characteristics. One said "we really do not
have ethnic groups as such." Another said that "even though
there are 200,000 Italians in Toronto, I know of no instance in
which they have spoken as a group on any issue, or have had a
spokesman." He wondered, incidentally, why this should not be
the case in all cities. The nearest anyone came to a conscious discussion of the racial impact of metro in Toronto was one statement that "Metro has not impeded access and has actually broken
down barriers to mobility by various races. The only barriers are
economic." He pointed out that in predominantly Protestant
Toronto the incumbent metro chairman was a Roman Catholic
and the Toronto mayor was a Jew.

The comparative data on Toronto, Miami, and Nashville
offer no support for the hypothesis that area-wide metropolitan
government tends to weaken the political access of Negroes and
other core city minority groups. On the contrary, the perceptions
of informed observers are just the reverse, by more than three to
one. If Toronto interviewees are dropped, the ratio increases to
more than seven to one. Three chief causes are cited for Negroes'
easier political access—greater professionalism means less racial
discrimination, the elimination of divided responsibility makes
racial pressure more effective, and increased Negro representation
on the local legislative body. It should be noted that these factors

cited as causes are only partly inherent in the concept of area-wide metropolitan government, if at all. This would weaken any effort to argue that metro will inevitably *strengthen* Negro political access, but it in no way affects the conclusion that metro will *not* inevitably *weaken* Negro political access.

POLITICAL ACCESS BY HIGHER AND LOWER INCOME GROUPS

One other variable that was included in the questions asked concerning effect on political access was the income level of residents. They were asked specifically about possible effect on the ability of higher and lower income residents to get an attentive hearing from responsible officials. It is often alleged in the literature concerning metropolitan reorganization that metro reform would amount to a take-over by higher income groups at the expense of the political access of lower income groups. The pattern of answers in all three areas is shown in Table 4 and it is im-

Table 4

EFFECT OF ADOPTION OF METRO ON POLITICAL ACCESS
BY HIGHER AND LOWER INCOME GROUPS

	Toronto	Miami	Nashville	Total
Access Rating for Higher Income Residents:				
Much easier	—	2	1	3⎫ 20
Somewhat easier	—	8	9	17⎭
No change	8	6	9	23
Somewhat harder	7	1	1	9⎫ 11
Much harder	—	2	—	2⎭
Total answering	15	19	20	54
Access Rating for Lower Income Residents:				
Much easier	—	1	1	2⎫ 20
Somewhat easier	—	8	10	18⎭
No change	8	4	7	19
Somewhat harder	6	2	2	10⎫ 13
Much harder	1	2	—	3⎭
Total answering	15	17	20	52

mediately made clear that the interviewees as a whole saw no difference in the effect of metro on higher and lower income residents' political access.

EFFECT ON OTHER GROUPS

To allow for the possibility that metro has had important effects on the relative strength or political access of other interest groups, the interviewees were asked in an open-end question to describe any such effects. The answers to this question are highly inconclusive, with a considerable number saying that metro had not caused any change, and no strong consensus among those who did name specific interest groups affected. In Toronto "ratepayers groups" were named by three interviewees as having less access at the metro level, and a similar number mentioned "areawide interest groups" as having stronger access because of metro, and no other group was mentioned by more than two Toronto interviewees. One said that the bargaining power of civil service groups had been strengthened by the metro structure, one said newspapers had weaker influence in the suburbs now, another said the newspapers' long-range planning interests had been strengthened by metro, and another said that "good government groups had been strengthened."

Over one-half of the Miami interviewees said there had been no change in the strength of interest groups, but of those stating that changes had occurred, four named the *Miami Herald* (daily newspaper) as having been strengthened and given greater political access because of metro. Three said that "chamber of commerce types" now had increased access, and another spoke of better access for "area-wide interests," the same term used by Toronto interviewees. One said metro has tended to weaken the access of the more narrow special interest groups because of the openness of the metro commission, in contrast to personalized basis for access to the old county commission.

Nashville interviewees were not agreed on any particular pattern of change in interest group strength or access, with four being the largest number naming a single group. School teachers were mentioned by these as having better political access under metro than under the previously divided structure of city and county governments. Three thought organized labor had been strengthened by the adoption of metro but one said that labor had been weakened. The pattern of answers was even more mixed for the others.

EFFECT OF METRO ON POLITICAL PARTIES

The effect of metro on political parties was the subject of one of the questions asked of the panels of informed observers. They were asked, "Has Metro changed in any way the relative strength (advantages or disadvantages) of the political parties in the metropolitan area, and if so how?" Over three-fourths of those answering said metro had no effect on political parties, and in Miami none of the interviewees disagreed with this view. (See Table 5.)

Table 5

WHAT EFFECT HAS THE ADOPTION OF METRO HAD ON THE RELATIVE STRENGTH OR ADVANTAGES OF POLITICAL PARTIES?

	Toronto	*Miami*	*Nashville*	*Total*
No effect	11	16	12	39
Helped Democratic party	—	—	1	1
Helped Republican party	—	—	7	7
"Perhaps pushed toward partisan local government"	4	—	—	4
Total answering	15	16	20	51

In Toronto a minority of about one-fourth of the interviewees felt that there had been some movement in the direction of local party government, but this was not at all a strong feeling and there was disagreement on whether this was the result of the adoption of metro. One or two did feel that the NDP (New

Democratic party) which had consistently advocated party government at the local level, had become stronger in recent years in
Toronto, and that this might be related in part to metro. More
seemed to believe that the NDP was simply helped by the growth
of big city problems and the appeal of more socialist oriented
solutions, rather than by the establishment of metropolitan government.

Nashville interviewees were the only ones to state flatly, in
considerable numbers, that the creation of metro had helped one
particular party. About one-third of the interviewees expressed
the opinion that the adoption of metro had actually helped the
Republican party in Nashville and Davidson County. It was said
to be true because the Republican strength is in the suburban
areas where it had been effectively "sidetracked" from participation in the more live political issues of the core city government.
Consolidation, coupled with the decision to have thirty-five single-
member districts in electing the metro council, was said to give
the Republicans a chance to elect a few officials for the first time.
Although a handful of Republicans were elected to the council,
they did not use the party label openly. While this is a significant
number of interviewees to express the opinion, it still is a minority of the Nashville "knowledgeables," with 60 per cent saying
metro has had no effect. One interviewee expressed the opinion
that the Democrats had been helped because the creation of
metro represented a consolidation of political power and the
Democrats were the "in group" reaping the benefit of this.

EFFECT ON CITIZEN ABILITY TO FIX POLITICAL RESPONSIBILITY

If the essence of representative democracy is holding governmental officials accountable for their performance, this should be
a key question to ask in seeking to evaluate the political effects of
a new structure of government for metropolitan areas. Interviewees were asked, "Has the adoption of Metro caused any change
(for better, for worse, or not at all) in the ability of the people to

fix responsibility for the deeds or misdeeds of governmental officials in the area—for local failures or achievements?" For the
three areas in the aggregate, 57 per cent said metro had made it
easier to fix responsibility, 30 per cent said metro made it harder,
and the remainder said metro had caused no change. (See Table
6.) Important differences occur in the pattern of answers between

Table 6

WHAT EFFECT HAS METRO HAD ON THE ABILITY OF THE PEOPLE
TO FIX RESPONSIBILITY ON GOVERNMENTAL OFFICIALS
FOR ACTION OR INACTION?

	Toronto	Miami	Nashville	Total
Easier	3	9	17	29
No change	3	2	2	7
Harder	8	6	1	15
Total answering	14	17	20	51

the three areas, however, with Nashville interviewees in rather
strong consensus that fixing responsibility has been made easier,
whereas only a bare majority in Miami answered "easier" and only
about one-fifth of the Toronto interviewees believed it had been
made easier. More than half of those answering in Toronto actually said that metro's establishment had made it more difficult
to fix responsibility for governmental action or inaction.

These three patterns of answers offer strong support for the
hypothesis that the particular kind of formal governmental structure does make a difference in the ability of people to fix responsibility. The key variable, of course, between Nashville's metro
and the other two systems is the number of levels of government
built into the system. The perceptions of the interviewees support
the rational, horseback judgment that fixing responsibility is more
difficult under a two-tier system than under a single consolidated
system. This still does not explain the difference between Miami
and Toronto, in which the Toronto interviewees indicated in
considerably larger percentage than in Miami that metro actually
made it harder to fix responsibility. Logic would indicate that the
additional variable in this case is the method of electing the gov-

erning body of metro, with direct election being used in Miami
and an indirect, ex officio system being used in Toronto.

CONCLUSIONS

The opinions of informed observers in three metropolitan
areas which have adopted area-wide government do not generally
support the hypothesis that such governments will make political
access more difficult. Approximately three-fourths of the interviewees said metro's adoption has made political access either
easier or had no effect on it. When asked about metro's effects on
the political access of specific categories of people, such as core
city residents, suburbanites, rural residents, lower income residents, and Negroes, two-thirds or more of the interviewees said
access is either easier or unchanged.

The hypothesis that metropolitan government will make
political access more difficult comes closer to being confirmed by
Toronto's experience than by that of Miami and Nashville, but
even in the case of Toronto about two-thirds of the knowledgeables thought there had been no change in political access. More
Toronto interviewees said access had been made harder than said
easier, however, and this actually constituted a majority of those
answering when asked separately about such specific groups as core
city, suburban, and rural residents. In no case did a majority of
either the Miami or Nashville interviewees say that access had
been made more difficult. Negro political access in Miami and
Nashville was actually said to be improved by almost 75 per cent
of the interviewees, and the percentage rises to 90 when those saying "no change" are added.

A comparative picture of the three metro's effects on political
access, at the risk of oversimplification, would indicate access as
clearly easier in Nashville, slightly easier in Miami, and slightly
more difficult in Toronto. Differences in formal structure of metro
are most frequently cited as explanatory factors related to the
three-city differences in political access, e.g., one tier versus two
tiers, and direct election of officials versus indirect election or

appointment. It would seem plausible to expect political access problems in Toronto to grow as its metro government becomes more involved in the social service functions delegated to it under the 1967 reorganization.

8 /

Explanatory Variables in the Comparative Study of Urban Administration and Politics

ROBERT R. ALFORD

THIS ESSAY PLACES A NUMBER of non-American studies of urban administration and politics into the context of a common analytical framework, in an attempt to see whether some clarification of the field of study and of appropriate strategies for further research can be attained. Comments on several studies, including chapters in this volume, are presented after a brief summary of the scheme.

INTRODUCTION: AN ANALYTIC SCHEME[1]

At any given point in time political actors make decisions, some of which carry the authority of law and government. These

---

AUTHOR'S NOTE: The authors of the works on which I comment have not had the opportunity to examine my manuscript, although there was considerable discussion of some of these points during our stimulating month together in Chapel Hill in July, 1967. But if I have misread or misinterpreted their works, it is my responsibility and not theirs. It should perhaps be added that in pushing and pulling their observations and interpretations to fit my analytic scheme, no criticisms of the original authors' work are intended.

[1] For a more detailed statement of and application of the scheme to five comparative studies of American cities, see Robert R. Alford, "The Comparative Study

decisions are influenced by three sets of factors: situational, structural and cultural. Situational factors are those which pertain to the contingencies influencing the concrete events of the decision itself and which cannot be predicted from structural or cultural factors. The fact that a certain type of man holds office, that a certain party has a majority, that certain members of the city council showed up to vote one day, that a certain person in an area to be annexed happened to choose to live there and to choose to become an opposition leader, are factors which may be situational, structural or cultural, depending on how recurrent and patterned they are.

Structural factors include size, complexity, number, distribution, differentiation, and division of labor, insofar as these factors have an effect independent of the values and norms that may be their causes. Cultural factors refer to the values and norms that infuse a structure with meaning, provide political actors with justifications for their actions, and legitimate various types of groups and their demands, insofar as these values and norms have an effect independent of the structural factors which may be their causes. Environmental factors include all of those factors which, for convenience, are regarded as operating outside the boundaries of the local political system. They may also be subdivided into situational, structural, and cultural aspects.

Situational factors, by definition, cannot be predicted from structural or cultural factors, but constitute the element of the random, contingent, accidental, which influences any particular series of events. Thus, whether or not a factor is situational or not cannot be known from the study of a single case, but only by comparison with a number of other cases similar or different in a number of respects. Also, exactly the same factor may be an important influence in one set of circumstances as in another, but have a situational character in one set of circumstances, but structural properties in another. For example, recruitment of a chief

of Urban Politics," in Leo F. Schnore and Henry Fagin (eds.), *Urban Research and Policy Planning* ("Urban Affairs Annual Reviews," Vol. I [Beverly Hills: Sage, 1967]). A later version, applying the scheme to four United States cities, appears in Robert R. Alford, with the collaboration of Harry M. Scoble, *Bureaucracy and Participation: Political Cultures in Four Wisconsin Cities* (Chicago: Rand McNally, 1969).

executive officer in council-manager cities may be determined by law in such a way as nearly to guarantee selection of a person with a certain training, skills, outlook, and sets of assumptions about the proper role of local government and its administration. A continuous series of decisions to select such a man as chief executive officer would thus be a policy determined by a structural factor. On the other hand, in mayor-council cities, the chief executive officer might infrequently have the combination of personal attributes usually found in city manager cities. But, in a particular case, the mayor, let us say, of a mayor-council city might be quite similar to the "normal" type of man chosen in council-manager cities. If that is so, then his behavior in comparable situations might be quite similar, let us assume, to most city managers. But the fact that a "city manager" type of man happened to hold the chief executive office in this mayor-council city at this particular time would be a situational factor, one not predictable from knowing anything about the political and administrative structures of the city.

A summary of the central analytical concepts may be useful:

DEPENDENT VARIABLES (FOR ANY GIVEN UNIT OF ANALYSIS)

Decision: An authoritative act

Policy: A high probability of a similar decision in an analogous situation

Role of government: A high probability of similar policies in a variety of substantive decision-areas

EXPLANATORY VARIABLES

Situational Factor: The contingencies of action

Structural Factor: A high probability that similar situations confronting actors will recur

Cultural Factor: A high probability that the same principles of behavior will be manifested in a number of structures.

These definitions focus principally upon the *consequences* of behavior as the central measurement tool. Because values, for example, cannot be directly measured, it is our assumption, for analytic purposes, that finding the same principles of behavior manifest in a variety of structures will manifest the presence of a cultural value. Similarly, structures are not directly measurable, and we assume that a useful approach is through assessment of the probabilities that given situational contexts for behavior will recur.

The analytic scheme is intended to be used as part of the strategy of attack upon comparative empirical studies of urban administration and politics, since we have not yet broken through the problem of vacillation between case studies of unique systems and abstract comparisons of variables torn from their context. The analytic scheme attempts to unify the "system" and the "variable" approaches to comparative analysis. A concern with systems leads to a focus upon the unique interdependencies of the phenomenon being studied; a concern with variables usually assumes implicitly that the framework or context is a constant.

Also, the analytic scheme is intended to bridge the gap between qualitative and quantitative techniques by linking qualitative characterizations to quantitative ones. The notions of probability and the consideration of the relative contribution of a variety of independent variables to a given dependent variable are quantitative concepts, but, as the discussion of various papers will show, they are applied here to essentially qualitative distinctions. At this stage in the comparative study of urban administration and politics, it is important to develop conceptual links between the qualitative data which are frequently all that are available and a quasi-quantitative analytic framework.

Much of social science vacillates between two modes of explanation, one focusing upon situations and individual participants in events, and one upon structural, cultural, and environmental factors. Seldom are these integrated, however. The series of riots in American cities are a case in point. A riot in Detroit could be "explained" by a series of precipitating events: acts of violence by individual policemen and rioters, speeches by civil rights leaders, and other events "close" to the wave of burnings and destruction, but also "explained" by the general level of poverty, deprivation, and indignities suffered by the Negro people in the city. Both levels of explanation are necessary to understand why riots break

out in one city and not in another, but a given act of violence is
not predictable from knowledge of the poverty level in the city.

The comparative studies of urban administration and politics
also vacillate uneasily between these modes of explanation, partly
because they have not first been conceptually distinguished and
then reintegrated into a broader analytical scheme. The behavioral
revolution in social science has partly been responsible for remind-
ing us that our data are ultimately linked to specific times, places,
and participants in particular sequences of events. The "systems"
approach reminds us that particular sequences of events are patterned within a larger, interrelated framework which reduces their
contingent and quasi-random character. But the dichotomy per-
sists between studies which describe events and actors and explain
them by situational factors, and studies which describe institutions
and their functions and explain them by structural and cultural
factors.

A word is necessary on the choice of studies. The purpose of
this essay is analytical and not bibliographic, and therefore not all
or even most of the relevant literature is cited. Because of the relatively few attempts at explicit comparative analysis, almost none
of the books and articles included refer to each other nor do they
place themselves within a common theoretical framework. Therefore, it has been impossible systematically to compare one substantive factor with another in several countries. The analytical
scheme, rather than a substantive problem, constitutes the unifying theme of the chapter.

Hopefully the analytical usefulness of these abstract categories will become clear in the course of presentation of studies
of particular nations and urban governments. We will deal with
the actual explanatory factors and dependent variables of concern
to the authors themselves, translating them into the analytic
scheme briefly summarized. Tables classifying particular substantive variables are presented in conjunction with the discussion of
several studies, to make the analytic distinctions more explicit.

"CREEPING" URBANISM IN MALAYSIA

The study by Professor James Guyot provides interesting case materials for the juxtaposition of two models of explanation of the development of an urban way of life among Malaysian settlers on rural development schemes.

Table 1 differentiates the various categories of independent and dependent variables with which Guyot deals. The dependent variable is the development of an "urban way of life" among the settlers on rural development schemes, as indicated by the various measures listed. Explanatory variables include the general social and political conditions mentioned under the "structural" and "situational" features of the environment. A last environmental variable is the policy of the government to establish the agricultural schemes as employing organizations rather than as communities comprised of land-owning peasants free to organize their own local institutions. "Environmental" variables, it will be recalled, are those which have an impact upon a local system but whose causal origins lie outside it. If each of the schemes was established by local decision, regardless of how similar these decisions were, the variable would be classified as an attribute of the local system. Cases where national officials make decisions after pressure from local officials are intermediate.

Characteristics of the local system which may possibly explain the development of an "urban way of life" include such demographic changes as increasing size, density, social and ethnic heterogeneity or homogeneity, and the landless economic position of the settlers. Guyot gives no information on what might be classified as "cultural" attributes of the rural development schemes, or on variations among them in types of leadership, or idiosyncratic features which could be classified as situational variables. Essentially, he assumes that the sixty-one schemes are relatively alike in these major independent *and* dependent variables so that collectively they constitute a test of the hypothesis that increasing size, density, and heterogeneity lead to a gradual (creeping) development of an urban way of life.

Table 1

DEPENDENT AND EXPLANATORY VARIABLES IN A STUDY
OF RURAL MALAYSIAN DEVELOPMENT SCHEMES

DEPENDENT VARIABLE
Development of "urban way of life" among settlers on rural development
schemes:
  1) nuclear family more important
  2) development of secondary organizations to resolve conflict
  3) labor discipline increases
  4) money economy more important
  5) expectations of future no longer traditional

EXPLANATORY VARIABLES (Characteristics of state and nation relevant to rural
  development schemes)
Environmental
  Structural
    Overrepresentation of rural areas in national political system
    Concentration of Chinese in urban areas, Malays in rural areas
  Cultural
    None mentioned by author
    Possible: Communal conflict between Malays and Chinese
  Situational
    Alliance of dominant Malay party (UMNO) with Chinese party (MCA)
    Shared English educational experience among Malay political elite
    Differentiation of two leading political roles into "instrumental" and
    "expressive" functions
  Policy
    To establish the agricultural schemes as employing "organizations" rather
    than as local "communities"
  Decision
    To implement this policy on each component scheme
Local System (Characteristics of rural areas)
  Structural
    Units of production larger in population than old rural land holdings
    Social units denser in population than old rural land holdings
    Ethnic homogeneity
    Settlers mainly landless
  Cultural
    None mentioned by author
    Possible: Level of achievement motivation among peasants
  Situational
    None mentioned by author (because no individual schemes discussed)
    Possible: Personalities of local leaders on each scheme

The image of "creeping urbanism" which Guyot uses to unify
his materials may be based upon a model of economic and social
development in which government and bureaucratic activity play

a relatively unimportant role. The movement of people from farms to cities is seen in the classic model of urban development as an almost purely voluntary activity, as a response to market conditions and job opportunities. The consequences of urbanization follow "naturally," as part of an unplanned, uncontrolled process of change of social and human relationships. As families move from farms to cities, the economic interdependence of family members dwindles, contact with the extended family is lost, and exposure to a variety of impersonal social controls increases. Such is the image of social change implied by the concept of creeping urbanism, as the size, density, and heterogeneity of the social unit increases. An urban community, in this view, is an open system, mainly influenced by market pressures, and the "typical" interrelationships of size, density, and the "urban way of life" may depend upon free occupational and geographic mobility remaining as parameters of the system.

Given this framework, Guyot's explanation for the development of an "urban way of life" among the settlers on these rural development schemes, thus, focuses upon the classic variables of demographic and ecological theory: size, density, and heterogeneity.

Yet, the picture which he presents is not one in which gradually increasing size and density of population bring in diverse social elements from a countryside and produce an "urban" way of life, a new urban "community." Rather, a number of "organizations" were established, with a hierarchy of officials possessing effective sanctions to control the behavior of their members or employees. The imperative tasks set for these organizations dictated the creation of specific conditions of life and work which may have had little to do, we suggest, with the size and density of the population forming the base of the organizations. In the terminology we are using here, the question is which factors produced the "urban way of life" characteristic of the settlers on the rural development schemes: the demographic ones of size and density or the political-organizational policies established by state and national leaders. Let us review the characteristics of these schemes in order to document this point. Guyot's conclusion is that "there is a perceptible and most likely significant increase in the intensity and diversity of personal contacts confronting a settler removed from the traditional, small *kampong* to the somewhat larger, more significantly dense, and someways more heterogeneous scene of the FLDA land development scheme."

The land development schemes are essentially agricultural factories located in "company towns" and the fact that they produce from the land is irrelevant to their social and organizational characteristics. Males are selected by their ages and physical condition for the work. They do not own the land, and may be ejected from employment for disciplinary reasons. The settlers report for roll call six days a week at 6 A.M. Income is based on both daily wages and piecework. So far, these aspects of the settler's life are not too much different from an ordinary industrial employee in the West. But the extent of social control and sanctions used on the schemes go far beyond this. The FLDA staff attempts, apparently successfully, to cut settler family ties with their extended kin network. Both the social and work life of the settler are "under the direction" of a block head appointed by the manager of the scheme. Purchases of household needs away from the cooperative store on the scheme are "frowned upon." These aspects of life on a development scheme sound much like the company towns organized by Henry Ford and other leading American capitalists in the days prior to the organization of the industrial unions. The author does suggest that the economic character of the settler is really close to that of the industrial employee, "a shift in the urban direction which we may expect to locate him at a different point in the political arena from the *kampong* bound peasant."

Professor Guyot is aware of the tensions and conflicts endemic to this sort of social structure. He suggests that "as the structure of political power becomes more localized, the settlers are more likely to win" when they demand something. Such a hypothesis assumes that the policy of centralization of production and control which resulted in the initial establishing of the pattern of organization of the schemes will at some stage of development be reversed, or at the very least, suggests that there are inherent strains and tensions between an open "community" and a semi-closed "organization."

Our analytic scheme allows us to see that there are two general models of social processes implicit in Guyot's presentation of the Malaysian case. One is a voluntaristic, market model which presumes the free movement of individuals responding to job opportunities and postulates a variety of gradual changes in social structure which Guyot expresses by the adjective "creeping" urbanism. The other model sees social structure as being shaped by decisions and policies of authoritative agencies possessing sanctions and exercising direct control over the movements, activities and relationships of individual persons. Probably both general kinds of independent variables are operative in every empirical case, but specialists focus on certain ones. Demographers and ecologists have, by and large, neglected the political forces at work in analyzing the causes of the changes they wish to explain. Political scientists, by and large, have neglected the slow but powerful social changes set in motion by demographic changes in the social composition of a population or the constraints upon the spatial distribution and relationships of a population by economic forces. It is only when a scheme of variables takes into account the possible explanatory power of a variety of different factors can theorizing be raised to a new level. It is a virtue of this study that both major types of factors are brought into the description of the empirical materials. In their absence, alternative explanatory possibilities would be less easy to discern.

To conclude, Guyot's article presents two implicit explanatory schemes which are not necessarily contradictory but which point in two directions, toward a model of gradual, evolutionary change of social relationships as the size, density and heterogeneity of a population increases and toward a model of immediate, directed, controlled change as authoritative decisions establishing productive organizations are made. The point is that these models suggest alternative explanatory factors. If the changes in social relationships among the settlers are due to authoritative decisions of administrative officials, then the size and density of the scheme may have absolutely nothing to do with the patterns of social relationships that have come to exist. Conversely, if increasing size and density have alone produced secondary, bureaucratic controls over the settlers' behavior, then the organizational context

within which they live and work is irrelevant. Probably neither
of these extreme alternative explanations is correct, but the *relative* explanatory power of the demographic changes versus the
organizational changes is not raised as a problem in the chapter,
partly, we suggest, because of the lack of explicitness of the analytic scheme of independent and dependent variables.

THE DECENTRALIZATION OF POLITICAL POWER

The problem of the nature, causes and consequences of political and legal autonomy among urban communities is one of the
more intriguing and important problems in the comparative
study of urban politics and administration. The chapter by Professor Frank Sherwood in this volume raises the issues in a way
that provokes some questions inspired by our analytic scheme.

First, what is the important dependent variable? There are at
least two for Sherwood: the extent to which a local community is
prized by its members (which Philip Selznick calls institutionalization) and the extent to which a local government has some measure
of real political and legal autonomy (devolution in Sherwood's
terminology). In our terms, these are cultural and structural characteristics, respectively, and they are assumed by Sherwood to be
closely associated. One of the basic conditions for institutionalization *is* devolution, according to Sherwood. He hypothesizes implicitly that it would be quite difficult for a community to be
prized by its members without possessing some real autonomy
vis-à-vis the national government. Table 2 presents the main distinctions between dependent and explanatory factors with which
Sherwood deals.

Sherwood applies a model of organizational decision-making
to the relationships of national government to local governments.
While useful, the range of explanatory variables which it leads one
to consider may be incomplete. For example, Sherwood cites the
organizational principle that "where the resources to support an
organization come from only one point in the environment, a

Table 2

FACTORS IN THE DEVOLUTION
OF POLITICAL POWER

DEPENDENT VARIABLES
   Cultural
      Extent to which local community is prized by its members (institutionalization)
   Structural
      Extent to which a local government has real autonomy (decentralization) (Indicator: proportion of total income received by local governments from the national government)

EXPLANATORY VARIABLES
   Environmental
   Structural
      Legal powers given to local governments
      Economic development of various regions
      Number of local units of government
      Level of development of communications system in nation
   Cultural
      Extent to which autonomy for local communities is a society-wide value
   Situational
      Particular national laws affecting municipalities in force at a given time
      Strategic commitment by national leaders to certain policies regarding local autonomy
   Local System
   Structural
      Economic base of the community
      Level of population growth
      Changes in economic structure of the community
   Cultural
      Extent of general value-consensus in community on goals to be served by local government
   Situational
      Initiative, honesty and political skills of mayor of community

single decision can mean the survival or demise of the organization." He infers from this principle that the more a municipality is dependent upon the national government for its financial support, the less likely it is to be valued by its members. Surely this does not follow, if only because a local community is not merely a lower-level unit of a hierarchical bureaucratic apparatus, regardless of its statutory role in the national political system. Even if in theory a local government can be eliminated by a "single decision," the social and political forces sustaining it are probably far stronger than those sustaining a branch sales office of General Motors or a lumber camp of American Box Company. By using an organization model, he suggests that a community's local government is just as dependent upon its environment as any subordinate unit in a bureaucracy. This point illustrates the incomplete explication of the possible relationship of explanatory variables to each other. By assuming a high correlation between formal devolution and institutionalization, he omits the possibly most frequent type in which the local population constitutes neither a fully autonomous and deeply prized community nor a totally dependent and purely instrumental organization.

Suppose we were to hypothesize that the structural and cultural aspects of devolution are not necessarily linked. Four types of local systems are possible, depending on whether or not they are prized by their members and on whether or not they possess real political autonomy. (Clearly these are continua in reality.) Table 3 shows the four resulting types.

Table 3

AUTONOMY AND VALUE: A TYPOLOGY

Cultural Characteristic
The Local Community is Valued

		+	−
Structural Characteristic The local government has real political autonomy	+	A Autonomous community	B Instrumental organization
	−	C Valued community	D Low-level bureaucratic unit

The labels of the cells are intended to do no more than provide a summary of the two characteristics which define them; they add no more meaning. Those aspects of local community life which are not controlled or limited by the national government and which enjoy the attachment and appreciation of local community residents fall into cell C. Those aspects of local community life which are not valued by residents but over which their local government has real control fall into cell B. These are the two cells that deviate from Sherwood's scheme, since he assumes that there is a high correlation between these structural and cultural characteristics. Either a local community is an organizational appendage of the national community—neither prized nor autonomous—or it is both prized and autonomous. Some aspects of community life may fall into the two deviant groups, and these would be important to analyze, precisely because of the tensions and conflicts that would lead to change (assuming they are "normally" correlated).

But the very distinction between these two characteristics raises the question of how integrated and homogeneous a community is likely to be. Surely *some* activities in every community —no matter how centralized or decentralized its local government system in theory—would fall into each one of these cells. The question is what kind and how much control is there by higher levels of government over which activities of local groups, individuals, and the local political system, and also, what kind and how much prizing of what there is by local individuals and groups. At the minimum, a more complex typology of types of devolution seems called for, to provide for more adequate comparative descriptions of local governments in terms of their structural and cultural characteristics.

A more complex typology of devolution could include measures of the following characteristics: (1) the number and type of functions assigned to local government by national law; (2) the number and type of functions performed by local government even though only permitted by national or state law; (3) the number and type of functions performed by local government even though forbidden by a national law which lacks effective sanctions; (4) the number and type of functions performed by local government even though forbidden by national law and carrying costs in the form of various levels of sanctions. Since we cannot assume that a national system is totally homogeneous, measures of each characteristic would have to be worked out for each local government. Such distinctions cannot easily be incorporated into Sherwood's scheme, because they embody the assumption of potential conflict between national and local government. A local government which *only* performs those functions assigned by law and one which performs others, at some cost to itself, clearly must be distinguished, although a single continuum of devolution may not suffice to do so.

Sherwood assumes that the level of devolution for any given nation is the same for all local governments, and this makes sense in a comparative international study, such as the one he relies upon by Professor Vieira dealing with the proportion of local government revenues deriving from the national government. But by assuming that the general level of devolution is a policy of the national government, implemented by a series of decisions with respect to each locality, in an important sense Sherwood is violating his own basic perspective on and commitment to devolution. If local communities are truly viable sociopolitical entities, they will act on their own behalf regardless of what the status of local government is in national law. We would expect considerable variation in this respect from local community to community. In fact, autonomy might better be seen as a community attribute influenced by two sets of policies and decisions, those taken at the national level, and those taken at the local level.

These points have been developed at some length to show that the perspective which Sherwood takes vacillates from that of the local community back and forth to that of the national government, and, in fact, is more often the latter, perhaps surprisingly. On the one hand, he is concerned with the conditions under which local governments can gain autonomy, on the other with the conditions under which national governments can develop a strategy of devolution which can serve their goals. At first glance, these seem like neutral and objective questions. But he does not deal with the two other logical possibilities: How can the national government dispose of obsolete local governments? And how can local governments defend themselves against unacceptable demands or regulations of the national government? These questions imply a conflict perspective which Sherwood implicitly rejects, accepting instead assumptions of consensus by both local and national government on ends to be served and means to achieve those ends. Or, to put the point more specifically, actual conflicts in particular nations, such as Brazil, are discussed, but the existence and nature of these conflicts does not enter explicitly into his theoretical framework. Analytic distinctions between different explanatory and dependent variables would have allowed him to raise certain questions which do not come up, given his view of an integrated and consensual system.

His acceptance of the point of view of the national government can be shown by several examples. On several occasions, Sherwood refers to devolution as a national "strategy" and, with reference to Brazilian experience, to the "seemingly unwarranted expansion of the number of municipalities . . . ," and to the failure of Brazilian municipalities "to achieve the goals set for them." These phrases indicate that the point of view is that of national leaders seeking to develop an appropriate machinery for local government, not that of local government officials seeking to find additional powers to make their institutions viable ones. Despite his insistence on devolution and institutionalization, Sherwood does not take the existing municipalities seriously as autonomous entities. His comparison of northern and southern municipalities in Brazil illustrates this point. New local governments were established in Northern Brazil "simply to secure a greater share of federal funds." More importantly, it cannot be assumed that important functions were not being performed by these new local units simply because they were created mainly because federal funds were available. Implicitly, Sherwood assumes that the "needs" of local communities are defined by national government officials, which contradicts the basic character of devolution, as he himself defines it.

Another example showing that he takes the point of view of national government is that "the essential idea of devolution is system separateness, in which local governments discharge obligations as part of a national political system." Such a formulation assumes consensus—that devolution can only take place if values and goals are shared and if local governments are willing to work within a framework established by the national government. (Such a point of view is consistent with Selznick's view of the conditions of decentralization in an organization, which can occur when subunits are imbued with the values of the center.)

Another instance that indicates that the perspective of national government is taken occurs when he remarks that the "institution-building model" conceives of the local government as a system "with sufficient independence and autonomy to discharge its full membership obligations in a larger system of governments." Structurally based conflict is blurred by that phrase, which presupposes that the entire purpose of autonomy is to serve the goals of national government. But, surely, the basic meaning of autonomy is that one has the power to refuse cooperation. At the very least, potential conflict between the structural framework established by the national government and a valued and instrumental local government should be allowed for in the categories of analysis, not denied by an a priori judgment about the relationships between key variables.

URBAN SERVICES IN LATIN AMERICA

Professor Francine Rabinovitz suggests, in her chapter in the present volume, that the "major functions of urban politics in Latin America will be found in the external sphere": implementing decisions made largely by the national government, or recruiting future national politicians. Her whole argument about the centralization or "nationalization" of politics in Latin America assumes that national policy controls local decision-making. To put the point in the language of our scheme, she assumes that variations from city to city in local political structures and political cultures do *not* have a significant effect upon local decisions and policy-making. Rather, variations in decisions and policies will be found to be related almost entirely to structural and cultural factors located at the national level. Or, to put the point another way, if local structural and cultural characteristics are correlated with local decisions and policies, it is only because local variations are taken into account by national leaders and officials, who differentiate the applicability of their decisions to local jurisdictions accordingly.

This point illustrates the sharp difference between the data and the problem which Professor Rabinovitz is dealing with and those of most other chapters discussed here. She is mainly concerned with the "environment" of urban political and administrative systems, and asserts that in Latin America the environment is decisive, that, in fact, one cannot usefully distinguish between the nation and the city as politico-administrative units which can be analyzed even partially as autonomous systems. But surely this assumption must remain empirically problematic, in the absence of data which in fact demonstrate that national policies explain far more about urban government than do local variations in social and political structure. The data are not yet assembled to test this assertion.

We shall assume, however, in the discussion to follow that it is possible to predict relationships at the urban level from the national data that Professor Rabinovitz presents, within a certain unknown range of probability.

Rabinovitz found that the national level of urbanization in Latin America was not strongly associated with the organization of urban institutions: a bureaucracy, stable mechanisms for changing executives, institutions for the control of group violence, the development of urban services. But these organizational features or consequences of a "developed" society were themselves associated. It is highly significant that all of the characteristics which have to do with features of social organization were interrelated, but that none of them were closely associated with the level of urbanization of the total society. (Note that we are here taking her data and basic interpretations as a given.)

The implication is not that differences in "urbanization" have no consequences, but rather that attention must be directed not only to national correlates of urbanization, but also to the infrastructure of urban life: the development of organizations which function at the urban level, *even though the society as a whole is not highly urbanized.* Her data imply that important interrelationships occur at the level of the organization of bureaucratic and participatory institutions at the local urban level, not only at the national level. The deaths from group violence which she uses as a measure of "constitutional stability" could, for example, equally as well be used as a measure of the adequacy of development of legal and police institutions in cities (assuming that much of the violence occurred in cities).

Even though the "functions" of politics may be national, the *location* of many of the behaviors which are the source of her national level data must be at the local urban level. City executives may indeed be "mainly important as influence wielders," but somebody has to administer the local water and police system. The implications of this inference will be developed below.

At the end of her chapter, Professor Rabinovitz suggests that one of the indicators of "urbanization" which she used earlier—the level of urban services—may in fact be an indicator of "urbanism," because of the very different pattern of relationships of political stability and political development to demographic urbanization than to organizational urbanism. This theoretical suggestion emerges from the analysis of her data and is left undeveloped. But it is one of the most interesting suggestions of her essay, and I propose to develop its implications further.

Let us clarify our terminology by restricting the word "urbanization" to its demographic meaning: the clustering of human populations into dense, relatively small areas. These are in fact the measures of urbanization which she uses, save the one referring to urban services (water and drainage). We shall *not* use the term "urbanism" for the latter although it is consistent with Louis Wirth's classic definition, and with Professor Guyot's usage in another article in this volume, because of dangers of misunderstanding. Rather, we shall substitute the term *bureaucratization,* which, we suggest, is the central meaning of urbanism as an organizational concept. A "bureaucracy" as a type of organization refers to a hierarchical and coordinated system of rules, differentiated into offices with defined tasks. But from a slightly different point of view, "bureaucratization" refers to the extension and penetration of segmented and role-specific behavior farther and deeper into previously non-bureaucratized human relationships, communities and societies, and is essentially what is meant —organizationally—by "urbanism."

Professor Rabinovitz had no direct measures of bureaucratization, but, I shall argue, her measure of urban service levels can be regarded as having as their direct and almost necessary *condition* the development of bureaucratic forms of organization of local government, and therefore, in the absence of more direct indicators, the level of urban services can be regarded as a *consequence* of bureaucratization. It seems plausible to assume that there must be some kind of formal organization developed to install, maintain, and control a water or drainage system in a city, which requires a staff of persons with differentiated skills and tasks. Such an organization would itself not come into being without an administrative framework which makes it possible to continue carrying out the routine decisions required by systems of urban services. In our terminology, the *policy* of providing urban services which has implied a series of *decisions* to install and maintain water and drainage systems requires a minimum level of bureaucratic *structure*. Whether or not the existence of such policies is the result of varying public commitments to certain social values—a *cultural* factor—is an empirical question. It may well be that there is considerable internal variation in these countries from city to city, which in turn reflects the dominance of social groups holding different values with respect to public welfare and amenities.

Assuming that the national data which Rabinovitz analyzes can be regarded as establishing probabilities that similar relationships exist at the urban level as well, we present the scheme in Table 4. The dependent variable is the policy of developing urban services, and thus a fairly high probability that decisions will be made in city after city to install and maintain water and drainage systems. Although Professor Rabinovitz initially regards urban services as an indicator of "urbanization" parallel to the size of cities and the proportion of urbanized population, the level of urban services can be regarded as a policy consequence which may or may not be empirically related to demographic urbanization. As a matter of fact, urbanization is *not* closely related to the level of urban services, as the parentheses around the environmental factor of societal urbanization are intended to show.

The lack of a correlation of urban services with voting turnout is an interesting finding, and we can only speculate on its meaning. Rabinovitz found that voting turnout was higher in

Table 4

FACTORS EXPLAINING THE LEVEL OF DEVELOPMENT
OF URBAN SERVICES IN LATIN AMERICA

DEPENDENT VARIABLES
  Policy
    To develop urban services
  Decisions
    To install and maintain a water system
    To install and maintain a drainage system

INDEPENDENT (EXPLANATORY) VARIABLES
  Environmental
    Political stability
    (Urbanization level of the society)
    (Voting turnout)
    (Political party development)
  Local System
  Structural
    Existence of minimum level of bureaucratization of local government (no
    data)
    Development of interest groups and political associations
  Cultural
    Lack of local political bosses (*caudillismo*)

CONSEQUENCES FOR POLITICAL PROCESSES
    Lack of group violence
    Political stability

more urbanized nations and in nations with largest single cities. It is impossible to know from these national-level data whether or not urban residents are more likely than rural residents to vote in both highly urbanized and lowly urbanized countries, since it is possible that rural-urban differences in voting turnout are small in more urbanized countries, where the rural-urban difference itself loses some of its political significance. Data on smaller than national units would be required to distinguish between these two possible patterns. It is possible, in other words, either that urbanization affects the entire population (the second case) or only the urban population (in which case higher voting rate in cities than in rural areas accounts for the higher national level). Regardless of which of these two "causes" of a given national level of voting turnout is correct, the meaning of any given national level clearly depends to a large extent on its composition. Urban-level data are required, not only to provide information on cities regarded as an important unit of analysis in their own right, but also to interpret properly the meaning of national-level data. It should not be assumed that data on cities as units have meaning only for cities, as such.

The policy of developing urban services is related to the level of political stability of the society, a lack of local bosses (*caudillismo*), and to the development of interest groups and political associations. The correlations of urban services are higher than is the level of demographic urbanization with those features of political development, according to Rabinovitz' data. Unfortunately, she had no direct measure of the level of bureaucratization of local governments.

Table 4 presents an interpretation of these data somewhat different than Professor Rabinovitz' own, although not inconsistent with it. A national environment of political stability may create the possibility of the development of urban administrative institutions which can move toward a provision of higher levels of local urban services. Stability almost by definition means that there is no periodic or continuous disruption of local government functioning by national upheavals, particularly in societies where national politics is so closely intertwined with local politics.

But certain features of the local system itself may produce higher or lower levels of urban services. We have arbitrarily distinguished them into structural and cultural factors, simply to raise the issue. Structural factors include bureaucratization and the development of participatory institutions such as interest groups and political associations which presumably would put forth demands for improvement of water and drainage systems, among others. Cultural factors could include the degree of acceptance of a boss system (*caudillismo*)—a personalistic, nepotistic, style of politics—as legitimate. The persistence of a boss system certainly depends also upon a variety of structural factors.

A test of the hypotheses implicit in these relationships would require both historical and comparative data from a number of Latin-American cities. A move away from a boss system would seem logically to imply an increase in bureaucratization, that is, decisions are made less on the basis of personal, particularistic power, and more on the basis of official, prescribed authority. The coming into existence of such public, legitimate, and visible loci of decision-making would seem to encourage the development of a variety of interest groups which for the first time perceive channels of influence. As such a bureaucratic machinery develops, together with instrumentalities of demands, we would expect consequences to follow in the form of the development of agencies specifically entrusted with urban services.

The intervening variable of bureaucratization may thus be an important one, but it is impossible, given cross-sectional data, to determine causal priority or even to distinguish various factors. Professor Rabinovitz does not go beyond two-variable statements about her data, although logically a series of statements about control and intervening variables, or even the interaction effects of several variables, could have been made. It is possible, for example, that highly bureaucratized systems which have few participatory institutions such as interest groups will be more "nationalized," and may well be those countries which have high levels of performance of national services (electricity, roads) but low levels of performance on local urban services (water, drainage). Conversely, those societies which are less bureaucratized but have highly developed interest groups may have high levels of urban services, but relatively low national services. The two other cells in this typology (high bureaucratization-high participation, low bureaucratization-low participation) may have distinctive patterns to urban and national services, as well as political stability and conflict. My purpose here is not to develop this kind of theoretical elaboration further, but merely to suggest alternative ways that the data could have been approached.

Can we infer that such structural changes as the development of bureaucratic and participatory institutions involve changes in the values of a population—that structural change produces cultural change? Not necessarily. Structural changes may involve the development of communication networks which activate or generate political organization and thus for the first time make the values of groups visible and consequential. It need not be assumed that the structural changes have created those values which are finally manifest in political or administrative conflicts. The whole point of attempting to separate explanations based upon structural and cultural factors is to avoid the presumption that either type of factor can be completely explained by the other.

POLITICAL INTEGRATION IN TWO AFRICAN COMMUNITIES

The relationship of ethnic cleavage to political integration in two African communities—Umuahia and Mbale—is the subject of the chapter by William John Hanna and Judith Lynne Hanna in the present volume. A "polyethnic community" is defined as one in which "ethnic group membership shapes political perspectives and practices" and also as one in which there is at least "some institutional duplication based upon ethnic group membership." "Integration" has two aspects: practices and perspectives. The integration of practices implies "cooperative interaction . . . common effort, collective action, and mutual facilitation." In our terminology, a social and political system which succeeded in organizing coordinated activities would have established a set of "structures" but would not necessarily possess a common "culture." This distinction is also explicitly made by the Hannas, who define the integration of perspectives as political culture: the "sharing of common prescriptions and proscriptions for conduct, belief, valuation." (They take this last phrase from Robin Williams, Jr.) But they immediately merge the two conceptually by saying that "both polyethnicity and integration should themselves be considered variables rather than attributes," thus reducing the two aspects of integration to a single variable called "integration" which is then related to another variable: polyethnicity. The definition of polyethnicity thus seems to blur the distinction between the independent and dependent variables by defining polyethnicity in terms of the consequences of ethnic membership for political perspectives and practices.

Given these definitions, any of the three different variables which they distinguish could be regarded as either dependent or independent variables. The three variables are polyethnicity (institutional duplication based on ethnic membership), the integration of practices (a structure of coordinated activities), and the integration of perspectives (a culture of common norms, identifications, preferences, beliefs). I shall call their second variable "structural integration" and the third one "cultural integration," for three reasons; to indicate the link between their terminology and mine, to abbreviate the phrases "integration of practices" and "integration of perspectives," and to keep distinct the two aspects of integration.

The independence of the concepts of structural and cultural integration can be illustrated by a simple example. A society which is culturally integrated but totally structurally unintegrated would be one in which two ethnic groups possessing exactly the same values and cultural norms occupied the same territory, but participated in no common activities. Picture a community in which people passed persons of another ethnic group silently on the street, rode in different buses, shopped in different stores, went to different churches, had only friends of the same ethnic group, worked in shops and industries owned, managed by and employing only persons of the same ethnic group, went to different schools. If separately organized around *all* forms of economic, political, and social activity, two completely independent sets of *structures* would occupy the same territory. Yet, it is theoretically possible that the *cultural* values of the two groups could be the same, and the two independent systems might be hidden by their complete physical and geographic merger.

Conversely, two groups could be structurally integrated without cultural integration. Exchanges of commodities, a common transportation system, common occupational recruitment, other coordinated activities of a complex division of labor could, in theory, occur between two ethnic groups without any sharing of values. Some procedural rules governing exchanges and interactions would be necessary, but basic identifications, beliefs, and values might differ radically.

Without expanding on these distinctions further, it is important to note that it is vitally important for the thesis of the article under discussion that the two aspects of integration be kept analytically distinct, because their problem is precisely that: what are the conditions under which cooperative activities are possible in a society split along ethnic lines? And does the continuing existence of those coordinated activities depend upon the existence of shared common values between the ethnic groups? Unfortunately, the way in which the authors define their terms blurs their key empirical and analytical distinctions. For example, they note that most African urban-centered communities can have no "single system of social norms," because they are divided by language, custom and religion (quoted from Kenneth Little). They infer that "this low degree of civility and norm homogeneity *permits* the prevalence of polyethnically structured integrative practices and perspectives" (italics added). As it stands, that sentence is nearly tautological, because "norm heterogeneity" is essentially the same thing as "polyethnically structured integrative practices and perspectives." That is, one could not have the latter without the former, given the basic definitions already summarized. Also, since an ethnic group is *defined* as a set of individuals who share "goal dispositions with associated normative strength," it is difficult to speak of norm heterogeneity "permitting" a low degree of integration of practices and perspectives, because the very existence of an ethnic group implies that different sets of norms exist.

Their basic focus is upon polyethnicity as an independent variable, structural and cultural integration as dependent variables. Their data on the different variables vary in extensiveness and completeness. For purposes of this discussion I shall accept all of their data and basic interpretations as given, even though the authors themselves regard many of their findings as quite tentative.

What did they find? First, both communities were polyethnic: geographic subareas were populated by persons largely of one clan or tribe, although this pattern was more evident in Mbale. Second, persons in both communities associated more frequently with members of their own tribe or clan than with outsiders. But, third, persons were both more politically active and more active with coethnics in Umuahia than in Mbale. Thus, in this respect at least, polyethnicity is *not* associated with structural integration. Umuahia has *less* geographic ethnic segregation, but *more* integration of political activities along ethnic lines. We thus have a negative finding with respect to one key proposition, that geographic polyethnicity is associated with integration of political practices along ethnic lines.

We might suggest another interpretation of these diverse findings. Geographic subareas heavily dominated by a single ethnic group may be more likely to have a "traditional" form of political organization than areas which are ethnically diverse. That is, leadership in ethnically homogenous areas is likely to emerge not from open competition between factions but as a result of informal agreements among hereditary or ascriptively designated heads of families or subclans. Because of this emphasis on private, relatively invisible politics, the ethnic public in the homogeneous area is less likely than in the heterogeneous area to be mobilized into visible interest groups and associations of various kinds. Therefore, they will be less likely to define their problems in political terms, and thus define their situation as one in which they seek political advice or take political action. Conversely, in the ethnically diverse community, political leadership will emerge from a process of competition in which ethnicity is one of a number of bases of cleavage which can be mobilized by aspiring leaders. Paradoxically, ethnicity will seem more important as a basis of political cleavage in the ethnically diverse community, although in fact such a community has actually moved along the path of political development farther away from a situation in which ethnicity is so much taken for granted that it is not visible in survey responses.

This interpretation may explain the seemingly contradictory findings that Mbale has more geographic segregation along ethnic lines but both less political activity in general and less political activity which is ethnically organized.

Cultural integration was studied by means of questions asked of respondents in the two communities about their political and social beliefs and attitudes. Indexes of "homogeneity" were computed for the different ethnic groups, and both intraethnic homogeneity and interethnic contrasts were found to be greater in Umuahia than in Mbale. In the language we are using, Umuahia has a less culturally integrated political system than Mbale, at least with respect to the measure of homogeneity used. Taking this finding as given, it now appears that Umuahia not only has less geographic segregation but more integration of political activities along ethnic lines, but also more integration of political perspectives along ethnic lines. This finding can possibly be explained by the reasoning already given, which we shall not elaborate further.

The "homogeneity index" of political perspectives allowed some inference about the degree to which any group or subgroup approached unanimity of opinion on any question, and thus the degree of cultural integration of each ethnic group. The authors compared two types of leaders—influentials and prominents—with rank-and-file citizens and found that the political perspectives of Umuahia's leaders were more homogeneous than Mbale's. They included only Ibo respondents in Umuahia, African and Asian respondents in Mbale. Their conclusion was that "the comparatively low level of Mbale locality homogeneity is probably a reflection of the politicized biculture which encompasses both Africans and Asians, in contrast with the pervasive Ibo culture of Umuahia."

In the language of our analytic scheme, they are dealing with three forms of social and political structure, one based on group organization without necessarily any territorial identity (ethnicity), one based on territorial location without any single group identity (locality), and one based on both (leadership). An important and interesting question is whether political perspectives are independently shaped both by non-territorial group memberships and by a territorial location which defines political identities. It would be possible, given their data, to assess the relative importance of three different aspects of structural location (ethnic membership, leadership position, territorial residence) for both the direction and the homogeneity of political culture. If the authors had computed their homogeneity indexes for Africans and Asians separately in Mbale (and any other ethnic group for which they had enough cases) and for Ibekus, Ohuhus, and others in Umuahia, and within each ethnic group, separately for leaders and rank and file, they could have assessed the relative importance of one form of social location over another for the homogeneity of political culture.

Another major finding concerned cultural integration. The authors found a "significant gap between the political perspectives of influentials . . . and those of the sampled adults . . . ," but the perspectives of the influentials in the two communities were quite similar to each other. The authors theorized that a "confluence of perspectives . . . takes place among persons who have to deal with each other regularly in order to manage the political affairs of an urban-centered community," or in our terms, that a cultural consequence follows from a structural cause. More specifically, the requirements for governing an urban community imposed by a given population size, group diversity, and objective tasks of public administration result in leaders coming to share similar views of the world. Granted, leaders must come to share a common perspective on the procedures which guide their interactions and negotiations. Otherwise they cannot deal with each other on a regular basis. But the authors seem to go farther than this. They argue that "the locality subunit serves to link the peaks of ethnic hierarchies so that a more 'cosmopolitan' culture emerges and at least a moderate degree of interethnic coordination is made possible." The possibility that all one means by a cosmopolitan culture is the activities implied by "interethnic coordination," is ruled out by the sentence just quoted, which clearly links them as two parts of a causal relationship. But coordination of activities between two groups might occur through bargaining or through sheer power and coercion. A common perspective which might be called a cosmopolitan culture might not be necessary for coordinated activity. To put the hypothesis another way, structures of coordinated activities may continue which enjoy agreement only on procedures for conducting and mediating conflicts, without agreement on general beliefs about society and politics. The authors assume a concordance between structural and cultural factors which is certainly plausible, but which might be left problematic, given their main concerns.

The implication that the differences between leaders and rank and file in political perspectives is a stage in the development of a class structure could be tested, to see whether the differences arise from location in a political structure (leadership) or from location in a class structure (education, occupation, and income).

If the rank and file had been compared to the leadership within comparable education, occupation and income groups, we would have had some hard evidence on the nature of the political and class structures emerging in the two communities. It would be significant to discover that persons similar in occupation, say, were quite similar in political perspectives, regardless of whether or not they were influentials. Or, vice versa, it would be most interesting to find that influentials differed greatly from the rank and file in political perspectives, even though they were similar in occupation and income.

The authors argue in another report from this same study that the high correlation of ethnicity with other social and political characteristics of persons—religion, occupation, political party —means that other "horizontal" group memberships do not significantly cut across ethnicity, and, therefore, that ethnicity can be regarded as the major structural variable which has to be taken into account in describing political processes in the communities.[2] But exactly the opposite could be argued. The high correlation of ethnicity with occupation and party might mean that ethnicity was *not* the salient structural cleavage which explains a pattern of events, but rather occupation or party. Why call a given coalition an "Ibeku" coalition, why not a "less educated" coalition? It is important to distinguish between the structural elements which are intercorrelated and which account for particular events and decisions. One set of political issues may activate the occupational, one the ethnic, another the political party basis for group solidarity, and the classificatory terminology used in describing the events may sneak in an implicit interpretation of the primacy of one or another variable.

Another difference between the two communities concerns their power structures. The authors found that influential persons in the community were more likely to be located in the formal institutions of local government in Mbale than in Umuahia, and thus, in their terms, there was more "bifurcation" of the power structure in Umuahia. This can be regarded as an aspect of polit-

[2] William John Hanna and Judith Lynne Hanna, "The Political Structure of Urban-Centered African Communities," in Horace Miner (ed.), *The City in Modern Africa* (New York: Praeger, 1967), pp. 151–84.

ical process in a community which derives from the nature of its structural and cultural integration. To put it another way, the formal institutions constitute one aspect of structure. The bases on which prestige is accorded, and the kinds of alliances possible between persons with varying interests, depends at least partly upon the values held by the members of the community: its political culture.

Is this finding consistent with others we have already discussed? Recall that Umuahia is more politically active than Mbale, and that its activity is organized more along ethnic lines than Mbale's politics. Would we expect a greater bifurcation of formal and informal leadership in one community than in another, given these findings? Other things being equal, we might presume that actual decision-making would occur outside formal channels if those channels were likely to intensify conflicts in a way which leaders would find disadvantageous, or defeat their chances of negotiating bargains for themselves and their constituencies. And this is really what is meant by bifurcation: the formal authorities are weak and do not make the "real" decisions. Probably the case could be argued both ways. The causal relationship might be the reverse. Given an existing and continuing set of power relationships, in which a group of persons outside formal leadership have succeeded in gaining influence, they might act in such a way as to mobilize ethnic groups on their behalf, in order to counteract the pressure toward universalistic decision-making which a publicly elected body might encourage.

One factor which the authors do not consider in attempting to explain the greater bifurcation of power in Umuahia is the relative proportion of persons in the various ethnic groups. In Umuahia, the two major tribal groups were nearly equally balanced in numbers.[3] This structural factor may help account for the development of important roles for informal groups of leaders who played negotiating and bargaining roles which would not have been necessary under different conditions. Where a single party or ethnic group has a decisive majority, it may be possible to make decisions and policies through the formal structure; there is no need to develop separate bargaining institutions, particularly in a culture which stresses consensus rather than conflict.

Their argument to explain the bifurcation of formal from informal authority is that local government was denigrated because it was based on a European model, was emasculated because rewards were outside its jurisdiction, and was isolated because it did not represent ethnic groups. But the latter two factors might be consequences rather than causes of the bifurcation of power and influence into local government officials and informal, mediating influentials. Given a need for informal mediators in a situation of nearly equal competing groups, the formal structure, once bypassed, would in fact no longer be the major arena for the allocation of rewards nor the major location of negotiations among ethnic groups.

From the point of view of decisions and policies as dependent variables, the authors in this chapter are dealing only with the interrelationships of a variety of independent variables, and *assume* that certain consequences follow. That is, they do not consider the *kinds* of coordinated activities in which the communities engage. In this stimulating exploratory study the authors have mapped some of the structural and cultural components of two African local political systems. It would be possible now to ascertain what difference the degree of polyethnicity or integration makes for authoritative decisions and policies of the two local governments.

METROPOLITAN GOVERNMENT IN NASHVILLE AND MIAMI

An example which shows that the scheme can be applied to analysis of events occurring over time can be drawn from Professor Daniel Grant's chapter in this volume, which we shall not deal with in as great a detail as the others.

Professor Grant suggests that more careful charter drafting may have accounted for the greater stability of metropolitan government in Nashville as compared to Miami. Accepting this as a given, can we ascribe this difference to situational or structural factors? And, regardless of what accounts for the difference in charter drafting, what are the likely consequences for stability?

A variety of situational factors might account for the differences among cities in the quality and political perspicacity of their constitutional charters, partly because there are few recognized guidelines which take the necessary parameters of constitution-drawing into account: financial resources, the heterogeneity, and intensity of political demands likely to be faced by the leaders produced by whatever system is established, and the human resources which can produce a competent and efficient staff. Rather, the exigencies of the political situation surrounding the establishment of the charter-drafting committee will account for the outcome: the skills of particular people who happen to get on the committee, and the emergence of alliances on the committee and the striking of bargains which could not be predicted from a knowledge of the committee members. Let us assume, thus, that a variety of situational factors account for the differential quality of the charters in the two cities, however quality is to be judged.

But, once a decision has been made on the charter, a structure is established: offices, electoral procedures, appeal procedures, a division of powers, legal sanctions, and other components of a political and administrative system. These structures have consequences which are not situational, although a new set of situational and structural factors will influence which aspects of the charter are in fact established and enforced or ignored and evaded.

More generally, this example shows that the sequence of events which occurs cannot be regarded as all predictable from the general characteristics of a "system," no matter how labeled and identified. Rather, the outcomes of processes must be regarded as incompletely determined by *any* set of structural and cultural factors. This incomplete quality allows for the emergence of new factors, new coalitions of forces, and, therefore, for innovation and change, by the very nature of the relationship of subsystems to a system as a whole.

LOCAL GOVERNMENT IN NAIROBI

The problems involved in distinguishing between situational factors, on the one hand, and structural or cultural factors, on the other, are well illustrated by a brief case study by Herbert Werlin of Nairobi, Kenya.[3] The author cites conflict between the Mayor of Nairobi and the Minister for Local Government as an instance which "exemplifies the general lack of cooperation in political life characteristic of underdeveloped countries such as Kenya" (p. 183). However, the events which Werlin describes may be explainable without reference to any "environmental" factors at all, but solely by factors pertaining to the particular sets of circumstances of the situation, and also by structural and cultural factors which may or may not be typical of underdeveloped countries.

I shall list the factors Werlin mentions under the analytical headings that I am utilizing, assuming that there is some validity in all of them, even though he suggests that some of them were used by the participants merely for strategic purposes.

Table 5 summarizes Werlin's discussion on pages 181 to 183 of his article, which gives this instance of conflict to illustrate a general point. The resignation of the mayor followed the demand for an accounting of his private business interests, and the various rhetorical points were made by the officials and by supporters and newspapers. It may be noted that both sides accepted the legitimacy of bureaucratic claims upon leaders to be "efficient," "responsible," and "competent." However, the "popular" governmental instrument—the city council—challenged the bureaucracy's right to interfere on the grounds that it represented the people.

Nothing in this account, nor in the set of explanatory factors I have distinguished, seems to me to establish the "general lack of cooperation" in Kenya local government which was Werlin's conclusion. If the national and ethnic labels were changed, this could well be an account of a conflict in Boston among ward representatives of Italians and Irish and city bureaucrats if we substitute "communist" for "imperialist." The legal structure of divisions of powers may not be substantively different in the two

[3] See Herbert Werlin, "The Nairobi City Council: A Study in Comparative Local Government," *Comparative Studies in Society and History*, VIII (January, 1966), 181–98. A comment by J. David Greenstone follows in the same issue: "Corruption and Self Interest in Kampala and Nairobi: A Comment on Local Politics in East Africa," pp. 199–210.

Table 5

CLASSIFICATION OF FACTORS IN NAIROBI

Structural
  Power of Minister to approve city council acts
  Inexperience of city councilmen
  Tribal composition of city (Luo and Kikuyu)
  British-type local government
Cultural
  Rhetoric used by competing groups to justify actions:
    (1) Bureaucratic: illegitimacy of "preferential" treatment of individuals
    (2) Bureaucratic: officials should be financially responsible and competent
    (3) Popular: local officials represent the people and therefore should not be brought into "disrepute"
    (4) Popular: officials who represent "imperialists" should be removed
Situational
  Tribal memberships of Mayor and Minister
  Personal ambitions of Mayor and Minister
Decisions
  Minister vetoed council actions
  Local Government Inspector asked Mayor to disclose business interests
  Mayor resigned

---

cases. The competing legitimacies of bureaucracy and popularly elected institutions, even the situational factors of ethnic memberships and personal ambitions of the particular individuals who happened to occupy the key offices, may not be peculiar to Kenya or any other underdeveloped country. In explaining a series of events, therefore, it may not be necessary in a comparative study of urban government and politics to resort to any explanatory factors above and beyond those which can be found operating in the particular situation. What Werlin is implying—perfectly validly—is that there is a different *probability* in Kenya of the *conjunction* of certain sets of structural and cultural factors than there is in the United States and Britain. But a specific series of events in a given situation may not differ at all from those likely in another country. It is the job of systematic comparative analyses to distinguish between those events which are not at all probable, given the national environment, and those which typify processes to be expected in the particular milieu.

    The fact that most of the population is illiterate and impoverished need not always influence political processes in the under-

developed countries. The consequence of poverty which is politically relevant is the great difficulty with which poor and unedu-
cated people can be mobilized to present political demands in
their own interests. But in many particular decisions, Western
politics exhibits exactly the same pattern of infrequent and partial
mobilization of the electorate or various publics within it. Although widespread poverty is a long-term structural factor deeply
affecting politics in countries such as Kenya, in many specific
political situations the extent of popular participation and concern may be no greater in Nairobi than in Chapel Hill, North
Carolina, or Madison, Wisconsin. To put the point another way,
the "system" within which political actors function may differ
considerably from issue to issue, decision to decision, and general
characteristics of the society and polity which are vital in some
long-range sense may not be at all important in a whole series of
particular situations.

Werlin himself uses our terminology of historical, situational,
cultural, and structural factors in his critique of the culturally
restricted definitions of power of Richard Neustadt, and in his
point that Neustadt ignores the "system" (or environment in our
terms) in which power is exercised. The main dimension which
Werlin chooses to contrast Western and Kenyan politics is that of
"elastic" versus "inelastic" political power. British local government is elastic: central-local government, relationships are relatively loose, flexible, advisory, guiding. Kenyan central-local relationships are inelastic and stiff, based on force and corruption. In-
effectiveness is combined with attempts to push decisions through
by authoritarian methods (p. 184–85).

But again, the difference may not be one between "developed" and "underdeveloped" *countries,* but between "developed"
and "underdeveloped" *local* systems. Exactly the same factors, processes and consequences may be operating in many Western cities
subject to the same conditions present in Nairobi. Let us pursue
this point a little farther, using more information from Werlin's
interesting article.

He focuses upon the Nairobi city council's composition and
political role in 1963–64 when he did his field work. To summa-
rize the situation, most of the Africans had poor housing, had low-

paying jobs, were male, and had no families in the area. They comprised over half of the population, which was 30 per cent Asian. The new council in 1963 was composed of twenty-eight Africans, only eight of whom had previous experience in such matters, and most of whom had little education. They were confronted with new functions, notably education, for which no procedures existed. Also, the new city chart expanded the boundaries of jurisdiction of the council to 266 square miles in place of 35. In addition, most of the chief administrative officers spoke a different native language than the councilors.

Werlin notes that "one immediate consequence of the African take-over of the Council was a doubling of the amount of time spent in the committee meetings . . ." (p. 193). He attributes this partly to the "inadequate understanding" of the African councilors, as well as the presumed cultural trait of Africans to be unwilling to end debate.

It seems possible, however, that the sheer problems created by the objective situation of poor housing, jobs and education, combined with the changes of political jurisdiction, the added functions, the almost completely new membership of the council, and the language barriers between council and its administrative staff, are structural factors sufficient to account for much of the conflict between council and staff, the "inefficient" committee meetings and the conflict between council and ministries. The Nairobi situation might be analogous to that in Washington, D.C., immediately after home rule had been achieved, after a majority of poorly educated blacks were elected to the city council, and after a new charter for the city had been promulgated. We would surely expect similar kinds of conflicts and prolonged committee meetings in Washington.

The exotic details of name and place should not lead us to overestimate the degree of distinctiveness required in either the unit of analysis or in the explanatory variables used in studying the structure and functions of local government in developed and underdeveloped countries. Explanations should be sought in features of the immediate situation and associated structural and cultural factors, before resorting to characteristics of the total society and culture. To put the point another way, the ways in which general characteristics of the society are reflected in particular characteristics of a local urban population and government may be not at all consistent and regularized, and analogies and contrasts among local governments in quite different societies, with quite different histories and traditions, may be used to advantage, sometimes completely disregarding—quite legitimately—the "effects" of the level of development of the society.

URBAN ADMINISTRATION AND POLITICS IN LATIN AMERICA

I turn now to a selective view of other literature on local government in Latin America, with particular reference to Brazil. Again, my concern is not substantive but analytical, and, therefore, I make no pretense of covering the relevant literature.

A case which illustrates the use of the analytic scheme is that of the removal of the mayor of Belo Horizonte, Brazil, during the course of the 1964 revolution in Brazil which ousted President Joao Goulart. Table 6 summarizes the factors included by the author of this case study, as tentatively categorized.[4] Belo Horizonte was in financial difficulties, its government was corrupt, and the mayor supported the prerevolutionary president. The author regards as significant the considerable length of time taken and the legalistic maneuvers which were used by the "revolutionary" government to remove these officials. Apparently the impeachments were illegal, since a court decided that it could not overrule them, holding that the revolutionary government could supersede any laws. But the very fact that it was felt necessary to use legal procedures seems significant. The author also ascribes the particular procedures used by the revolutionary government to a culturally based reluctance to use extreme measures, a willingness to compromise with existing structures.

---

[4] See Frank Sherwood, *Institutionalizing the Grass Roots in Brazil: A Study in Comparative Local Government* (San Francisco: Chandler, 1967), pp. 43–44, for details of this case.

Table 6

CLASSIFICATION OF FACTORS IN REMOVAL OF MAYOR
OF BELO HORIZONTE, BRAZIL

ENVIRONMENT
Historical
  Successful resolution of internal conflicts
  No external threats to nation
  No expanding frontier
Structural
  Federal constitution
  General inflation
  Relative expenditures higher by national than by local governments (as
    compared to U. S.)
  Restricted franchise
Cultural
  Emphasis on compromise rather than ideological principles
  Personalized leadership
  Legitimacy of patronage
Situational
  Revolution succeeded nationally
  Governor of state supported Revolution

LOCAL SYSTEM
Structural: Belo Horizonte, 1965–1966
  [Extent to which above characteristics true of a given city]
  Plurality election system
  Candidates must run on party labels
  Power of executive
  Municipalities encompass urban areas plus surrounding rural areas
Cultural: Belo Horizonte, 1965–1966
  [Extent to which above characteristics true of a given city]
Situational
  Corrupt government
  Financial difficulties
  Mayor supported prerevolutionary president
Decisions
  Removal of Mayor of Belo Horizonte
  Removal of Vice-Mayor of Belo Horizonte
  Court decision that removals were revolutionary acts and not subject to laws

In this case, the particular "decision" to remove an official
may not seem important, but it is just such cases which may clarify
the constraints upon political, even revolutionary processes and
allow us to distinguish between patterns that are likely to be
recurrent and typify an entire system, and those that are only
found in nearly unique situations. We can thus ask to what ex-

tent do the structural and cultural factors which are part of the environment of all Brazilian cities influence a particular series of events? Take the emphasis upon legalism, for example. Was this a political tactic, used to avoid losing certain supporters in Belo Horizonte? Or was it a procedure taken for granted as the appropriate way to do things? One Latin-American scholar has asserted that there is a tremendous need for legitimacy of authority in Latin America, but legitimacy accorded to the *actor,* not the *act,* unlike the Anglo-America tradition.

Latin-American states have been termed "patrimonial regimes," lacking a "rationalized legal order" and dependent for their "operation and claims to assent upon personalistic intervention by the highest athority." [5] Morse points to the "importance of sheer legalism in Latin-American administration as constant certification for the legitimacy, not of the act, but of him who executes it." [6]

Thus, the removal of the mayor of Belo Horizonte can be explained by increasingly general explanatory variables. The situational factors of corrupt government and the unfortunate political allies of the mayor explain why the act was contemplated in the first place. The structural factors of the particular powers of local executives, and their political role as mobilizing centers for influence for or against the national government, account for the necessity for the revolutionary government to remove obstreperous mayors. The cultural factors of the emphasis upon legalism account for the particular procedures employed.

The above sentences, attempting to classify what seem to be some of the important factors, may or may not be accurate. But in any case, the point is that a series of cases of similar observations of events, in which the range of possible explanatory variables is kept in mind, would be necessary to distinguish between the relative probabilities of one or another type of event. It is possible that the events in Belo Horizonte were determined by situational factors entirely unrelated to any elements of the structure or culture, factors, let us say, which are common to most

---

[5] Richard M. Morse, "The Heritage of Latin America," in Louis Hartz (ed.), *The Founding of New Societies* (New York: Harcourt, Brace & World, 1964), p. 161.
[6] *Ibid.,* p. 175.

"revolutionary situations." The decisions to remove the officials may have been entirely due to the political necessities of the immediate situation.

To take another case, Table 7 shows the classification of factors which were involved in the 1963 decision by the electorate of the state of Guanabara, Brazil, not to create municipalities.[7] In 1960 the new city-state of Guanabara was created from the city of Rio de Janeiro when the capital of Brazil moved to Brasilia. The new constitution provided for a referendum in 1963 on the question of creating municipalities, and the case study is the story of the issues and the campaign leading up to the overwhelming vote to keep the state as it was.

A number of questions can be raised, prompted by the classification of factors into the scheme.

Would an effective majority for Labor in Guanabara have resulted in a different constitution and probably a legally established system of municipalities in the state? How firmly established was the conservative majority? If political factors had been different in the previous few elections, possibly the weight ascribed to patronage and the opposition of interest groups would have operated in the opposite direction. And the attachment of citizens to Rio as a single unit might have been offset by the legitimacy of unanimous support of decentralization by the ruling party and major interest groups. To put the point more abstractly, a series of previous situational factors in the environment may have created the particular situation in Guanabara which led to defeat of decentralization, and explanation of the outcome need not involve recourse to any structural or cultural factors at all. Conversely, it is possible that the high level of citizen attachment to Rio as a single governmental unit (a cultural factor) may have overridden any conceivable combination of political advantages which could have fallen to the proponents of decentralization as a result of favorable outcomes of a series of previous situations. The failure of the proposed change to win more than 7 per cent support even in a district with strong Labor support indicates this (al-

---

[7] All of the information for this case study is drawn from Sherwood, *op. cit.*, pp. 138–59.

Table 7

CLASSIFICATION OF FACTORS IN DECISION NOT TO DECENTRALIZE
THE STATE OF GUANABARA, BRAZIL

ENVIRONMENT
Structural, Cultural and Historical
[Same as for Belo Horizonte situation; see Table 6]
Situational
   Failure of any one party to command an effective majority in state of Guanabara
   Consequent provision of new 1960 constitution that voters should decide municipal structure of Guanabara in 1963 election
   Successful passage of new federal law giving states without any internal municipalities all of the tax resources assigned hitherto only to municipalities
   Conservative party (National Democratic Union) control of Gunabara state legislature
   Success of state conservative leadership's (Governor Lacerda) program of establishing "regional administrations" (deconcentration without true delegation of power)

LOCAL SYSTEM
Structural
   Size of population for which governmental unit being debated (3,000,000)
   Relatively highly developed party and interest group structures
   Absence of two particular interest groups which might have favored decentralization: suburbs and ethnic groups
   Proportional representation system, which reduced the pressure to create small, single district elections areas
   Business groups wanted unhampered, unified political system for economic reasons
   Part of Labor party wanted to strengthen political base in municipalities
Cultural
   High level of citizen attachment to Rio as single governmental unit (100-year history and great "love" for the city)
   Lack of citizen perceptions of connections between small municipal institutions and high level of governmental outputs
   General predisposition against organizational change
Situational
   Labor party split over issue: some felt that dividing the state into municipalities would reduce the power of the conservative party in the state, others felt that the labor movement would be divided if political jurisdictions were fragmented
   Political dynamics: the proposal to decentralize failed to pick up critical support at decisive points in the political process, so support began to fall off
Decisions
   Advisory Committee opposed decentralization
   All interest groups opposed decentralization
   Electorate voted 20–1 against decentralization

---

though the Labor incumbent from that district ultimately opposed decentralization).

A few other points drawn from this case study of Brazil may be made in passing. The author summarized a survey of attitudes toward local services in Rio de Janeiro and in Los Angeles by noting that more persons were satisfied with police services in Los Angeles than in Rio, and concluded (from other data as well) that people see more of a relationship between inputs and outputs of specific governmental agencies in the U.S. than they see in Brazil (pp. 86–90). This inference raises acutely the problem of situational versus structural explanations of such survey findings. Suppose the same question had been asked in Los Angeles immediately after the Watts riots. It seems highly likely that the level of dissatisfaction with policing would have risen sharply, and yet the general relationship seen between inputs and outputs might remain the same. The very recent experience of citizens with government, elections and leaders can sharply alter patterns of survey responses, and it cannot be concluded that deep values, commitments to policies, or semipermanent party or leadership attachments exist on the basis of any survey response, no matter how overwhelmingly one-sided. Situational factors can alter majorities almost instantly. Empirically it may be very difficult, particularly where data are drawn from a single point in time, a single survey, and a single issue, to distinguish patterns of response that are relatively stable from those that are extremely transitory. A variety of alternative factors may explain a given series of events.

Another case given in the same monograph illustrates the point. In 1958 a rancher was elected mayor of Campo Grande, Brazil. He tried to change the "clientelistic" policies of the local government to one more technically and service oriented. His main concern was with tax reform, which he succeeded in getting passed over the opposition of part of his own party. A key issue arose in which a big rancher refused to pay the considerable increase in taxes. The mayor got a retired slaughter house operator to re-enter business in competition with him (see pages 103–7). The rancher soon came to terms. The situational contingencies are clear. If the mayor had not had this political resource available, it seems possible that he would not have been able to force the rancher to pay taxes, others might have followed suit, and the mayor would have lost his credibility and his political effectiveness. It cannot be inferred that the outcome was due to more than situational factors. As Sherwood puts it himself, in assessing the prospects for long-run change in the "instrumental" direction the mayor advocated, it is likely that "traditional mechanisms reasserted themselves" (p. 107). This statement is a prediction that this particular decision (to raise taxes) would not have a substantial impact on the structural and cultural factors pulling the system away from instrumental performance.

To take a last example, the author attended a single council meeting in the city of Resende. He notes the lack of public participation in the meeting, the lack of interest group and press participation, and assesses the council as essentially a "debating society," rather than a "working group," contrasting Brazilian councils with his estimate of the typical U.S. council on this score. But many U.S. city councils also resemble debating societies, haggling about minor procedural issues rather than big issues of policy. Again, the problem of how far one can generalize from particular instances and their circumstances to overriding features of the "system" is an extraordinarily difficult one.

An interesting example of a purely structural analysis of administration in Brazil is a study underway by Professor John T. Dorsey, Jr.[8] He classified thirteen state administrative agencies in São Paulo into those whose programs were or were not closely related to the economic development of the state ("economic" and "noneconomic" agencies) and into those which were administratively "effective" or "ineffective." Then he interviewed all of the persons in each agency who "played a significant role in the formulation of policies and programs" (p. 32), concerning the level of conflict in the agency, their interpersonal contacts, their perceptions of the amount of change their agency's policies encouraged, and the range of information normally taken into account by the agency.

The particular findings are unimportant here, except to note

[8] The discussion here is based on a preliminary paper reporting only a part of his data: "Bureaucracy and Modernization in the State of São Paulo" (unpublished manuscript, 1967).

that the "effective economic" agencies—those he considers to be most deeply involved in development administration—were found to be the most different from the others. What is important to note is that in explaining his findings he nowhere finds it necessary to refer to cultural factors, although in his historical introduction, he calls attention to the well-established patterns of patronage and nepotism in Brazilian administration.

The author assumes that subjective reports by administrators provide adequate data upon the actual processes of communication and other aspects of day-by-day functioning of their offices. More importantly he assumes that he has a fair sample of agencies and not merely of individual work environments. The unit of analysis is the agency, and yet the data are consistently reported for individuals. Different proportions of individuals reporting patterns of communication, conflict, and search activities are assumed to reflect the agencies from which they are drawn, and yet a skewed distribution of individuals from agencies might alter the patterns found considerably. This point illustrates the problem of inferring structural characteristics from individual responses. It is conceivable (although not necessarily likely) that the findings which the author reports pertain to the particular set of role responsibilities peculiar to the individuals he interviewed, and that he happened to get a biased sample of individuals within an agency. Probably, we can assume that if that were the case, the relationships would appear to be random.

Note again that the strategy of design and analysis which Dorsey uses is one that has no explicit reference to any "Brazilian" or cultural factor. The same variables which he attempts to measure could equally as well be used in any political or cultural context. Even the notion of "development administration" is not confined to the "developing countries," since almost every American state has an agency which is entrusted with the goals of attracting industry, of encouraging appropriate investment decisions, and of encouraging the allocation of state resources to uses which will further economic development. The classification of administrative agencies by their major economic function and by their administrative effectiveness as a way of establishing the environment within which officials work is an approach by this author which offers yet another beginning of systematic comparative analysis of urban politics and administration.

A cultural factor of considerable importance in Brazil seems to be the permeation of political and economic institutions by responsibilities and obligations based upon one's membership in an extended family, which is allied with other families, in efforts to improve the political, social and economic position of members.[9] This institution, called the *panelinha,* in its political and administrative aspect is a general norm or principle governing behavior which is found in many different kinds of structures. If the organization of families into such alliances is indeed a pervasive fact of Brazilian society, then presumably any organization which offers a chance for considerable material or prestige rewards should be the object of "attack" by "outposts" of one or another coalition of families, and the recruitment, allocation of incomes, promotion, and policies of the organization should be found to be influenced by considerations that have little to do with the ostensible purposes and functions of the organization. To put the point into the language of the scheme, internal structural imperatives of the organization should compete with external commitments of members of the organization.

A recent study of Brazilian development administration offers another illustration, although this case is at the national rather than local level.[10] The author was concerned to explain the low performance of the agencies committed to economic development and their poor material and administrative resources. The series of administrative and political upheavals in Brazil between 1945 and 1967 made it necessary for him to distinguish (not in our

[9] See Gilberto Freyre, "The Patriarchal Basis of Brazilian Society," and Charles Wagley, "Luso-Brazilian Kinship Patterns: The Persistence of a Cultural Tradition," in Joseph Maier and Richard W. Weatherhead (eds.), *Politics of Change in Latin America* (New York: Praeger, 1965), pp. 155–90, for relevant recent articles. For an interesting parallel attempt to devise an analytical terminology which will encompass both micro- and macrosociological levels of explanation and units of analysis, see Anthony Leeds, "Brazilian Careers and Social Structure: An Evolutionary Model and Case History," *American Anthropologist,* LXVI (1964), 1321–47. Leeds's empirical focus is upon case studies of the "careers of individuals moving through the social network" and he attempts to deal with the "ties between localities and national institutions" (p. 1321). Leeds deals explicitly with the *panelinha's* role in Brazilian social structure and politics.

[10] See Robert T. Daland, "Development Administration and the Brazilian Political System," *Western Political Quarterly,* 21 (June, 1968), pp. 325–339.

terms, however) between situational, structural, and cultural factors which explain the recent history of development administration in that country. (See Table 8.)

Table 8

FACTORS IN BRAZILIAN ADMINISTRATIVE DEVELOPMENT, 1967

Structural Factors
  Insulation of Brazil from external military threat
  Impermanence of governmental institutions (?)
  Internal frontier allowing migration of dissidents
  Institutionalization of "clects" (in Brazil, the *panelinha*, or alliance of individuals
    and families to gain influence through economic and political bureaucracies)
Cultural Factors
  Commitment to compromise as a method of political struggle (party politics
    non-ideological)
  Psychological tolerance of political and administrative disorder
  Lack of consensus on rules of the game (?)
  Attachment to Brazil as national unit
Situational Factors
  Impermanence of governmental institutions (?)
  Great variety of demands directed toward the bureaucracy
  Lack of consensus on rules of the game
  Political domination by the military
  Continuation of Brazil as single political system
Decisions
  Not to carry out a systematic plan of national economic development

---

SOURCE: Taken from Daland, *op. cit.* For the term "clect," see Fred Riggs, *Administration in Developing Countries: The Theory of Prismatic Society* (Boston: Houghton Mifflin, 1964). The "clect" is a typical social formation in "prismatic" society, an intermediate and transitional form between traditional or "fused" society and modern or "diffracted" society. The clect combines the functions of primary and secondary groups, kinship and bureaucracy.

The impermanence of top leadership and the removal of many elected and appointed officials by the military rulers were clearly situational factors which operated to reduce whatever commitment to development and administrative effectiveness existed in any agency. Just the uncertainty about what was expected of them undoubtedly affected the behavior of many officials, who may have failed to introduce planned innovations just because it was safer to do nothing. The very nature of a revolutionary regime made it necessary to remove officials without regard for their commitment to economic development, if they were in the political opposition, even if they agreed abstractly with the new regime's economic goals.

Cultural factors suggested by the author to help explain the lack of sustained and consistent administration of development programs include Brazilian tolerance for administrative chaos and a preference for compromise over principle in political battles. Thus, policy preferences no matter how widespread or deep, are not easily translated in Brazil into organizational commitments.

The author singles out, however, as the major factor explaining the lack of systematic planning of national economic development the "great variety of demands . . . directed toward the bureaucracy" (p. 7), and the lack of insulation of the bureaucracy from interest groups presenting demands. In our terms, this factor might best be regarded as an intervening situational factor, dependent upon the series of political upheavals which have torn the bureaucracy apart on several occasions and exposed it to many "uncontrolled" and inconsistent demands. These upheavals were not predictable from any knowledge of Brazilian social structure and culture. Whether or not it is necessary to go further and postulate cultural values supporting chaos and disorder seems problematic. The structural and situational factors seem well able to account for the lack of decisions to set up autonomous and well-supported development administrative units. But our point, once again, is merely to raise alternative possibilities for explanation of a series of events, not to argue a particular case.

An hypothesis offered by Latin American historian Richard Morse concerns another cultural factor. He suggests that a principle systematically differentiating Catholic from Protestant civilizations is the view of society as a differentiated whole versus a multitude of unrelated societies. In Catholic cultures, the world is viewed as "composed . . . of one highly differentiated society for which certain common forms, acts, and ceremonies are needed binding force . . . ," in Protestant cultures, the world is seen as a "multitude of unrelated societies, each of them a congregation of similar persons which is finite in time and place and ordered by the declarative terms of a compact rather than by common symbolic observances." [11] Morse goes on to quote Kenneth Burke on a further contrast. The Catholic church's "organic" theory "puts a going social concern together by the toleration of *differences*, the Protestant sects stressed the value of complete uniformity. Each time this uniformity was impaired, the sect itself tended to split, with a new 'uncompromising' offshoot reaffirming the need for a homogeneous community, all members alike in status." [12]

The description provides us with a set of hypotheses about organizational behavior in Latin America as compared to the United States. If this difference is a cultural factor, providing (by definition) normative principles guiding behavior in many structural contexts, then we would expect that bureaucracies, for example, would operate quite differently in Latin America and the United States. Boundaries between agencies and parts of agencies would be far less sharply drawn in Latin America. Schisms— the formation of new departments from the splitting of old ones —should be far more frequent in American bureaucracies. Tasks should be less narrowly assigned to particular offices in Latin America than in the United States. Role conflict between primary and secondary group memberships should be experienced more frequently in the United States. Membership in one bureaucracy should be seen far more in the United States as defining the major role obligations for the person and excluding other bureaucratic memberships, or at least providing a more well-defined set of expectations of behavior. At least some of these predictions from the hypothesized cultural norms are consistent with the emphasis upon personal obligation, upon the principles of *caudillismo* and clientage, and upon the extensive formation of family coalitions within and among bureaucracies (*panelinha*).

Let us assume that these differences are indeed found in the functioning of government bureaucracies in Latin America and the United States. Can they be attributed to deep-seated cultural values? Could we find a structural explanation for these patterns of behavior and these orientations? One possible explanation

[11] Morse, *op. cit.*, p. 152.
[12] *Ibid.*

might be in the ascriptive and personal structure of power within organizations in Latin America as contrasted to the achievement-based and bureaucratic structure of power within United States organizations. Where power is organized around persons and the rewards which persons can allocate to others, boundaries between organizational roles will tend to be weak, and vice versa.

This "explanation" for the differences we have assumed to exist reverses the presumed causal order. Instead of explaining the strength of organizational boundaries and bureaucratic role-definitions by a world view that sees society as a single differentiated society versus many isolated societies, we are explaining the emergence of views of the proper way to organize collectivities by the legitimacy requirements of the actual way in which power is gained and exercised in a given society. Clearly matters are not so simple because the congruence of the historic domination of a given religious world view with pervasive patterns of social and political organization cannot be readily "explained" by transitory features of structures of power and stratification. And our point here is neither to contrast Latin America and the United States, nor to judge between alternative possible explanations, but to suggest varying possible explanations of the same observations.

Note that the Morse hypothesis is a quite general one, and if true, should help to "explain"—in the sense of including a wide range of phenomena under a set of explanatory variables—some of the events that other articles we have cited describe. Yet some of them do not mention this "cultural" variable. Is it relevant? We do not know. Yet, it seems reasonable to argue that an adequate explanatory scheme should take a wide range of such variables into account.

Lastly, the problem of "metropolitan government" may have very different dimensions in Latin America than in the United States because of a related cultural difference between the two areas.

> The substitution of locality groups for kin groups which Weber felt to be so characteristic of the medieval European town often failed to occur in Latin America. This meant that the city was not politically differentiated from the country; it was not a "commune" trying to expand its

jurisdiction over a rural area. A municipality in fact included rural lands, and there were no interstices between municipal jurisdictions.[13]

Such historical differences in the differentiation of city boundaries and functions from the rural hinterlands—a difference which may be linked to the general lack of boundaries among different "parts" of the society in Catholic countries, already suggested as a hypothesis—would seem to provide important comparative hypotheses about the functioning of urban politics and administration in different societies. Is it easier to organize governmental services on a metropolitan area basis in Latin America, given similar resources and needs? Can political authority be more easily "transferred" from one type and level of jurisdiction to another in Latin America? Answers to such questions would require that such structural factors as size, population mobility, economic base, wealth, age of the housing stock, and technological modernity of industry be "held constant" in comparing the political functioning of cities in the United States and Latin America,

CONCLUSIONS

We shall offer no extended conclusions, since the purpose of this essay has been to test the usefulness of an accounting scheme embodying several "sensitizing" concepts and distinctions to a number of disparate studies in the general area of urban administration and politics. The test of the scheme is whether it is found by readers to provide a useful analytical framework. We shall not attempt the task here of bringing the various studies discussed into juxtaposition, although a number of suggestive hypotheses could be constructed.

But a few closing remarks may be in order. The accounting scheme is not designed to be a private language, but a way of raising questions about the relationships between dependent and

---

[13] Richard M. Morse, "Recent Research on Latin America Urbanization: A Selective Survey with Commentary," in *Latin American Research Review*, I (1965), 38. Morse's reference to Weber comes from *The City* (Glencoe, Ill.: The Free Press, 1958), chap. 2.

independent variables and the data that are relevant to test such relationships. It provides a way to unify theoretical approaches oriented toward "systems" and those around "variables." Also, it attempts to link qualitative observations to quasi-quantitative propositions about the probabilities of events, and the relative weight to be assigned different independent variables. It is not a theory, since it contains no implicit or explicit hypotheses about the importance of any substantive variable, and is not intended as a new systematic framework to replace an old one, but rather only as a codification of existing implicit modes of thinking. It is a way of approaching the basic data which underlie any study, in a way that does not take for granted the conceptual framework of the original author, and yet does not impose a contrary set of substantive assumptions.

Ambiguous classifications and gross theoretical generalizations are inherently connected with a paucity of data. In the absence of quantitative and qualitative indicators for each major theoretical variable of interest, it is impossible either to distinguish various dimensions of a phenomenon and label them separately, or to decide that the high correlation of various indicators means that one is really dealing with a single phenomenon and that a single term is all that is needed. Excessive reliance on highly abstract terms in early stages of investigation may blind one to the need for breaking down the abstractions into their component and not necessarily interrelated dimensions. At some point in the development of criteria for the gathering of data necessary to handle both practical and theoretical problems, these abstractions must be criticized.

Part of the methodological problems, broadly conceived, facing comparative urban studies concern the ways in which the general characterizations of the historian abstracted from narratives of events can be converted into variables that can be measured by the techniques of the social scientist. The appropriate and legitimate division of labor between the traditional disciplines concerned with the study of man and society has not yet been turned to advantage through assimilation of each other's perspectives and particular form of understanding and communication. To take an example, a history of São Paulo begins with the note that "in the course of the study it will become clear that São Paulo is not a replica of Chicago, that the mesh and action of its society are influenced by traditions of the Brazilian hinterland, and that what there exists of the 'ethos of capitalism' crystallizes in forms often unfamiliar to North Americans." [14] The easy prose of the historian must be converted to the purposes of the social scientist. Clearly "traditions" and "ethos" refer to the cultural base of Brazilian society, and "mesh and action" and "crystallization" to the ways in which social structure incorporates cultural imperatives. Also, for various other historical (situational?) reasons, São Paulo is both like and unlike Chicago. These tantalizing implicit comparisons are not in fact developed in the book explicitly, because the genius of the historian is not to state comparative hypotheses in propositional and variable form, but rather to create an evocative picture of a society through a series of artfully constructed narratives.

The general problems here may be the need by scholars both to develop general guiding concepts which characterize an entire system and to state sets of variables embedded in propositions. The notions of "command systems," "underdeveloped" or "modern" systems, "prismatic" society, and so on, are summary, typological concepts which implicitly present propositions about the form and content of an enormous number of concrete political and decision processes, and about the correlations of a large number of variables. To some extent, such conceptions are necessary before a great deal of data are gathered, to order impressions and to facilitate the gathering of further data. Yet, the concrete relationships of variables which constitute the meaning of such system concepts must be specified at an early stage of investigation, and the general descriptive categories clarified, modified, or abandoned, if they no longer fit the discoveries of concrete empirical processes. [15]

[14] Richard M. Morse, *From Community to Metropolis* (Gainesville: University of Florida Press, 1958), p. xiii.

[15] To take a not-so-remote example, even Slavic specialists are increasingly calling for the abandonment of the "totalitarian" or "Communist," "developed," and "underdeveloped" distinctions in the studies of comparative politics as lacking analytical usefulness. See the symposium in the *Slavic Review*, XXVI (March, 1967), by five scholars of Soviet and Slavic political systems.

Selective Bibliography

THE BIBLIOGRAPHY IS organized under three broad headings, one general, one focused on industrialized societies, and the third—containing well over half the entries—concerned with modernizing societies. Within the second and third headings items are grouped by broad geographic regions. With few exceptions the items listed have been published during the nineteen-sixties. Relatively few entries represent comparative studies of urban administration and politics; indeed, many are not directly concerned with urban life. But all are relevant to the researcher who seeks to build the foundation of understanding for comparative analysis of urban political and administrative processes.

I. GENERAL

A. BIBLIOGRAPHIES AND BIBLIOGRAPHIC ESSAYS

African Studies Program, Boston University. *A Selective Bibliography of Books, Articles, and Documents on the Subject of African Administrative Problems.* Boston: Development Research Center, Boston University, 1964.

Bazzanella, Waldemiro. *Problemas de urbanização na América Latina: Fontes bibliográficas.* Rio de Janeiro: Centro Latinoamericano de Pêsquisas em Ciencias Sociais, 1960.

Bicker, William, Brown, D., Malakoff, H., and Gore, W. J. *Comparative Urban Development: A Bibliography.* Washington: American Society for Public Administration, 1965.

Booth, David A. *Council-Manager Government: 1940–1964: An Annotated Bibliography.* East Lansing: International City Managers' Association and the Institute for Community Development and Services, Michigan State University, 1965.

Edinburgh University, Department of Social Anthropology. *African Urbanization: A Reading List of Selected Books, Articles, and Reports.* London: International African Institute, 1965.

Heady, Ferrel, and Stokes, Sybil L. *Comparative Public Administra-*

tion: A Selective Annotated Bibliography. 2nd ed. Ann Arbor: Institute of Public Administration, University of Michigan, 1960.

Jenkins, George. "Africa as it Urbanizes: An Overview of Current Research," *Urban Affairs Quarterly,* II (March, 1967), 66–80.

Morlan, Robert L. "Foreign Local Government: A Bibliography," *American Political Science Review,* LIX (March, 1965), 120–36.

Morse, Richard. "Recent Research on Latin American Urbanization: A Selective Survey with Commentary," *Latin American Research Review,* I (Fall, 1965), 35–75.

Rabinovitz, Francine F. "Sound and Fury Signifying Nothing?: A Review of Community Power Research in Latin America," *Urban Affairs Quarterly,* III (March, 1968), 111–24.

———, Trueblood, Felicity, and Savio, Charles J. *Latin American Political Systems in an Urban Setting: A Preliminary Bibliography.* Gainesville: Center for Latin American Studies, University of Florida, 1967.

Raphaeli, Nimrod. "Selected Articles and Documents on Comparative Public Administration," *American Political Science Review,* LVII (March, 1963, and subsequent issues).

Simms, Ruth P. *Urbanization in West Africa: A Review of Current Literature.* Evanston: Northwestern University Press, 1965.

Spitz, Alan A., and Weidner, Edward W. *Development Administration: An Annotated Bibliography.* Honolulu: East-West Center Press, 1963.

Wallace, Rosemary H. (ed.). *International Bibliography and Reference Guide on Urbanization.* Ramsey, N.J.: Ramsey-Wallace, 1966.

B. THEORETICAL, CONCEPTUAL, METHODOLOGICAL

Agger, Robert, Goldrich, Daniel, and Swanson, Bert. *The Rulers and the Ruled.* New York: Wiley, 1964.

Alford, Robert R. "The Comparative Study of Urban Politics," in Leo F. Schnore and Henry Fagin (eds.). *Urban Research and Policy Planning.* Beverly Hills: Sage Publications, 1967.

Berry, Brian. "City Size Distributions and Economic Development," *Economic Development and Cultural Change,* IX (July, 1961), 573–87.

Bonjean, Charles M., and Olson, David M. "Community Leadership: Directions of Research," *Administrative Science Quarterly,* IX (December, 1964), 278–300.

Boskoff, Alvin. *The Sociology of Urban Regions.* New York: Appleton-Century-Crofts, 1962.

Crain, Robert L., and Rosenthal, Donald B. "Community Status as a Dimension of Local Decision-Making," *American Sociological Review,* XXXII (December, 1967), 970–84.

Cutright, Phillips. "National Political Development: Measurement and Analysis," *American Sociological Review,* XXVIII (April, 1963), 253–64.

Daland, Robert T. *A Strategy for Research in Comparative Urban Administration.* Bloomington: CAG Occasional Paper, 1966.

D'Antonio, William V., and Erickson, Eugene C. "The Reputational Technique as a Measure of Community Power," *American Sociological Review,* XXVII (June, 1962), 362–76; (December, 1962), 848–54.

Durand, Oswald, and Durand, Jacques. "Rôles et finalités des villes," *Civilisations,* XV (1965), 360–75.

Flanagan, Dennis (ed.). *Cities.* New York: Knopf-Random House, 1965.

Form, William H., and Sauer, Warren L. "Labor and Community Influentials: A Comparative Study of Participation and Imagery," *Industrial and Labor Relations Review,* XVII (October, 1963), 3–19.

Gibbs, Jack. *Urban Research Methods.* New York: Van Nostrand, 1961.

Gugler, Josef P. "Measuring Urbanization." Evian: paper prepared for the Sixth World Congress of Sociology, September, 1966.

Gutman, Robert, and Rabinovitz, Francine. "The Relevance of Domestic Urban Studies to International Urban Research," *Urban Affairs Quarterly,* I (June, 1966), 45–64.

———, and Popenoe, David (eds.). "Urban Studies," *American Behavorial Scientist,* VI (February, 1963), entire issue.

Hauser, Philip M., and Schnore, Leo (eds.). *The Study of Urbanization.* New York: Wiley, 1965.

Herson, Lawrence J. R. "In the Footsteps of Community Power," *American Political Science Review,* LV (December, 1961), 817–30.

Jacob, Philip E., and Toscano, James V. (eds.). *The Integration of Political Communities.* New York: J. B. Lippincott, 1964.

Kornhauser, William. *The Politics of Mass Society.* Glencoe: The Free Press, 1959.

Lipset, Seymour Martin. *Political Man.* Garden City: Doubleday Anchor, 1963.

Long, Norton E. "The Local Community as an Ecology of Games," *American Journal of Sociology,* LXIV (November, 1958), 251–61.

Loomis, Charles P. *Social Systems.* Princeton: Van Nostrand, 1960.

Maass, Arthur (ed.). *Area and Power.* Glencoe: The Free Press, 1959.

McArthur, Robert E. "The Impact of Metropolitan Government on the Rural-Urban Fringe." Nashville: unpublished Ph.D. dissertation, Vanderbilt University, 1967.

McCrone, Donald J., and Cnudde, Charles F. "Toward a Communications Theory of Democratic Political Development: A Causal Model," *American Political Science Review*, LXI (March, 1967), 72–79.

Mumford, Lewis. *The City in History*. New York: Harcourt, Brace, 1961.

Ostrom, Vincent, Tiebout, Charles M., and Warren, Robert. "The Organization of Government in Metropolitan Areas: A Theoretical Inquiry," *American Political Science Review*, LV (December, 1961), 831–42.

Overly, Don H. "Decision-Making in City Government: A Proposal," *Urban Affairs Quarterly*, III (December, 1967), 41–53.

Pitts, Forrest R. (ed.). *Urban Systems and Economic Development: Papers and Proceedings*. Eugene: School of Public Administration, University of Oregon, 1962.

Polsby, Nelson W. "The Sociology of Community Power: A Reassessment," *Social Forces*, XXXVII (March, 1959), 232–36.

————. "Three Problems in the Analysis of Community Power," *American Sociological Review*, XXIV (December, 1959), 796–803.

Popenoe, David. "On the Meaning of 'Urban' in Urban Studies," *Urban Affairs Quarterly*, I (September, 1965), 65–82.

Reissman, Leonard. *The Urban Process*. New York: The Free Press, 1964.

Rosenblüth, Guillermo. "Problemas socio-económicos de la marginalidad y la integración urbana." New York: UN Economic Commission for Latin America, Department of Social Affairs, 1966, mimeo.

Rosenthal, Donald B. "Problems in Comparative Analysis of Urban Political Systems." Chapel Hill: unpublished paper based on a presentation at University of North Carolina, January, 1967.

Schnore, Leo F. (ed.). *Social Science and the City: A Survey of Urban Research*. New York: Praeger, 1968.

————. "The City as a Social Organism," *Urban Affairs Quarterly*, I (March, 1966), 58–69.

————. "The Statistical Measurement of Urbanization and Economic Development," *Land Economics*, XXXVII (August, 1961), 229–46.

————. *The Urban Scene: Human Ecology and Demography*. New York: The Free Press, 1965.

Sherwood, Frank P. "The Correlates of Decentralization: Interpretations, Speculations, Strategies." Chapel Hill: unpublished paper presented at CAG Urban Studies Seminar, August, 1967.

Sjoberg, Gideon. *The Pre-Industrial City.* Glencoe: The Free Press, 1960.

———. "Theory and Research in Urban Sociology," in Philip Hauser and Leo Schnore (eds.). *The Study of Urbanization.* New York: Wiley, 1965.

Smith, Paul A. "The Games of Community Politics," *Midwest Journal of Political Science,* IX (February, 1965), 37–60.

Taylor, John L., and Maddison, Richard N. "A Land Use Gaming Simulation: The Design of a Model for the Study of Urban Phenomena," *Urban Affairs Quarterly,* III (June, 1968), 37–52.

Vereker, Charles, and Mays, J. B. *Urban Redevelopment and Social Change.* Liverpool: Liverpool University Press, 1961.

Vieira, Paulo Reis. "Toward a Theory of Decentralization: A Comparative View of Forty-Five Countries." Los Angeles: unpublished Ph.D. dissertation, University of Southern California, 1967.

Walsh, Annmarie Hauck. *The Urban Challenge to Government: An International Comparison of Thirteen Cities.* New York: Praeger, 1969.

Walton, John. "The Vertical Axis of Community Organization and the Structure of Power," *Southwestern Social Science Quarterly,* XLVIII (December, 1967), 355–68.

Weiner, Myron. "Urbanization and Political Protest," *Civilisations,* XVII (1967), 44–53.

Wilkinson, Thomas O. "Urban Structure and Industrialization," *American Sociological Review,* XXV (June, 1960), 356–63.

Williams, Oliver P. "A Typology for Comparative Local Government," *Midwest Journal of Political Science,* V (May, 1961), 150–64.

Wirth, Louis. *Community Life and Social Policy.* Chicago: University of Chicago Press, 1956.

Wolfinger, Raymond. "Reputation and Reality in the Study of Community Power," *American Sociological Review,* XXV (October, 1960), 636–44.

———, and Field, John O. "Political Ethos and the Structure of City Government," *American Political Science Review,* LX (June, 1966), 306–26.

C. MISCELLANEOUS

Anderson, Nels. *Industrial Urban Community.* New York: Random House, 1968.

————. *Our Industrial Urban Civilization.* New York: Asia Publishing House, 1964.

————. "The Urban Way of Life," *International Journal of Comparative Sociology,* III (December, 1962), 175–88.

Banks, Arthur, and Textor, Robert. *A Cross Polity Survey.* Cambridge: The M.I.T. Press, 1963.

Davis, Kingsley. "The Urbanization of the Human Population," *Scientific American,* XLI (September, 1965), 213–28.

Gibbs, J. P., and Martin, T. W. "Urbanization and Natural Resources," *American Sociological Review,* XXIII (June, 1958), 266–77.

Halpern, Joel Martin. *The Changing Village Community.* Englewood Cliffs: Prentice-Hall, 1967.

Hoselitz, Bert F., and Moore, Wilbur E. (eds.). *Industrialization and Society.* The Hague: UNESCO, 1963.

Humes, Samuel, and Martin, Eileen M. *The Structure of Local Government Throughout the World.* The Hague: M. Nijhoff, 1961.

Ito, Hanya. "Self-Government, Local Finance, and Democracy," *Public Finance/Finance Publique,* XX (1965), 118–36.

Ogburn, William F. "Technology and Cities: The Dilemma of the Modern Metropolis," *Sociological Quarterly,* I (July, 1960), 139–54.

Pauvert, J. C. "Urbanisation et planification de l'education," *Civilisations,* XVII (1967), 30–43.

Russett, Bruce, *et al. World Handbook of Political and Social Indicators.* New Haven: Yale University Press, 1963.

Schnore, Leo F., and Fagin, Henry (eds.). *Urban Research and Policy Planning.* Beverly Hills: Sage Publications, 1967.

Thompson, Wilbur R. *A Preface to Urban Economics.* Baltimore: Johns Hopkins Press, 1965.

United Nations. *Decentralization for National and Local Development.* New York: United Nations Technical Assistance Programme, 1962.

United Nations. Bureau of Social Affairs, Population Division. *Urbanization and Economic and Social Change.* New York: 1960.

Weber, Adna Ferrin. *The Growth of Cities in the Nineteenth Century.* Ithaca: Cornell University Press, 1964.

Weissmann, Ernest. "The Urban Crisis in the World," *Urban Affairs Quarterly,* I (September, 1965), 65–82.

————. "The Urban Crisis: Its Meaning for Development," *UN Monthly Chronicle,* III (April, 1966), 48–56.

White, Morton, and White, Lucia. *The Intellectual versus the City.* New York: The New American Library of World Literature, 1964.

II. URBAN DEVELOPMENT IN INDUSTRIALIZED SOCIETIES

A. WESTERN EUROPE

Bulpitt, J. G. "Party Systems in Local Government," *Political Studies,* XI (February, 1963), 11–35.

Fried, Robert. "Urbanization and Italian Politics," *Journal of Politics,* XXIX (August, 1967), 505–34.

Gutkind, E. A. *Urban Development in Central Europe.* New York: The Free Press, 1964.

————. *Urban Development in Southern Europe: Italy and Greece.* New York: The Free Press, 1968.

————. *Urban Development in Southern Europe: Spain and Portugal.* New York: The Free Press, 1967.

————. *Urban Development in the Alpine and Scandinavian Countries.* New York: The Free Press, 1965.

Humphreys, Alexander J. *New Dubliners: Urbanization and the Irish Family.* New York: Fordham University Press, 1966.

Kinch, M. B. "Qualified Administrative Staff in the Local Government Service," *Public Administration* (London), XLIII (1965), 173–90.

LaPalombara, Joseph. "Italy: Fragmentation, Isolation and Alienation," in Lucian Pye and Sidney Verba (eds.). *Political Culture and Political Development.* Princeton: Princeton University Press, 1965.

Miller, Delbert C. "Decision-Making Cliques in Community Power Structures: A Comparative Study of an American and an English City," *American Journal of Sociology,* LXIV (November, 1958), 299–310.

Smallwood, Frank. *Greater London: The Politics of Metropolitan Reform.* New York: Bobbs-Merrill, 1965.

Walsh, Annmarie Hauck. *Urban Government for the Paris Region.* New York: Praeger, 1968.

Waterston, Albert. *Planning in Yugoslavia.* Washington: The Economic Development Institute, 1962.

B. NORTH AMERICA (excluding Mexico and Puerto Rico)

Abney, F. Glenn, and Hill, Larry B. "Natural Disasters as a Political Variable: The Effect of a Hurricane on an Urban Election," *American Political Science Review,* LX (December, 1966), 974–81.

Adrian, Charles R. "Leadership and Decision-Making in Manager Cities: A Study of Three Communities," *Public Administration Review,* XVIII (Summer, 1958), 208–13.

———. "Public Attitudes and Metropolitan Decision-Making," in Thomas R. Dye and Brett W. Hawkins (eds.). *Politics in the Metropolis.* Columbus, Ohio: Charles E. Merrill Books, 1967.

Alford, Robert R. "Forms of Government and Socioeconomic Characteristics of Suburbs," *Administrative Science Quarterly,* VIII (June, 1963), 1–17.

———, and Lee, Eugene C. "Voting Turnout in American Cities," *American Political Science Review,* LXII (September, 1968), 796–813.

———, with Scoble, Harry M. *Bureaucracy and Participation: Political Culture in Four Wisconsin Cities.* Chicago: Rand McNally, 1969.

Banfield, Edward C. "The Politics of Metropolitan Area Organization," *Midwest Journal of Political Science,* I (May, 1957), 77–91.

——— (ed.). *Urban Government: A Reader in Politics and Administration.* New York: The Free Press, rev. ed., 1969.

———, and Wilson, James. *City Politics.* Cambridge: Harvard University Press and The M.I.T. Press, 1963.

Bollens, John C. (ed.). *Exploring the Metropolitan Community.* Berkeley and Los Angeles: University of California Press, 1961.

Booth, David A. "Are Elected Mayors a Threat to Managers?" *Administrative Science Quarterly,* XII (March, 1968), 572–89.

———. *Metropolitics: The Nashville Consolidation.* East Lansing: Institute for Community Development and Services, Michigan State University, 1963.

Campbell, Alan K., and Sacks, Seymour. *Metropolitan America: Fiscal Patterns and Governmental Systems.* New York: The Free Press, 1967.

Cleaveland, Frederic N. "Congress and Urban Problems: Legislating for Urban Areas," *Journal of Politics,* XXVIII (May, 1966), 289–307.

Coulter, Philip, and Gordon, Glen. "Urbanization and Party Competition: Critique and Redirection of Theoretical Research," *Western Political Quarterly,* XXI (June, 1968), 274–88.

Cutright, Phillips. "Urbanization and Competitive Party Politics," *Journal of Politics,* XXV (August, 1963), 552–64.

Dahl, Robert. *Who Governs?* New Haven: Yale University Press, 1962.

Dye, Thomas R. (ed). *Comparative Research in Community Politics.* Athens: University of Georgia Press, 1967.

———. "Governmental Structure, Urban Environment, and Educational Policy," *Midwest Journal of Political Science,* XI (August, 1967), 353–80.

———. "Urban Political Integration: Conditions Associated with Annexation in American Cities," *Midwest Journal of Political Science,* VIII (November, 1964), 430–46.

———, and Hawkins, Brett W. (eds.). *Politics in the Metropolis.* Columbus, Ohio: Charles E. Merrill Books, 1967.

Form, William H., and Sauer, Warren L. *Community Influentials in a Middle-Sized City.* East Lansing: Institute for Community Development and services, Michigan State University, 1960.

Froman, Lewis A., Jr. "An Analysis of Public Policies in Cities," *Journal of Politics,* XXIX (February, 1967), 94–108.

Gans, Herbert. *The Urban Villagers.* New York: The Free Press, 1962.

Gilbert, Charles E. "National Political Alignments and the Politics of Large Cities," *Political Science Quarterly,* LXXIX (March, 1964), 25–51.

———. "Some Aspects of Non-Partisan Elections in Large Cities," *Midwest Journal of Political Science,* VI (November, 1962), 345–62.

———, and Clague, Christopher. "Electoral Competition and Electoral Systems in Large Cities," *Journal of Politics,* XXIV (May, 1962), 323–49.

Gilbert, Claire W. "Some Trends in Community Politics: A Secondary Analysis of Power Structure Data from 166 Communities," *Southwestern Social Science Quarterly,* XLVIII (December, 1967), 373–81.

Gold, David, and Schmidhauser, John R. "Urbanization and Party Competition: The Case of Iowa," *Midwest Journal of Political Science,* IV (February, 1960), 62–75.

Greer, Scott. *The Emerging City: Myth and Reality.* New York: The Free Press, 1962.

———. *Metropolitics: A Study of Political Culture.* New York: Wiley, 1963.

Grodzins, Morton. "Local Strength in the American Federal System," in Marian D. Irish (ed.). *Continuing Crises in American Politics.* Englewood Cliffs: Prentice-Hall Spectrum Books, 1963.

Grumm, John. *Metropolitan Area Government: The Toronto Experience.* Lawrence: University of Kansas Publications, Governmental Research Series No. 19, 1959.

Gulick, Luther. *The Metropolitan Problem and American Ideas.* New York: Knopf, 1962.

Hawkins, Brett W. *Nashville Metro: The Politics of City-County Consolidation.* Nashville: Vanderbilt University Press, 1966.

Holden, Matthew Jr. "The Governance of the Metropolis as a Problem in Diplomacy," *Journal of Politics,* XXVI (August, 1964), 627–47.

Hunter, Floyd. *Community Power Structure.* Chapel Hill: University of North Carolina Press, 1953.

Jennings, M. Kent. *Community Influentials: The Elites of Atlanta.* New York: The Free Press, 1964.

Jones, Victor. *Metropolitan Government.* Chicago: University of Chicago Press, 1942.

Kaplan, Harold. *Urban Political Systems: A Functional Analysis of Metro Toronto.* New York: Columbia University Press, 1967.

Kaufman, Walter C., and Greer, Scott. "Voting in a Metropolitan Community: An Application of Social Area Analysis," *Social Forces,* XXXVIII (March, 1960), 196–204.

Kessel, John H. "Governmental Structure and Political Environment: A Statistical Note about American Cities," *American Political Science Review,* LVI (September, 1962), 615–20.

Lineberry, Robert L., and Fowler, Edmund P. "Reformism and Public Policies in American Cities," *American Political Science Review,* LXI (September, 1967), 701–16.

McQuown, Ruth, Hamilton, William R., and Schneider, Michael P. *The Political Restructuring of a Community.* Gainesville: Public Administration Clearing Service, University of Florida, 1964.

Main, Eleanor C. "The Impact of Urbanization: A Comparative Study of Urban and Non-Urban Political Attitudes and Behavior." Chapel Hill: unpublished Ph.D. dissertation, University of North Carolina, 1966.

Martin, Roscoe C. *The Cities and the Federal System.* New York: Atherton Press, 1965.

———, et al. *Decisions in Syracuse.* Bloomington: Indiana University Press, 1961.

Masters, Nicholas A., and Wright, Deil S. "Trends and Variation in the Two-Party Vote: The Case of Michigan," *American Political Science Review,* LII (December, 1958), 1078–90.

Mueller, John E. "The Politics of Fluoridation in Seven California Cities," *Western Political Quarterly,* XIX (March, 1966), 54–67.

Norton, James A. "Referenda Voting in a Metropolitan Area," *Western Political Quarterly*, XVI (March, 1963), 195–212.

Putnam, Robert D. "Political Attitudes and the Local Community," *American Political Science Review*, LX (September, 1966), 640–54.

Presthus, Robert. *Men at the Top: A Study in Community Power*. New York: Oxford University Press, 1964.

Rosenthal, Donald B., and Crain, Robert L. "Executive Leadership and Community Innovation: The Fluoridation Experience," *Urban Affairs Quarterly*, I (March, 1966), 39–57.

Salisbury, Robert H. "Urban Politics: The New Convergence of Power," *Journal of Politics*, XXVI (November, 1964), 775–97.

Sayre, Wallace S. "The General Manager Idea for Large Cities," *Public Administration Review*, XIV (Autumn, 1954), 253–58.

———, and Kaufman, Herbert. *Governing New York City*. New York: Russell Sage Foundation, 1960.

———, and Polsby, Nelson W. "American Political Science and the Study of Urbanization," in Philip M. Hauser and Leo F. Schnore (eds.). *The Study of Urbanization*. New York: Wiley, 1964.

Scott, Anne Firor. "The Study of Southern Urbanization," *Urban Affairs Quarterly*, I (March, 1966), 5–14.

Scott, Thomas M. "Metropolitan Governmental Reorganization Proposals," *Western Political Quarterly*, XXI (June, 1968), 252–61.

Smallwood, Frank. *Metro Toronto: A Decade Later*. Toronto: Bureau of Municipal Research, 1963.

Sofen, Edward. *The Miami Metropolitan Experiment*. Bloomington: Indiana University Press, Metropolitan Action Studies No. 2, 1963.

Warren, Roland L. *The Community in America*. Chicago: Rand McNally, 1963.

Williams, Oliver P. "Life-Style Values and Political Decentralization in Metropolitan Areas," *Southwestern Social Science Quarterly*, XLVIII (December, 1967), 299–310.

———, and Adrian, Charles. *Four Cities*. Philadelphia: University of Pennsylvania Press, 1963.

Wissink, G. A. *American Cities in Perspective with Special Reference to the Development of Their Fringe Areas*. New York: The Humanities Press, 1962.

Wood, Robert C. *1400 Governments*. Cambridge: Harvard University Press, 1961.

———. *Suburbia: Its People and Their Politics*. Boston: Houghton Mifflin, 1959.

Wright, Deil, and Mowitz, Robert. *Profile of a Metropolis*. Detroit: Wayne State University Press, 1962.

Zisk, Betty H., Eulau, Heinz, and Prewitt, Kenneth. "City Councilmen and the Group Struggle: A Typology of Role Orientations," *Journal of Politics*, XXVII (August, 1965), 618–46.

III. URBAN DEVELOPMENT IN MODERNIZING SOCIETIES

A. GENERAL

Alderfer, Harold F. *Local Government in Developing Countries*. New York: McGraw-Hill, 1964.

Almond, Gabriel, and Coleman, James (eds.). *The Politics of the Developing Areas*. Princeton: Princeton University Press, 1960.

————, and Powell, G. Bingham. *Comparative Politics*. Boston: Little, Brown, 1966.

Apter, David. *The Politics of Modernization*. Chicago: University of Chicago Press, 1965.

Bent, Frederick T., and Shields, Luise Lackland (eds.). *The Role of Local Government in National Development*. Ankara: Central Treaty Organization, 1965.

Breese, Gerald W. *Urbanization in Newly Developing Countries*. Englewood Cliffs: Prentice-Hall, 1966.

Davis, Kingsley, and Golden, Hilda H. "Urbanization and the Development of Pre-Industrial Areas," *Economic Development and Cultural Change*, III (October, 1964), 6–26.

De Briey, Pierre. "Control of Urbanization," *Civilisations*, XVII (1967), 3–11.

————. "Country and Town," *Civilisations*, XVI (1966), 160–66.

————. "The Political, Economic, and Social Role of Urban Agglomerations in Countries of the Third World," *Civilisations*, XVII (1967), 166–84.

————. "Town and Country," *Civilisations*, XV (1965), 291–305.

————. "Urban Agglomerations and the Modernization of the Developing States," *Civilisations*, XV (1965), 452–68; XVI (1966), 3–23.

————. "Urbanization and Underdevelopment," *Civilisations*, XV (1965), 2–12.

Deutsch, Karl W. "Social Mobilization and Political Development," *American Political Science Review*, LV (September, 1961), 493–514.

Eisenstadt, S. N. "Modernization and Conditions of Sustained Growth," *World Politics*, XVI (July, 1964), 576–94.

Esman, Milton J., and Bruhns, Fred C. "Institution-Building in National Development: An Approach to Induced Social Change in Transitional Societies," in *Comparative Theories of Social Change*. Ann Arbor: Foundation for Research on Human Behavior, 1966.

―――, and Blaise, Hans C. *Institution-Building Research: The Guiding Concepts*. Pittsburgh: Research Headquarters, Inter-University Research Program in Institution Building, 1966.

Field, Arthur J. *Urbanization and Work in Modernizing Societies*. Detroit: Glengary Press, 1967.

Firth, Raymond, and Yamey, B. S. *Capital, Saving, and Credit in Peasant Societies: Studies from Asia, Oceania, the Caribbean and Middle America*. Chicago: Aldine, 1964.

Frankenhoff, C. A. "Elements of an Economic Model for Slums in a Developing Economy," *Economic Development and Cultural Change*, XVI (October, 1967), 27–36.

Friedmann, John. "Two Concepts of Urbanization: A Comment," *Urban Affairs Quarterly*, I (June, 1966), 78–84.

Hanna, William John. "The Cross-Cultural Study of Local Politics," *Civilisations*, XVI (1966), 81–96.

Hicks, Ursula K. *Development From Below*. Oxford: Clarendon Press, 1961.

Hoselitz, Bert F. "The Role of Cities in the Economic Growth of Underdeveloped Countries," *Journal of Political Economy*, LXI (June, 1954), 195–208.

Huntington, Samuel P. "Political Development and Political Decay," *World Politics*, XVII (April, 1965), 386–430.

LaPalombara, Joseph (ed.). *Bureaucracy and Political Development*. Princeton: Princeton University Press, 1963.

―――. *Theory and Practice in Development Administration*. Bloomington: CAG Occasional Paper, 1967.

LeVine, Robert. "Political Socialization and Cultural Change," in Clifford Geertz (ed.). *Old Societies and New States*. New York: The Free Press, 1963.

Maddick, Henry. *Democracy, Decentralization and Development*. London: Asia Publishing House, 1963.

Park, Richard L. "Local Government and Political Development." Washington: paper presented at American Political Science Association Convention, 1965.

Pye, Lucian W. (ed.). *Communications and Political Development*. Princeton: Princeton University Press, 1967.

————. "The Political Implications of Urbanization and the Development Process," in *Social Problems of Development and Urbanization.* Geneva: U.S. papers prepared for the United Nations Conference on the Application of Science and Technology for the Benefit of the Less Developed Areas, Volume 7, 1963.

————, and Verba, Sidney (eds.). *Political Culture and Political Development.* Princeton: Princeton University Press, 1965.

Riggs, Fred W. *Administration in Developing Countries: The Theory of Prismatic Society.* Boston: Houghton Mifflin, 1964.

————. *The Ecology of Administration.* New York: The Asia Publishing Company, 1961.

————. *The Political Structures of Administrative Development.* Bloomington: CAG Occasional Paper, 1967.

Rivkin, Malcom. "Urbanization and National Development." Pittsburgh: paper presented at the Inter-Regional Seminar on Development Policies in Relation to Urbanization, 1967.

Santos, Milton. "Le rôle des capitales dans la modernisation des pays sous-développés," *Civilisations,* XVI (1966), 45–56.

————. "Le rôle du tertiaire primitif dans les villes du Tiers Monde," *Civilisations,* XVIII (1968), 186–203.

Siffin, William J., (ed.). *Toward the Comparative Study of Public Administration.* Bloomington: Indiana University Press, 1959.

Silvert, Kalman H., and Bonilla, Frank. *Education and the Social Meaning of Development.* New York: American Universities Field Staff, 1961.

B. ASIA

Ahmad, Qazi Shakil. *Indian Cities: Characteristics and Correlations.* Chicago: Department of Geography, University of Chicago, Research Paper No. 102, 1965.

Bopegamage, A. *Delhi: A Study in Urban Sociology.* Bombay: University of Bombay, 1957.

Braibanti, Ralph, and associates. *Asian Bureaucratic Systems Emergent from the British Imperial Tradition.* Durham: Duke University Press, 1966.

Bruner, Edward M. "Urbanization and Ethnic Identity in North Sumatra," *American Anthropologist,* LXIII (June, 1961), 508–21.

Bungwu, Wang, *Malaysia: A Survey.* New York: Praeger, 1964.

Carpenter, David B. "Urbanization and Social Change in Japan," *Sociological Quarterly,* I (July, 1960), 155–66.

Chang, Sen-Pou. "The Historical Trend of Chinese Urbanization,"

Annals of the Association of American Geographers, LIII (June, 1963), 109–43.

Cressey, Paul F. "Urbanization in the Philippines," *Sociology and Social Research,* XLIV (July–August, 1960), 402–9.

Dore, R. P. *City Life in Japan.* Berkeley: University of California Press, 1958.

Garry, R. "L'urbanisation au Cambodge," *Civilisations,* XVII (1967), 83–109.

Ginsburg, Norton S. "The Great City in Southeast Asia," *American Journal of Sociology,* LX (March, 1955), 455–62.

Guyot, James F. "Bureaucratic Transformation in Burma," in Ralph Braibanti and associates. *Asian Bureaucratic Systems Emergent from the British Imperial Tradition.* Durham: Duke University Press, 1966.

Hauser, Philip M. *Urbanization in Asia and the Far East.* Calcutta: UNESCO Research Center on the Social Implications of Industrialization in Southern Asia, 1957.

Hollnsteiner, Mary. *The Dynamics of Power in a Philippines Municipality.* Quezon City: University of the Philippines, 1960.

Isomura, Eiichi. "The Problems of the City in Japan," *Confluence,* VII (Summer, 1958), 150–56.

Jakobson, Leo, and Prakash, Ved. "Urbanization and Regional Planning in India," *Urban Affairs Quarterly,* II (March, 1967), 36–55.

Kuroda, Yasumasa. "Measurement, Correlates, and Significance of Political Participation in a Japanese Community," *Western Political Quarterly,* XX (1967), 660–68.

Lewis, John W. "Political Aspects of Mobility in China's Urban Development," *American Political Science Review,* LX (December, 1966), 899–912.

McGee, T. G. "The Cultural Role of Cities: A Case Study of Kuala Lumpur," *Journal of Tropical Geography,* XVII (May, 1963), 178–96.

———. *The Southeast Asian City.* New York: Praeger, 1967.

Milone, Pauline D. *Urban Areas in Indonesia: Administrative and Census Concepts.* Berkeley: University of California, Institute of International Studies, 1966.

Miner, Horace. *The Primitive City of Timbuctoo.* 2nd ed. Garden City: Doubleday, 1965.

Murphey, Rhoads. "New Capitals of Asia," *Economic Development and Cultural Change,* V (April, 1957), 216–43.

Ness, Gayl D. *Bureaucracy and Rural Development in Malaysia.* Berkeley: University of California Press, 1967.

Pethe, Vasant P. "Changes in Economic Conditions of an Urban Community," *Artha Vijnana,* III (June, 1961), 169–76.

Riggs, Fred W. *Thailand: The Modernization of a Bureaucratic Polity.* Honolulu: East-West Center Press, 1966.

Rosenthal, Donald B. "Administrative Policies in Two Indian Cities," *Asian Survey,* VI (April, 1966), 201–15.

———. "Factions and Alliances in Indian City Politics," *Midwest Journal of Political Science,* X (August, 1966), 320–49.

Saikia, P. D. "Village Leadership in North East India," *Man in India,* XLII (June, 1963), 92–99.

Sovani, N. V. "The Analysis of 'Overurbanization'," *Economic Development and Cultural Change,* XII (January, 1964), 113–22.

———. "The Urban Social Situation in India," *Artha Vijnana,* III (June, 1961), 85–105, 195–222.

———. *Urbanization and Urban India.* New York: Asia Publishing House, 1966.

Steiner, Kurt. *Local Government in Japan.* Stanford: Stanford University Press, 1965.

Turner, Roy (ed.). *India's Urban Future.* Berkeley: University of California Press, 1962.

Vakil, C. N., and Roy, Krishna. "Growth of Cities and Their Role in the Development of India," *Civilisations,* XV (1965), 326–59.

Wilkinson, Thomas O. "Agricultural Activities in the City of Tokyo," *Rural Sociology,* XXVI (March, 1961), 49–56.

———. "Agriculturalism in Japanese Urban Structure," *Rural Sociology,* XXVIII (September, 1963), 262–70.

C. THE MIDDLE EAST AND NORTH AFRICA

Abu-Lughod, Janet L. "Migrant Adjustment to City Life: The Egyptian Case," *American Journal of Sociology,* LXVII (July, 1961), 22–32.

———. "Urbanization in Egypt: Present State and Future Prospects," *Economic Development and Cultural Change,* XIII (April, 1965), 313–43.

Ashford, Douglas E. *National Development and Local Reform: Political Participation in Morocco, Tunisia, and Pakistan.* Princeton: Princeton University Press, 1967.

———. *Political Change in Morocco.* Princeton: Princeton University Press, 1961.

Baur, Gabriel. "Urbanization in the Arab East," *New Outlook*, II (May, 1959), 33–39.

Bose, Ashish. "Urbanization in the Face of Rapid Population Growth and Surplus Labour: The Case of India." New Delhi: paper submitted to the Asian Population Conference, 1963.

Cankaya, Ali. "The Growth of Cities and the Role of Local Administration," in Frederick T. Bent and Luise Lackland Shields (eds.). *The Role of Local Government in National Development*. Ankara: Central Treaty Organization, 1965.

Gable, Richard W. "Government and Administration in Iran." Los Angeles: School of Public Administration, University of Southern California, 1959, mimeo.

Gulick, John. "Old Values and New Institutions in a Lebanese Arab City," *Human Organization*, XXIV (Spring, 1965), 49–52.

Khadduri, Majid. *Modern Libya: A Study in Political Development*. Baltimore: Johns Hopkins Press, 1963.

Lerner, Daniel. *The Passing of Traditional Society*. Glencoe: The Free Press, 1958.

Lewis, Bernard. *The Emergence of Modern Turkey*. London: Oxford University Press, 1961.

Moore, Clement H. "Politics in a Tunisian Village," *Middle East Journal*, XVII (Autumn, 1963), 527–40.

Naraghi, Ehsan. "Problèmes sociaux de l'industrialization dans un pays du Tiers Monde," *Civilisations*, XV (1965), 504–18.

Raphaeli, Nimrod. "Development Planning in Iraq, Israel, Lebanon, and the United Arab Republic." Ann Arbor: unpublished Ph.D. dissertation, University of Michigan, 1964.

Weinryb, Bernard D. "The Impact of Urbanization in Israel," *Middle East Journal*, XI (Winter, 1957), 23–36.

Zartman, I. William. *Government and Politics in Northern Africa*. New York: Praeger, 1963.

D. Sub-Saharan Africa

Badenhorst, L. T., and Unterhalter, B. "A Study of Fertility in an Urban African Community," *Population Studies*, XV (July, 1962), 70–86.

Bailey, Norman A. "Local and Community Power in Angola," *Western Political Quarterly*, XXI (September, 1968), 400–8.

Bascom, William. "Some Aspects of Yoruba Urbanism," *American Anthropologist*, LXIV (August, 1962), 699–704.

―――. "Urbanization Among the Yoruba," *American Journal of Sociology*, LX (March, 1955), 446–53.

Burke, Fred G. *Local Government and Politics in Uganda*. Syracuse: Syracuse University Press, 1964.

Coleman, James S. *Nigeria: Background to Nationalism*. Berkeley: University of California Press, 1958.

Denis, Jacques. "Les villes d'Afrique tropicale," *Civilisations*, XVI (1966), 26–44.

Epstein, A. L. *Politics in an Urban African Community*. Manchester: Manchester University Press, 1958.

Gellar, Sheldon. "West African Capital Cities as Motors for Development," *Civilisations*, XVII (1967), 254–62.

Gluckman, Max. *Custom and Conflict in Africa*. Glencoe: The Free Press, 1959.

Greenstone, J. David. "Corruption and Self Interest in Kampala and Nairobi: A Comment on Local Politics in East Africa," *Comparative Studies in Society and History*, VIII (January, 1966), 199–210.

Gutkind, Peter C. W. "Some Problems of African Family Urban Life: An Example from Kampala, Uganda, British East Africa," *Diogenes*, No. 37 (Spring, 1962), 88–104.

―――. "The Energy of Despair: Social Organization of the Unemployed in Two African Cities: Lagos and Nigeria," *Civilisations*, XVII (1967), 186–214, 380–405.

―――. *The Royal Capital of Buganda: A Study of Internal Conflict and External Ambiguity*. The Hague: Mouton, 1963.

―――. "Urban Conditions in Africa," *Town Planning Review*, XXXII (April, 1961), 20–33.

Hanna, William John. "Image-Making in Field Research: Some Tactical and Ethical Problems of Research in Tropical Africa," *American Behavioral Scientist*, IX (January, 1965), 15–20.

―――, and Hanna, Judith Lynne. *Leadership and Politics in Urban Africa*. Chicago: Rand McNally, forthcoming.

―――. "The Integrative Role of Urban Africa's Middleplaces and Middlemen," *Civilisations*, XVII (1967), 12–29.

―――. "The Political Structure of Urban-Centered African Communities," in Horace Miner (ed.). *The City in Modern Africa*. New York: Praeger, 1967.

————. "The Problem of Ethnicity and Factionalism in African Survey Research, *Public Opinion Quarterly,* XXX (Summer, 1966), 290–94.

Harvey, Milton. "Implications of Migration to Freetown: A Study of the Relationship between Migrants, Housing, and Occupation," *Civilisations,* XVIII (1968), 247–69.

Henderson, Richard N. "Generalized Cultures and Evolutionary Adaptability: A Comparison of Urban Efik and Ibo in Nigeria," *Ethnology,* V (October, 1966), 365–91.

International Africa Institute. *Social Implications of Industrialization and Urbanization in Africa South of the Sahara.* Paris: UNESCO, 1956.

Jacobson, David Ellis. "Social Order Among Urban Africans: A Study of Elite Africans in Mbale, Uganda," Rochester: unpublished Ph.D. dissertation, University of Rochester, 1967.

Kuper, Hilda (ed.). *Urbanization and Migration in West Africa.* Berkeley: University of California Press, 1965.

Le Divelec, Marie-Hélène. "Les 'nouvelles' classes sociales en milieu urbain: le cas du Sénégal et celui du Nigeria du Nord," *Civilisations,* XVII (1967), 240–53.

Little, Kenneth L. "The West African City: Its Social Base," *Diogenes,* No. 29 (Spring, 1960), 16–31.

————. *West African Urbanization: A Study of Voluntary Associations in Social Change.* Cambridge: Cambridge University Press, 1965.

————. "West African Urbanization as a Social Process," *Cahiers d'Etudes Africaines,* I (October, 1960), 90–102.

Lloyd, Peter, Awe, Bolanle, and Mabogunje, Akin (eds.). *Ibadan: A West African City.* Cambridge: Cambridge University Press, 1967.

Mabogunje, Akin. "The Growth of Residential Districts in Ibadan," *Geographical Review,* LII (January, 1962), 56–77.

————. "Urbanization in Nigeria: A Constraint on Economic Development," *Economic Development and Cultural Change,* XIII (July, 1965), 413–38.

————. *Yoruba Towns.* Ibadan: Ibadan University Press, 1962.

Marris, Peter. *Family and Social Change in an African City.* Evanston: Northwestern University Press, 1962.

Meillassoux, Claude. *Urbanization of an African Community: Voluntary Associations in Bamako.* Seattle: University of Washington Press, 1968.

Miner, Horace (ed.). *The City in Modern Africa*. New York: Praeger, 1967.

Mitchell, J. C. "Theoretical Orientations in African Urban Studies," in Michael Banton (ed.). *The Social Anthropology of Complex Societies*. London: Tavistock Publications, 1966.

Mwepu-Kyabutha, Gaspard. "Quelques aspects des conséquences sociales de l'industrialisation au Katanga," *Civilisations*, XVII (1967), 53–71.

Nsarkoh, J. K. *Local Government in Ghana*. Accra: Ghana Universities Press, 1964.

Ohadike, Patrick O. "Urbanization: Growth, Transition, and Problems of a Premier West African City (Lagos, Nigeria)," *Urban Affairs Quarterly*, III (June, 1968), 69–90.

Poirier, Jean. "Aspects de l'urbanisation à Madagascar: les villes malgaches et la population urbaine," *Civilisations*, XVIII (1968), 80–112.

————. "Etude de l'urbanisation et sociologie urbaine à Madagascar," *Civilisations*, XVIII (1968), 285–98.

Powdermaker, Hortense. *Copper Town: Changing Africa*. New York: Harper and Row, 1962.

Proceedings of the Conference on the Government of African Cities. Lincoln University, Pa.: Lincoln University Press, 1968.

Richards, Audrey I. "Multi-Tribalism in African Urban Areas," *Civilisations*, XVI (1966), 354–64.

Verhaegen, Paul. *L'Urbanisation de l'Afrique Noire*. Brussels: Centre de Documentation Economique et Sociale Africaine, 1962.

Wallerstein, Immanuel. "Ethnicity and National Integration in West Africa," *Cahiers D'Etudes Africaines*, I (October, 1960), 129–39.

Werlin, Herbert. "The Nairobi City Council: A Study in Comparative Local Government," *Comparative Studies in Society and History*, VIII (January, 1966), 181–98.

Williams, Babtunde A., and Walsh, Annmarie Hauck. *Urban Government for Metropolitan Lagos*. New York: Praeger, 1968.

E. Latin America (including Mexico and Puerto Rico)

Anderson, Charles W. *Politics and Economic Change in Latin America*. Princeton: Van Nostrand, 1967.

————. "Toward a Theory of Latin American Politics," in Peter G. Snow (ed.). *Government and Politics in Latin America*. New York: Holt, Rinehart & Winston, 1967.

Banco Interamericano de Desarrollo. "El financiamiento del gobierno local," in *Reunión sobre financiamiento municipal en Latinoamérica: Informe.* Washington: Inter-American Development Bank, 1966.

Bazzanella, Waldemiro. "Industrialização e urbanização no Brasil," *América Latina,* VI (January–March, 1963), 3–27.

Beyer, Glenn H. (ed.). *The Urban Explosion in Latin America.* Ithaca: Cornell University Press, 1967.

Blanksten, George. "Local Government in a Rising Technology: Problems and Prospects for Latin America," Chicago: paper presented at the American Political Science Association Convention, 1964.

Bonilla, Frank. *Rio's Favelas: The Rural Slum within the City.* New York: American Universities Field Staff, 1961.

Bourricaud, François. "Lima en la vida política peruana," *América Latina,* VII (October–December, 1964), 89–96.

———. "Structure and Function of the Peruvian Oligarch," *Studies in Comparative International Development,* II (1966), 17–31.

Browning, Harley. "Recent Trends in Latin American Urbanization," *Annals of the American Academy of Political and Social Science,* CCCXVI (March, 1958), 111–20.

Calderón Alvarado, Luis, with Dorsalaer, Jaime, and Calle, Arturo. *Problemas de la urbanización en América Latina.* Fribourg, Switzerland: Oficina Internacional de Investigaciones Sociales de FERES, 1963.

Caplow, Theodore. *The Modern Latin American City.* Chicago: University of Chicago Press, 1952.

———, Stryker, Sheldon, and Wallace, Samuel E. *The Urban Ambience: A Study of San Juan, Puerto Rico.* Totowa, N.J.: Bedminster Press, 1964.

———, and Wallace, Samuel. "Social Ecology of the Urban Area of San Juan," *América Latina,* VIII (July–September, 1965), 97–111.

Cardoso, Fernando Henrique. *Empresario industrial e desenvolvimento econômico.* São Paulo: Difusão Europeio do Livro, 1964.

Centro Latino-Americano de Pêsquisas em Ciencias Sociais. "L'Urbanisation en Amérique Latine," *Civilisations,* XIV (1964), 398–406.

Currie, Laughlin. *Una política urbana para los países en desarrollo.* Bogotá: Tercer Mundo, 1965.

Daland, Robert T. "Development Administration and the Brazilian Political System," *Western Political Quarterly,* XXI (June, 1968), 325–39.

D'Antonio, William V., and Suter, Richard. "Primary Elections in a Mexican Municipio: New Trends in Mexico's Struggle toward Democracy." South Bend: Department of Sociology, University of Notre Dame, 1966, mimeo.

Davis, Kingsley. *Las causas y efectos del fenómeno de primacía urbana con referencia especial a América Latina.* México: Instituto de Investigaciones Sociales, 1962.

Deutschmann, Paul, and McNelly, John T. "Characteristics of Latin American Countries," *American Behavorial Scientist,* VIII (September, 1964), 25–29.

Dietz, A. G. H., Koth, M., and Silva, J. *Housing in Latin America.* Cambridge: The M.I.T. Press, 1965.

Dollfus, Olivier, "Remarques sur quelques aspects de l'urbanisation péruvienne," *Civilisations,* XVI (1966), 338–53.

Donald, Carr L. "Brazilian Local Self-Government—Myth or Reality," *Western Political Quarterly,* XIII (December, 1960), 1043–55.

————. "The Politics of Local Government Finance in Brazil," *Inter-American Economic Affairs,* XIII (Summer, 1959), 21–37.

Dorselaer, Jaime. "Quelques aspects régionnaux du phénomène urbain en Amérique Latine," *Civilisations,* XVII (1967), 263–79.

————, and Alfonso, Gregory. *La urbanización en América Latina.* Bogotá: Centro Internacional de Investigaciones Sociales de FERES, 1962.

Durand, John, and Peláez, César. "Patterns of Urbanization in Latin America," *Milbank Memorial Foundation Quarterly,* XLII (October, 1965), 166–96.

Eagleton Institute of Politics, Rutgers University. *Urban Leadership in Latin America: A Report to the U.S. AID.* New Brunswick: 1964.

Edwards, Harold T. "Power Structure and its Communications Behavior in San José, Costa Rica," *Journal of Inter-American Studies,* IX (April, 1967), 236–48.

Fitzgibbon, Russell H. "A Statistical Evaluation of Latin American Democracy," *Western Political Quarterly,* IX (September, 1956), 607–19.

————, and Johnson, Kenneth. "Measurement of Latin American Political Change," *American Political Science Review,* LVI (September, 1961), 515–26.

Form, William H., and D'Antonio, William V. "Integration and Cleavage Among Community Influentials in Two Border Cities," *American Sociological Review,* XXIV (December, 1959), 804–14.

Frank, Andrew G. "Urban Poverty in Latin America," *Studies in Comparative International Development*, II (1966), 75–84.

Friedmann, John. "Economic Growth and Urban Structure in Venezuela." Cambridge: Harvard-M.I.T. Joint Center for Urban Studies, 1963, mimeo.

———. "The Strategy of Deliberate Urbanization." Santiago de Chile: The Ford Foundation Urban and Regional Advisory Program in Chile, 1967, mimeo.

———, and Lackington, Tómas. "Hyperurbanization and National Development in Chile: Some Hypotheses," *Urban Affairs Quarterly*, II (June, 1967), 3–29.

Geiger, Pedro Pinchas. *Evoluçao de rede urbana brasileira.* Rio de Janeiro: Brasil, Ministerio de Educaçao e Cultura, Instituto Nacional de Estudos Pedagógicos, Centro Brasileiro de Pesquisas Educaciones, 1963.

Germani, Gino. "El proceso de urbanización en Argentina," *Revista inter-americana de ciencias sociales*, II, segunda época (1963), 287–345.

———. "Urbanización, secularización, y desarrollo económico," *Revista mexicana de sociología*, XXV (May–August, 1963), 625–46.

Goldkind, Victor. "Sociocultural Contrasts in Rural and Urban Settlement Types in Costa Rica," *Rural Sociology*, XXVI (December, 1961), 365–80.

Goldrich, Daniel, Pratt, Raymond B., and Schuller, C. R. "The Political Integration of Lower-Class Urban Settlements in Chile and Peru," *Studies in Comparative International Development*, III (1967), 3–22.

Gonzáles, Alfonso. "Castro: Some Economic Benefits for Latin America." Atlanta: paper presented at the Southeastern Conference of Latin Americanists, 1967.

Gonzales Casanova, Pablo. *La democracia in México.* México: Era, 1965.

Graham, Lawrence S. "Politics in a Mexican Community." Austin: Institute of Public Affairs, University of Texas, 1966, mimeo.

Hauser, Philip M. *Urbanization in Latin America.* New York: Columbia University Press International Documents Service, for UNESCO, 1961.

Heath, Dwight B., and Adams, Richard N. (eds.). *Contemporary Culture and Societies of Latin America.* New York: Random House, 1965.

Herrick, Bruce M. *Urban Migration and Economic Development in Chile.* Cambridge: The M.I.T. Press, 1966.

Holden, David. "La estructura del liderazgo y sus características en una communidad de Costa Rica," *Journal of Inter-American Studies,* VIII (January, 1966), 129–41.

Horowitz, Irving L. "Electoral Politics, Urbanization and Social Development in Latin America," *Urban Affairs Quarterly,* II (March, 1967), 3–35.

———. "Modern Argentina: The Politics of Power," *The Political Quarterly,* III (October–December, 1959), 400–10.

——— (ed.). *Revolution in Brazil.* New York: E. P. Dutton, 1964.

Hoskins, Gary. "Community Power and Political Modernization: A Study of a Venezuelan City." Urbana: unpublished Ph.D. dissertation, University of Illinois, 1966.

———. "Patterns of Power and Politics in a Venezuelan City." Ithaca: Paper presented at Cornell University, 1966 (mimeo).

Hutchinson, Bertram. "Fertility, Social Mobility and Urban Migration in Brazil," *Population Studies,* XIV (March, 1961), 182–89.

———. "The Migrant Population of Urban Brazil," *América Latina,* VI (April–June, 1963), 41–71.

Imas, José Luis de. *Estructura social de una ciudad pampeana.* La Plata, Argentine Republic: Instituto de Historia de la Filosofía y el Pensamiento Argentino, Universidad Nacional de La Plata, 1965.

Jesús, Carolina Maria de. *Child of the Dark.* New York: E. P. Dutton, 1962.

Johnson, Dale L., "Industrialization, Social Mobility, and Class Formation in Chile," *Studies in Comparative International Development,* III (1967), 127–51.

Johnson, John J. (ed.). *Continuity and Change in Latin America.* Stanford: Stanford University Press, 1964.

———. *Political Change in Latin America: The Emergence of the Middle Sectors.* Stanford: Stanford University Press, 1958.

Johnson, Kenneth. "Causal Factors in Latin American Political Instability," *Western Political Quarterly,* XVII (September, 1964), 432–46.

———. "Urbanization and Political Change in Latin America." Los Angeles: unpublished Ph.D. dissertation, University of California at Los Angeles, 1963.

Kahl, Joseph. "Social Stratification in Metropoli and Provinces: Brazil and Mexico," *América Latina,* VIII (January–March, 1965), 23–35.

————. Urbanização e mundanças ocupacionais no Brasil," *América Latina*, V (October–December, 1962), 21–30.

Klapp, Orrin E., and Padgett, L. Vincent. "Power Structure and Decision-Making in a Mexican Border City," *American Journal of Sociology*, LXV (December, 1960), 400–6.

Kling, Merle. "Toward a Theory of Power and Political Instability on Latin America," *Western Political Quarterly*, IX (March, 1959), 21–35.

Labelle, Ivan, and Estrada, Adriana. *Latin America in Maps, Charts, and Tables*. Cuernavaca: Center for Inter-Cultural Formation, 1963.

Lambert, Denis. "L'urbanisation accélérée de l'Amérique Latine et la formation d'un secteure tertiaire refuge," *Civilisations*, XV (1965), 158–74, 309–25, 477–92.

————. "Urbanisation et développment économique en Amérique Latine," *Caravelle*, III (1964), 266–74.

Lambert, Jacques, "Le rôle politique des capitales en Amérique Latine," *Caravelle*, III (1964), 130–37.

Lewis, Oscar. *La Vida*. New York: Random House, 1966.

————. "Urbanization Without Breakdown: A Case Study," *Scientific Monthly*, LXXV (July, 1952), 31–41.

Lipman, Aaron. "Social Backgrounds of the Bogotá Entrepreneur," *Journal of Inter-American Studies*, VII (April, 1965), 227–35.

Lipset, Seymour Martin, and Solari, Aldo (eds.). *Elites in Latin America*. London and New York: Oxford University Press, 1967.

McCallum, James D. *Urbanization, Development, and Regional Planning in Latin America: A Conceptual and Analytical Study*. Bogotá: Centro Interamericano de Vivienda y Planeamiento, Summer Research Fellowship Program, 1966.

————. "The Place of Latin America in the Study of Comparative Politics," *Journal of Politics*, XXVIII (February, 1966), 57–80.

Martz, John D. *Acción Democratica: Evolution of a Modern Political Party in Venezuela*. Princeton: Princeton University Press, 1966.

Miller, Delbert C., Chamorro, Eva, and Aguila, Juan Carlos. *De la industria al poder*. Buenos Aires: Ediciones Libera, 1966.

————. "Community Power Perspectives and Role Definitions of North American Executives in an Argentine Community," *Administrative Science Quarterly*, X (1965), 364–80.

Morse, Richard M. *From Community to Metropolis: A Biography of São Paulo, Brazil*. Gainesville: University of Florida Press, 1958.

————. "Latin American Cities: Aspects of Function and Structure," *Comparative Studies in Society and History,* IV (July, 1962), 473–93.

————. "Some Characteristics of Latin American Urban History," *American Historical Review,* LXVII (January, 1962), 317–38.

Municipios do Brasil. Rio de Janeiro: Instituto Brasileiro de Administração Municipal, 1960.

Needler, Martin. *Political Development in Latin America: Instability, Violence and Evolutionary Change.* New York: Random House, 1968.

Peattie, Lisa Refield. *The View from the Barrio.* Ann Arbor: University of Michigan Press, 1968.

Pinto, Aluizio Loureiro. "The Brazilian Institute of Municipal Administration (IBAM): A Case Study of Institution-Building in Brazil." Los Angeles: unpublished D.P.A. dissertation, University of Southern California, 1967.

Powelson, John P., and Solow, Anatole A. "Urban and Rural Development in Latin America," *Annals of the American Academy of Political and Social Science,* CCCLX (July, 1965), 48–62.

Problemas de la urbanización en Guatemala. Guatemala City: Ministerio de Educación, Departamento Editorial "José de Pineda Ibarra," 1965.

Rabinovitz, Francine F. "Urban Development Decision-Making in the Mexican Federal District," in C. M. Haar (ed.), *Programs for Urban Development in Latin America.* Washington: U.S. Agency for International Development, 1965.

Ratinoff, Luis. *La urbanización en América Latina: El caso de Paraguay.* Santiago de Chile: Instituto Latinoamericano de Planificación Económica y Social, 1964.

————. "The New Urban Groups: The Middle Classes," in S. M. Lipset and Aldo Solari (eds.). *Elites in Latin America.* London and New York: Oxford University Press, 1967.

Rochefort, Michel. "Le rôle regional de Rio de Janeiro," *Civilisations,* XVI (1966), 365–75.

Rodwin, Lloyd. "Ciudad Guayana: A New City," in Dennis Flanagan (ed.). *Cities.* New York: Knopf-Random House, 1965.

Santoro, Gustavo. "La estratificación y la movilidad social en la ciudad de San José," *Revista salvadoreña de ciencias sociales,* I (January–March, 1965), 9–88.

Schmitt, Karl, and Burks, David. *Evolution or Chaos: The Dynamics of Latin American Politics.* New York: Praeger, 1961.

Scobie, James R. *Argentina: A City and a Nation.* New York: Oxford University Press, 1964.

Sherwood, Frank. "Industrialization and Urbanization in Brazil." Chicago: paper presented at American Political Science Association Convention, 1964.

———. *Institutionalizing the Grass Roots in Brazil.* San Francisco: Chandler, 1967.

Silvert, Kalman, and Germani, Gino. "Politics, Social Structure and Military Intervention in Latin America," *European Journal of Sociology,* II (1961), 62–81.

Snyder, David F. "Ciudad Guayana: A Planned Metropolis on the Orinoco," *Journal of Inter-American Studies,* V (July, 1963), 405–12.

Soares, Glaucio. "The Political Sociology of Uneven Development in Brazil," in Irving L. Horowitz (ed.) *Revolution in Brazil.* New York: E.P. Dutton, 1964.

———, and Hamblin, Robert L. "Socio-economic Variables and Voting for the Radical Left: Chile, 1952," *American Political Science Review,* LXI (September, 1967), 1053–65.

Solari, Aldo. "Impacto político de las diferencias internas de los países en los grados e índices de modernización y desarrollo económico en América Latina," *América Latina,* VIII (January–March, 1965), 5–22.

Stepan, Alfred. "Political Development Theory: The Latin American Experience," *Journal of International Affairs,* XX (1966), 223–34.

Tavares, J. Nilo. "Marginalismo social, marginalismo político," *Revista brasileira de estudos políticos,* XIII (January, 1962), 69–86.

Tricart, J. "Quelques caractéristiques générales des villes latino-americaines," *Civilisations,* XV (1965), 15–30.

Tumin, Melvin M. *Social Class and Social Change in Puerto Rico.* Princeton: Princeton University Press, 1961.

United Nations, Economic Commission for Latin America, Social Affairs Division. "Recent Changes in Urban and Rural Settlement Pattern in Latin America." Pittsburgh: paper presented at the Inter-Regional Seminar on Development Policies and Planning in Relation to Urbanization, 1966.

Violich, Francis. *Cities of Latin America.* New York: Reinhold, 1944.

Wagner, P. L. "Political Implications of Rapid Urbanization in Caribbean Countries," *Annals of the Association of American Geographers,* LII (Summer, 1962), 367, abstract.

Whiteford, Andrew. *Two Cities of Latin America.* Beloit: Logan Museum of Anthropology, 1960.

Whitten, Norman E., Jr. "Power Structure and Socioeconomic Change in Latin American Cities," *Social Forces,* XLIII (March, 1965), 320–29.

Wilhelm, Jorge, *São Paulo Metrópole*. São Paulo: Difusão Européia do Livro, 1965.

Williamson, R. C. "Some Factors in Urbanism in a Quasi-Rural Setting: San Salvador and San José," *Sociology and Social Research*, XLVII (January, 1963), 187–200.

Wingo, Lowdon, Jr. "Recent Patterns of Urbanization among Latin American Countries," *Urban Affairs Quarterly*, II (March, 1967), 81–110.

The Authors

ROBERT R. ALFORD is Professor of Sociology at the University of Wisconsin (Madison). He is the author of *Party and Society: The Anglo-American Democracies* (1963), *Bureaucracy and Participation: Political Cultures in Four Wisconsin Cities* (1969), and a number of articles and reviews for professional journals in the fields of sociology, political science, and public administration. He is currently engaged in a study of decisions and policies in the 676 American cities over 25,000 population in 1960.

ROBERT T. DALAND is Professor of Political Science and Director of the Public Administration Program at the University of North Carolina. He has published in the fields of urban politics and development administration, including *Brazilian Planning: Development Politics and Administration*. Having just completed a year of data collection in the field, his current research is a study of the Brazilian bureaucratic elite.

JAMES F. GUYOT, of the Political Science Department at the University of California, Los Angeles, is currently a Visiting Senior Lecturer in Political Science at Columbia University and a Research Associate of the Southern Asian Institute. He has written on American and Asian bureaucratic behavior and is now com-

pleting an analytical comparison of Burma and Malaysia as polar
models of political and economic development.

DANIEL R. GRANT is Professor of Political Science, Vanderbilt
University, and Director of its Urban and Regional Development
Center. He is co-author of *State and Local Government in America* (2nd ed., 1968), *The States and the Metropolis* (1968), and
Government and Politics: An Introduction to Political Science
(1966). He has served as consultant for the U.S Advisory Commission on Intergovernmental Relations, and for numerous metropolitan area studies.

WILLIAM JOHN HANNA, Professor of Political Science in the
City University of New York, is author-editor of *Independent
Black Africa: The Politics of Freedom* (1964) and the forthcoming
Students and Politics in Africa. JUDITH LYNNE HANNA, Consultant in New York University's Program of Dance, has published
articles on urban affairs and African dance. Together, the Hannas
are authors of *Urban Dynamics in Black Africa* (in press) and are
completing *Leadership and Politics in Urban Africa* and *Nkwa di
Iche Iche,* both scheduled for publication next year.

FRANCINE F. RABINOVITZ is Assistant Professor of Political
Science at the University of California at Los Angeles. She is the
author of several studies in the field of international urbanization,
including *Urban Government in the Stockholm Region* and *Latin
American Political Systems in an Urban Setting.* She is currently
engaged in studies of urban policy outputs in Latin America.

FRANK P. SHERWOOD is Director of the Federal Executive
Institute in Charlottesville, Virginia. Before assuming his present
position in 1968, he was Director of the School of Public Administration, University of Southern California. His studies of local
government include *Institutionalizing the Grass Roots in Brazil*
and *California's System of Governments,* of which he was co-
author.

DEIL S. WRIGHT is Professor of Political Science at the University of North Carolina (Chapel Hill) and Research Professor at the Institute for Research in Social Science. He is the author of *Public Administration and the Public, Profile of a Metropolis,* and *Federal Grants-in-Aid: Perspectives and Alternatives.* He is currently pursuing research on U.S. state and local executives, health administration, and the structure and organization of the planning function in state and local government.

Index

Access to the political process:— and interest groups, 266-267;— and political parties, 266-268; —in central cities, 257-262;— in incorporated suburbs, 257-262;—in Miami, 256 and ff.;— in Nashville, 257 and ff.;—in rural areas, 257-262;—in Toronto, 255-256 and ff.;—in unincorporated suburbs, 257-262; —of ethnic and racial minorities, 262-266;—under metropolitan government, 249-250. (*see also:* integration)

Anomic urban agitation, 120.

Autonomy:—as a non-hierarchical concept, 67;—as a variable in the study of urban politics, 20-21;—as devolution, 68-69.

Brazil:—constitutional provisions for local government in, 76-77;—industrialization and urbanization, and relationships to devolution in, 77-78; —financial aspects of devolution in, 78-79;—local government in, from Frank Sherwood study of, 309-315;—public administration in, studies of:–by John Dorsey, 315-316;–by Robert Daland, 316-321.

Budgets and budgeting process; —as an indicator of city manager–council relationships, 220-228.

Centralization:—definition of, 66;—of decision-making in council-manager government, 246-247.

Centralization-decentralization continuum, 65-67.

City managers and development: —in council-manager government, 218-219;–city manager as a development administrator, 241-243;–managerial role of the city manager, 219-224;–policy role of the city manager, 224-228;–political role of the city manager, 228-235.

Communications and development:—in Malaysia, 151-154; —mass media in council-manager government, 214-218;— role of the city manager in communications, 220-231.

Community influentials:—role of, in the integration process, 194-202.

Community political integration:—political culture as an indicator of, 42-44;—political socialization as an indicator of, 44;—role of elites in, 46;— study of, as a variable in comparative urban studies, 41 and ff.

Comparative analysis:—methodology of, 26-28.

Comparative urban studies:—as a component of the study of national political systems, 16-19;—as a distinct field of study,